D1061091

Controller's and Treasurer's Desk Reference

Christopher R. Malburg, CPA, MBA

McGraw-Hill, Inc.

New York San Francisco Washington, D.C. Auckland Bogotá
Caracas Lisbon London Madrid Mexico City Milan
Montreal New Delhi San Juan Singapore
Sydney Tokyo Toronto

Library of Congress catalog card number 94-075620

1 2 3 4 5 6 7 8 9 0   DOH/DOH   9 0 9 8 7 6 5 4

ISBN 0-07-911604-3

*The sponsoring editor for this book was David J. Conti; the production supervisor was
Donald F. Schmidt. It was set in Palatino by North Market Street Graphics.*

Printed and bound by R. R. Donnelley & Sons Company.

This book is printed on recycled, acid-free paper containing a
minimum of 50% recycled de-inked fiber.

This publication is designed to provide accurate and authoritative information
in regard to the subject matter covered. It is sold with the understanding that
the publisher is not engaged in rendering legal, accounting, or other professional service. If legal advice or other expert assistance is required, the services
of a competent professional person should be sought.
    —*From a declaration of principles jointly adopted by a committee of the
    American Bar Association and a committee of publishers*

This book is dedicated to Marilyn—
that one special person in my life
who has helped fulfill my dream and
vocation as an author.

Contents

4. Audit: Internal and External

5. System of Internal Accounting Controls

18. Financing and Borrowing 294

21. Risk Management

Preface

Read this book; use it as a reference source. Take it with you into the field. Make sure your staff, colleagues, and clients get a copy. This work represents the current thinking, techniques, methods, and observations on the subject. Rely on it for answers to the complex questions encountered every business day. Once you use this book, you'll seldom allow it beyond arm's reach. I hope this book is as enjoyable for you to use as it was to write. Best wishes for a prosperous career.

Acknowledgments

Every author has a special group of people on whom he or she counts. For me, these select individuals provided their counsel, encouragement, technical expertise, and, most importantly, their time: Mr. A. J. Melrose; Ms. Francis Adams of F. G. Adams, Inc.; Mr. John Watters of Zusman, Cameron and Watters, Inc.; and Mr. Pat Banister of Capital Insight Brokerage. Thanks to each of you.

Chris Malburg

Introduction

Overview

Controller's and Treasurer's Desk Reference provides a comprehensive look into the financial operations of small- to medium-sized companies. The book addresses the unique information needs of the individuals who run such firms. Each area under the responsibilities of a modern controller and treasurer is detailed.

Within these functions, the book describes specific tasks. Where technical or analytical tools are used, the book identifies them, puts them into simple terms, and walks you through easy-to-use applications relevant to your situation.

Whether you've been newly promoted to your financial job or simply wish to better understand the financial operations of your company, this book delivers the what-to-do and how-to-do-it essentials.

We won't waste time on things that are of little or no direct use to financial managers at small- and medium-sized companies. For example, how many small businesses need to know the intricacies of floating a public stock offering? On the other hand, access to investment capital and business financing is very relevant. Five chapters are devoted to the various aspects of financing small businesses:

- Cash management (Chapter 10)
- Banking relationships (Chapter 16)
- Capital expenditures (Chapter 17)
- Financing and borrowing (Chapter 18)
- Investor relations and corporate communication (Chapter 20)

Purpose of the Book

The *Controller's and Treasurer's Desk Reference* serves two functions:

1. Provides a complete and detailed view of a small company's financial operations when read in its entirety
2. Furnishes a handy reference guide that readers can pick up, quickly answer a specific question (such as, How do you compute fully diluted earnings per share?), then put back on the shelf until next time

Everywhere practical, real-life examples, charts, and graphs are used to simplify and illustrate the presentation. The book gathers information normally found only in a variety of reference works such as finance and accounting texts and the internal revenue code. The style purposely separates accounting and treasury issues into their component parts, then addresses each one individually. Experience teaches that even people already knowledgeable in the subject matter appreciate streamlined, simplified explanations. This accelerates the reference task of busy financial decision makers.

Scope

The subject of business accounting and treasury operations is vast. The topics covered were carefully selected for:

- Relevance
- Ease of application
- Predictable results
- Quick implementation and fast solutions

Most discussions begin with the basics—you don't have to be a financial whiz to use this book. In fact, I assume you aren't. We'll then advance to the details you need in order to apply the concepts to your particular situation.

No author can honestly claim to relate all there is to know about a subject. I certainly don't. However, I can promise that those subjects included in this desk reference are complete and of immediate use to you. Further, I won't waste your time on subjects that probably aren't relevant right now to a company the size of yours.

Here's a partial list of the topics covered:

- Use of most common financing vehicles
- How to adjust the capital structure
- Design of an efficient cash management system
- Potential cash risks and opportunities
- Ways to accelerate cash inflows and to delay cash outflows

- Control of accounts receivable and payable
- Cost accounting systems and their use in profit management
- Inventory management
- How to create a successful financial plan
- Ways to streamline financial reporting
- Internal accounting control issues essential to the financial department
- Financial impact and operation of export/import activities
- Use of computer networks in the financial department
- Assessment and control of interest rate risk and foreign currency risk
- Management and avoidance of bankruptcy

Who Can Benefit from This Book?

The book was written for a variety of individuals:

- Experienced financial, accounting, and treasury personnel
- People whose jobs are not in the finance area, but who need to understand how it works
- Persons newly promoted either into the treasury or accounting department or who have been moved up within the department to a position of higher authority
- People such as consultants and auditors who provide professional services to small- and medium-sized companies
- Directors with limited financial backgrounds who appreciate the support of a clear and concise reference book on the subject

Many people just promoted have been so involved in the technical details of their jobs that they haven't the time to gain an overview of the entire financial operation necessary for their new position. *Controller's and Treasurer's Desk Reference* helps bridge the gap between technical expert and financial executive. It explains in plain English how each area in the finance department folds into the others. Additionally, the book brings in other areas of the company to illustrate how they impact the company's financial position and vice versa.

How This Book Differs from Others

It's difficult enough understanding the financial function. You don't need to wrestle with a reference book that's difficult to use as well. Therefore, the style emphasizes a user-friendly approach. The objective is quick access to simplified techniques that answer your specific questions and help you do your job. Period. Absent are long, irrelevant discussions on the theory behind each issue—that's for textbooks.

Each chapter employs major and minor headlines for the topics. This helps in locating the exact discussion you want without wasting time thumbing through the parts you don't need immediately. All examples and illustrations appear within the text where they'll be of most benefit—not elsewhere in the book where space permits.

Features of the Book

Along with the use of streamlined headers and concise discussions often followed by examples that demonstrate the techniques, you'll see aids such as the following:

Charts and Diagrams

These demonstrate:

- Flow of cash through the business cycle
- Internal controls designed to manage and safeguard company assets
- Methods used for cash inflow acceleration and outflow deceleration
- Banking services
- Features and characteristics of investment vehicles
- The role of key personnel in the financial department

Graphs

These illustrate:

- Cash fluctuations at various stages of the business cycle
- Interest rate risk of various financial structures
- The consequence of changes in the elements of cash
- How assumptions in business planning models can change key financial targets and what to do about them

Worksheets

What better way to structure a problem and lead you to its solution. Worksheets contained in this book are intended to be copied from the book and used for "live" problem-solving applications.

Examples

Examples offer practical illustrations that quickly clarify a method by showing how someone in a similar situation solved the problem. Some of the examples:

- Identify financial risk and opportunity
- Demonstrate the consequences of particular financial decisions
- Illustrate the risk presented by an absence of specific internal controls
- Quantify the benefits of cash inflow acceleration and cash outflow deceleration techniques
- Assess the benefits of different financing alternatives
- Inject the appropriate balance of safety, liquidity, and yield into investment strategy
- Separate duties among financial executives

How to Use the Book

There are four areas of the book to help you locate the exact topic, problem, or issue in which you're interested. These are:

- The Contents at the front of the book
- Index
- The "Overview" beginning each chapter
- Subheads within each chapter

To locate a subject, look first in either the Contents or Index. Then locate the exact discussion using the subheads within the text.

Additionally, the book also was intended for reading from cover to cover. Each topic builds on prior discussions. The chapters begin with the basics and progress to state-of-the-art practices in the field of accounting, cash management, and treasury operations.

Chapter Summaries

Chapter 1: Financial Organization and Structure. Identifies how the financial department is organized and who is responsible for particular activities.

Chapter 2: The Accounting System. Identifies the components of the accounting and treasury systems, how they interact, and the information provided by each.

Chapter 3: Automated Systems. Illustrates the application of various types of computer systems in the controller's and treasurer's departments. Identifies how to select an integrated hardware/software system.

Chapter 4: Audit: Internal and External.   Demonstrates the link between audit and consistent application of company policies and procedures. Illustrates the role of the controller in administering the audit responsibility. Identifies the types of independent audit services and which are needed under various circumstances.

Chapter 5: System of Internal Accounting Controls.   Shows the components of this critical system, how they are maintained, and ways they are used to prevent fraud, theft, and embezzlement.

Chapter 6: Internal Treasury Controls.   Because the treasury department handles cash and other liquid assets, its control requirements are unique. This chapter shows what works and what doesn't to protect these easily convertible assets.

Chapter 7: Business Planning.   Leads you through the planning process. Includes design, implementation, and monitoring of results.

Chapter 8: Financial Reporting.   Identifies the key reports that track financial performance and plan implementation. Demonstrates how to create them, use them, and tell if they're correct.

Chapter 9: Financial Analysis and Support.   Describes how modern controllers analyze financial performance, what tools they use, and how their results are employed throughout the firm.

Chapter 10: Cash Management.   Provides techniques to accelerate cash inflow, slow cash outflow, prepare cash projections, manage interest rate risk, and arrange capital structure.

Chapter 11: Accounts Receivable.   Details the most up-to-date receivables management techniques to stay on top of receivables growth and delinquent customers.

Chapter 12: Accounts Payable.   Identifies the best ways to pay when you want to without jeopardizing business relationships.

Chapter 13: Inventory Control.   Takes you by the hand through the most current methods used to keep the minimum amount of salable inventory on hand without running short.

Chapter 14: Cost Accounting.   Shows how this system tracks production costs. Includes components, reporting responsibilities, uses for information, and tests of results.

Chapter 15: Tax Preparation, Management, and Planning.   Overview of controller's responsibilities for compliance with laws, filing dates, identification of transactions with tax implications, and techniques to plan business transactions that minimize tax consequences.

Chapter 16: Banking Relationships.   Shows what banks can do for small companies and how to use them without overpaying. Defines banking terms so the small business manager is on a level playing field with bankers.

Chapter 17: Capital Expenditures.   Combines mathematical analysis with the art of assessing the viability of proposed expenditures.

Chapter 18: Financing and Borrowing.   Identifies responsibilities of the financing function. Explains the pros and cons of raising money using various techniques and instruments. Demonstrates the inner workings of most financing vehicles.

Chapter 19: Investments.   Describes how investment of excess cash reduces the cost of carry without compromising the company's liquidity. Various types of investment vehicles are described along with methods to assess their risk.

Chapter 20: Corporate Communications.   Identifies those who comprise the investment community for small- to medium-sized companies along with their role and importance in raising capital and influencing stock price. Demonstrates proven methods to deal with press releases, financial reporting requirements, and shareholder meetings. Provides instructions on how to form a crisis management team along with contingency planning.

Chapter 21: Risk Management.   Describes methods to protect financial stability. Includes ways to assess potential risk and the company's ability to cope with it.

Chapter 22: Managing Bankruptcy.   Explains the various sections of the bankruptcy code and how to use them. Walks through the process from filing to preparation and court approval of a workout plan, creditor relations, and bankruptcy protection emergence.

Chapter 23: Personnel Management.   Shows the legal dos and don'ts of personnel administration. Demonstrates how to legally hire and fire employees, and offers interview techniques and questions to ask prospective financial employees.

1

Financial Organization and Structure

Overview

Understanding the financial operations of a small- to medium-sized business requires a grasp of both the financial responsibilities and the financial structure of the company. This isn't always obvious. The smaller the company, the more hats any given individual wears. Often you'll see the same person acting as the chief financial officer, the controller, *and* the treasurer. Because these jobs entail different responsibilities, the larger the company, the greater the tendency to specialize. As the firm grows, the first split usually separates the controller from treasury operations.

Conversely, the smaller the company, the simpler the financial structure. At small businesses, capital often comes from nothing more than the owner's pockets. As the company grows, bank loans enter the financial structure. If the firm is successful, obtaining growth capital may come from outside investors in the form of a stock or bond placement (or both).

Large companies have complex capital structures that often include several series of stocks—sometimes preferred stocks as well as common. Companies issue bonds over the years in many different tranches. There may even be a high-yield bond offering (the so-called junkers) somewhere along the line.

The CFO, controller, and treasurer administer all this. That's what we'll illustrate in this chapter—who does what in the financial department and how we organize the capital structure.

Organization Structure

Organization of financial operations depends on the structure of the rest of the firm. Companies with stand-alone operating divisions may have separate financial operations to serve them. Sometimes this extends to the treasury functions as well. These may even include cash management and short-term investments.

However, more often we'll see treasury responsibilities executed at the corporate level even if a division has its own accounting system. This is desirable. The firm gains more clout (the professionals call it leverage) the larger its borrowing and investment accounts grow. The larger their deposits, the more attention and services they can demand from banks.

However, centralized treasury operations at a company with decentralized accounting operations make recording and transfer of cash tricky. The company needs to keep records of how much each division transferred and when the transfers occurred. Even with the added record keeping, the benefits of having all treasury operations in one place usually outweigh the slight burden.

Centralized Financial Functions

If your company has more than one operating division, here are some additional financial functions that might be profitably taken over by the corporate financial staff:

- Computer operations
- Tax planning and preparation
- Employee benefits
- Insurance
- Collection of accounts receivable
- Payment of accounts payable
- Payroll

Some companies throw purchasing into the centralized functions as well. The theory is that separate divisions may order the same items for themselves. The company can gain a better price if one person who knows everyone's requirements does all the buying.

Management Style

Another determinate of the financial organization structure is that of style. Executives with a hands-on style usually want detailed financial information instantly. Companies with two or more divisions may find centralizing the financial information system gives them the information they want when they need it.

Where companies have truly delegated operational responsibility to their executives, a decentralized financial function may work most effectively. The senior executives at the corporate level are more bottom-line-oriented and don't want to see all the financial detail.

Division Specialization

Some companies have divisions with such diverse businesses that they really need separate financial staffs. An example would be a company with one division that franchises hamburger stands and another division that owns and leases the real estate under them.

The accounting and taxation expertise required for both divisions is so specialized that the same people probably couldn't do it.

Responsibility for the Accounting System

The controller is the company's chief accounting officer. This person may do other things at small companies; however, accounting is usually the top priority.

Figure 1-1 gives a good listing of what the controller does.

Accounting Systems

The controller maintains the company's accounting systems. These include:

- General ledger
- Accounts receivable and payable subledgers
- Inventory control
- Order entry and its interface with inventory control and accounts receivable
- Cost accounting
- Fixed assets
- Backup and source documents for transactions

The controller maintains each of these systems with respect to:

- Accuracy of data input
- Timeliness of reporting
- Suitability of systems and procedures
- Backup and recovery of systems

The financial operations of so many small businesses are often the heaviest users of the firm's computer equipment. Therefore, the controller often acts as the data processing manager along with performing all of the other accounting duties. This entails:

Controller's Responsibilities

1. Chief accounting officer. General responsibility for accounting entries, preparation of financial statements, and related reports.

2. Oversees and operates all financial systems including: general ledger, cost accounting, inventory accounting, fixed-asset accounting and reporting, planning, and budgeting.

3. Compiles monthly financial results for senior management. This package often compares actual performance against the business plan.

4. Designs, implements, and maintains the system of internal accounting controls.

5. Runs the company payroll system. Issues all governmental reports and year-end payroll tax forms to employees.

6. Gathers all information for preparation of the financial plan.

7. Acts as focal point for outside financial reporting and for regulatory agencies such as the SEC.

8. Assists with the internal audit function. However, does not supervise the internal auditors, nor do they report to the controller—to do so would compromise their independence.

9. Formulates and executes tax policies for the company.

10. Drafts and files company tax returns.

11. Maintains authorized-signature list along with individual authority levels to obligate the company.

12. Advises the board on addition and removal of signatories.

13. Operates the check disbursement system. Maintains custody of check stock. But does not have custody of the check signature plate or check signing authority.

14. Responsible for the checking-account reconciliations, review, and approval.

Figure 1-1. Responsibilities of the controller.

- Acquisition and maintenance of hardware
- Identification and acquisition of appropriate software
- Managing both hardware and software system upgrades
- Maintaining library of user manuals
- Staff and user training
- Security and protection of computer equipment

Financial Reporting

The controller provides financial reports to company executives, its owners, and any third parties having a need to know (such as lenders). At a minimum these include:

- Balance sheet
- Income statement
- Statement of cash flows

Beyond that, most controllers maintain specific reports for internal use regarding:

- Accounts receivable
- Cash flow projections
- Fixed assets
- Capital expenditures programs

Certainly the list goes on and varies widely among companies. Chapter 8, "Financial Reporting," discusses each of these reports in detail. The controller's job with respect to financial reporting is to provide the information required to those with a need to know. The information must be accurate, timely, and presented in a manner that doesn't confuse or allow the possibility for misinterpretation. Finally, these reports are often confidential—especially at smaller companies not publicly held and not subject to SEC disclosure requirements. The controller is responsible for maintaining the security of the company's financial information.

This may sound odd. Who cares about a company's financial information? Consider a small manufacturing business engaged in a tightly competitive market. Their edge could be low prices brought about by an advantageous cost of production. Perhaps the smaller firm is able to compete against companies many times its size only through a patented production process.

Leaking key production or cost information could give away the advantage if it fell into the hands of a competitor. In any case, it's the controller's job to see that this information isn't distributed beyond those with a need and a right to know.

Types of Financial Reporting.   The controller is responsible for keeping accurate books and records and for maintaining a system of internal accounting controls that ensure this accuracy. Company executives and owners have every right to expect their financial statements and any other information coming from the finance department to be accurate.

Figure 1-2 identifies the financial reporting concerns of the controller.

Management Accounting Information System

From a profit standpoint, maintaining the management information system is one of the most important jobs of the controller. The system tracks company perfor-

---

Controller's Financial Reporting Concerns

1. Fairness of presentation of the company's financial position both monthly and at year end
2. Adequacy and competency of the accounting system
3. Production of financial reports including internal, external, and regulatory requirements
4. Overall system of internal accounting controls such that it ensures accurate financial reporting and safeguards the firm's assets

---

Figure 1-2. Controller's reporting concerns.

mance against its business plan. It also provides key information regarding such things as:

- Production costs
- Equipment downtime
- Purchase price variances
- Labor costs and variances from standards
- Inventory turnover—the speed at which inventory is converted to cash
- Customers who are delinquent in paying their bills
- Sales force commission schedules
- Projected cash outflow and balances

These are just a few of the vital pieces of management information that comes from the finance department. Figure 1-3 summarizes the controller's responsibility with respect to management information.

Traditional Treasury Functions and Responsibilities

Small companies often combine treasury responsibilities with those of the controller. As the firm's size increases, so does the complexity of its capital structure, borrowing, and cash management requirements. Eventually, the specialization necessary to execute the treasurer's responsibilities demands a full-time professional. Companies with extensive international operations often have an international treasurer (or assistant treasurer in charge of international operations) to

---

Management Accounting Requirements

1. Provides accurate and reliable information. The system must have a high degree of credibility among users of the information.

2. System of management information reporting is designed to anticipate potential risks.

3. Provides information within the time frame to be of use in management decision making. Management must have time to interpret the information and act on it. In this regard, financial information has a high spoilage factor. Problems have a habit of exploding out of control quickly. Conversely, opportunities pass by just as fast.

4. Reports are designed for ease of use and point to the decision that needs to be made. Most good reporting systems follow a consistent format so information can be found quickly and easily.

5. Indicators out of range from management expectations are highlighted. Likewise for actual performance that differs from the business plan or past performance.

6. The management information system targets information that's important to the company. Such information might include cash flow increase/decrease, profitability, or sales by product.

7. Not only does the management information system identify problems, it provides optional courses of action for decision makers to choose from and identifies the likely outcomes.

Figure 1-3. Management information system requirements.

oversee such prickly issues as currency conversion, hedging, and offshore funds transfer.

One of the most traditional treasury responsibilities is that of running the cash concentration system. Chapter 10, "Cash Management," details this subject. Briefly, the cash concentration system acts as a giant funnel that gathers incoming cash from all the sources of the firm. Think about where your firm draws its cash. Among these sources are probably:

- Customer payments
- Interest income
- Maturing investments or loans
- Income tax refunds
- Settlements of lawsuits

- Insurance claims reimbursements
- Income from the sale of assets

Once in the funnel, the cash concentration system accelerates the funds through the company. It converts incoming receipts to spendable cash, records it in the accounting system, and puts it in the firm's cash concentration checking account. It is from this single account that the treasurer (or controller who wears the treasurer's hat) manages the company's cash.

The job of the treasurer focuses on these things:

- Cash management
- Providing funds for operations
- Maintaining investor and owner contact
- Managing the company's stock
- Credit approval
- Managing receivables, collections, and payables
- Banking relations
- Maintaining credit lines
- Risk management—interest rate risk, foreign currency risk, and insurance

Figure 1-4 summarizes the treasury departments duties.

Financial Structure

What Is Financial Structure?

It's also called *capital structure*. Whatever the term, it relates to the way a company capitalizes and finances itself. For example, the capital structure of a small partnership probably consists of:

- Partner's contributions
- Capital calls contributed by partners
- Loans from partners to the firm—this may take on the form of such things as waiver of partnership distributions by some partners
- Loans provided by outside lenders such as banks

Corporations have a much more complex capital structure. This can consist of:

1. *Stock.* Often a single company can have several different classes of stock. It may also have issued preferred stock.
2. *Bonds.* Bonds are the liability side of the firm's balance sheet. These are obligations of the company to repay the bondholders. Don't think that only large cor-

---

Responsibilities of the Treasurer

- Maintains the system of internal control in the areas of:

  Cash collections and disbursements

  Cash concentration system

  Investment of excess cash

- Maintains banking relationships. Includes compliance with lending covenants and restrictions and furnishing lenders with specific financial information.

- Administers the employee benefit plans such as the employee stock purchase plan, 401K plan, employee stock options, and pension fund.

- Coordinates issues between the stock transfer agent and registrar.

- Maintains relationships with the investment public including shareholders, investment bankers, and financial analysts.

- Manages company stock transactions in accordance with board's instructions with regard to changes in par value and stated value of stock.

- Signs the company's stock certificates, replaces and cancels certificates when necessary. Maintains the company's stock book.

- Provides the long-term and short-term capital necessary to sustain the company's operations.

- Authorizes restrictive covenants and all other terms of borrowing.

- Supervises the cash concentration system.

- Administers the credit policy and credit extension function.

- Runs the collections function.

- Oversees foreign exchange operations and manages currency risk.

- Authorized signatory for disbursement checks for payables and for payroll. Treasurer may also be custodian of the automatic signature plate.

- Responsible either for the checking account reconciliations or their review and approval, but not both.

- Determines and executes risk management policy including interest rate risk, foreign currency risk, and insurance coverage.

- Responsible for investment of excess cash. Safeguards company's investment securities.

- Supervises company compliance with financial rules of stock-governing bodies including the SEC, NASD, and any exchanges on which the firm's stock is traded.

Figure 1-4. Treasurer's responsibilities.

porations may issue bonds. Private placements of debt offerings are also common among smaller companies and provide a ready supply of needed capital.

3. *Long-term financing.* Mortgage loans reside here. These often form the core financing of the company. This is money that isn't due for repayment for many years.

4. *Short-term loans.* These take on the form of installment credit and other loans usually due within two years. Often assets of the firm such as machinery, equipment, and accounts receivable secure the loans.

5. *Credit lines.* These are the so-called revolvers. They were so named because they are drawn down, then repaid during the course of the year, in a revolving manner. Lines of credit fund such working capital requirements for businesses with seasonal sales. They are often unsecured because they are so short term in nature and are callable.

Responsibility for Maintaining the Financial Structure

Maintenance of a company's financial structure is usually a treasury function. Smaller companies without a full-time treasurer may ask the controller to assume these duties.

The larger and more complex a firm's financial structure, the larger the task to keep everything under control and in compliance. Figure 1.5 summarizes many of the tasks associated with maintaining the financial structure.

Funds for Working Capital

Though technically not part of a company's capital structure, working capital is the lifeblood of most small- to medium-sized businesses. Whoever is in charge of the treasury function at the company is responsible for providing sufficient working capital to keep the business running.

Definition of Working Capital. Working capital simply means the excess of current assets over current liabilities. It's the money that remains after payment of liabilities due within the operating period. Some people compute working capital as:

Cash

Plus accounts receivable

Plus inventory

Equals working capital

Companies require working capital to pay for purchases of inventory that they've sold on credit to customers. It takes time for customers to pay, yet vendors demand payment. Where does that cash come from? Further, where does payment for obligations such as payroll and rent, along with all the other expenses that come due before collecting accounts receivable, come from? Working capital, that's where.

Figure 1-5. Tasks to maintain financial structure.

Tasks to Maintain Financial Structure

Partnerships

- Maintain partner's capital account balances.
- Provide Forms K-1 at year end.
- Manage capital calls.
- Manage distribution of profits to partners.

Stock

- Maintain the stock records book.
- Issue stock certificates.
- Cancel stock certificates.
- Retire stock certificates.
- Oversee stock transfer.
- Manage shareholder voting for directors at the annual meeting.
- Keep the firm in compliance with all rules and regulations of any stock exchanges on which the firm's stock is publicly traded.
- Maintain officers and associated persons in compliance with current insider trading rules.
- Maintain firm compliance with the rules of every state in which the stock is offered for sale.
- Pay dividends when so declared and ordered by the board of directors.

Bonds

- Maintain the firm's compliance with the bond indenture.
- Pay bond interest in accordance with bond requirements.
- If bonds are publicly traded, maintain firm compliance with all exchange requirements.
- Manage the bond's call provisions in the event the firm wishes to call them back.
- In the event the firm is working with industrial development bonds, manage legal requirements such as arbitrage profit and use of bond proceeds.
- In the event the bonds are sold to the Small Business Administration from a qualified small business investment company, maintain the statutory requirements regarding ownership percentage and investment limits.
- Properly account for any bond premium or discount when the securities are issued.

(Continued)

Figure 1-5. (*Continued*)

> *Loans*
> - Maintain the firm's compliance with all lending covenants and restrictions.
> - Pay principal and interest payments when due.
> - Provide financial reports as required by the loan terms.
> - Maintain relationship with lenders.

Where working capital demand exceeds trade credit, a funding gap occurs. The treasurer must somehow close this gap for the firm to meet its obligations and the company to remain solvent. A working capital loan—sometimes in the form of a line of credit (LOC)—sometimes works.

Another point about the volatility of working capital: It changes over time. For example, if the general economy worsens, customers become reluctant to part with their cash. Collection of accounts receivable slows. From the equation above, this increases working capital required to keep the firm in business.

Additionally, companies that suddenly become better inventory managers and can do with less stock on hand liberate working capital required to fund operations. That's good news for a treasurer, who can more profitably employ the extra money elsewhere in the company rather than in slow-moving inventory. Alternatively, the firm can use this money to pay down existing LOCs. As a last resort, if it's not needed elsewhere, short-term investment of excess cash is a possibility.

The components of working capital that change over time concern treasurers. Figure 1-6 shows an example of the commonly used Statement of Changes in Working Capital.

Figure 1-6 shows a decrease in working capital between the two years under review. The firm caused cash and receivables to fall and payables to rise. Inventory increased and accrued liabilities decreased—but not so much that we lose the benefit of a drop in working capital requirements. The net effect decreased the working capital required to run the firm.

Composition of Working Capital.   A change to a working capital account can alter the composition of working capital without actually changing the amount of working capital required to run the company. Notice that collection of receivables causes a rise in the balance in cash and a fall in the balance in receivables. Working capital stays the same; its composition was just rearranged. If you are responsible for the treasury function, chances are you've worked hard to cause this event to occur. Suddenly, more cash has become available for use in running the company. Cash is always preferable to the same amount in accounts receivable.

Effects of Noncurrent Items on Working Capital.   By a *noncurrent item* we mean things that go beyond this operating period or are of a noncash nature—such as depreciation, issuance of common stock, and the purchase of capital assets

TDO Enterprises, Inc.
Statement of Changes in Working Capital
For the Year Ended December 31, 19X2

	December 31		Working Capital	
	19X1	19X2	Increase	Decrease
Current assets:				
Cash	$21,000	$10,000		$11,000
Accounts receivable	30,000	20,000		10,000
Inventory	26,000	30,000	4,000	
Total current assets	$77,000	$60,000		$17,000
Current liabilities:				
Accounts payable	$10,000	$15,000		$ 5,000
Accrued liabilities	2,000	0	2,000	
Total current liabilities	$12,000	$15,000		$ 3,000
Working capital	$65,000	$45,000		$20,000

Figure 1-6. Statement of Changes in Working Capital.

(to name a few). So that the controller and treasurer may readily capture the effects of these noncurrent items, they compute the Statement of Changes in Financial Position prepared on a working capital basis. Figure 1-7 continues the example begun with TDO Enterprises, Inc.

See how this statement provides a more complete picture of where the money actually went?

Funds Required to Execute the Business Plan

The capital structure must provide the funds necessary to implement the firm's business plan this year and in the coming years. Astute treasurers include any required changes to their capital structure as a major ingredient of the business plan.

For example, let's say that a company plans on introducing a new product in two years. The funding required for this project is as follows:

Research and development—year 1	$ 500,000
Purchase of production equipment—year 2	1,000,000
Marketing and advertising—year 2	750,000
Increase in required working capital from accounts receivable—year 2	350,000
	$2,600,000

TDO Enterprises, Inc.
Statement of Changes in Financial Position—Working Capital Basis
For the Year Ended December 31, 19X2

Financial resources provided:
Working capital from operations:

Net income		$10,000
Plus nonworking capital expenses:		
Depreciation		5,000
Total working capital from operations		$15,000
Issuance of common stock		30,000
Total financial resources provided		$45,000

Financial resources applied:

Purchase of plant assets	$20,000	
Dividends expenditure	45,000	65,000
Decrease in working capital		$20,000

Schedule of changes in working capital components:
Increase (decrease) in current assets:

Cash		$(11,000)
Accounts receivable		(10,000)
Inventory		4,000
		$(17,000)

Increase (decrease) in current liabilities:

Accounts payable	$(5,000)	
Accrued liabilities	2,000	(3,000)
Decrease in working capital		$(20,000)

Figure 1-7. Statement of Changes in Financial Position—Working Capital Basis.

The treasurer may get the $2.6 million using different methods of financing and sources of capital. Further, since the company doesn't need it all at once, it is drawn as necessary. A possible scenario might be:

- R&D funds come from existing cash on hand.

- Production equipment and marketing expenses are funded from a private placement of bonds.

- Finance working capital needed from the increase in A/R by raising the working capital line of credit. Secure the needed increase with the new receivables.

Regardless of where the funds come from, the treasurer is responsible for having the funds available to execute the business plan.

Risk

Design of the capital structure should address two types of risk:

- Interest rate risk
- Financing risk

Chapter 21, "Risk Management," details the various elements of risk associated with the controller's and treasurer's job. However, here's a quick overview from the standpoint of capital structure.

Interest Rate Risk. Whenever a company's capital structure produces financing expense that changes with movements in interest rates, there is risk. For example, say a company is 100 percent financed using variable-rate loans. That company is at substantial risk if rates rise. It is the treasurer's responsibility to reduce interest rate risk to a level acceptable by the firm's management.

For many companies, that's easier said than done. However, in theory it simply requires a little financial common sense. Take, for example, the company completely financed by variable-rate loans. The treasurer considers two things when determining the acceptability of that risk:

1. The range over which interest rates are most likely to fluctuate
2. The potential damage to the bottom line if rates did fluctuate within that range

Using these guides the treasurer identifies the amount of debt needed in a fixed-rate instrument or some other method of controlling costs when interest expense moves against the firm. One such strategy would be the use of interest rate futures or an interest rate swap whose benefits move opposite the damage done by rising rates. Chapter 21, "Risk Management," discusses these techniques in more detail.

Financing Risk. By this we mean the company may be at risk of having to completely repay a loan when it comes due. If the firm considers the money part of its core financing, then it would likely want to roll the loan over. Indeed, it may not even have the funds to repay the loan.

Financing risk usually moves in relation to the creditworthiness of the company. As a firm's credit rating deteriorates, so does its ability to attract financing when necessary. The treasurer is responsible for lining up lenders and other sources of capital as the financial structure matures and comes due.

Return on Investment

The entire management team is responsible for providing owners and investors with an acceptable return on their invested capital. However, the treasurer is in a unique position. The treasurer must attract investment and lending capital. The investment community looks to the treasurer for assurance as to the stability and competitive return from the company. Unsatisfied investors won't invest again. However, treasurers seldom have a controlling vote on company strategy to fulfill investor's expectations. That's the treasurer's unique position: responsibility without the authority to act.

Add to this regulatory restrictions and the normal competitive influences of the investment market. Suddenly the treasurer has a huge job in promoting the financial structure of the company.

2

The Accounting System

Overview

Accounting systems vary from company to company. The sophistication and importance of a company's accounting system depends on management's orientation. For example, if management assumes a high level of daily involvement, the operational detail provided by the accounting system may be less—understandably so because of management's involvement in the firm's daily operations. They know what's going on before the accounting system can report it.

Conversely, firms with several divisions all reporting to a single holding company (sometimes called the *corporate entity*) require more detail. Here, corporate management cannot involve itself in daily operations of the divisions. The accounting system and system of internal accounting controls must provide senior executives with two things:

- *Financial information.* Including performance data, cost of operations, and warning signs that performance is moving out of the planned range.

- *Control.* Essentially a system of checks and balances that ensures the operation is running in accordance with management's already-established policies and procedures.

This chapter demonstrates the types of accounting systems found at small- to medium-sized businesses. We'll also identify the different components that make up the accounting system, how they interact with one another, and what information goes in and comes out.

The Accounting Cycle

We're not going to teach accounting here. However, to understand the accounting system, it's important that you have a grasp of the accounting cycle. The accounting system has a definite beginning, middle, and end—that's what we'll describe first.

Beginning of the Accounting Cycle

If we start at the beginning of the accounting period (either the start of the new month or year) we have balance sheet accounts, income accounts, and expense accounts, all with particular balances. The balance sheet accounts start the new accounting period with the balances from the end of the prior period. For example, say we had $100,000 in our bank account at the end of last year. We would begin this year with the same $100,000 balance reported on the balance sheet.

However, if our revenue accounts all added up to $5 million in revenue last year, what do we start the new year with? *Zero*. The income and expense accounts are all zeroed out as part of the controller's year-end closing routine. Absent this, we couldn't track our company's profit or loss from year to year (or accounting period to accounting period).

This doesn't mean that the income and expense balances have gone away. They are all added up at year end. We close the resulting profit or loss to:

- Retained earnings (a balance sheet item) if the firm is a corporation
- Partner's capital (also a balance sheet item) if the firm is a partnership

We carry the balance in retained earnings or partner's capital forward from year to year because it is part of the company's balance sheet. Here are the accounting entries for a simple closing:

	Debit	Credit
All income accounts	X	
All expense accounts		X
Retained earnings	X	X

Note, the entry to retained earnings can be either a debit or a credit depending on whether the firm had a profit (then it's a credit) or a loss (then it's a debit). The entries bring the income and expense balances to zero in preparation for the new accounting period.

One last reminder: Since people unfamiliar with accounting sometimes forget, Figure 2-1 shows what entries increase and decrease particular types of accounts.

Middle of the Accounting Cycle

Actually, the middle of the accounting cycle begins right after the new accounting period starts and the income and expense accounts are at zero. Now is when the controller begins recording the company's transactions in the general ledger and all of the subledgers.

For example, when invoices from vendors come in, they get posted to the accounts payable subledger individually. From there, the general ledger accounts receive batch totals from the invoices. At the general ledger level we debit the individual expense accounts (to increase them) and credit the accounts payable balance (to increase it).

Accounting Entry Refresher		
	Debit	Credit
Assets:		
Increase	X	
Decrease		X
Liabilities:		
Increase		X
Decrease	X	
Income accounts:		
Increase		X
Decrease	X	
Expense accounts:		
Increase	X	
Decrease		X

Figure 2-1. Increasing/decreasing accounting entries.

Cutoffs. Most well-run accounting departments pay close attention to the cutoff of each accounting period. They want to be consistent. If the financial statements say they are for a particular year, there can be no transactions contained in them from either the prior or succeeding years.

When an accounting period ends, it doesn't mean we close the books on that day. Invoices for expenses incurred in that period may not have come in yet. Likewise (though this is often stretching the point), invoices may lag behind items sold in that period. That's why some companies hold open the books for a week or more. This allows time for recognition and accounting of all the transactions associated with that period.

End of the Accounting Cycle

After accounting for all the transactions associated with a particular accounting period, it's time to close the books. Here are the steps most controllers follow in their period-end closing procedures:

- Post all subledgers.
- Post all transactions appearing in the subledgers to the general ledger.
- Prepare a trial balance.
- Prepare the financial statements.
- Conduct the period-end closing procedures.
- Prepare management review package.

Note that the trial balance is simply a listing of all the account balances (both balance sheet and income statement accounts) with a net profit/loss figure at the bottom. Review each account in the trial balance for accuracy. Investigate and correct any items that appear wrong.

Often, in automated accounting systems, closing procedures automatically roll balance sheet items forward to the new accounting period and close out income and expense items to retained earnings (or partner's capital). This begins the new period with zero income and expense balances.

Components of the Accounting System

The controller carries ultimate responsibility for establishing and maintaining the firm's accounting systems and procedures. Depending on the company's size and requirements, the accounting system may include some or all of the following components:

- General ledger
- Accounts receivable and payable
- Inventory control
- Order entry and its interface with inventory control and accounts receivable
- Cost accounting
- Fixed assets
- Backup and source documents for transactions
- Hardware and software necessary to run the accounting system
- Personnel requirements

Where Does Accounting Information Come From?

Accounting information comes from all over the company. Here are the most common sources:

- Invoices from vendors for purchases
- Invoices sent from the company to customers to record sales
- Shipping confirmations of inventory received
- Invoices and/or purchase contracts for capital assets
- Insurance claims certificates to record receipt of cash from insured losses
- Lawsuit settlement agreement documents to record payment or receipt of cash

Where Does the Accounting Information Go?

Audit trails concern accountants. This is a mechanism used to determine the reason and details behind each and every entry that hits the accounting system.

Accountants want the ability to identify the reasons for each entry into the books. Therefore, many companies retain most of the source documents associated with entries made to the books. They organize and file these records to allow for easy retrieval. Vendor invoices, for example, are retained in invoice-number sequence for a specified period as the source documents for accounts payable. Retain company invoices by number as support for customer sales already recorded in accounts receivable.

Most automated accounting systems provide space for a reference number and a brief description as to the nature of each transaction. This greatly expedites tracing an entry. The general ledger, for example, uses journal entry (J/E) numbers as reference aids. We can tie these to hard-copy records ordered by J/E number for future reference.

Concerns of the Controller

The controller has several objectives other than just getting the numbers right—though that certainly is important. Here are the main concerns of a modern controller:

- Fairness of presentation of the company's financial position
- Adequacy and competency of the accounting system
- Internal and external financial reporting
- Compliance with regulatory requirements
- Overall system of internal accounting controls

Fairness of Presentation

This is what the CPAs call a term of art. It means that the financial statements correctly portray the company's financial situation as of the period ending indicated on their face. However, there are several techniques the controller uses to ensure fairness of presentation:

Account Classification.   The accounting system must correctly classify transactions affecting the balance sheet and income statement. For example, the reader of the balance sheet must have confidence that a particular account contains activity *only* for that account.

Timing.   The controller is responsible for maintaining proper accounting cutoffs for the firm's transactions. Readers of the financial statements must have confidence that when the income statement says we made a million dollars profit, that doesn't mean that a few hundred thousand leaked in from the prior year to make this year look better.

Cutoffs are very precise and require vigorous enforcement. Indeed, they're so important that if your firm undergoes a certified audit by an independent CPA firm, one of their procedures will be to test the cutoff of the accounting system from which they are attesting to the fairness of presentation of your financial statements.

Conformity with Generally Accepted Accounting Principles.   The controller is responsible for the accounting system being run with consistent adherence to generally accepted accounting principles (GAAP). For example, there are specific procedures for recognizing the depreciation of an asset. The controller is responsible for following these procedures. To arbitrarily change from straight-line depreciation to sum of the year's digits in the middle of the month without good reason is not applying GAAP consistently.

The point is that the controller's audience for the firm's financial accounting data must have a common reference point for recording and reporting transactions. That reference point is GAAP.

Adequacy and Competency of the Accounting System

The controller is responsible for maintaining an accounting system that meets the needs of the company. This includes not only the physical aspects of the department but competent personnel as well. Too often small- to medium-sized businesses overlook deficiencies in their accounting system and attempt to limp along. Some rationalize this tendency, saying, "It's an overhead cost and we don't need any more of those."

True. The accounting department may not contribute directly to the profitability of the company. However, without adequate books and records the firm would have no basis to file accurate tax returns. Further, a reliable cost accounting system serves management every day by tracking production costs that help keep the company profitable.

Here are some of the things that go into an adequate and competent accounting system:

Books of Original Entry.   Most businesses of any size at all run their accounting system on a computer. It may be only a small personal computer, but it's better than making entries into a book of columns using a quill pen. Therefore, the books of original entry are more and more often found resident on a hard disk.

The computer and the software that runs it must be adequate for the job. For example:

- The memory capacity must be adequate to hold all the transaction records needed.

- Employees charged with running the accounting system must understand the system.

- All the modules needed by the accounting system (general ledger, accounts receivable, etc.) must be available from the software.

Personnel.   The people who work in the accounting department must be qualified. Their level of education and experience must have prepared them to do their jobs. Further, most companies provide a program for ongoing education of their technical personnel. Finally, the personnel interview and reference-checking process must be adequate to ensure that only competent and trustworthy people enter the accounting organization.

Adequate Documents and Records.   Have you ever walked into your controller's office and asked for an explanation of a particular cost? Controllers who competently run an accounting system that's adequate for their company's requirements can find the answer without any problem. In this regard, the system of document storage and retrieval must be sufficient to meet the company's needs.

Physical Aspects.   The accounting department doesn't need to be the most beautifully decorated part of the company. Most aren't. However, because the nature of the work demands it, at least two physical requirements must be met:

1. *Limited access to the books and records.*   These are irreplaceable documents of the firm. Often contained in the accounting and treasurer's offices are original articles of incorporation, stock certificate books, backup computer media, leases, and other important documents.

2. *Adequate storage facilities.*   Due to the sensitive nature and value of documents in the controller's and treasurer's offices, the storage facility becomes an issue. Many offices use fireproof safes or specially designed cabinets. Key entry doors sometimes control access to particular storage areas. In certain cases (stock certificates, for example), on-site facilities are inadequate. Some companies rent space from special commercial facilities (such as safe-deposit boxes at a bank).

Internal and External Financial Reporting

For most small- and medium-sized companies, internal reporting is the most important. The world at large does not generally care much about financial reports of nonpublicly held companies. The accounting system must provide these things in its financial reporting:

- Accuracy and reliability
- Timeliness
- Objectivity
- Relevance

Financial reports usually have a certain urgency about them. Management may need them to make a decision. Investors may require them by a particular date because that's when the indenture says they're due. The IRS requires calendar-year companies to file their income tax by April 15 (unless they are granted an extension).

However, it never makes sense to put out financial information that is suspect just to meet a deadline. Credibility is the controller's most valuable commodity. If you ever face the dilemma of getting it right or meeting a deadline, get it right, then worry about your deadline.

Next, the financials must tell the facts without any embellishments designed to soften the blow of bad news. That's not the controller's job. The numbers are the numbers. Nothing can change that.

Finally, the financial reports must provide the precise information needed by those who use it. Astute controllers identify what their audience wants before they prepare it. That's what they get. Providing anything more runs the risk of being misinterpreted and confusing the reader.

Compliance with Regulatory Requirements

The controller's office is often the focal point of regulatory reporting. Controllers are usually good at this sort of thing. Besides, much of the information required by regulatory authorities is financial in nature. Governmental entities and other regulators are usually after some sort of tax or other assessment based on financial performance.

However, providing the reports is not enough. That deals only with historical issues. The controller's job extends to keeping the company out of trouble with the regulators. In this sense, the controller's office may very well be the chief compliance authority. It's up to the controller to:

Understand Regulatory Requirements.   Many small- to medium-sized businesses are in regulated industries. The securities brokerage industry is one. For example, a small boutique brokerage firm with annual gross sales of only $1 million is probably overseen by the Securities Exchange Commission, the National Association of Securities Dealers, the Commodities Futures Trading Commission, the National Futures Association, and the department of corporations for the state in which they conduct business. Each of these entities has their own regulatory requirements with which the firm must comply. Each entity requires its own monthly and quarterly reporting package.

Stand with Regulators.   Financial executives help maintain the firm in good standing with regulators. The best way to do this is to keep the firm in compliance with all rules and regulations of the governing bodies. Again, the controller often assumes the role of chief compliance officer. Further, there must be a single knowledgeable person in authority at the company whom the regulators may contact concerning questions or problems.

Overall System of Internal Accounting Controls

The controller and treasurer are responsible for maintaining the system of internal controls for their departments. Chapters 5 and 6 deal with the technical aspects extensively. However, from our present standpoint, internal control is an integral part of the accounting system.

The system of internal controls provides several features:

- Safeguards the firm's assets
- Checks the reliability and accuracy of accounting data
- Promotes operating efficiency
- Encourages adherence to prescribed managerial policies

The controller is responsible for designing, implementing, and maintaining the system of internal accounting controls. Your firm may undergo a certified audit by an independent CPA firm. One of their procedures probably includes a study of the system of internal control as a basis for reliance on the firm's numbers. They use their conclusions to determine the extent of the tests included in their auditing procedures. If your CPA firm determines it can rely on the system of internal controls, chances are their tests of transactions will be less extensive—their bill may even be lower.

Internal Audit.   Maintaining the system of internal control concerns some firms so much that they have created an internal audit function. This acts as part of the built-in checks and balances that ensures management policy is followed. The internal audit staff is *independent* of the controller. They don't report to the controller, nor does the controller have anything to say about their hiring, firing, raises, or promotions. Instead, most internal audit organizations report directly to the audit committee of the board of directors. This ensures independence from the organization under review.

Management Information System

The most important part of the accounting system from a management standpoint is its reporting system. This is the part of accounting everyone depends on to help them make accurate, timely decisions.

The management information system must provide the data needed in a timely manner. For example, say a company conducts a test-marketing program on a prototype product. The accounting system reports on sales revenue, costs of production, and collection of accounts receivable related to the new customers buying the test product. Each of these items is important to judge how the new product is doing.

Components of the Management Information System

Size and sophistication of the company define the areas of specialization. Small companies usually incorporate all the components of their accounting information system into a single software package that's run by one person—often the controller/treasurer. Larger companies have special information needs and tend to split up the areas of specialization.

Here are the major areas of accounting information:

Management Reporting.   Every month the management and owners of most companies like to see how their companies performed. The management information system produces the reports used for this assessment. Month-end reporting packages vary among companies and management. However, most include at least the following:

- Complete set of financial statements including balance sheet, income statement, and statement of cash flows
- Aging of accounts receivable with analysis showing the tendency of accounts to roll through the aging buckets to write-off
- Cash flow projection showing anticipated sources and uses of cash in the upcoming days, weeks, and months
- Accounts payable as related to compliance with company aging policies and what expenses are being purchased from specific vendors
- Production analysis including costs and variances

There are other parts of the financial reporting package for specific types of companies. Yours will likely vary. However, the above list is a good start.

General Ledger Accounting.   The general ledger (G/L) is the part of the accounting system to which all financial information eventually flows. All financial reports come from the G/L system. Balances as reported in the G/L accounts all tie to either the subledgers or reconcile to their source documents (such as the bank statements).

Often the requirements of maintaining the G/L system at large firms are so demanding that it requires a supervisor and a staff. Most small- to medium-sized companies, however, get by with a single person.

Accounts Receivable.   The receivables system is a component of the G/L system. All transactions concerning credit purchases and payments or adjustments to customer account balances flow first through accounts receivable (A/R). From there they flow up to the A/R account in the G/L system. The A/R subledger balance must tie in exactly to the accounts receivable balance in the general ledger. If it doesn't, there's a problem.

The A/R system generates all the management information regarding credit sales, payment collections, delinquent accounts, and write-offs. Use this information to make decisions regarding:

- Credit authorization policy
- Cash flow projections
- Actions against delinquent customers
- Legal action necessary to perfect the firm's position for customers likely to go into bankruptcy (or already there)

Accounts Payable. Payables are something small- and medium-sized businesses can and should control. There's a fine line between being an astute cash manager by stretching payment terms and abusing vendors. Nevertheless, perceptive A/P policy takes the firm to the point of payment that meets its cash requirements without impugning the firm's creditworthiness.

The monthly report from the payables system generally includes such information as:

- Average aging of payables before payment
- Cash requirements for payables aging over the next days, weeks, and months for use in the cash forecast
- Invoices in dispute and what's being done to resolve them

Fixed Assets. The monthly financial reporting package does not always report fixed assets. In small- and medium-sized companies, there's usually not that much to report. However, many companies have a capital-asset acquisition plan—especially those firms that are growing. This often requires the purchase of substantial amounts of capital equipment.

Reporting the status of fixed assets tracks the purchases and deliveries against the plan and gives everyone a progress report. Further, this information is necessary for the cash flow projection.

Cost Accounting. Chapter 14 details cost accounting. However, the monthly management package often reports significant variances from standard costs. These may include such things as:

- Variance from standard material prices
- Labor variances from those that were planned
- Material rework costs

Management needs to know two things about these variances reported from the cost accounting system:

- How much will it affect the bottom line?
- What can be done to correct problems or capitalize on opportunities?

If the firm has a factory, here are some of the added cost-related responsibilities sometimes assigned the accounting department:

- Inventory control
- Timekeeping
- Cost distribution

Tax.   Taxation is a specialized area. Some companies have a tax professional on staff who prepares the firm's tax returns and assists in structuring transactions to lessen the tax burden. Small businesses often seek the help of an outside tax consultant as needed rather than incur the expense of a full-time employee.

Payroll.   The payroll system usually falls within the controller's responsibility. Associated with this function are such things as:

- Payroll computation
- Distribution
- Payroll tax payments
- Payroll tax forms at year end
- Time cards
- Maintenance of payroll history files

Many companies use some sort of automated payroll—either on their own computer or through a service bureau. Regardless, there is someone in the controller's department who generates payroll on time and accurately.

Organizational Structure of the Accounting Department

Structure the accounting department along lines of responsibility. Large companies may have a person or (if they're really large) an entire department dedicated to each of the disciplines discussed above.

Regardless of whether each area has its own supervisor or a single manager overseeing everything, these are the lines of organization in the accounting department. Most often the controller oversees the entire area and is responsible for everything related to accounting.

The controller may report to a vice president of finance. This person is responsible for all the firm's financial affairs, not just those belonging in the controller's office.

Audit Committee

Many companies have an audit committee within the board of directors. This committee selects the outside auditors if the firm uses one. It also oversees the internal audit function. The controller does not directly report to the audit committee. Nevertheless, the audit committee greatly influences parts of the controller's job.

Internal or external auditors bring controller-related problems to the attention of the audit committee. If this happens too often, the committee may issue a recommendation that the controller be replaced.

Delegation of Duties

Most of the disciplines have sufficient internal control points that allow delegation of the function, while the controller maintains oversight. Such an area is accounts receivable. The A/R subledger must balance with accounts receivable in the G/L. That's one control. Another is routine contact with customers by someone independent of the A/R function—say, a salesperson. Verification of account balances is done at that time. A third check would be routine random polling of selected credit customers to verify that they exist. Finally, the controller is usually familiar with the names of the customers.

Probably the most serious breach of internal control points when delegating financial duties is giving too much responsibility to one person. The controller must be sure that a single person doesn't have what are called *uncomplementary duties.* Those are tasks that if done by the same person could open the door to potential risk. For example, most companies don't delegate to the same person tasks of running the A/P system, check writing, signature authority, and bank account reconciliation. Doing so would present an opportunity for embezzlement.

Organization of the Treasury Department

The treasury works closely with the controller's department as well as most other departments. For control purposes we want the actual handling of cash—done in the treasurer's department—separated from the task of transaction recording—done in the controller's department.

Here are some of the functions undertaken by the treasurer. Recognize that not every company has the need for a separate individual handling each of these areas.

Cashier

The cashier pays out and receives cash on a limited basis for various functions in the company that need it. However, most cash payout transactions use checks or some other means. After all, the company's function is to take in cash, not pay it out.

Credit Authorization

Separate the receivables manager from the person who authorizes credit. Separate departments doing A/R supervision and credit authorization ensure that collusion between two or more people would have to occur before compromising the control.

Both the people granting credit and the receivables manager must work closely together. After all, receivables will suffer on the back end if mistakes in granting credit occur on the front end. The monthly management report should summarize the types of credit extended and the changes made in credit policy. It should link these changes in strategy to the results in collection of accounts receivable.

Mail Room

Does it sound odd to have something traditionally unsophisticated like the mail room under the control of the relatively complex treasury department? Consider the most important pieces of mail coming into the company—customer payments. It's the treasury's responsibility to capture these payments, rush them through the cash concentration system, and convert them to spendable funds. What better department to make responsible for the mail room?

There's another reason—internal control. We want the people who handle funds (i.e., checks received in the mail) separated from those who record their receipt (the people who run A/R in the controller's department).

Further, we also want separation of duties when the company's payment checks go out. The controller's department writes the checks and records their payment. The treasurer's department signs the checks and mails them out.

Payment Processing.   Every company has some system of processing payments received through the company. The method ranges from informal, word of mouth at small companies to very structured high-tech systems at large companies. The degree of sophistication depends on the average daily amount of funds received.

For companies receiving millions of dollars a day (like a credit card company) the treasury may demand heavy involvement (if not complete control) in the mail room. Chances are they've installed state-of-the-art automated optical scanning equipment that opens the payment envelope, reads the bar code of the payment stub, records the customer's name, account number, and amount paid in the computer, and prepares the bank deposit computer tape all in a matter of seconds per customer.

From the mail room the deposit goes to the bank and the payment records go to the accounting department for posting to the A/R subledger.

Cash Manager

This is a traditional treasury task. The cash manager is responsible for:

- Maintaining adequate cash balances to meet the company's obligations
- Forecasting future cash requirements
- Maintaining compliance with lending covenants and compensating balances
- Management and administration of the cash concentration system

This job requires a complete knowledge of the company. Working capital requirements can suck up cash like nothing else in the company. Keeping track of working capital reduction opportunities includes assessment of:

- Cash
- Accounts receivable
- Inventory
- Accounts payable
- Accrued liabilities

Many cash managers take a holistic point of view of their jobs. That is, cash management relates to all aspects of the company. There isn't one part of the firm whose work doesn't in some way either take or give cash to the operation. It's the cash manager's job to accelerate the giving and slow down the taking.

Investment Manager

Companies fortunate enough to have excess cash need something to do with it. That's where short-term investments come in. Naturally, the more money there is to invest, the more important will be the job. Some very large firms have hundreds of millions to invest. It becomes very expensive if this money isn't working as hard for the company as everyone else.

Whoever does the investments must control the safety, liquidity, and yield of the instruments purchased. Further, they must manage the schedule of maturing investments. In this regard, the investment manager works closely with the cash manager. Both know how much interest and principal are coming due and when. If the cash manager doesn't have a ready use for this excess cash, then the investment manager reinvests it for a term that matches the company's cash requirement.

Additionally, the investment manager is responsible for maintaining the investment portfolio. Where investments are collateralized (such as in repurchase agreements—see Chapter 19, "Investments"), the underlying assets must be appropriate. If the firm owns stock certificates, it must inventory them and keep them in a safe place.

Finally, the investment manager must keep the board of directors (or owners if there is no board) apprised of the firm's investment portfolio. The person investing the firm's money can purchase only those securities specifically authorized by the board. This authorization considers such things as:

- Duration of the investment
- Liquidity—can they get out of it easily without risk of loss?
- Safety
- Return on the investment

Often, inexperienced investment managers take on more risk for the company than management had planned. They may do this by investing in instruments with too long a term. Alternatively, they may stray from their normal AAA-rated bonds to AA or less to get a higher yield. Regardless, it's the investment manager's job and ultimately the treasurer's responsibility to keep the firm's excess cash working without excess risk of loss. The money was too hard to make in the first place to risk losing it for the sake of another point or two of interest income.

3
Automated Systems

Overview

Most companies have some sort of automated accounting systems. More advanced firms have expanded their computer capabilities into the treasurer's department. The issue today is not how to or whether we should automate the accounting and treasury functions. Rather, financial executives want to know the best way to take advantage of modern computer capabilities. The most frequently asked questions are along the lines of, "What's new out there that could help us do our job better."

This chapter takes you through the various types of computer systems commonly used in modern accounting and treasury shops. It separates hardware issues from those related to software and demonstrates how to match the two. Chapter 3 teaches you how to select the most appropriate systems if you're thinking of upgrading what you currently have.

You don't have to be a computer expert. Indeed, most of the successful accounting and treasury users are not. They learn through doing. Where we can't avoid using buzz words I'll define them right after their use. There's a lot to cover, so let's get started.

Use of High Technology

Computer technology is changing at an increasing rate. Fact is that software has a tough time keeping up with advances being made in the hardware that runs it. Microchip technology is a case in point. Suddenly we have computer horsepower that has surpassed the needs of currently available software. The few programs able to use the advanced capacity—such as computational speed—are light years ahead of the competition.

The problem comes in compatibility between the advanced software and other programs companies may have that need to communicate with it. Introduction of the Windows operating system by Microsoft Corporation created just such a software gap. Suddenly software could take advantage of the larger random access memory (RAM) and the faster processor chips unveiled seemingly every year. RAM is the electronic memory that goes away after turning off the power. It differs from the "memory" on the hard disk in the sense that data stored on the hard disk in the sense that data stored on the hard disk is permanent.

The capabilities of Windows were enormous. However, the application programs that could take this powerful hardware/software combination to its limit were not available for some time after its introduction. An application program is the program that users interact with—like general ledger or accounts receivable. It took well over a year before we began to see the programs that really used this new capability. Even then people were reluctant to install them for fear the rest of their systems could not interface with the new technology.

Speed

Like kids with cars, the speed of computers seems to be of great concern to many people. For practical managers, computer speed (again like cars) need only be sufficient to get the job done without overkill. Again, like cars, the faster the computer, the more expensive it's likely to be.

We measure computer speed two ways:

- Megahertz
- Chip speed

These are just indices of speed—the actual value means little except when compared with a competitor. Back to our car analogy. Computer speed is similar to measuring potential engine speed using cubic inches and liters. Who cares if an engine has 450 cubic inches or 5.3 liters (just so it's more than the car next to you)?

However, if you really want to know what they mean, the following should help.

Megahertz.   Megahertz (MHz) identifies the clock speed of the central processing unit (CPU), the computational brain of the computer. MHz measures the simplest mathematical operation a machine can do in one cycle of its clock frequency.

The larger the MHz index, the faster the computer's capability. Modern computers measure MHz in 25, 33, 50, and 66 MHz. There is also a direct correlation between price and MHz.

Chip Speed.   Chips refer to the silicon chips most popularly made by Intel that run the CPU. These form the processing brain of the computer. Generally, the higher the chip number (286, 386, 486, etc.), the faster the computer.

Beware of Speed Indices.   Computer sellers tout their latest and greatest megahertz and chip combinations. They use all sorts of figures to emphasize their enhanced speed (and cost). However, the fact is that most programs need to access some sort of data storage device (such as a hard disk). The technology for these electromechanical devices lags far behind that of the chips. Therefore, the computer can run your program only as fast as the access speed allows it to read and write on the disk.

In this regard, often chips and MHz make little if any difference in job processing speed when constrained by comparatively slow disk access.

Another caution: Chip speed must synchronize with clock speed measured in MHz. This means that you can't simply switch from a 286 to a 486 processing chip without doing anything else to your machine and expect it to run faster (or sometimes run at all).

Finally, think of computer speed logically. Most modern computers (say 286, 386, or 486) process transactions in the blink of an eye. Yes, a 66-MHz, 486 machine might process the same transaction twice as fast—in half of a blink of an eye. What benefit is there? You can't tell the difference anyway.

Enhancements to System Speed

There are some inexpensive and easy ways to accelerate the *throughput* of a system. Throughput is simply the elapsed time from data input to usable output. Following are a few simple enhancements.

Upgrade Printers.   Printers are usually the bottleneck in most systems. No matter how fast the computer runs, it's still of no use until a human can read the output. That requires a printer. By investing in higher-speed printers, we enhance the throughput of a system to acceptable levels.

Upgrade Disk Storage Devices.   Another cause of slow operation is the mass data storage facility. This is usually some form of disk system. The more information loaded on a disk, the longer the access time. This isn't noticeable on PCs which use only between 40- and 100-megabyte disks. However, fully loaded disks larger than these do take time for the computer to access.

The easiest way to free up wasted disk space is to remove unneeded, seldom-used, or redundant files. A second way is to install additional smaller disk systems to isolate entire sections of data. The theory here is the smaller the disk, the faster the access time.

A third way is more exotic. It's called *defragmentation*. This is simply a repositioning of stored data on a disk. The program positions related data next to each other. This process eliminates wasted space. It also puts files in a more orderly sequence. Defragmentation programs are available from PC Tools and Norton Utilities.

Use of Networks.   Often duplicate software wastes needed disk space. This could occur when, say four people, need to access the same system. Using stand-alone PCs, each user needs a complete system. That takes up valuable disk space and could slow down throughput.

An alternative is to network the PCs into workstations. The common software resides just once in the network and is accessible by all four users.

Types of Systems

Accounting and treasury computer systems vary in cost, capability, and sophistication. The system should match your needs for today and sometime into the foreseeable future—and that's all.

Technology in both hardware and software, as well as business requirements will continue to grow. Overcomplicating a computer system so it can "grow with the firm" is often a waste. The chances of correctly guessing the firm's requirements and matching them with a technology accepted (just by luck) as the industry standard of the future are slim.

Most forward-looking controllers and treasurers design and upgrade their computer systems using a time horizon of two to five years. Beyond that, there's little way of telling the firm's needs and technology's ability to meet those needs. Here are the most popular configurations of financial computer systems:

- Stand-alone PCs
- Networks of PCs
- Minicomputers
- Mainframe computers

Stand-alone PCs

For many small companies a dedicated computer that works all by itself is sufficient. This environment lends itself to companies that are security-conscious and that have limited separation of duties. For example, the accountant who does the general ledger posting may also do receivables and payables as well as any other accounting functions on the computer. In this case, there's virtually a one-person accounting shop. Issues of internal control aside, chances are the company needs only a stand-alone accounting computer.

Some firms try to limp along with several stand-alone computers in the accounting department. What happens when they need to transfer batches from, say, accounts receivable to the general ledger for posting? Assume that both the A/R and G/L modules are on different machines and there's enough work to keep two accounting clerks busy. They have two choices:

Manual Entry.   They can do a manual journal entry into the G/L that reflects the A/R activity. Beware, however, that there is often resentment at having to make redundant manual entries from one machine to another when everyone knows the technology exists to automate this procedure. The inference is that the company is too cheap to buy it.

Disk Transfers.   The second alternative is to copy the transaction batch from the A/R computer to a disk, then load the disk into the G/L computer and copy the batch file for posting to the general ledger.

This method is less time-consuming than manual entry and doesn't require so much human intervention—therefore, less chance for errors.

Networks of PCs

A PC network is simply a group of PCs linked together through a local area network (LAN) by a common data storage device called a *file server.* The server contains the application software (all the accounting systems, for instance) as well as the data files being used. Multiple users can access the file server at the same time.

A constraint on many of the network systems is that only one user may access a given module at once. This is logical since someone printing a balance sheet from the G/L module wouldn't want the A/R balance changed by someone else in the middle of printing. The balance sheet wouldn't balance.

Networks are among the most popular advances in computer technology today. Communication between various components of the computer system is fast, electronic, and accurate. Unlike stand-alone systems, there's little chance a batch posted to a subsystem (like accounts payable) will fail to make it into the G/L. Often the first things many of these accounting systems check for when they come up are batches in the subledgers not yet transferred to the G/L and posted. The system immediately notifies users of existing unposted batches.

Types of Networks

The configuration of a computer network depends on the firm's requirements. One of the most popular configurations is the hub-and-spoke (Figure 3-1). Here, separate people perform most functions in the accounting department. Each needs a dedicated computer workstation. The central file server or the mini- or main-

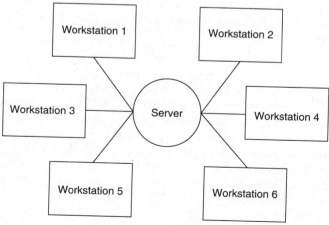

Figure 3-1. Hub-and-spoke configuration.

frame computer at larger firms acts as the hub. All outlying workstations form the spokes. The same file server stores all work done by the various people in the accounting department. All data transfers take place within the file server.

One potential problem with the hub-and-spoke configuration is the potential disaster if something goes wrong at the hub. Suddenly, data needed by other parts of the financial system is no longer available. However, if each workstation is also a stand-alone computer, at least some of the work can probably get done. The completed work is stored at the spoke workstations until the hub comes back up.

Access to different parts of the system is both password- and access-controlled according to workstation. For example, if you want to separate the bank reconciliation from possible entries in the general ledger, just turn off password access to the G/L module to the person who performs the reconciliation.

Treasury Computers.   Treasury departments use the hub-and-spoke method too. Here's how. There may be several outlying locations that take in cash each day. The treasurer needs to know the daily deposit amounts. Using the computer, the treasurer "polls" all daily cash transactions at each location. The network of computers shown in Figure 3-1 works this way.

If there's no need for a continuous daily computer connection between the corporate office and outlying locations, then connect only when needed using a modem and regular telephone lines. Many of the advanced telecommunications software packages provide for programmed calling. That feature allows the computer to automatically poll the sources of cash, download the collection information, and place it in a file at the headquarters computer. This requires no human intervention. First thing in the morning, the treasurer accesses the files collected the night before and determines how much cash to transfer from the outlying depository banks.

Another way to capture the same information is to have the treasury computer poll the banks used by the outlying locations. Information captured in this way can include the actual deposits as well as availability of those funds for use. Most banks with a cash management department provide for such on-line access by their treasury clients.

Minicomputers

There's an increasingly fine line between the capabilities of a sophisticated network system of microcomputers and a true minicomputer. Minisystems generally require more care and a higher level of sophistication to maintain. The software usually runs faster and you can "hang" more user workstations on the minisystem.

Financial departments often use minis where more than 10 people need access to the computer at the same time. The minisystem takes care of all the firm's financial computer requirements including:

- All financial accounting and reporting
- Cost accounting

- Treasury operations and analysis
- Cash forecasting
- Planning and budgeting

If the firm has other computer systems scattered throughout its operations, chances are the financial minisystem can exchange data with these other systems.

Differences between Minis and Micros. Let's state the obvious—minicomputer systems are just plain bigger than a network of microcomputers. By bigger, we mean that there is:

- More random access memory
- More internal data storage capacity
- More peripheral supporting equipment
- More workstation ports available

The software that runs these minicomputers is significantly more complicated than that found on micros. Often companies using minisystems have one or two professional programmers on staff.

Still, most minicomputers are capable of using specially adapted application software packages similar in function to those found on microsystems. You will find the various accounting system modules (G/L, A/R, A/P, etc.) and word processing, as well as some of the spreadsheet programs available for minisystems.

Finally, some of the minicomputer manufacturers recommend a special physical environment in which to set the equipment. They require environments with specially controlled temperature, humidity, and dust.

Mainframe Computers

Mainframe computers are big, complex, and expensive. Generally, large companies employ mainframes to execute all of the firm's data processing requirements—not just those of the financial department.

Many large companies purchase canned accounting software packages. Because they run them on the mainframe computer operated by a professional programming staff, they have the capability of customizing the program to exactly meet their needs.

This customization raises issues of:

- Programming standards
- Understanding of program specifications
- Review of program code
- Testing of program enhancements
- Documentation of changes
- Training of staff to operate and maintain modified programs

Certainly companies large enough to employ mainframe computers have the resources to address and manage these issues.

Centralized versus Distributed Data Processing

This question has been raging for years. Centralized data processing (DP) uses a single computer (a network of PCs, mini- or a mainframe). Users process their data through remote terminals or workstations connected to the central point.

Distributed DP means that users or groups of users have their own computers that process their work. They aren't dependent on a central computer or a professional programming staff to interpret their requirements and then program them. Instead, distributed users find their own canned software and run it. This means they are more dependent on a software seller's ability to survive and continue supporting their products after the sale.

One of the more compelling arguments in favor of distributed DP is the fact that no one knows what a user (or a group of users) needs better than themselves. Further, if the end user documents and maintains the system, chances are they'll do a better job because they have a direct and vested interest in seeing that it's right.

Software

Software is where "the rubber meets the road" in computer operations. Inefficient or cumbersome software makes even the most modern computers appear inadequate. This is especially true in computationally intensive operations such as accounting.

Here are the general features we want from financial software:

- User-friendly
- Reference capability
- Reliability
- Flexibility
- Fast and easy transfer of data within the system
- Interfaces with other systems
- Clear documentation
- Manufacturer support
- System updates responsive to changing needs

System Modules

Most systems divide accounting sections into modules. This is usually a distinct part of the system that can either stand alone (if purchased by itself) or be used as a component of a larger system. Earlier we talked about the responsibilities of the controller. The various modules usually found in accounting systems closely parallel these. They include:

- General ledger
- Accounts receivable
- Accounts payable
- Inventory control
- Order entry
- Cost accounting
- Fixed assets
- Payroll

Every accounting system module interfaces with the general ledger module. The key to finding an accounting system appropriate for your company is that it have the modules required both now and in the future. However, which modules will the company need?

This isn't very hard to figure out. For example, most smaller securities brokerage firms don't have accounts receivable of a size that requires an entire separate subledger to manage those few transactions. That means such a company probably won't need an A/R module in its accounting system—as long as it just does brokerage. However, it would be negligent to buy an accounting system that did not have an A/R module ready to plug in if needed. What happens if the business changes or if the firm acquires a subsidiary that needs an A/R system?

In that unhappy case, the controller faces either converting to a new system or using two different systems—one for the brokerage firm and one for the new firm. Wouldn't it have been easier to anticipate the possible need from the start?

Interfaces. How many times have you heard people who should know better say they need to *interface* with this or that. Everyone seems to overuse the word. However, there are some critical points of interaction within the accounting system software that you must be aware of. These include communication between:

- All subledgers and the general ledger
- Accounts receivable and the cash management system
- Order entry, accounts receivable, and inventory control
- Accounts payable and inventory control
- Fixed assets and the general ledger
- Payroll and the general ledger

These components of the system must communicate with one another. Without it, the power and utility of the computer system is diminished. Take, for example, the critical interface between order entry, inventory control, and accounts receivable. Order takers must be able to see on their computer screens the following information:

- Inventory status of each product
- Backorder status of each product
- Cost of each product
- Payment status of each customer

More sophisticated systems provide the customer's payment status when accessed on the order-entry screen. At that point order takers know whether they can even sell to particular customers or must advise them to bring their accounts current before attempting any further purchases.

Additionally, as order takers enter the inventory items they can tell instantly if these items are in stock and ready for shipment. If not, the O/E system automatically advises the purchasing department to order them through a backorder routine.

These are the kind of automatic interfaces that computers are good at. They make the difference between having simply a numbers-crunching computer and an *integrated system* that actually contributes to the firm's profitability.

Linkage

This refers to the accounting or treasury system's ability to communicate with another system such as spreadsheets, word processing, or database management software. Treasurers need to predict cash collections in order to forecast cash flow. All the historical information needed probably already exists in the A/R subledger system. However, the ability to access it, convert it, and load it into software needed to perform the computations must also exist.

Particular links between stand-alone software packages and the accounting system are sometimes important. It's best to determine these requirements in the beginning. Then narrow the search to systems that have these linkage capabilities.

References

Computer software information is in abundant supply. Most firms that service and sell the hardware also provide software or references to software manufacturers. Figure 3-2 shows some of the sources.

Security

Paying attention to financial systems security is just common sense. It really doesn't cost much in terms of time or dollars. Yet it presents a deterrent against future problems. Insiders help perpetrate most thefts of company assets. A well-designed security system keeps honest employees honest.

The Requirements Analyst

This is a database of accounting software. It's available from Training Services, 11708 Ibsen Drive, Rockville, MD 20852, (800) 433-8015.

The Accounting Library

Just what its name describes. Accounting software information is available from Solutions, 244 Early Settlers Road, Richmond, VA 23235, (804) 330-0000.

Computer Select

Descriptions on different types of accounting software. Available from Computer Library, 1 Park Avenue, 5th Floor, New York, NY 10016, (212) 503-4400.

Software Digest Ratings Report

This periodical publishes a detailed review of most popular software systems. Additionally, it issues a complete annual report on accounting software. Obtain from National Software Testing Labs, Publications Division, P.O. Box 1000, Plymouth Corporate Center, Plymouth Meeting, PA 19462, (800) 328-2776, ext. 2346.

The Center for Accounting Software Evaluation

Part of the University of Texas, CASE is a software testing lab open to the public for purposes of running software searches and evaluations. It also provides on-line access of its facilities via modem. CASE can be contacted at P.O. Box 19466 Arlington, TX 76019, (817) 273-3023.

Magazines

There are many magazines devoted to business computer systems. They may be found on most newsstands or in computer stores:

- *BYTE*
- *Computers in Accounting*
- *Info World*
- *PC Magazine*
- *PC World*

Figure 3-2. Sources of accounting software information.

Physical Security

The first step in implementing a financial security system is to harden physical access to the equipment. Many firms allow only limited entry to the accounting and treasury departments. Employees with a reason to be there are admitted, others are not.

If it's impractical to limit access, then separate the computer terminals from the main floor in a secured area. If that is also impractical, then there are software controls (passwords, access privileges) that make it more difficult (though not impossible) for unauthorized personnel to make valid entries into the accounting or treasury systems.

Terminal Access Privileges

Computer terminals or workstations tied into a local area network, minicomputer, or mainframe should be limited to specific tasks. The system controller manages terminal access privileges. For example, treasury terminals are capable of executing electronic funds transfers out of the company's bank account. We wouldn't want this access privilege in a terminal available to just anyone.

Some companies have *information only* terminals for those who simply need to look up references. These terminals cannot change any data. Other terminals that do make changes (such as posting financial transactions or recording cash receipts) sit on the desks of those authorized to make the entry.

Generally, authorization controls restrict use of a terminal to a select few for each task. For example, the terminal that posts accounts payable and the one that authorizes check printing are often different. We wouldn't want the same person to be able to enter their own invoice and have the company pay it for them, would we?

Access Checklist.   How do you keep track of who goes where within the system? One way is by assembling an access checklist like the one shown in Figure 3-3.

Passwords

Most of us are familiar with the password protection features offered by modern computer systems. By themselves, passwords provide little assurance of security. Why? Because people tend to be cavalier about the risk of compromising their systems. Also, they're afraid of being embarrassed if they forget their password. As a result, many people use passwords commonly known around the firm, such as:

- Their own names
- Their birthdays
- Children's birthdays
- Children's names
- Their maiden names
- Parent's or spouses names

This worksheet answers the questions: What areas of the system are accessed? Who has access? What can they do? From where can they do it?

System module	Terminal no.	Personnel granted info only?	Access
General ledger			
Accounts receivable			
Accounts payable			
Inventory control			
Order entry			
Invoicing			
Cost accounting			
Fixed assets			
Payroll			
Word processing			
Database systems			
Funds transfer			
Investments			

Figure 3-3. Computer system access checklist.

Still others write their passwords on those yellow post-em's and affix them right to the terminal. The more secretive tape their passwords either under blotters or inside desk drawers. Some really paranoid types attach them to the underside of their keyboards.

Often computer programs print out the entire list of passwords for maintenance purposes. Neglectful system managers simply throw them away (rather than shred them) after updating. Suddenly the master key is available to anyone knowing where to look and what to look for.

Maintaining Passwords. Some users look upon password maintenance as a pain. Just when you finally memorized your personal password, it's changed for security purposes. This could be once a month, once a quarter, or just annually. Often, system supervisors change passwords randomly.

Perform password changes as frequently as needed. Certainly when people leave the firm or change jobs within the firm, or changed jobs within the firm, cancel their passwords and issue new ones to the successors.

Rotate people who conduct password maintenance frequently. This reduces the chance of on-going fraud by the password maintenance person. Additionally, the program to change passwords itself must require at least one access password. The more advanced systems require different passwords from two people before granting access. This makes collusion a necessity in order to breach the system.

Encryption

Installations often used data encryption when security is a necessity between the sender and receiver of computer information. It works like a telephone scrambler. The process converts data into code before it goes out over the telephone lines. The end point decodes the data stream. For anyone who intercepts the data stream to have anything meaningful, they must be able to decode the message. Such unauthorized decoding requires sophisticated mainframe computers. This deterrent eliminates all but the very resourceful hackers. The objective is to make decoding the data more expensive than the value of the data.

Surprisingly, cryptographic algorithms are in common use even on PC systems.

Data Backup

The best way to protect valuable financial data is by backing it up, then storing the backups in a secured facility away from the company. After all, it doesn't make much sense watching your backup media go up in flames with the rest of the plant.

Most computer installations serious about backup procedures use a grandfather, father, son routine. This requires three separate generations of data (tapes, disks, disk packs, whatever). Tape 1 is the grandfather. Store it offsite. Tape 2 is the father. Store it perhaps in a vault on the premises. Tape 3 is the son. That's the working copy of the backup.

Cycle the tapes (if that's the media used)—the son becomes the father, which becomes the grandfather, which comes full circle to become the son. This way you never have to go too far back in case something should happen to one of the backups.

Periodic Backup.   Most companies for which security is important have regular backup procedures. For example, every day they back up that day's work. Then each Friday they back up the entire week's work and take it to the offsite storage facility. The same thing occurs at the end of each month, quarter, and year.

This procedure allows re-creation of most any time frame, if necessary.

Recovery Procedures.   Reliable recovery procedures are necessary to ensure that the backup measures work. It would be foolhardy (not to mention terribly embarrassing) to religiously back up data only to find there was a flaw in the backup procedure and the system proved unrecoverable.

Therefore, test all backup procedures to ensure they produce a recoverable tape, disk, or whatever. The only way to do this is to actually try a recovery. Many astute financial executives require a full-scale recovery periodically.

Threats to Automated Systems

Name it and it has probably happened to a computer system—everything from the mundane (spilling coffee into the CPU) to the exotic (a computer virus injected into the system).

The key to dealing with computer threats is to identify those that are most likely and protect against them. The degree of protection needed is proportional to the likelihood an incident may occur. Figure 3-4 illustrates a simple way to assess system threats.

There are three ways to deal with the risk of loss to company-owned computer systems:

- Treat it as a normal business expense.
- Share risk through trade associations.
- Purchase insurance coverage.

Threat	Probability of occurrence	Expected value of loss	Protection
Physical threat:			
Power failure			
Disk crash			
Telephone modem failure			
Telephone line failure			
Earthquake			
Fire			
Flood			
Electromagnetic discharge			
Pollution			
Gases			
Temperatures (extreme hot or cold)			
Deliberate hostility:			
From employees			
Viruses/worms			
Sabotage			
Espionage			
Fraud			
Piracy			
Theft			
Bombs and bomb threats			
Human threats:			
Incompetence			
Error			
Hackers			
Unauthorized intrusion			

Figure 3-4. Assessment of threats.

Figure 3-4 identifies a method to compute the expected value of a loss from the most common threats to computer installations. Simply identify the probability of an event occurring and multiply it by the estimated loss from an incident. The product is the expected value of the loss. Normally, the cost of countermeasures should not come close to the expected value of a loss. Otherwise, the end doesn't justify the means.

How to Select an Automated Accounting System

The issue for most treasurers and controllers is how to maximize the use of computer equipment in their operations. This requires a combination of software, hardware, and people who know how to get the most out of each. All three components are equally important. Failure of any one to perform means the system won't deliver the most bang for the company's buck.

Identify System Requirements

The first thing controllers and treasurers do when considering a new system is determine what changes they want. The enhancements may be in areas of:

- Efficiency
- Better outside systems interface
- Faster throughput
- Larger capacity

Figure 3-5 shows a checklist of some questions that are helpful in determining general ledger systems requirements. Use this checklist to compare the differences between:

- Your current system and the one under consideration
- Your wish list and the one under consideration

Software

Upgrades to existing software systems should fulfill at least these criteria:

- Compatibility with existing systems
- Tested and proven track record
- Adequate documentation
- Manufacturer support
- Existing hardware supported by new software

System requirements	Current system	New system
Financial reporting:		
Frequency: Daily		
Weekly		
Monthly		
Quarterly		
Semiannually		
Annually		
On demand		
Contents of reports:		
Balance sheet		
Income statement		
Statement of cash flows		
Statement of changes in financial position		
Financial ratio reports		
Special management reports (specify)		
Comparative reports needed?		
Historical reports?		
Provides month-to-date reports?		
Provides quarter-to-date reports?		
Provides year-to-date reports?		
Capable of separate department reporting		
Capable of consolidating two or more companies		
General ledger:		
Accounting method used:		
Accrual		
Cash		
Modified cash		
Batch posting?		
Frequency of posting		
JE referencing capability		
Trial balance		
Month-end closing		
Year-end closing		
Postclosing entries handled?		
Number of G/L accounts possible		
Capable of doing recurring JEs		
Capable of automatically repeating JEs		
Maximum nnumber of characters in a given transaction		
Separates account codes by department		
Does account code sequence match your company's requirements?		

Figure 3-5. Software requirements checklist.

Beware of the last point—hardware support. It's surprising how enthusiasm for new software wastes away if it doesn't support the hardware that stays in place. For example, packaged word processing systems require specific printer driver files, called *printer action tables* (PATs), to print the document on a given printer. It's time-consuming and a real pain to create these PATs yourself if the software setup program doesn't specifically call out your printer in its installation routine. Suddenly you have a shiny new state-of-the-art word processing system that's useless.

Another point is the windowing software that's become almost an industry standard. It makes little sense to upgrade your software to take advantage of these new features if the random access memory (RAM) in your computer is insufficient to support windows.

Staff Skills

Identify the level of skill people who run the system must have. Different computer systems require varying levels of both computer familiarity and accounting and treasury expertise. It's probably fine to train someone to use the computer, but it's not fine having to upgrade their job skills.

Training

This is where so many companies get their lunch eaten. It makes little sense to acquire software that's beyond your staff's ability to master. Generally, software is much less expensive than people. Make sure that the people who will be using the system have a say in its acquisition. Computer systems live and die by their user's enthusiasm. Many of the more progressive software houses provide training on their systems for new users.

Documentation and on-line tutorials help too. Regardless of the method, make sure that your people get adequate training on the new system. Many controllers and treasurers take this one step further. They insist that both the old and the new systems run parallel for a time.

This provides a get acquainted period for the new system. The company isn't dependent on the new system while all the kinks are being removed. Second, it identifies all differences in operating procedures and informs everyone of the changes. Finally, it highlights the benefits (as well as any deficiencies). Dropping the old system and adopting the new one is a welcome change.

4

Audit: Internal and External

Overview

Few companies look forward to their annual audit. They are expensive, time-consuming, and usually rarely tell you anything you don't already know. Then why do so many companies insist not only on annual audits by independent accounting firms, but interim reviews done by their own internal auditors as well? Chapter 4 explains why and describes the various procedures conducted during an auditor's work.

Chapter 4 also explains the difference between audits done by independent accounting organizations and those done by the company's own employees. We define the controller's and treasurer's roles during an audit. Additionally, we explain the situations that call for different types of services performed by CPA firms.

Further, Chapter 4 identifies what the auditors are looking for. It's a lot easier to pass a test if you know the questions in advance. So, let's get started.

What Does an Audit Accomplish?

First of all, companies with stock traded publicly on an organized exchange must have an annual certified audit by an independent accounting organization. That's the law. The SEC entitles investors and shareholders to fairly presented financial statements provided by their company. That's what an audit accomplishes: an opinion on the fairness of presentation of the financial statements.

Indeed, many people think the only point of an independent audit is to obtain an opinion on the fairness of presentation in accordance with generally accepted accounting principles. With this so-called clean opinion, most people rely on the accuracy of the financial statements.

Here are some other things audits accomplish.

Removes Questions About Financial Statements

Audited financial statements have less of a tendency to prompt questions regarding such issues as:

Uncertainty of the Numbers Presented.   Presentation of company assets and liabilities is one potential source of uncertainty. For example, how do investors know that future benefits of machinery and equipment shown as assets on the balance sheet are likely to continue? They don't, unless the auditor certifies that the balance sheet fairly presents the financial position of the firm.

Accurate Financial Performance.   The income statement classifies and summarizes financial events. Without examination by a qualified independent professional, investors and creditors must simply take the word of management that the statements aren't misleading. If you read the financial press at all, you know that deliberately misstated financials have taken in more than their share of unwary investors.

Proper Choice of Accounting Alternatives.   Accounting is not an exact science. Management often has choices to make among accounting alternatives. All may be perfectly justifiable by themselves. The problem comes when managers intentionally use a combination of choices to produce a desired effect.

A certified audit identifies such abuses of accounting principles before release of financial statements to the public. Incorrect usage or consistent choices designed to skew the presentation may cause the statements to unfairly present the company's financial position.

Other Uses of Audit Results

Financial statements certified as to their fairness of presentation are more credible than those coming straight from management without independent audit or review. Indeed, lenders, investors, and partners often require certified financials as part of their formal agreements.

Additionally, the annual audit does provide a slight deterrent against fraud, embezzlement, defalcations, and other irregularities. Though discovery of this is not the mission of an audit, it sometimes exposes such things. At any rate, a perpetrator may think twice about such action, knowing that a crew of trained professionals will one day pour over the books and records.

Linkage with Overall Checks and Balances

When administered correctly, the audit function provides a necessary link in the company's system of checks and balances. The audit function doesn't have to end in certification of the financial statements. The accountant's report can reflect a review (giving no assurance on fairness of presentation) or simply a compilation using unverified numbers provided by management. Further, the accountant may be an employee of the company acting as an internal auditor.

Regardless, the work done by these professionals provides an important link in the overall control that lenders and owners of the firm have in the financial operations of the company. They have a vested interest in seeing consistent application of company policies.

Types of Engagements

Too often, people who should know better refer to CPAs as auditors. They call the work these professionals do *auditing*. Neither is correct. Certainly, only a licensed CPA can perform a certified audit. However, there are many other services a company may use to get what they need. Here are the types of financial engagements most often used and their indications.

Certified Audit

This is the highest level of service the CPA provides. It's usually the most expensive too. The objective of a certified audit is to attest to the fairness of presentation of the financial statements. To accomplish this, the CPA must prove all material aspects of the financials on which his or her opinion appears.

CPAs conduct procedures designed to provide reasonable assurance that the statements are fairly presented. Additionally, they include notes to readers of the financials explaining items that may not be obvious as they appear on the face.

The company distributes certified financial statements to third parties. Indeed, that's usually the point of having the audit conducted in the first place.

When Is an Audit Indicated?   Certainly, publicly held companies require a certified audit. Other circumstances that require audits include:

- Lending covenants
- Securities indentures
- Provision of partnership agreements
- Special cases such as the sale of a firm where the purchase price is based on financial performance

Review

Review by a CPA, regardless of whether the CPA is independent or associated with the company, is substantially smaller in scope than an audit. Reviews generally don't include tests of transactions sufficient to form an opinion on the financial statements—presented fairly or otherwise. Instead, the accountant in a review applies analytical procedures to the financial data and makes inquiries of those responsible for financial and accounting matters.

The review report states that the accountant is not aware of any material modifications required to conform the financial statements to GAAP. Professionals call this *negative assurance.*

The work involved in a review is less costly than that performed in an audit. Generally, the financial statements coming out of a review are not for release to third parties. They assume the reader is familiar with the specifics of the company.

When Is a Review Indicated?   Interim periods such as for quarterly reports usually call only for a review of financial statements. Additionally, management may request a review for their own internal use. Do this when management wants to verify the accuracy of information received from the firm's internal accountants.

Compilation

This is one step removed from a review. During a compilation, accountants simply present information provided by management in the form of financial statements that represent management. Compilations do not express an opinion or any other form of assurance on the statements. The CPAs simply act as number crunchers, converting management's numbers into financial statements. You will see the disclaimer of opinion in the accountant's report.

When Is a Compilation Indicated?   Compilation tells little about the integrity of the information provided in preparing the financial statements. Essentially, the task puts numbers in the right formats and computes them. Small companies without the internal accounting staff to perform this job engage an accounting professional to do it for them. Accuracy of the information provided by its accountants does not concern management. Chances are that management helped develop this same information in the first place. Finally, there's no need to release the compiled financial statements to third parties.

Agreed-Upon Procedures

This format comes in handy for consulting engagements. Accounting professionals conduct procedures designed to deal with just a portion of the financial operation. This is where the client wants answers to specific questions. It may be almost anything. For example, management may ask its accounting firm to conduct certain procedures only on accounts receivable for the purpose of verifying their existence.

The accountant's report describes the limitations of the engagement scope and the procedures conducted. It goes on to disclaim any opinion on the financial statements taken as a whole. Finally, it reports the results.

In any case, the issue is one of needing to limit the scope of the engagement to a specific area and conducting only those procedures previously agreed to. The accountant usually won't stray from these procedures or outside the scope as originally defined without modifying the engagement letter. This protects both parties. Bills for unauthorized work don't catch the client by surprise. The professionals don't assume responsibility for work beyond the engagement's scope.

Indications for Use of Agreed-Upon Procedures.

Use agreed-upon procedures when management wants to know something in particular about the firm's financial operation. The circumstances generally include the following:

- No opinion on the financial statements is required.
- The report and results won't be distributed to third parties.
- The accountant has specific expertise in the required procedures not found in the client company.

Role of Controller
and Treasurer in an Audit

Controllers and treasurers have specific boundaries with regard to their involvement in an audit. The reason is simple—the audit verifies the work of the controller and treasurer. If these two individuals participate in the audit, it loses its independence.

Therefore, the auditors ask a lot of questions of the controller and treasurer. Their in-house staffs may even assist in preparing schedules. However, the conclusions drawn about the fairness of the financial statements and the system of internal control are always those of the accountant rendering the opinion.

An independent auditor must:

1. Have no financial interest in the company

2. Have no jointly held business relationship with an officer or other official of the company

3. Not have had any loan to or from the company or its officers or directors

4. Not have been connected with the company as an employee, executive, trustee, or director

5. Not have been a trustee of any trust or estate that has an interest in the company

6. Not have a fee arrangement contingent on the outcome of any aspect of the engagement

An internal auditor must:

1. Not report to the executive being audited

2. Not be subject to review (for either performance or salary) by the executive being audited

3. Not receive any form of gifts from those being audited

4. Maintain an attitude of independence from the entity under review

5. Avoid developing and installing procedures or other activities that would normally fall under their responsibility for review

Figure 4-1. Attributes of independence.

We want to make sure that the auditors are independent of the company, the controller, and the treasurer. Their opinion reflects freedom from any sort of rela-tionship *or the appearance* of a relationship that might influence their independent judgment. Figure 4-1 illustrates a list of independence requirements for auditors.

Internal Audit

Internal audit functions as a management tool for verification that prescribed poli-cies and procedures are being consistently followed. Certainly, small companies with lots of attention from hands-on management have little need for internal audit. Senior executives involve themselves in the daily operations of the firm. Any internal audit would probably not tell them anything they didn't already know.

However, as companies grow, the extent of daily management involvement in the details decreases. To neutralize the risk of prescribed policies and procedures not being followed, companies often delegate this responsibility to an internal auditor (or entire department). The internal audit staff reports directly to senior management. In publicly held companies, this is usually to the audit committee of the board of directors.

Mission of Internal Audit

Unlike an independent CPA, internal auditors go beyond the financial operations of the company. Remember, the independent CPA is usually there to conduct an audit of the financial statements for purposes of forming an opinion of fairness of presentation. Internal auditors don't do that. They can't. They are not independent with respect to the company—they are its employees.

Instead, the valuable function internal auditors perform includes things such as:

Evaluating Internal Controls. Internal auditors review and judge the effectiveness, adequacy, and operation of internal controls in the areas of:

- Accounting
- Treasury
- Operations

The objective is to balance the cost of internal controls against the risk of loss they are designed to avoid.

Verification. One of the essential tasks internal auditors perform is that of verification. This is particularly important for companies with geographically remote operations. Senior management cannot be on site to see what is there and what isn't. Yet guess who's head will roll if there's a problem? Therefore, internal auditors conduct verification procedures regarding:

- Accounting records
- Accuracy of reports to corporate headquarters
- Underlying assets
- Equities
- Operating results

Figure 4-2 illustrates typical procedures conducted for these activities.

Evaluation. A company's internal auditor takes the position of an outsider looking at the operation. From this vantage point they are in a position to evaluate the adequacy of the things they see. Figure 4-3 lists some of the points where an internal auditor's evaluation is useful.

Compliance. This is probably one of the most critical areas in which the internal auditor works. It makes little sense to have adequate and sufficient controls and procedures if the staff doesn't follow them.

Accounting records

- Compare inventory quantities with inventory records.
- Compare accounting reports with source information.
- Account for all prenumbered forms such as checks, purchase orders, and credit memos.
- Prove all subledgers (A/R, A/P, fixed assets, inventory) with G/L control accounts.

Accuracy of report to corporate headquarters

- Prove reports against source documents using footing, tracing of posting, and analytical procedures.
- Test accuracy of expense distribution codes on vendor's invoices.
- Prove statistical and analytical reports such as A/R collection performance used to estimate bad debt reserve requirements.
- Prove specific critical reports such as unfilled sales orders, production backlog, open purchase orders, employee absences, accidents, and insurance claims.

Underlying assets

- Count cash.
- Reconcile bank account.
- Verify undeposited receipts.
- Confirm A/R by direct correspondence with sample of customer base.
- Physically inventory finished goods, work in process, and raw materials.
- Physically inventory plant machinery and equipment.

Equities

- Confirm loan balance with lenders.
- Confirm stock ownership with shareholders.
- Confirm book (or market) value of assets.
- Confirm amounts and existence of liabilities.

Operating results

- Prove performance reports against source documents.
- Conduct analytical procedures for verification of results.

Figure 4-2. Internal audit procedures.

Internal control, from the standpoint of:

- Adequate information
- Accurate information
- Effective systems
- Adequate supervision
- Sufficient separation of uncomplementary duties
- Safeguard of assets from theft, embezzlement, and carelessness

Accounting efficiency, from the standpoint of:

- Effective procedures
- Competent personnel
- Proper use of computers in the accounting operation
- Records retrieval, retention, and destruction of unneeded records

Overall departmental performance, from the standpoint of:

- Organization structure
- Competency of personnel
- Sufficiency of staff
- Adequacy of machinery, equipment, software
- Inventory control and management
- Policies
- Procedures
- Performance measurement
- Management control

Figure 4-3. Internal audit evaluation points.

Verification of compliance doesn't end after installation of a new system or control. People have a habit of reverting back to the old way of doing things. They often change prescribed procedures to make their work easier without knowledge of what it may do to controls in other parts of the company.

If the corporate headquarters designed policies and procedures for use in outlying branches, a compliance review can point out deficiencies. After all, the corporate office may have created something in a vacuum without knowledge of the unique requirements at each branch. It may be that a compliance review uncovers flaws in new procedures and policies already fixed at the branch level.

In this sense the internal auditor provides an expert line of communication between branch offices and corporate headquarters.

Internal Audits at Small Businesses

Few small businesses can justify a full-time professional internal auditor. Nevertheless, the procedures conducted are just as essential—more so, some argue, because smaller companies enjoy a smaller margin of error than large companies.

Small businesses usually have the owners, partners, or CEO perform many of the traditional internal audit functions. To get the most bang for the buck, the concentration is usually on readily negotiable assets such as inventory and cash or their equivalents. Here are some of the things small business managers and owners should look for when they are performing their internal audit function.

Cash.   Some of the easiest ways to prevent conversion of cash receipts is to conduct frequent surprise examinations. These are simple, don't take much time, and act as a huge deterrent against theft. Some of these procedures include the following:

- Examine cash register tapes and compare against cash count.
- Verify that checks in the cash drawer are endorsed "For Deposit Only" to the company's checking account.
- Match bank deposits against sales records and cash receipts.
- Account for all missing prenumbered invoices, sales slips, and credit memos.
- Thumb through the posted invoices to be sure there are no missing numbers.
- Test sales records against daily cash count and invoices.
- Trace the posting of sales to the accounts receivable subledger.

Don't keep these procedures and their purpose a secret. The owner or manager of the business does the review for a reason—to make sure the firm is being run according to management policies. The fact that people know about the review serves as a deterrent against future override of these policies.

Differences Between Internal and Independent Audit

Managers who look upon the accounting and audit function as a necessary evil often see little difference between the function of an internal auditor and that of an independent auditor. They sometimes ask, "If we've got our own people looking at the company, why pay an outsider for the same service?"

Figure 4-4 contrasts the internal and independent auditors' functions.

Internal audit	Independent audit
Auditors must have no affiliation with the controller, treasurer, or any of the departments which they audit.	Auditors are not employees of the company being audited. They must maintain independence in both appearance and in fact.
They work for the company as an employee.	Auditors are engaged as independent contractors.
They conduct a continuous review program of company operations.	Work is done only periodically— usually once a year.
Objective is to serve company management. Orientation of the work is to verify, evaluate, and determine compliance with company policies and procedures.	Objective is to provide an opinion as to fairness of presentation for financial statements to be used by third parties.
Work does not always deal strictly with financial matters.	Primary focus is financial in nature.
Examines operations and systems of internal accounting control to recommend improvements.	Examines operations and systems of internal accounting control to determine scope of work and nature and extent of tests of transactions.
Divides projects by operation, department, and management responsibility.	Divides audit work by chart of account classification.
Concerned about detection of fraud, irregularities, and defalcation.	Nature of the engagement is not to detect fraud. Concern with fraud comes only if it materially affects financial statements.

Figure 4-4. Internal versus independent audit.

Planning for an Independent Audit

Here's what happens when you engage an independent CPA firm to conduct an audit:

- CPA provides a proposal and engagement letter.
- CPA reviews client's system of internal accounting control.
- CPA plans the work to be done for your company.

- Start and end dates of engagement are determined.
- CPA furnishes a list of schedules and information required from company management.
- CPA commences field work—CPA is usually physically on site.
- Audit procedures are conducted, including

  Test of transactions

  Determining if financial statements conform to generally accepted accounting principals

  Test of cutoffs

  Tie-in of account balances to trial balance

  Tie-in of trial balance to financial statements

  Review of financial statements for account classification and disclosure

  Confirming receivables balances

  Searching for unrecorded liabilities

  Searching for related party transactions

- Field work ends and CPA pulls out of company.
- Conclusions are formulated.
- Draft client representation letter for client's signature.
- Discussion between CPA and client of any changes that are required on the financial statements.
- CPA renders opinion on the financial statements as of the date appearing on their face.
- Financial statements are rendered by CPA along with notes and any supplemental information that goes with them.
- CPA issues a management letter discussing any issues or problems observed during the course of the work.

Sound like a lot of work? It is. That's why the CPA's opinion on financial statements carries so much weight. The work is thorough and designed solely to determine the fairness of presentation of the financial statements. Failure on the part of the professional to follow audit guidelines prescribed by the American Institute of CPAs can result in forfeiture of his or her license.

Client Responsibilities

Even though the auditor includes a copy of the financial statements with the opinion letter, notes, supplemental information, and management letter, the statements themselves are those of the company. The CPA didn't prepare them—the company did. Nowhere on the statements do you see the CPA's name.

Clients are responsible for providing their auditors with the necessary schedules and information they ask for. Of course, the auditor verifies the procedures and accuracy of these schedules. Not only does it make the work go faster, it reduces the cost if the CPA can expedite the work without compromising its integrity.

Client Representations

The auditor relies on the client to provide accurate answers to questions and not to withhold information. To this end, the auditor asks specific questions regarding such things as the existence of contingent and unrecorded liabilities.

Further, the auditors will ask the company's officers to provide them a signed letter (on company letterhead) representing that:

- They did not withhold any material information.
- There are no undisclosed contingent liabilities.
- There are no unrecorded liabilities not included in the financial statements.

If the audit subsequently fails due to the existence of these things, then the company and its executives defrauded the auditor. At least that's what the CPA firms have tried to prove in court when the shareholders sued them.

Audit Committee

The mission of an audit committee is to oversee the internal audit process as well as hiring and working with the external auditor. Because the firm's internal auditors report directly to the audit committee, they are frequently the first to sniff out any irregularities. They can then direct the independent auditor to examine the problem. This helps in preventing a failed audit.

Audit committees are not a new idea. In 1940 the Securities and Exchange Commission endorsed the use of audit committees on the boards of directors of publicly held companies. Since that time, the SEC has on occasion required problem companies to establish an audit committee as part of settlement agreements.

Audit committees are part of the board of directors. In their most effective configuration, they consist entirely of outside directors. Indeed, in 1991 the Federal Deposit Insurance Corporation Improvement Act required financial institutions with assets exceeding $150 million to have an audit committee composed entirely of outside directors.

Effectiveness of an Audit Committee

Not all audit committees are effective in carrying out their tasks. They need to have member directors strong enough to challenge the policies, procedures, and practices of top management when necessary. They must also have the power to direct the external auditor's examination of specific parts of the company brought to their attention by the internal auditor.

Figure 4-5 shows a checklist of things to look for in judging the effectiveness of your audit committee.

Questions to Determine Effective Audit Committees

1. How many outside directors are on the audit committee? The more the better. 100 percent is ideal.

2. Did the entire board of directors define in writing the audit committee's responsibilities and authority? Are there any restrictions which appear to prevent them from doing their job?

3. Does the audit committee have authority to request the presence of all levels of employees, internal auditors, and external auditors at their meetings? They should. If not, they can't do their job.

4. Does the audit committee also meet privately without management present? If not, then management knows beforehand what they are looking at and can take steps to further conceal any wrongdoing.

5. Does the audit committee have a say in determining the independent auditor's scope and approach to an upcoming audit?

6. Is the audit committee available during the audit to discuss progress, questions, and problems with the external auditors?

7. Does the internal auditor report directly to the audit committee?

8. Are the audit committee members sufficiently knowledgeable to review the internal auditor's reports and make decisions?

9. Do concerns of the audit committee include such topics as:
   - Internal accounting control
   - Financial reporting
   - Internal audit results
   - External audit results and the management letter
   - Audit reports from regulatory agencies
   - Risk management as related to financial reporting

10. Must the audit committee submit a periodic report to the board of directors with recommendations for enhancement of internal controls as related to:
    - Financial reporting
    - Internal audit
    - External audit

Figure 4-5. Audit committee effectiveness checklist.

5
System of Internal Accounting Controls

Overview

If company owners did everything themselves there would be little need for a system of internal accounting controls. However, business doesn't work that way. By its nature, the accounting and treasury functions involve a number of different people. The company is subject to risk of:

- Unauthorized conversion of assets
- Failure to safeguard assets
- Inaccurate transaction reporting
- Loss of vital documents
- Entry of bogus documents into the accounting system
- Disregard for management policies

The treasury area deals with liquid assets. The accounting area provides for the recording of these liquid asset transactions. When combined, both areas—treasury and accounting—must work together to establish an effective system of internal controls. Failure of controls in both areas at the same time creates a situation that allows for an immediate problem that could go undiscovered for some time.

Here's an example:

Joe had just taken over as general manager for a small label-making company. After hearing him complain how unsophisticated almost all their systems were, his independent auditor suggested he conduct an internal control review. "It never hurts to find out what you're up against at the beginning of your watch," said the auditor. "That way if there's a problem you come out a hero for finding it."

"No problem," said Joe. "The controller has been here for ten years. She's so dedicated she refuses to take her vacations. Why, they practically have to push her out the door at night. A control review would be insulting to her as well as wasting everyone's time."

Six months later Joe's auditor discovered the trusted controller had embezzled $50,000 over a five-year period. She ran the payables system, printed the checks, signed the checks she printed, and reconciled the checking account. In fact, there were no controls over the company's cash.

Chapter 5 identifies the points of effective accounting and treasury control systems. It determines the design requirements of internal control. Additionally, Chapter 5 illustrates how someone clever enough can beat the system. Forewarned is forearmed.

Purpose of Internal Control

Certainly, reducing the threat of theft or fraud on the part of employees and others is one purpose of establishing an effective system of internal accounting and treasury controls. However, most controllers and treasurers would agree that preventive controls are far better than methods that merely detect the occurrence of a problem after the fact. Such detection controls do little to prevent a problem from occurring in the first place.

Deterrence

Effective systems of internal accounting and treasury controls that are strictly enforced act as a lock on a door. Honest people see the mechanism at work and don't even try to beat it. Those inclined to steal will go somewhere else that presents an easier target.

Nevertheless, every company needs to understand that if people really want to steal, they will. Internal controls—regardless of how effective they may be—won't stop them. The best we can hope for is that controls make it harder, increase the risk of being caught, and decrease the amount available for taking in each fraudulent transaction.

Reliance on Reporting

The internal control system is responsible for maintaining the accuracy of transaction reporting. We learned in Chapter 4 that independent auditors examine the system of internal accounting controls to determine the nature, timing, and extent of their procedures when planning the audit.

A task of the internal audit staff is to test the control mechanism to ensure that it functions as intended. We want to verify that when our inventory drops it's due to a sale and not from some unauthorized person loading the item onto a truck and simply driving it out the back door.

Records Control

An important component of control is the records involved in the company's business transactions. Without an ability to retrieve the records that can reconstruct a transaction, the door is open to such problems as:

- Payment of invoices from vendors for work that was never done
- Payment to fictitious vendors or employees
- Sales without the proper recording of a receivable
- Investments improperly recorded
- Cash forecasting that fails to recognize future obligations
- Incorrect reporting of cash deposits
- Improper inventory count
- Misstatement of cost of goods sold

Design of Internal Control System

Large firms sometimes employ experts in the controller's and treasurer's departments or on the internal audit staff who design, implement, and monitor internal controls.

However, at smaller companies, the treasurer or controller may have little or no experience in designing a system of internal controls. These companies often rely on outside consultants or their independent auditors to design their control systems.

Here are the five things experts try to include in the design of internal control systems:

- A plan for the segregation of functional responsibilities
- Operations and custodianship (treasurer) separated from record keeping (controller)
- System of authorization and recording procedures
- Sound policies and procedures
- Personnel capability commensurate with their responsibilities

Figure 5-1 illustrates the different areas of control that usually fall to the controller and treasurer.

Delegation of Responsibility

You can see from Figure 5-1 that internal control systems delegate responsibilities in such a way that no single person has complete authority over a specific func-

Controller	Treasurer
Records transactions in the general ledger, accounts receivable and payable subledgers, fixed assets transactions such as depreciation and inventory control	Holds or gets funds used to finance operations
Invoices customers	Maintains capital structure required to meet needs of the business plan
Personnel timekeeping	Holds and manages cash and other liquid assets of the firm
Prepares payroll	Approves payment checks and acts as signatory on checks
Management reporting	Reconciles checking accounts
Acts as planning director	Manages the credit function of the firm
Performs tax computations	Acts as cashier
Records transactions and reconciles company investment account at brokerage firms	Makes short-term investment of excess cash on behalf of the company
Manages company policy related to granting trade discounts and receivables aging policies	Establishes company policy with regard to vendor payment aging and taking of trade discounts

Figure 5-1. Internal control responsibilities.

tion. Take, for example, check payment. The controller (or staff) posts invoices to the accounts payable subledger. This includes printing payment checks. However, the treasurer has signature authority over the checks. Once signed, the treasurer mails the checks.

If the company uses a signature plate, the treasurer maintains custody of it. The treasurer may keep custody of the check stock as well. Further, the treasurer probably maintains a log of the prenumbered checks. This records the checks issued to the controller for payments. The treasurer receives back any void or damaged checks to account for all consecutively numbered checks. Finally, the controller reconciles the checking account.

Collusion and Sabotage

Ugly words, aren't they? Yet the necessity for collusion is the objective of an effective system of internal control. Properly designed control systems require at least two unrelated people (in different departments) working together to perpetrate a fraud or defalcation. The chances of this happening are more remote than allowing just one person complete access to a control point.

Designing a system that requires collusion to subvert a control prevents more than just fraud or theft. For example, disgruntled employees (and former employees) have been known to sabotage the company.

Becoming of increasing concern are the company's software systems. These are vulnerable to attack from computer viruses and logic bombs. At one aerospace company a programmer installed such a software device. Each day it searched for the programmer's name on the payroll list. When the computer discovered he was fired and his name was scratched from the list of active employees, the virus erased engineering data valued in six figures.

Maintenance of Internal Control Systems

Internal control systems must be flexible and should change with the company. For example, let's say that two unrelated employees worked in the company—one as the A/P supervisor who runs the checks and the other in the treasurer's office who authorizes check signatures and acts as custodian of the signature plate. No problem so far. There's a solid separation of duties. Neither employee is related to the other. Except, the backup person for the A/P supervisor during sick time and vacations just married the treasury employee's brother. Now these two are in-laws—*related* parties.

A smoothly functioning system of internal controls would discover this change shortly after it occurred. Management would then take steps to either replace the backup person or implement another type of control that would mitigate the risk of collusion among family members. Of course, some may argue that a sister-in-law relationship is far enough removed to present little risk. Perhaps. This is a judgment call. There are no definite guidelines. Maybe the two people involved hate each other. But maybe they don't.

Another example is the person who has responsibility for investing excess cash. What if the individual is undergoing a personal bankruptcy? Maybe this job is inappropriate right now.

The point is that the control system must identify the problem quickly and present possible solutions.

Cost versus Benefit.   Every control procedure carries a cost. It may be in people's time taken to generate a report or to review a document for approval. It may be a real dollar cost. Regardless, the control procedure should never cost more than the risk of loss it is trying to prevent. There comes a point where the risk doesn't justify the cost of control. Protecting certain assets can be hot buttons for management. Frequently, their controls outdistance the risk or even the value of the asset being protected. Petty cash is often a case in point. Many firms have elaborate systems of checks and balances, vouchers, reconciliations of receipts, dual control of the cash box—you name it—to protect a fund valued usually at less than $1000.

Money is a common yardstick used to determine the effectiveness of controls. Here are the three questions you should ask when evaluating a control procedure:

1. What value is it in terms of preventing or detecting errors, sloppiness, defalcations, or other problems?
2. What are the expected frequency and cost of an occurrence without the control?
3. What is the cost of the control procedure?

Here's an example of how to quantify the value of a control.

Problem: There's a backlog in the sales invoicing department. This results in delayed invoicing. A solution under consideration is to establish a daily sales invoice backlog report. The cash manager and receivables manager would review this report. The invoicing manager estimates the cost of producing the report to be $50 per day or $13,500 per year.
Here's how we compute the expected value of the cost of loss: Say an average invoice is $500. The maximum backlog is two full days of invoices at 100 invoices per day without the control. We use a 10 percent interest rate for ease of computation. Cost of the backlog if ignored for an entire year is $10,000:

$$(($500 \times 100 \text{ invoices per day}) \times 2 \text{ days}) \times 10\% = $10,000$$

Implementation of the control would actually cost the firm $3500 ($13,500 − $10,000 = $3500). In this case the control does not make economic sense as designed. However, an astute manager might look at this problem and try finding a way to reduce the cost without compromising the control's effectiveness. For example, why not decrease the report frequency to weekly rather than daily? Another possibility would be to prepare a streamlined version each day. Then distribute this exception report only if the backlog exceeds a predetermined level.

Personnel

Of all the control mechanisms available, both the best and the worst are people. Employees delegated the responsibility of maintaining control procedures can either make it work or cause exposure to increase. The best way to ensure proper maintenance of the control system is to emphasize its importance. Some companies even include specific control objectives in employee job descriptions and as part of their performance reviews.

Competency

It may sound obvious, but all employees assigned to do a particular job must demonstrate the ability to execute that job. This isn't always the case. In one company, I've seen the president hire the children of his largest clients. The kids are suddenly thrust into a job they weren't trained for but given the salary as if they were. Nobody is happy: not the kids or their client/parents or the other employees who must work their way up without the benefit of such nepotism. The president's theory is that the parents are such good clients they'll make up whatever loss the kids create. But that's no way to run a business—a kindergarten, maybe, but not a business.

Education and Training

Many positions in the finance department require specific levels of education and training. The controller and treasurer usually establish the education and training levels for prospective employees. The hiring process should verify that candidates have indeed attained the education and backgrounds they claim.

Some managers feel it's an insult to request college transcripts, talk with prior employers, and ask candidates technical questions to verify their command of the job. However, not doing so breaches the manager's responsibility to the employer.

Further, progressive companies encourage employees to take additional training to maintain proficiency and familiarity with current business practices. Many larger companies provide either in-house training programs or offer tuition reimbursement programs for their employees.

Experience

Here's another obvious fact, but one that is often overlooked: People assigned the oversight of any control procedure must understand the nature of the procedure, how the control works, and the ways potential abuses are most likely perpetrated. Internal controls and those who maintain them must be one step ahead of those who may try subverting the system.

This knowledge usually comes with experience. Employees having little or no experience can be taken advantage of by others possessing greater familiarity with the system. Check carefully a candidate's employment record. Probe into any unexplained gaps. They might be trying to hide a termination with cause or even a period of imprisonment for embezzlement.

Authorization Control

Authority to approve company transactions is a symbol of one's status in the organization. It says that the company trusts you and your judgment. The higher the dollar amount of someone's authorization limit, the greater the status.

Yet this control won't work unless the list of employees' authorization responsibilities and limits is kept up to date. Verify all transactions requiring authorization against the documents reviewed prior to giving authorization. This ensures the control is working.

Bonding

Many jobs in the finance area—particularly in treasury—either handle money or provide an opportunity to handle money. Carrying a fidelity bond on each employee with access to the firm's liquid assets provides insurance against theft, negligence, and other compromises that could place the firm at risk of loss. Some companies get a group rate on their fidelity bonds. They often don't bother determining just who should be bonded—instead, all employees are bonded.

Monitoring for Compliance

Just like regular policies and procedures, internal controls require monitoring to ensure compliance. This is especially true when employees don't see the logic or the need for a particular control. Call on the internal audit staff (if one exists) to assess control compliance.

Tests of Transactions

The best way to ensure compliance with control procedures is to take a representative sample of transactions and test them. The persons testing should have a thorough understanding of the procedure they are testing, along with an idea of the ways to fool the control. Record each incidence of noncompliance. From this representative sample, formulate a conclusion as to overall compliance with the control.

Following are the steps to test transactions.

Define the Test.   Narrow the focus of your investigation to one particular control point. For example, some controllers and treasurers measure their internal deposit float—the time it takes to record and deposit a customer payment check. The test consists of comparing the list of checks received against the daily deposit slip and the bank statement. The number of days from receipt to deposit is the internal deposit float. By the way, deposit float should be one day or (preferably) less. Compare the results with management policy.

Select Transactions for Testing.   We want a representative sample. For some tests, where noncompliance could mean significant loss, we take a more formal approach. In these tests we select a statistically significant sample. For this type of sample, the size is important. Though statistical analysis is beyond the scope of this book, consider two things when selecting sample size:

- A predetermined rate of tolerable error
- The expected rate of error in the population

There are tables published that provide sample sizes based on tolerable error and expected error.

Two common selection techniques include selection from a table of random numbers or systematic selection (every nth item with several random starts). Whatever the method, we now have the sample transactions we're going to test.

Conduct the Test.   Use the test methodology, selection method, and the sample size to conduct the test. The results of the test will be the number of exceptions that fall outside the rate of tolerable error already established. For example, continuing with the internal deposit float, assume we establish a 5 percent tolerable error rate. That is, internal float can be greater than one day no more than 5 percent of the time. However, the results of our test find that float exceeds one day 10 percent of the time.

Let's say our test concludes that the float is actually closer to two days than one. Assume that our average daily deposit is $1 million, and our borrowing rate is 10 percent. Here's how to compute the cost of noncompliance with this control:

Daily deposit:	$1,000,000
Exception rate less tolerable rate (10% − 5% = 5%)	5%
Daily deposit not in compliance	50,000
Annual interest rate	10%
Annual cost of noncompliance	$ 5,000

Of course, $5000 is not significant to a company that takes in $1 million a day. However, if we can find enough of these types of things, it quickly adds up to real money. Further, we reduced the amount of work involved by using a sample of the transactions to draw valid conclusions on the entire procedure.

Components of the Internal Control System

There are three main elements to the system of internal controls:

- Control environment
- Accounting system
- Control procedures

Each works with the others to provide reasonable assurance that the firm's assets are safeguarded and transactions are recorded according to generally accepted accounting principles in line with management policies.

Control Environment

This is the overall environment for control created by management's attitude, awareness, and actions. It runs through the entire company—from the board of directors to senior officers, owners, and employees.

Three factors that influence the control environment are:

- Assignments for monitoring control responsibilities
- Personnel policies and practices
- External requirements such as regulatory reporting and independent audits

An effective control environment does not make routine override of management policies and procedures the rule rather than the exception. The control requires managers to seek approval from an established authority hierarchy when they must circumvent policies or procedures. Such adherence to the rules makes everyone aware how serious the company is about internal control.

The attitude of adherence to internal control begins with senior management and works its way through the entire organization.

Accounting System

This provides the means and method to identify, classify, record, report, and determine accountability for the company's assets and liabilities. The accounting system and those who run it should have a high level of credibility. The department should have an attitude of accuracy over expediency. Personnel should be well trained and have experience consistent with their responsibilities.

The hardware and software that form the company's books of original entry should be adequate for the job. It makes no sense to require convoluted procedures and overtime hours just to keep an antiquated system limping along. Most companies receive back many times over the money spent on an efficient accounting system in more timely and accurate information needed for management decisions that increase profits.

Control Procedures

Management establishes and maintains control procedures. They must be well designed and function in the capacity intended. For example, let's say the treasurer invests the company's excess cash but is frequently out of the office in the morning. In the treasurer's absence, the controller fills in and executes that day's investment. This division of executing and recording transactions by two separate people is poorly designed. Not only does the controller record all investment activity, sometimes this person makes the investments as well.

Management must train personnel in how the control system operates. They must also share management's attitude of treating internal control seriously. Further, there should be a regular review of control points to verify compliance.

When the business changes, control procedures must change with it. When people leave the firm, change controls such as passwords, keys, and combinations to locks. Additionally, update authorized signatures at the bank and any other place required.

Accounting Controls

The most common controls found in the accounting department revolve around recording transactions. There, the risk of error or losing vital documents is usually of greater concern than theft.

Following are some of the accounting controls you're likely to encounter.

Unrecorded Sales. Management supervision is probably the best deterrent against failure to record a sale and pocket the money. Another way is to match cash register totals with totals from prenumbered sales tickets and the daily cash count.

If inventory is dropping at a rate inconsistent with recorded sales, there may be some unrecorded sales. Another method larger companies use to track point-of-sale performance is with "shoppers." These are employees of the firm who make purchases only to look for violations of company policy.

Unissued Sales Receipts. Why would a clerk deliberately fail to issue a sales ticket or receipt with a purchase? So that the clerk need not record the next sale but can give a valid sales ticket to the customer and pocket the money.

The best defense against unissued sales tickets are the customers themselves. Most demand a receipt with their purchases in case they have to return an item. Another safeguard is to use prenumbered consecutive sales tickets in duplicate. The original goes to the customer, the copy goes in the daily report. Someone other than the sales staff audits the sales tickets to verify the number sequence and account for any missing tickets.

Credit Vouchers. Also called *credit memos*, these are valuable slips of paper. Most companies require approval by an authorized signatory, depending on size of the credit. Use these to credit a customer's account or sometimes to issue a refund check.

The custodians and writers of credit memos should be separate from both the check-writing function and from posting accounts receivable. That way, perpetration of a fraudulent transaction requires collusion.

Additionally, consecutively number the credit vouchers themselves. Make someone responsible for explaining any missing numbers.

Accounts Receivable. There are a variety of controls over the receivables system. Those discussed above also help to keep the receivable portfolio correct.

Another control over receivables is periodic reporting to management. Review such reports for things like:

- Excessive aging
- Growth beyond the treasurer's working capital projections
- Shrinkage beyond the bank's collateral requirement
- Write-off

Both internal and independent auditors like to verify the existence of the receivables portfolio. Employ this control by taking a representative sample of the receivables customers and writing to them requesting verification that the balance stated in the letter is indeed the correct balance they owe.

Accounts Payable.   The risk in A/P is more likely to be in failing to record a liability. The internal control system must effectively get all invoices approved for entry in the A/P system and posted properly.

The treasury department usually requires some sort of tickler system so they know the cash requirements needed to honor the company's payment obligations and to take advantage of trade discounts.

Payroll.   Fictitious employees are one target for payroll system controls. Another is time for which the company pays its hourly employees. Most common breaches of payroll control come when a naive company designs its control system in such a way that collusion is not necessary to create and pay a fictitious employee.

The best control procedure in this case is common sense. Make sure that someone independent of payroll but who knows each employee reviews the payroll list. Also, have someone with knowledge of who worked what hours review the time sheets.

Another control is to reconcile the total payroll amount from one payroll to another. This explains the changes resulting from terminations, vacations, overtime, bonuses, and new hires.

Beating the System

No system of internal controls is foolproof. Otherwise, they would be so expensive and cumbersome to operate that no work would get done. The trick is to match cost of control points against both risk and expense of a potential loss. A determined individual can beat the system for a time. Under certain circumstances, we'll take that risk.

1. *Failure to separate uncomplementary duties such as check writing and reconciliation of the checking account.* The check writers are then free to write themselves checks and forge the signatures.

2. *Lapping the receivables system.* This is done by an A/R clerk who takes a payment from customer A and pockets it. Then A's account is credited with a payment from B. Customer B's account is credited with C's payment and on and on. Confirmation of the A/R portfolio and requiring personnel to take their vacations or at least rotate them out of the job for a time can correct this problem. Resistance of a clerk to take earned vacation is sometimes a symptom of lapping.

3. *Failure to mark invoices as having been paid.* This opens the door for the same invoice being put through the system again.

4. *Failure to control and safeguard inventory.* Without accurate inventory counts and security for valuable inventory, the possibility of theft exists. Further, the amount of the loss may never be known.

5. *Wire transfer confirmations going back to the person who ordered them.* Confirms should go to someone independent of the wire order. This ensures independent verification that the confirm matches the properly recorded entry.

6. *Failure to verify new employee's backgrounds.* In this age of litigation, honest references are almost impossible to get. Yet a diligent search will usually uncover the most obvious lies.

Figure 5-2. Ways to beat the system.

Figure 5-2 shows some of the more common ways management neutralizes its control systems.

Internal Control Checklist

The internal control checklist shown in Figure 5-3 is reprinted from *The Cash Management Handbook* by Christopher R. Malburg, copyright 1992, with permission of the publisher, Prentice-Hall, a division of Simon & Schuster, New York.

Figure 5-3. Cash management system internal control points.

Page 1 Date:	Cash Management System Internal Control Points		
Control point	Acceptable (yes/no)	Workpaper reference	Comments

I. Overall control environment:
   A. Is management's awareness of the importance of the control system appropriate?
   B. Does management stress the importance of internal control and compliance with procedures?
   C. Are personnel assigned tasks using appropriate policies?
   D. Does the accounting system provide means to identify, classify, record, and report cash transactions?
   E. Does the control environment:
      1. Segregate responsibilities appropriately?
      2. Record transactions correctly?
      3. Build checks and balances into the system?

II. Treasury policy manual:
   A. Does a treasury operations policy manual exist?
   B. Is it kept current?
   C. Is it adequate for the purposes of policy control?

III. Employee controls:
   A. Are there procedures to verify employee competency?
   B. Are there procedures to verify employee experience?
   C. Are employees adequately trained?
   D. Are employees bonded?
   E. Are authorization responsibilities listed?
   F. Are employees required to take annual vacations? While on vacations are their jobs done by other employees?
   G. Are uncomplementary duties not executed by any single individual?

Figure 5-3. (*Continued*)

Page 2 Date: Control point	Acceptable (yes/no)	Workpaper reference	Comments
H. Are employees with family ties prevented from sharing uncomplementary duties?			
I. Are employees held accountable for their work?			
IV. Bank accounts:			
A. Are authorized signatories designated with due diligence?			
B. Are account reconciliations done regularly by personnel independent of the bank account? Are bank statements received directly by the person doing the bank reconciliation? Are the reconciliations reviewed by a qualified, appropriate, independent person?			
C. Are the number of accounts appropriate for the firm?			
D. Are compensating balances managed?			
V. Funds inflows and deposits:			
A. Are cash receipts listed by the person who opens the mail?			
B. Are over-the-counter cash receipts compared against register tapes and a count of sales tickets?			
C. Does the bank confirm deposits directly to someone independent of the cash deposit function?			
D. Does the bank alert the cash manager to incoming wires? Are they recorded properly?			
E. Are cash receipts managed according to policy?			
VI. Fund outflow:			
A. Are checks prenumbered and accounted for by someone independent of the disbursement function?			
B. Are custodianship of checks, check writing, authorization signature, and accounting all done by separate people?			

(*Continued*)

Figure 5-3. (*Continued*)

	Acceptable (yes/no)	Workpaper reference	Comments
Page 3			
Date:			
Control point			

    C. Is there an appropriate disbursement approval and authorization process in place? Is it followed?

    D. Does the bank confirm with someone independent of the wire transfer function prior to sending out a wire?

    E. Are invoices marked "PAID" so they cannot be used again?

    F. Is the signature plate controlled by someone independent of the disbursement and check-stock custodianship?

    G. Are checks sent out promptly after signature by someone independent of the check function?

VII. Petty cash:

    A. Is the petty cash fund adequately controlled?

    B. Are vouchers used for disbursement?

    C. Are periodic reconciliations of the petty cash fund conducted by someone independent of the task?

    D. Is the petty cash fund appropriate in size?

    E. Is the fund kept in an appropriately safe place?

VIII. Trade credit:

    A. Is there an appropriate trade credit policy?

    B. Is the credit manager qualified for the job?

    C. Do formalized credit authorization limits exist for all customers?

    D. Are there credit authorization guidelines?

    E. Are credit decisions reviewed by management?

    F. Does a timely and accurate communication link exist between order entry, A/R, and the credit manager?

Figure 5-3. (*Continued*)

Control point	Acceptable (yes/no)	Workpaper reference	Comments

Page 4
Date:

IX. Investments:
   A. Is there a formalized investment policy?
   B. Are investment securities of the type specified by management policy?
   C. Do the investment maturities fit the current cash flow plan?
   D. Do the returns of the portfolio warrant the risks?
   E. Are brokers' statements reconciled to the G/L and the investments ledger by someone independent of the function?
   F. Do employees have personal accounts at brokerage firms used by the company?
   G. Are brokerage confirmations sent directly to someone independent of the investment function?
   H. Is collateral sufficient to secure positions?
   I. Is the physical possession of investment securities appropriately safeguarded?
   J. Are periodic inventory counts made of the securities portfolio?
   K. Are securities registered in the company's name?

X. Financing:
   A. Do nonroutine financing activities carry the approval of a board resolution?
   B. Is the person authorized to negotiate financing transactions qualified?
   C. Are terms of the financing in accordance with board authorization? Do they violate any restrictive covenants already in place?
   D. Are documents with instrinsic value properly controlled and accounted for?
   E. Are financing documents signed by authorized officers of the firm?
   F. Are securities records properly maintained?

(*Continued*)

Figure 5-3. (*Continued*)

	Acceptable (yes/no)	Workpaper reference	Comments
Page 5 Date: Control point			

XI. Accounts receivable:
   A. Does the A/R subledger tie to the general ledger?
   B. Is there proper control of invoices? Are gaps in the invoice numbering sequence accounted for?
   C. Is there a reliable method to ensure all invoices are posted to the A/R subledger and the general ledger?
   D. Are receivables statistics computed and monitored?
   E. Is there an effective control procedure for credit memos?
   F. Are collections managed and aggressively pursued?
   G. Are monthly statements sent to all customers?
   H. Is there proper approval for all accounts that are written off?

XII. Accounts Payable:
   A. Is the disbursement officer independent from the accounting function?
   B. Are purchase orders matched with receiving reports prior to authorization of an invoice for payment?
   C. Are A/P statistics computed and monitored?
   D. Does the A/P subledger tie to the general ledger?
   E. Are trade discounts taken?

XIII. Cash Projections:
   A. Are cash projections regularly made?
   B. Is the cash projection integrated into the overall business plan?
   C. Are projected receipts and disbursements compared against the plan with differences explained?

Figure 5-3. (*Continued*)

Control point	Acceptable (yes/no)	Workpaper reference	Comments
XIV. Interest rate risk:			
A. Have interest rate risk limits been established by the board?			
B. Is there a mechanism in place to measure and control interest rate risk?			
XV. Insurance:			
A. Are insurance reviews done periodically?			
B. Are insurance claims analyses done periodically?			
C. Is insurance coverage adequate?			

Page 6
Date:

6
Internal Treasury Controls

Overview

Chapter 6 describes the most effective system of internal controls for the treasurer's special needs. This section emphasizes controls appropriate for the risk being managed. We'll take a close look at what works and what doesn't to protect the easily convertible assets most often found in the treasury department.

By its nature the treasury department deals with large amounts of liquid assets. For this reason, treasury controls are among the most important of any found in the company. Professionals design these internal controls not only to prevent and detect misappropriation of assets, but to assure the proper recording of treasury transactions and accurate reporting to the right people.

Treasury controls generally affect cash and investments. Additionally, the treasury department verifies some of the accounting controls.

Controlling Authorized Signatories

The accounting department matches authorized signatures against transactions prior to recording them. However, who maintains the list of authorized signatories? Often it's the treasurer. This responsibility includes maintaining the authorization limits for various sizes of transactions. It also includes providing replacement signatories in the event the primary person is unavailable.

Probably the most recognized signature in any company appears on the accounts payable and payroll checks. This signatory is usually responsible for verifying the payment is correct and authorized according to company policy.

It may sound elementary, but many businesses have absurdly large authorized signature lists. Senior management is on the list to authorize relatively insignificant transactions. We see these phenomena more often in small companies. The business grows, but management's trust in its ability to maintain control does not. Therefore, management insists on approving everything.

Pushing Authority Down the Line

The most efficient authorization limits are those established in a hierarchical format. That way, we establish signature authority for particular individuals up to a specified dollar limit. Transactions exceeding that limit require approval from the next-higher level.

Using this method, the work does not stop while senior executives create a bottleneck for their approval on small dollar amount transactions. The higher up the ladder, the farther away from the issues is the authorizer. It wastes time bringing them up to speed on minor decisions where there's little risk. More often than not their conclusion simply mimics that which subordinates have already reached. So why not let subordinates make the decision on their own? Subordinates whose decisions are too often vetoed usually get removed from the authority hierarchy anyway.

Figure 6-1 shows a typical authorization hierarchy for progressive dollar amounts of credit. The objective is that we give the maximum authority to the lowest level in the organization considering these things:

- Risk of loss
- Competence and experience of personnel
- Monitoring for decision quality
- Internal controls

Controlling Cash

Managing the Mail Room

Earlier we said that the treasury department was responsible for cash from the moment it enters the firm. This is why so many companies put at least part, if not all, of the mail room under supervisory control of the treasury. Further, the trea-

Person responsible	$5,000	$10,000	$50,000	$100,000	$300,000	$500,000
Credit clerk	X	X	X	X	X	X
Credit supervisor		X	X	X	X	X
Credit manager			X	X	X	X
Treasurer				X	X	X
VP finance					X	X
President						X

Figure 6-1. Authorization hierarchy—credit department.

sury usually signs payroll and disbursement checks, then mails them directly without returning them to the originator.

When cash (usually in the form of checks) arrives in the mail room two things should happen:

- Checks are separated from the receivables payment vouchers.
- The cashier prepares a deposit ticket.

The checks go directly to the bank and the payment vouchers go to the accounting department. At this point, accounting records the payment and matches the batch against the amount deposited.

Differences between the deposit reported by the bank and the receipts reported by the mail room usually result from errors caused by the:

- Deposit ticket
- Bank
- A/R clerks

In any case, the control requires resolution of the differences.

Separate individuals receive cash, deposit it, and record its receipt. Circumvention of this combination of internal controls in order to misappropriate cash requires collusion. Figure 6-2 illustrates additional checklist items for the cash area.

Keep an eye out for the warning signs shown in Figure 6-3. Each by itself probably is of little concern. It could be just sloppy management. However, when combined they may indicate a lack of cash control.

Protecting Petty Cash

Petty cash is one of those areas needlessly pounded by internal control. The trick is to design petty cash controls sufficient to keep the risk of loss at an acceptable level. Beyond that, you gamble that the controls cost more than the expected value of any loss.

Following are the standard petty cash controls that work for most companies.

Recording Vouchers

Treat these records as source documents for petty cash disbursement. They should contain:

- Date of disbursement
- Recipient
- Purpose

1. Separation of duties: Make sure those who receive cash are segregated from those who do these tasks:

   - Work on customer invoices or credit memos
   - Work on customer A/R subledger
   - Collections
   - Mail customer invoices and statements
   - Accept and authorize sales discounts and allowances
   - Reconcile bank accounts
   - Post subledgers or general ledger

2. Is there independent verification of mail receipts?

3. Are receipts issued to the payer for all currency received?

4. Are receipts compared against the daily cash count?

5. Are collections deposited daily?

6. Are cash receipts used to cash payroll or personal checks?

7. Is one person accountable for cash receipts from the time of mail-opening to bank deposit?

8. Are differences in deposits claimed by the bank investigated by someone independent of the cash receipt function?

9. Are all people handling cash and checks properly bonded?

10. Are all wire transfers and electronic funds transactions (EFTs) confirmed by the bank to someone independent of the requester?

Figure 6-2. Cash control checklist.

In theory, the sum of the vouchers plus the cash balance should equal what's supposed to be in the box at all times. That's how we balance the cash box.

Additionally, use the vouchers to record petty cash expense by the accounting department and to replenish the cash box.

One last point about the vouchers: By balance sheet date the accounting department must receive them to properly record expenses for the period. The petty cash fund then gets reimbursed back to its stated amount.

Reconciling Petty Cash

Reconcile the petty cash fund periodically. Some companies with an active petty cash box reconcile at the end of each day. Whenever, someone independent of the petty cash fund should do it.

1. Do cash-related indices such as the quick ratio, inventory turnover, asset turnover, and profit margin suggest a better cash position than is actually present?

2. Does the company keep excessive balances in superliquid non-interest-bearing accounts for emergency purposes?

3. Are below-normal short-term cash investment yields the result of surprise cash inflows? (If items 2 and 3 are true, there's probably little cash forecasting being done.)

4. Are emergency borrowings the rule rather than the exception?

5. Does the firm needlessly keep too many bank accounts?

6. Are bank accounts reconciled and independently reviewed on a regular basis?

7. Does the firm practice the antiliquidity policy of slow collections and fast payments? If so, its cash management procedures have broken down.

8. Does the firm's bank negotiating position suffer from poor banking relationships?

9. Is bank float information not used to negotiate better availability of deposited funds?

Figure 6-3. Cash warning signals.

Establishing the Amount

The amount of cash in the fund should be sensible. Ideally, we'd like it to be as low as possible. Remember, this is where we keep the most liquid asset there is—cash. Therefore, we want to reduce our risk exposure to the minimum.

Additionally, the less cash there is, the less work in maintaining the fund. Most companies have a policy stating a maximum amount for a petty cash transaction. For payments over that amount, vendors submit invoices to the accounts payable system for normal processing.

Securing the Petty Cash Fund

The actual cash should be in a container that reasonably ensures its security. For most small petty cash funds this requires nothing more than a strongbox. Make sure yours requires either a key or combination to open. Keep the box in a controlled access area.

Protecting Receivables
and Customer Payments

The primary control of receivables is a good separation of duties between those who receive cash (actually handle it) and those who record its receipt. That way collusion would have to occur between two different people to circumvent the control.

The relationship between receipt of customer payments and accounts receivable is often complicated. Some of the most effective controls to protect receivables and customer payment will now be discussed.

Separation of Duties

Make sure those in the controller's department who record cash receipts don't do any of the following:

- Handle any incoming cash from customers
- Open the incoming mail
- Mail or deliver customer statements

This control reduces the temptation of appropriating a cash receipt and recording a credit to a customer's account as if the money were deposited in a company account. With such controls it would be difficult to perpetrate a check-lapping scheme. That's where money received from customer A is pocketed, then payment from customer B is credited to A's account, payment from customer C is credited to B's account, and so on. Separation of duties goes a long way in keeping people honest.

A possible symptom of lapping can be where employees working in the A/R department refuse to take vacations. They can't. Their replacement would immediately see all the incorrect posting of payments.

Balancing the Receivables Ledgers

Someone completely independent of receivable recording should balance the A/R ledgers against the control account periodically. A good person to do this is someone with a vested interest in the firm collecting all the cash it's due—such as the treasurer.

Another way to verify the customer's receivables balance is to confirm it. Again, someone independent of A/R recording—like the treasurer—should do this task. Confirmation consists of taking a representative customer sample and sending a confirmation letter. The letter states a customer's balance and requests a reply to the treasurer if it's wrong.

Take care with the addresses of customers on the confirmation list. Individuals who knew what they were doing could change addresses on the confirm list so they go to *their* home rather than the customer's. Of course, they would respond that the account balance was right on the money. That's why someone independent of the A/R function should generate the A/R confirm list.

Another caution is in the mailing of the confirmations. The person conducting the confirm audit must actually drop the envelopes in the mail box personally. Giving the confirms back to the A/R staff for mailing compromises independence of the test.

Doctoring Statements

Perpetrators of fraud are crafty. Many times their crime goes undetected because neither the company nor the customer suspects what is really happening. One way is for someone who handles cash and records customer payments (a breach of common business sense) to install a statement-doctoring scheme that works something like this:

1. Appropriate the payment when it arrives.
2. Omit the payment from the daily deposit.
3. Omit recording the payment in the A/R ledger. The books are still correct.
4. Intercept the account statement before it goes to the customer.
5. Change the customer's account statement to read as if the payment had actually been credited to the account.
6. Send the doctored account statement on to the customer.

Of course, independent confirmation of customer balances would catch this type of embezzlement. Customers would raise the flag when they read on the confirms that their balances were much higher than is correct, given all of the (appropriated) payments.

Controlling Bad Debts and Other Account Credits

People responsible for recording new receivables should not be in a position to credit those same accounts. Such credits include:

- Bad debt write-off
- Credit memos
- Account balance adjustments
- Discounts
- Refunds

Disbursement functions include:

- Supervising the disbursement function
- Preparing checks
- Maintaining custody of check stock

Separate these duties from the following:

1. Reconciliations such as bank accounts, vendor payables accounts, and partner capital accounts
2. Mailing or otherwise delivering payment checks
3. Compiling and approving payroll records such as time sheets, piece work chits, and vacation payment requests
4. Approval of discounts, credits memos, and refunds
5. Approving payment vouchers and petty cash reimbursement requests
6. Posting of general ledger and subledgers
7. Custody or access to books of original record having to do with disbursements (including the general ledger, vendor invoice register, A/P subledger, payroll records, list of employees)
8. Requesting, approving, and posting of wire transfers and EFT transactions; receipt of confirmations for wires and electronic funds transfers

Figure 6-4. Separation of duties for disbursements.

The reason is that such authority gives them the opportunity to reduce or eliminate their own balances or those of family and friends. No one in the company would be the wiser.

Managing Disbursements

As usual, the issue of uncomplementary duties comes up. Figure 6-4 lists some of the duties *not to share* with those responsible for disbursement.

As a further measure, the controller often maintains custody of the check stock and issues only enough checks for a specific check run. The controller also maintains a log documenting the check number sequence. This control requires explanation of any breaks in the preprinted number sequence of the checks. Finally, the treasurer reconciles the checking accounts since the controller is responsible for recording transactions.

Part of the bank account reconciliation procedure should require comparison of signatures on the checks with specimen copies of original signatures.

Protecting the Check-signing
Machine and Signature Plate

If your company uses a check-signing machine with a signature plate, keep both in a secure location with limited access. Separate the custodian of the signature machine (often the treasurer) from the check stock custodian (often the controller). Store the machine and check stock in separate secure areas where neither person has access to both. That way there would have to be collusion to write negotiable checks without forging the signature.

Preventing Payroll Fraud

Payroll controls are not always effective at many companies. Some of the most common problems we want to guard against include:

- Payment to fictitious employees
- Overpayment to employees for work not done
- Theft by disbursing officer if payroll is paid in cash
- Inaccurate tax deductions and withholding from payroll
- Improper payment to governmental taxing entities
- Inaccurate accumulation of payroll statistics

Fictitious Employees.   This is one of the most common forms of fraud found in the payroll department. It can occur by simply entering an employee who doesn't exist in the payroll system and sending the check to the perpetrator's address or bank account. It may also occur by not removing an employee already terminated from the check run. A quick change of address is all it takes to send the check on its way to the perpetrator's address.

A good way to prevent this is to start when an employee is first hired. At that time someone separate from the payroll function completes the Form W-4 for payroll withholding and all other new-hire payroll forms specifying such things as rate of pay and mailing address. This person is responsible for verifying correct entry of the employee into the payroll system. Such verification can simply be a computer report that bypasses any payroll staff and goes directly to the person authorizing new staff.

The reverse works for employees dropped from the payroll. Someone separate from the payroll function completes the termination forms and sends them to the payroll department. A separate confirming report comes directly back to verify the change.

Timekeeping Abuses.   Separate this function from payroll preparation and disbursement. If you don't, the door is open for fraudulent time reporting. Probably the best timekeeper is a designated person whose job it is to accumulate and report time. Supervisors often do this task.

Many companies use time clocks to record time in and out on employees' time cards. However, this requires strict enforcement of employees punching only their own cards. Some firms count punching someone else's card as cause for dismissal.

Sophisticated computer systems are also available that allow a person to enter their personal ID number and record their time in and out. The system then accumulates all the time and feeds it into the payroll system.

Controlling Piecework Records.   Some sort of verification for the number of acceptable pieces made by each employee is used to compute piecework payments. This should never be the responsibility of the employee alone. Such honor systems don't work. Rather, many companies employ inspectors whose job it is to count acceptable pieces, then record them for payroll purposes.

An extension of internal control is to match the number of acceptable pieces counted for payroll purposes against those added to finished goods inventory.

Controlling Investments

More often than not, the treasurer's office is responsible for investment of excess cash on behalf of the company. These investment "positions" are usually of substantial size. Without adequate controls, a risk exists of circumventing management policy or, worse, of misappropriation of investment funds.

Investment controls deal specifically with these issues:

- Accountability
- Authorization
- Dual-controlled custody
- Execution

Figure 6-5 illustrates some commonly asked questions regarding investment controls.

Establishing Accountability

We want a single individual accountable for the investment portfolio of the company. However, this person must act under instructions from the board of directors. The board usually passes a resolution entered into the minutes of the meeting authorizing specific investment transactions.

Many times the board resolution incorporates an entire investment policy into its minutes. Such policies identify instructions to the treasurer and investment executives. These instructions include:

- Overall responsibility
- Authorized persons

1. Is the person responsible for investing qualified to do so?

2. Has the board of directors passed a resolution authorizing specific investment securities be purchased by this individual on behalf of the firm?

3. Does someone knowledgeable oversee the investments made each day by the investment officer?

4. Are those who reconcile the investment account separated from the investment officer?

5. Is the investment officer allowed to have a personal account at a brokerage firm used by the company? It may seem odd, but allowing this practice can be tempting. Either the investment officer or a broker, trying to be helpful, can move profitable trades to a personal account and unprofitable ones to the firm's account.

6. Is physical possession of investment securities safeguarded adequately?

7. Is collateral sufficient to secure all positions, such as repurchase agreements the company has bought?

Figure 6-5. Questioning investment controls.

- Acceptable securities
- Term
- Risk
- Brokerage firm qualifications
- Broker qualifications
- Transaction reporting
- Custodianship
- Procedures for policy change

Granting Authorization

Authorization covers several areas:

- Persons who trade the firm's account
- Authorized brokers and their firms
- Securities
- Collateral

We need to be sure that only those qualified to make investment decisions on behalf of the company can do so. Verbal rather than written investment orders are the rule. That makes this control difficult. That's why most companies select their brokerage firms and the brokers who service the company's account with care. Use only those of the highest integrity. This usually limits the search to only established firms and individuals that can produce a verifiable track record and sufficient references.

A quick way to investigate broker-dealers and the registered representatives who work for them is by calling the National Association of Securities Dealers (NASD) Public Disclosure service. Their toll-free number is (800) 289-9999. They will provide you with information on individual brokers and their companies regarding:

- Arbitration disputes
- Complaints
- Investigations
- Criminal convictions

They obtain their information from sources such as the Central Registration Depository (CRD), the FBI, the SEC, and sometimes individual states. Public Disclosure provides information only on the final resolution of cases—not ongoing or pending cases. Further, be aware that information from the CRD is broker-provided, so its credibility may be suspect. Nevertheless, it's a good start.

Maintaining Dual-controlled Custody

Investment assets are liquid and usually of large amounts. Often the securities are valuable on their face. Though now rare, bearer bonds are one example. In any case, these are not documents we can risk losing.

Most companies that invest excess cash with a brokerage firm do not take physical delivery on the securities. They keep them with the brokerage firm. That way, there's no risk of loss. Further, it minimizes the record keeping involved in the often frequent trading of short-term securities.

An exception to this is a repurchase agreement. Repos are essentially loans a company makes to a brokerage firm or a bank. The bank agrees to repay the loan at a specified interest rate at a certain time—usually the next morning. The borrower provides collateral in the form of U.S. government securities with a face value in excess of the repo amount. The borrower transfers collateral to either the lender or a third-party custodian. For control purposes, never leave the collateral with the borrower. If the borrower defaults, it's difficult to get the collateral for repayment.

A common method of dual control custody is to keep delivered securities in a bank safety-deposit box requiring two keys. The controller has one key and the treasurer may have the other. Alternatively, some firms prefer to keep them on site in a fireproof vault requiring two different combinations.

Executing Investments

The guidelines prescribed by the board's investment resolution give specific treasury staff limited authority to transact the company's investments. Any transaction outside these boundaries requires special authority by the board or its investment committee prior to execution.

There are three controls that can help ensure compliance with company investment guidelines:

Reconciling the Investment Account.   Periodic—at least monthly—reconciliation of the firm's investment account at the brokerage firm assures an independent look at all of the transactions. Someone completely independent of the investment function reconciles the investment accounts. They should also be aware of the firm's investment guidelines and review each transaction for compliance.

Companies that don't follow the common sense of independent reconciliation give the investment officer an invitation to convert company funds while blaming the disappearance on losses in the market.

Confirming Investment Transactions.   Someone in the company who is independent of the investment function receives all transaction confirmations coming from the brokerage firm. That person should inspect the confirm for compliance with company investment guidelines. After review, forward the confirm to the accounting department for recording of the transaction.

Limiting the Brokerage Firm.   In the brokerage agreement, the company has the right to enter language that restricts the types of transactions it authorizes the brokerage to execute on its behalf—regardless of its investment officer's orders. This provides a final safeguard against unauthorized transactions.

This allows the company to hold the brokerage firm liable if it executes an order that goes beyond the written restrictions of the board. Changes to these limits must come from the board in writing.

The limitations on the brokerage firm usually are in the form of:

- Specific securities (T-bills, for instance)
- Rating of securities
- Amount
- Term
- Collateral type and rating for repos

Controlling Capital Stock and Dividends

Fraud or theft in this area does not overly concern us. Instead, our controls verify:

- Proper recording of transactions
- Conduct in accordance with management directives
- Compliance with state and federal laws

Using a Registrar

The law requires all publicly traded firms to engage the services of an independent stock registrar. A stock registrar issues stock in accordance with the corporate charter. The registrar's signature on the stock certificate states that the issue is in compliance. Without the registrar's certification the possibility exists that a company may attempt to issue more stock than its charter authorizes. In this case investors would be buying fraudulently issued stock.

For stock issued in a private placement and not publicly traded, the company's board of directors designates officers to handle the transaction. Private placements do not require an independent registrar. Officers named by the board sign and countersign the stock certificates. The corporate secretary usually keeps the shareholder records.

Using a Transfer Agent

If a company appoints an independent registrar, it will usually engage an independent transfer agent at the same time. This provides an added measure of control. The transfer agent is responsible for maintaining all shareholder records and executing the transfer of stock ownership.

Another of the transfer agent's duties is to provide a certified list of shareholders to the company. This important list determines on dividend declaration date which shareholders should get a dividend check. Additionally, this list is prepared for the annual meeting to determine the number of votes each common stock shareholder gets.

Some companies use the transfer agent to disburse dividends. In this case, the firm sends just one check to the transfer agent to cover the entire amount of the dividend. The transfer agent then prepares and issues all dividend checks.

Implementing an Internal
Control Policy Manual

Many small businesses choose to fly by the seat of their pants when it comes to internal control. Without written procedures, the firm has to make them up as they go along. They try to pass these procedures along by word of mouth. However, like folklore, they often get altered as time goes by. The changes are usually for the convenience of the employees rather than to enhance internal control.

During a certified audit, the auditors can't tell what was originally intended. Consequently, they must expand tests of transactions to assume no reliance on internal control—a costlier undertaking.

Targeting Topics for the Manual

Internal control policy and procedure manuals don't have to be elaborate tomes. They can (and should) be short and sweet. Figure 6-6 shows the topics to include.

Insuring against Loss

Usually somewhere in either the controller's or treasurer's department is a part of the internal control mechanism dealing with asset protection. Insurance is one aspect of this. Large companies often employ insurance specialists or engage the help of professional consultants. The best such experts are those who offer their expertise without selling insurance. Such professionals don't take a referral fee from insurance sales people either.

Most people understand that every possible loss does not necessarily require insurance. Doing so would make insurance premiums prohibitively expensive. Most companies insure against catastrophic loss. These losses cause such damage that the firm could not continue operations.

Reviewing Insurance Needs

Professionals recommend an annual insurance review and claims analysis. This process evaluates the company's overall risk of loss. Here are some of the changes that could require an adjustment in coverage:

- Increases or decreases to fixed assets
- Inventory levels
- Numbers of employees
- Businesses in which the firm engages

The internal control procedures should include:

- Listing all the policies
- Verification that no policies are redundant in coverage
- Ensuring that all policies are stored in a safe place
- Written assessment that coverage is adequate and not excessive

Getting the Right Types of Coverage

Even small companies can have complex insurance requirements, depending on their business. Following are some of the more common insurance policies and what they do.

Personnel

- Current organization chart
- Educational and professional requirements named for each job
- Job descriptions of the treasurer, controller, and staff
- Bonding requirements by job function and copies of bonding documentation for each person under bond

Banking

- List of corporate banks and account numbers
- Automated account inquiry phone numbers
- Positions having access to passwords and account numbers
- Copies of banking agreements
- Location of original banking agreements

Authorized signatories

- List of authorized signatories for each transaction requiring authorization
- Authorization limitation hierarchy by dollar amount and by person
- Procedures for adding and removing signatories

Investments

- Types of investment securities authorized for purchase
- Board of directors resolution authorizing purchase of particular investment securities
- Persons authorized to execute investments
- Brokerage firms authorized for use
- Investment reporting requirements
- Specification as to who gets confirmations
- Policy on brokerage account reconciliation and approval process
- Policy on safekeeping of securities

Accounts receivable and payable

- Acceptable ratios and aging criteria
- A/P payment aging policy

Figure 6-6. Target topics for internal control manual.

- Cash discount policy
- Areas of responsibility by position
- Disbursement approval procedures
- Collection and write-off policies
- Policies on credit memos, account adjustments, and refunds

Petty cash

- Position responsible for petty cash
- Daily/monthly balancing requirements
- Amount of petty cash authorized
- Policy on petty cash receipts, vouchers, and IOUs

General and subledgers

- Persons authorized to make entries
- Policy on computer access for G/L and subledger systems
- Balancing procedures
- Policy on storage of backup documentation for entries
- Method of referencing backup documentation
- Policy on separation of duties

Figure 6-6. (*Continued*)

Using Blanket (or Umbrella) Policies.   Blanket policies insure against all risks not covered specifically on any other policy. They are sometimes called *excess liability coverage*. This policy takes over when claims exceed the coverage of other policies. Blanket policies cover true catastrophes. For example, say a personal injury judgment exceeds the liability policy's coverage. The excess liability policy takes over up to its limitation. If the judgment still goes beyond that, the insured is on his or her own.

Insuring Autos.   Be sure that your company's auto policy covers special equipment such as trucks and rental cars along with the vehicle pool. Additionally, make sure the firm carries insurance coverage for heavy equipment it uses.

Insuring against Business Interruption.   Business interruption insurance covers the loss of profits as in the case of a catastrophe. Cover such occurrences as:

- Civil commotion (riots)
- Flood

- Storm
- Fire and sprinkler leakage
- Explosions
- Computer failure and loss of data

Anything is insurable. Some firms are dependent on an uninterrupted supply of goods or services from another company. They may buy a policy against interruption of that supply.

Insuring against Workers' Claims.   Some states require businesses to carry workers' compensation insurance. They may not recognize the blanket policies carried for all employees. Premiums are usually based on a percentage of the previous year's payroll expense. Be sure to contact each state in which you have employees for their requirements.

Insuring the Health of Your Workers.   Employee health plans are now almost a standard perk. Companies must provide a competitive plan to attract qualified people. To defray the expense, some companies provide a policy where the employees contribute a portion of the premium each month.

Insuring against Employees.   Fidelity bonds cover the actions of employees against the company or its customers. A comprehensive fidelity bond frees the employer from having to apply separately for each employee. Some companies cover their entire work force with a comprehensive bond at a set maximum. Employees whose jobs place the firm at greater risk—such as investment officers—get an additional separate bond.

Covering Failure to Perform.   Performance bonds cover a third-party beneficiary in case your company fails to perform as agreed. Use these bonds in cases where nonperformance could cause material damage. Such a case could be in the construction of a building or other large capital asset. Additionally, many governmental entities require their vendors to carry a performance bond with the entity named as beneficiary.

Insuring the Lives of Key Executives.   Many companies have an insurable interest in the lives of their key executives. If they were to suddenly die, the loss to the firm would be material. Payment of an insurance policy would help compensate for the loss of those individuals' services and the profits obtained from them.

One point to note: Life insurance premiums, if the company is the beneficiary, aren't considered ordinary and necessary business expenses. Therefore, they are not tax deductible.

Computing Coinsurance.   Watch for coinsurance clauses in your insurance policies. They mean that you may share some of the liability for loss with the insurance company. Such coinsurance policies cover only a percentage of replacement value. The most common percentage is 80 percent.

Use this formula to compute a claim against an insurance company with a coinsurance clause:

$$\text{Claim against the insurance company} = \frac{\text{face amount of policy}}{80\% \times \text{property value}} \times \text{loss}$$

7

Business Planning

Overview

Most controllers and treasurers play a major role in creating their company's business plans. Since their departments are closest to the numbers, often the task of quantifying the goals and objectives of management falls on them. Further, most business plans employ computers in some manner. Financial personnel are often the most computer-literate in small- to medium-sized companies.

This chapter identifies differences between the types of planning you are likely to see. Included in this section are topics such as:

- Strategic, tactical, and financial planning
- Operational planning
- Financial planning
- Inventory control
- Plan implementation
- Monitoring

For many companies the act of creating a business plan is just as valuable as the plan itself. The exercise gets managers talking to one another and working together toward a common goal.

Characterizing Types of Business Plans

People produce business plans for a variety of reasons. For example, when new companies are trying to raise initial capital, they usually create a business plan for investors and lenders. It often serves as a sales tool. Along with the idea behind the new firm comes prospective financial statements. Professionals usually compile these. Such forecasts represent management's best guess as to what will happen given their chosen course of action. We won't spend much time with this type of pie-in-the-sky planning.

Instead, our planning program puts the company in gear and drives it toward management's targets. This is an organized and controlled process. We'll clearly define our goals. Particular individuals undertake responsibility for achieving milestones. Indeed, a workable business plan requires three elements in the planning process:

- Clearly defined goals
- Delegation of responsibility
- Accountability for results

Such goal-oriented plans are not usually designed for use by people outside the firm. Often such planning documents are proprietary and not widely distributed. These types of business plans include:

- Long-range strategic plans
- Short-term tactical plans
- Cash flow plans
- Manufacturing and production plans

You would not find such a candid account of the company's goals and intents in the prospectus of a securities offering.

Planning for the Long Term

Strategy is just a fancy term for long-range planning. All companies need to determine their direction over the next five years and beyond. They consider variables like:

- Competition
- Goals of the owners and investors
- Changes in the marketplace
- Technological innovation

However, formalizing strategic plans is less useful to small companies than to the corporate giants. This comes from smaller firms' perceived inability to influence their market.

Further, formulation of long-term strategies doesn't help the immediate bottom line. For most entrepreneurs and small business executives, that's what really counts. Strategic plans function more as road maps, used to guide the company's general direction over a long period of time. Smaller firms could go bankrupt by then.

Planning for the Short Term

Tactical plans go out a year or two. Such plans address essential everyday questions like:

How will next season's sales affect working capital requirements?

How much more inventory do we need to meet the additional demand created by our sales force?

Should we change our purchasing terms and accounts payable policy because of the added strain on cash resources?

In their most simplistic form, tactical plans serve as budgets. That's because most people focus on the financial targets that result from this planning effort. However, when done correctly, tactical planning actually provides the step-by-step blueprint for attaining longer-range strategic goals.

The short-term plan comes up with specific targets for each discipline within the firm. These are called *operational benchmarks*. There's a high degree of responsibility assigned each member of the planning team to reach his or her assigned benchmark. Unless they do (and by the time required), it may delay other parts of the plan.

Fueling the Engine—Cash

Once the strategy is formulated and the blueprint for its implementation is drafted in the form of a one- or two-year plan, someone must pay for it. This falls on the treasurer's shoulders (or those of the person acting as treasurer).

The cash flow plan needs to answer these questions:

- How much money do we need to implement the plan?

- Where will this money come from?

- When is it needed?

- What do we do with any excess cash?

Almost every part of the tactical plan has some influence over the cash position of the company. Therefore, the cash flow plan draws input from all over the firm including:

- Sales

- Production

- Inventory

- Capital expenditures

- Accounts receivable and payable

- Credit and collections

Whenever a change occurs to the business plan, it's likely to affect cash flow. Likewise, if there's a sudden change in the cash flow plan, it could require an adjustment to the business plan.

Structuring the Planning Effort

Business planning takes time from the most valuable people in the company. We want it structured to be productive and organized. The leader should have authority to assemble a team and make decisions regarding elements of the plan. Additionally, hold team members accountable both for providing the information required to assemble the plan and for reaching their plan goals by the time specified.

Structure of the planning effort guides department heads toward an integrated solution that gets the firm to the point it wants to be. Within the plan structure is room for periodic review and adjustments. Additionally, include an organized monitoring system to track actual performance and make midcourse corrections.

Figure 7-1 shows the key structure points of a business plan.

Involving the Controller and Treasurer

Both the controller and treasurer are well positioned to take responsibility for design and implementation of the business plan. They possess sufficient authority to make key decisions. They also have the trust of the firm's senior management. If not designated as the chief planning officer, then the controller or treasurer should at least have a place on the planning team.

Leading the Plan Team

If designated as planning director, the controller or treasurer probably has as many as six tasks to control:

Establishing a Clear Chain of Command.   Everyone involved with the planning effort must know who is in control and who has authority to make specific decisions. Within the planning organization, here's a typical chain of command (in descending order):

- Investors or shareholders
- Board of directors
- Chief executive officer
- Leader of the planning team

Mobilize the team:

- Select the team members.
- Design plan components.
- Meet plan goals.
- Make team members accountable for their parts.
- Delegate sufficient authority.
- Set up deadlines.

Direct the team:

- Establish decision-making authority.
- Institute a participative management style.
- Team leader retains ultimate decision authority.
- Record and communicate decisions.
- Determine impacts of decisions on team member's activity.
- Demand timely and accurate feedback.

Control the plan:

- Guide, don't chaperon.
- Define quantitative benchmarks to track the plan progress.
- Track plan against actual results.
- Monitor departure from plan on specific components.
- Adjust plan to react to changes.

Figure 7-1. Structuring the plan.

- Members of the plan design team
- Members of the implementation team
- Members of the monitoring team

Note that investors and directors don't participate in the planning exercise. Nevertheless, if the plan doesn't meet their profit expectations they have the ability to remove those responsible—that's why they're included in the planning hierarchy.

Choosing the Plan Team.   We want team players on the planning team. Look for people with a commitment to the company and its success. Those primarily

1. Commitment to the company and the leader of the planning organization
2. Ability to work with other members of the planning team
3. Oral and written communication skills
4. Origination of and receptiveness to new ideas
5. Sensitivity to impacts from actions in one area to other areas in the company
6. Ability to encourage and tap the best in their team members
7. Thinks and reasons beyond the obvious
8. Identifies specific actions that promote other parts of the plan

Figure 7-2. Planning-team-member attributes.

interested in self-promotion probably won't work out. Figure 7-2 shows a list of attributes that make a good plan team member.

Designing the Plan.   Most planning exercises begin with a series of objectives drawn up by senior management. Some companies call this the *strategic plan.* It's the planning team's responsibility to reach these long-term objectives.

With these goals defined, the group forms work units. These include team members from the individual departments within the company. Each determines the specific target that unit must hit in order for the company to reach its ultimate goals.

For example, say we target a 25 percent increase in profits by year end. That means the following must occur:

- Sales revenue must rise.
- Cost of goods sold must work with sales to maintain or improve profit margins.
- Working capital must rise to allow for increased receivables.
- Lines of credit must rise to pay for increased working capital requirements.

The result is a business plan designed to integrate each department's individual targets with the overall goals of the business plan.

Assigning Responsibilities.   The fewer people responsible for specific areas, the better. Excuses don't interest plan team leaders—they want results. Having more than one person responsible for a particular area of the plan invites the possibility of assigning blame.

Therefore, make one person responsible for each section of the plan design. If you are in a small company, a single individual may take responsibility for several sections of the plan. That's OK. Just make sure *someone* has responsibility for designing and implementing each section of the plan.

Identifying Work Products.   Specify the format each work unit should use for its part of the plan. They should all be the same. This speeds incorporation of each department plan into the overall business plan. It also makes monitoring progress toward plan goals easier.

Be sure each department plan includes these four things:

1. Demonstration of how each plan section reaches specific targets in the overall business plan.

2. Demonstration of how the section assists other sections of the plan. Additionally, it provides indication of the risk to other departments of missing targets.

3. Exact dates should be supplied for achievement of each milestone.

4. Quantified description of how plan targets will be achieved.

Acquiring Authority.   The plan leader and team members must make decisions at the planning stage that exceed their usual authority limits. That's normal. Delegate the authority necessary for them to design these decisions into the plan. When the plan leader, CEO, and board of directors accept the plan, the decisions made using delegated authority become ratified through the normal chain of command.

An example would be the increased working capital loan needed to bridge a cash shortfall from more credit sales. Such an increase in company liabilities may require board approval. This comes after final review and approval of the business plan by the board.

Implementing the Plan

The controller and/or treasurer are often responsible for implementing the business plan. They are close to the numbers and have a feel for the overall organization. Their job requires knowledge and involvement with every department in the company. Further, when one part of the business plan requires a change to compensate for developments affecting other parts of the plan, they have the authority to make them.

Smart plan leaders make sure those responsible for implementation also had a say in the plan design. To some extent the design and implementation teams overlap. That's fine. We don't want the business plan developed in a vacuum. Without such participation by those responsible for making it work, there would be no commitment to the plan's success.

Defining Expected Results

If the plan was carefully designed, expected results for the implementation phase are already in place. These are the quantified results for key parts of the plan. They should be in the form of milestones on a time line. We want to show our people the specific goals needed by particular dates.

Without clearly defined targets, when (not if) misses occur, we can't see the impact on other parts of the plan. Further, the relationship between plan targets isn't as clear without quantified and time-specified results.

Avoiding the Authority Gap

Authority gaps occur when the firm holds managers responsible for achieving particular goals, but fails to give them the authority to make decisions to get the job done. This often occurs at small companies where the owners do little more than pay lip service to delegating authority. Existence of authority gaps gives someone separated from departmental targets the ability to detrimentally affect their achievement.

The impact of authority gaps is a shift in accountability for the plan's success. This removes responsibility for achievement of the plan from those charged with making it happen. They are *responsible* but no longer *accountable*.

Trusting Employees

Owners who have grown the company from their own sweat are often the worst offenders in creating an authority gap. They are sometimes unwilling to delegate authority because they can't trust their employees. Consequently, they retain too much approval authority. People are afraid to make decisions. Consequently, they don't take responsibility for things they should.

The answer for distrustful owners is either to fire those employees they cannot trust to do the job right or train them to do it right, give them full authority, and hold them accountable. Not allowing employees to use their background, creativity, and skill to execute their jobs leaves over half the value of their salaries just lying on the table.

If you're an owner or CEO, don't shortchange yourself or your company by creating an authority gap.

Using Key Areas of the Plan

When creating your business plan, there are three areas that you should focus on:

- Goal setting and benchmarks
- Operational plans
- Financial plans

Setting Goals and Benchmarks

Every business plan begins with goals. They need to be consistent with the overall direction management wants to go (resulting from the strategic plan). They must also be compatible with the individual goals of those responsible for implementing the plan. If managers don't agree with the targets assigned their departments, they'll give a half-hearted effort at best to achieve them.

For example, if a target is the implementation of an automated warehouse management system, the warehouse manager may view it as:

- Overly complicated
- Ignorant of the manager's expertise
- Threatening to his or her position

Finally, all must agree the plan is achievable. Targets put too far out of reach have a negative motivational effect.

Specifying Goals.   The best goals used in business planning are those that are quantifiable and have milestones against which we can track their progress. For example, a good goal might be to provide a 12 percent annual return on invested capital.

There's no mistaking how to compute the goal (profit after tax divided by average invested capital equals return on invested capital). Monitor progress toward the goal every month. Adjust specific components of the plan to guarantee reaching the goal. And, most importantly, make sure the goal is significant to those who matter most within the company—the investors.

Planning Operations

Just like symphony orchestras, business plans must work in concert with the various departments in the company. Departments that must coordinate their individual parts of the plan include:

- Sales
- Marketing
- Accounting
- Credit and collection
- Production, manufacturing, and assembly
- Warehouse, inventory, and shipping
- Human resources
- Capital expenditures
- Administration

Each department creates and implements a subplan that fulfills its responsibility for that part of the plan. If the targeted benchmarks are not met on time, then another department suffers.

Planning Finances

The biggest question any financial plan must answer is: *How much money do we need and when will we need it?* The financial plan derives its assumptions from all the other departments in the company. With the exception of borrowing and financing assumptions, there's little original work done in the financial plan.

Its purpose is to quantify objectives, tactics, and policies over the planning horizon and put them into a standard format—projected financial statements.

Using a Computer

Most companies use some sort of automated planning tool for their financial plans. It can be as simple as a spreadsheet that prints out financial statements or as complex as some of the mathematical simulation software packages available. Regardless, it allows users to ask "what if" questions. That's the utility of using a computer. It eliminates the drudgery of manual computations in order to make a change on only one assumption.

Focusing the Financial Plan

Financial plans have three objectives:

- Identify financial results at the end.
- Provide financial milestones along the way.
- Determine financial resources required.

The components of most financial plans consist of assumptions, work papers, and financial schedules. These all support answers to the question, *How much do we need and when do we need it?*

Assumptions come from departments all over the company. It's best to understand the derivation of each assumption—using work papers if necessary.

Financial plans can be complicated. Further, they last for at least one year. Seldom can one person remember the thought process involved in assuming that, say, gross margin on product A was going to be 43 percent. Yet these are the questions requiring an answer when making decisions on midcourse corrections.

Figure 7-3 shows assumptions used in the financial plan derived from other departments around the company.

Items in the Financial Plan

The actual contents of a financial plan include:

- Projected balance sheet
- Projected income statement

Department	Assumption
Sales and marketing	Sales Customer mix Credit criteria Sales commissions Warranty service expense Cost of product development Advertising Response to advertising
Manufacturing	Cost of goods sold for each product Price increase from suppliers Manufacturing overhead expense Shipping and packing costs Warehousing costs Costs of material-handling equipment Cost of equipment repair Quality control rejects Rework costs Production engineering
Human resources	Salary increases scheduled out Overtime expense Bonuses Recruiting expenses Legal fees
Finance	Interest rates on all forms of financing Dividends Receivables collection forecast—derived in part from the sales forecast Cost of write-off Payables forecast Minimum level of required cash Company's ability to borrow funds
Capital expenditures	List by project: amount, when, and sources of funding for purchase
General and administrative	Utilities expense Postage and messenger service Interest and rental income Travel and entertainment Insurance expense Taxes: federal, state, local, real, and personal property

Figure 7-3. Department assumptions for the financial plan.

- Projected statement of cash flows
- Projected statement of changes in financial condition
- Assumptions used
- Illustrative material

We want to communicate what the contribution of each department means to the financial objectives of the company as a whole. The last item—illustrative material—helps cement that concept. Often they are things like charts, graphs, and pictures. Sometimes they are sensitivity analyses that anticipate questions like, *What happens if we don't make our sales objectives?*

Checking the Financial Plan

We want the financial plan to carry a high degree of credibility. Mathematical mistakes and other inconsistencies don't help further that objective. Figure 7-4 shows a checklist designed to quickly find glaring mistakes in your financial plan.

---

1. Does the balance sheet balance?

2. Does cash as projected on the balance sheet tie with cash as projected on the statement of cash flows?

3. Do accounts receivable, accounts payable, inventory, capital expenditures, salaries, and fixed assets projections (net of projected accumulated depreciation) from any submodels tie to the equivalent account balances shown on the projected balance sheet?

4. Retained earnings as projected in the owner's equity section of the balance sheet each month should equal *prior month retained earnings plus the current month net income taken from the projected income statement.*

5. Net income on the income statement must match the net income figure at the top of the statement of changes prior to conversion into working capital sources.

6. Any subplans created by other departments should tie with the corresponding numbers in the financial plan. If they don't, then the financial plan doesn't have the most current departmental projections.

If any of these don't match, there's a computational problem somewhere in the financial plan.

Figure 7-4. Financial plan checklist.

Controlling Inventory Plans

Planning inventory requirements is just another of the vital subplans that go into the overall business plan. Often the inventory plan is at the mercy of two power- ful groups. The operations and manufacturing groups want to hold a large raw materials inventory. This allows for economies of purchase and ensures long unin- terrupted production runs.

The sales force supports this inventory buildup because it assures them of suffi- cient finished goods inventory. There is little chance of ruining a sale because some of the order was unavailable.

On the other hand, the financial group wants inventory to be as low as possible. This frees working capital needed for other things within the firm that have a faster turnover.

So, how do we reconcile these opposing forces? Following are two useful tools to balance inventory objectives.

Balancing Inventory Levels.   The inventory plan should match timing of pur- chases with collections of accounts receivable. This smooths cash flow. There are two inventory balancing equations:

1. Beginning inventory + planned production = projected sales + target ending inventory

2. Target inventory = normal inventory + growth stock (if any) + safety stock

You don't have to be an inventory expert to determine the approximate level where inventory should be. Let's say we know that our cost of goods sold runs about 60 percent of the sales price for all goods and that we need a month-and-a- half supply of inventory to avoid stock-out costs. How much should we hold in finished goods inventory? The calculation is easily made, assuming monthly sales average $500,000:

$$(\$500,000 \times 60\%) \times 1.5 = \$450,000$$

If inventory has ballooned to, say, $600,000, something is wrong.

Inventory Ratios.   Ratios provide a quick index to make sure the inventory plan is consistent with management policy. Here are the three most common inventory ratios:

Average investment period:

Average investment period = current inventory balance / (annual cost of goods sold / 360)

Inventory turnover ratio:

Inventory turnover = annual cost of goods sold / average inventory balance

Days of inventory on hand:

Days of inventory = total inventory / daily demand

Here are two examples of signals these ratios can provide:

1. The days of inventory on hand rises, yet the production plan still shows three shifts running. Why? If something doesn't change, the company will soon be awash in excess inventory.

2. Inventory turnover begins to slow. However, the inventory purchase plan shows no intent of slowing. Something must be done. Further, credit policies should begin tightening and the receivables collection effort should be increased.

Monitoring Plan Implementation

Even if the treasurer or controller isn't the overall plan leader, he or she is likely made responsible for achieving the plan. Monitoring implementation includes:

- Gathering data
- Comparing actual results against the plan
- Reading trends and deciding on midcourse corrections

Plan monitoring requires keeping a record of how each section of the implementation is proceeding. The monitors are responsible for alerting the team when there's a risk in meeting the benchmarks. They also compute the impact that missing these targets has on other parts of the plan.

Those who monitor implementation of the plan should be familiar with every part of the plan and each department. Monitors often help initiate the solutions for getting the plan back on track. However, the plan implementer usually retains the authority to actually make such decisions. After all, that's the person responsible for making the plan happen.

No matter how perfect a business plan may be, it requires careful monitoring. There will always be deviations that require correction. The only way to control plan implementation is by reporting actual results against those planned. The ultimate objectives don't change, but the way we get there does.

Figure 7-5 illustrates a sample plan-monitoring package for Autumn Manufacturing, makers of plumbing supplies.

T-D-O Partners, Ltd.
Month of October 199X
Summary of Company Performance

	October actual	October plan	Act'l. B(W) plan	Actual YTD	Plan YTD	YTD Act'l. B(W) plan	YTD Act'l. Last year	Oct. YTD B(W) Last yr. YTD
Revenue	$450,000	$425,000	$25,000	$1,500,000	$1,375,000	$125,000	$1,350,000	$150,000
Cost of goods sold	275,000	275,000	0	730,000	575,000	(155,000)	750,000	20,000
Gross margin	$175,000	$150,000	$25,000	$770,000	$800,000	($30,000)	$600,000	$170,000
Total expenses	117,075	101,075	(16,000)	713,025	617,025	(96,000)	636,500	(76,525)
Net income before tax	$57,925	$48,925	$9,000	$56,975	$182,975	($126,000)	($36,500)	$93,475
Dollars in inventory	$450,000	$455,000	$5,000	N/A	N/A	N/A	$500,000	$50,000
Units in inventory	15,000	14,000	(1,000)	N/A	N/A	N/A	30,000	15,000
Days of sales in inventory	15	20	5	N/A	N/A	N/A	22	7
Accounts receivable balance	$300,000	$275,000	($25,000)	N/A	N/A	N/A	$450,000	$150,000
Accounts receivable turnover	25	22	−3	N/A	N/A	N/A	36	11
Number of employees	26	28	2	N/A	N/A	N/A		
Direct labor costs	$25,000	$29,000	$4,000	$150,000	$174,000	$24,000	$180,000	$30,000
Total salary expenses	$32,000	$35,000	$3,000	$192,000	$210,000	$18,000	$250,000	$58,000
Cash balance	$50,000	$55,000	($5,000)	N/A	N/A	N/A	$40,000	$10,000
Available line of credit	$250,000	$250,000	$0	N/A	N/A	N/A	$200,000	$50,000

Figure 7-5. Sample plan-monitoring package.

T-D-O Partners, Ltd.
Month of October 199X
Comparative Income Statement

	October actual	October plan	Act'l. B(W) plan	Actual YTD	Plan YTD	YTD Act'l. B(W) plan	YTD Act'l. Last year	Oct. YTD B(W) Last yr. YTD
Sales	$450,000	$425,000	$25,000	$1,500,000	$1,375,000	$125,000	$1,350,000	$150,000
Cost of goods sold	275,000	275,000	0	730,000	575,000	(155,000)	750,000	20,000
Gross margin ($)	$175,000	$150,000	$25,000	$770,000	$800,000	($30,000)	$600,000	$170,000
Gross margin (%)	39%	35%	0.04	51%	58%	-0.07	44%	0.07
Advertising	6,000	4,000	(2,000)	36,000	24,000	(12,000)	36,000	0
Bad debt expense	13,500	9,000	(4,500)	81,000	54,000	(27,000)	80,000	(1,000)
Commission expense	31,000	25,000	(6,000)	186,000	150,000	(36,000)	142,000	(44,000)
Depreciation:								
Corporate offices	3,500	3,500	0	24,500	24,500	0	21,000	(3,500)
Machinery & equipment	4,350	4,350	0	30,450	30,450	0	28,000	(2,450)
Furniture & fixtures	1,025	1,025	0	7,175	7,175	0	7,000	(175)
Leasehold improvements	1,700	1,700	0	11,900	11,900	0	10,500	(1,400)
Insurance	4,000	4,000	0	24,000	24,000	0	23,000	(1,000)
Salaries & wages	37,000	35,000	(2,000)	222,000	210,000	(12,000)	183,000	(39,000)
Payroll taxes	9,000	8,000	(1,000)	54,000	48,000	(6,000)	46,000	(8,000)
Utilities	3,000	4,000	1,000	18,000	24,000	6,000	41,000	23,000
Travel & entertainment	3,000	1,500	(1,500)	18,000	9,000	(9,000)	19,000	1,000
Total costs and expenses	$117,075	$101,075	($16,000)	$713,025	$617,025	($96,000)	$636,500	($76,525)
Net income before tax	$57,925	$48,925	$9,000	$56,975	$182,975	($126,000)	($36,500)	$93,475
Tax accrual	17,000	13,000	(4,000)	22,790	73,190	50,400	(14,600)	(37,390)
Net income	$40,925	$35,925	$5,000	$34,185	$109,785	($75,600)	($21,900)	$56,085

Figure 7-5. (Continued)

T-D-O Partners, Ltd.
Month of October 199X
Miles Stone Sales by Product
(Units sold)

	October actual	October plan	Act'l. B(W) plan	Actual YTD	Plan YTD	YTD Act'l. B(W) plan	YTD Act'l. Last year	Oct. YTD B(W) Last yr. YTD
Shower sprayers	178	150	28	1,246	1,050	196	1,150	96
Lav. faucets and knobs	292	295	–3	2,044	2,065	–21	2,200	(156)
Kitchen faucets	201	250	–49	1,407	1,750	–343	1,700	(293)
Pre-fab shower stalls	67	70	–3	469	490	–21	480	(11)
Cast iron bath tubs	55	30	25	385	210	175	328	57
Plastic bath tubs	75	50	25	525	350	175	502	23
Bath sinks	231	175	56	1,617	1,225	392	1,310	307
Kitchen sinks	82	100	–18	574	700	–126	800	(226)
Total units sold	1,181	1,120	61	8,267	7,840	427	8,470	(203)

Figure 7-5. (Continued)

T-D-O Partners, Ltd.
October 199X
Accounts Receivable Flow

Beginning A/R balance	$358,000
Increase to A/R:	
Credit sales <$150	30,000
Credit sales >$150<$400	83,000
Credit sales >$400<$1,000	92,000
Credit sales >$1,000<$6,000	42,000
Credit sales >$6,000	10,000
Total increase to A/R	$257,000
Collections on A/R balances:	
Current	90,000
30 days	55,000
60 days	43,000
90 days	29,000
120 days	7,000
Over 120 days	4,500
Total collections	$228,500
Ending A/R balance	$386,500

Figure 7-5. (*Continued*)

T-D-O Partners, Ltd.
October 199X
Summary of A/R Aging

	Current Month	Last Month	Current B(W) Last
Current balance	$153,000	$142,000	($11,000)
30 days	73,500	72,000	(1,500)
60 days	38,000	44,000	6,000
90 days	74,000	44,000	(30,000)
120 days	21,000	18,000	(3,000)
Over 120 days	27,000	38,000	11,000
	$386,500	$358,000	($28,500)

Figure 7-5. (*Continued*)

T-D-O Partners, Ltd.
Sales Actual vs. Plan

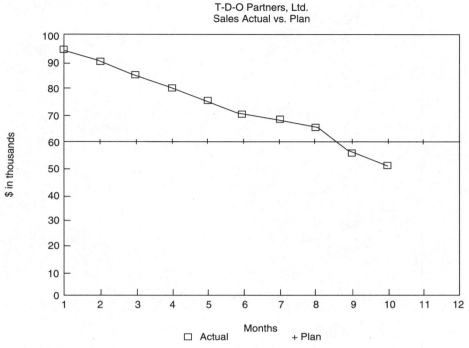

Figure 7-5. (*Continued*)

T-D-O Partners, Ltd.
Sales Composition—October 199X

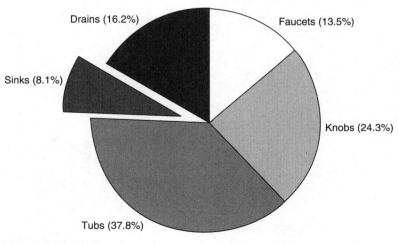

Figure 7-5. (*Continued*)

Figure 7-5. (Continued)

T-D-O Partners, Ltd.
Month of October 199X
Analysis of Gross Margin by Product

	October actual	October plan	Act'l. B(W) plan	Actual YTD	Plan YTD	YTD Act'l. B(W) plan	YTD Act'l. Last year	Oct. YTD B(W) Last yr. YTD
Margin analysis by product:								
Shower sprayers								
Gross revenue	$25,000	$23,000	$2,000	$150,000	$140,000	$10,000	$155,000	($5,000)
Cost of goods sold	6,500	6,000	(500)	32,500	28,500	(4,000)	70,900	38,400
Gross margin ($)	$18,500	$17,000	$1,500	$117,500	$111,500	$6,000	$84,100	$33,400
Gross margin (%)	74%	74%	0%	78%	80%	−1%	54%	24%
Lav. faucets and knobs								
Gross revenue	$15,000	$13,500	$1,500	$70,000	$66,000	$4,000	$67,500	$2,500
Cost of goods sold	8,500	7,000	(1,500)	35,000	43,000	8,000	50,350	15,350
Gross margin ($)	$6,500	$6,500	$0	$35,000	$23,000	$12,000	$17,150	$17,850
Gross margin (%)	43%	48%	−5%	50%	35%	15%	25%	25%
Kitchen faucets								
Gross revenue	$65,000	$67,000	($2,000)	$410,000	$425,000	($15,000)	$483,000	($73,000)
Cost of goods sold	20,000	23,000	3,000	175,000	197,000	22,000	240,500	65,500
Gross margin ($)	$45,000	$44,000	$1,000	$235,000	$228,000	$7,000	$242,500	($7,500)
Gross margin (%)	69%	66%	4%	57%	54%	4%	50%	7%
Prefab shower stalls								
Gross revenue	$21,000	$24,000	($3,000)	$80,000	$67,000	$13,000	$75,500	$4,500
Cost of goods sold	8,000	10,000	2,000	37,000	43,000	6,000	51,250	14,250
Gross margin ($)	$13,000	$14,000	($1,000)	$43,000	$24,000	$19,000	$24,250	$18,750
Gross margin (%)	62%	58%	4%	54%	36%	18%	32%	22%
Cast iron bathtubs								
Gross revenue	$33,000	$28,000	$5,000	$170,000	$186,000	($16,000)	$198,500	($28,500)
Cost of goods sold	18,500	16,000	(2,500)	75,000	88,000	13,000	120,250	45,250
Gross margin ($)	$14,500	$12,000	$2,500	$95,000	$98,000	($3,000)	$78,250	$16,750
Gross margin (%)	44%	43%	1%	56%	53%	3%	39%	16%

Plastic bathtubs								
Gross revenue	$45,000	$37,500	$7,500	$177,000	$160,000	$17,000	$175,000	$2,000
Cost of goods sold	20,000	25,250	(5,250)	75,000	78,000	(3,000)	110,000	35,000
Gross margin ($)	$25,000	$12,250	$12,750	$102,000	$82,000	$20,000	$65,000	$37,000
Gross margin (%)	56%	33%	23%	58%	51%	6%	37%	20%
Bath sinks								
Gross revenue	$37,000	$32,000	$5,000	$148,000	$120,000	$28,000	$135,000	$13,000
Cost of goods sold	15,000	12,000	3,000	60,000	57,000	3,000	75,250	15,250
Gross margin ($)	$22,000	$20,000	$2,000	$88,000	$63,000	$25,000	$59,750	$28,250
Gross margin (%)	59%	63%	-3%	59%	53%	7%	44%	15%
Kitchen sinks								
Gross revenue	$9,000	$15,000	($6,000)	$45,000	$36,000	$9,000	$60,500	($15,500)
Cost of goods sold	3,500	10,750	(7,250)	10,500	15,500	(5,000)	31,500	21,000
Gross margin ($)	$5,500	$4,250	$1,250	$34,500	$20,500	$14,000	$29,000	$5,500
Gross margin (%)	61%	28%	33%	77%	57%	20%	48%	29%
Total revenue	$250,000	$240,000	$10,000	$1,250,000	$1,200,000	$50,000	$1,350,000	($100,000)
Less total cost of goods sold	100,000	110,000	(10,000)	500,000	550,000	(50,000)	750,000	250,000
Total gross margin ($)	$150,000	$130,000	$20,000	$750,000	$650,000	$100,000	$600,000	$150,000
Total gross margin (%)	60%	54%	6%	60%	54%	6%	44%	16%

8
Financial Reporting

Overview

We see the controller's efforts most frequently in the periodic financial reports issued by the company. Chapter 8 identifies each of these reports, their content, audience, and use. Along with the standard financial statements presented to senior management and sometimes the public, we'll cover the reports necessary for internal management of the firm as well.

Composing Financial Reports

Financial reporting involves a variety of performance and statistical schedules including:

- Comparison of financial results
- Computation of disposable cash
- Inventory
- Fixed assets and their depreciation schedules

Providing Information

We don't want any of these reporting areas to merely give our audience raw data. Instead, they should provide useful information. We use information *in the form presented* to identify a trend or a problem or to make decisions. On the other hand, we must take the time to *interpret* raw data and relate it to the issues at hand before using it for decision making.

Presentations of just raw data irritate many decision makers. There's a feeling that the analysts don't really know what they're doing. We certainly don't want anyone thinking this of you.

Another thing about presenting useful information: Don't lead the audience to a biased conclusion based on your presentation. Remember, financial reporting should present the facts, period, not the opinion of some analyst with an ax to grind. It takes just one incident of being misled by someone's interpretation to damage that person's credibility.

Here are the things we want your audience to recognize about your presentation:

- It's accurate.
- It's on time.
- It's easily understood.
- It's complete.

Indexing Your Information.   Relate new information to something with which the reader is already familiar. For example, it's not very useful to say inventory turned over this month at a rate of 4. So what? Is that good? Is it an improvement or a deterioration? Raw data such as this prompts more questions than it answers.

A better way of presenting that number is to tie it to an index such as:

- Planned inventory turnover rate
- Last month's figure
- Year-to-date figures
- Figures for this month last year

Any of these gives the reader an idea of how to interpret the information.

Adopting a Standard Format

Using the same standard formats every month may be dull. However, they sure save the reader time trying to find needed pieces of information. Financial reporting is not the time to demonstrate your creativity. Adopt a standard format for your monthly presentation of financial results. Then stick to it. People will thank you.

Here's a suggested format:

- Executive summary of key numbers in chart form
- Brief narrative of results
- Comparative financial statements
- Supporting schedules and ratios
- Graphical presentations

Using Graphics

Graphs, charts, diagrams, and pictures all provide a nice break from reading dull financial statements, schedules, and the narrative explanations that often accompany them. Keep your graphics presentations simple. Try not to put more than two or three lines on a single graph. More than that detracts from the benefits of instantly recognizing your point.

Using Colors

Colors are nice. They provide an eye-catching impact for your point. However, light blues, yellows, and most pastels don't reproduce well. Further, your audience won't get the benefit of colors if they receive a black-and-white *copy*. Except under special circumstances, colors are not usually worth the effort.

A good alternative is various types of cross-hatching (especially on bar graphs and pie charts). These copy well and are almost as eye-catching as different colors.

Computing Trend Lines

Some graphics packages have the ability to compute trend lines using actual data up to the current month. These are great for making the point: *at this rate, here's what we'll look like by year end.* It's a mathematical computation so there's no analytical judgment involved.

Indeed, trends are one of the strongest visual impacts provided by graphs. In just one quick look the reader can extrapolate the graph's trend. Using that information a judgment is made regarding problem situations and the timing of critical decisions.

Summarizing Results

Busy people appreciate seeing a summary of the most important information contained in long reports. That way they can go right to the place where they see a problem. The most effective summaries are simply charts showing key numbers such as:

- Cash balance
- Accounts receivable and payable balances
- Inventory balance
- Gross revenue
- Cost of goods sold
- Total expenses
- Net income

Often, summaries include comparisons of other indices to give readers an idea how the company is doing. Such comparisons include between three and five columns and read from left to right. For example, try these column headings:

- Current month actuals
- Last month

- Current month better (worse) than last
- Plan
- Current month better (worse) than plan

Some of the most effective summaries integrate the reporting-package table of contents into the summary chart. That way, readers can flip right to a section whose summary comparison prompts a question.

Narrating Results

The purpose of most narrative explanations is to anticipate questions readers may ask regarding the financial results. The narrative should be clear, get to the point quickly, and give the answer. It should *not* be creative writing.

Explanations should also be free of words that impart a value judgment as to the explanation. Avoid words like:

- *any*
- *all* or *almost all*
- *huge, heavy* (as in losses)
- *substantial*

We're after the facts. Words like these imply a universal truth. They are red flags. Every reader can think òf at least one instance where your point isn't true. This shoots credibility of the presentation down in flames.

Adjectives are another problem. They mean different things to different people. This makes them easily misunderstood. Don't use them.

Figure 8-1 shows an acceptable narrative explanation.

Financial Statements

The backbone of any report on financial results is the financial statements. These usually include:

Cost of goods sold for axle assemblies rose $24,500 (12 percent) as the result of 7 hours unscheduled downtime on the bearing-grinding machine. This increased costs as follows:

Negative labor variance	$11,500
Additional finished product rework costs	9,750
Negative material usage variance incurred before machine problem was discovered and fixed	3,250
	$24,500

Figure 8-1. Narrative explanation.

- Balance sheet
- Income statement
- Statement of cash flows

Descriptions of how these statements work and the information they present is beyond our scope here. A good elementary accounting book can provide this information. Instead, we'll concentrate on how to make the most of their use.

Relating Financial Statements

For financial statements to tell their story, they must relate to one another. That is, all three statements interact with one another to communicate particular parts of the firm's financial performance during the operating period. Here's the kind of information that each statement should provide to readers of the financial performance package:

Balance Sheet. The balance sheet shows the ending balance of each lead account in the general ledger. These are ongoing balances that are additive from period to period. That is, the balance in, say, accounts receivable in month five consists of:

Ending balance from month 4

Plus credit sales during month 5

Less payments received during month 5

Equals ending balance for month 5

The balance sheet relates to the income statement to the extent that income and expense items during the operating period change the balance sheet account balances. Cash is certainly one of these.

Revenue on the income statements shows credit sales. They flow to the balance sheet to increase accounts receivable. Likewise, cash sales are a part of sales revenue on the income statement and also increase cash on the balance sheet (but not receivables).

Invoices generally go into the accounts payable system for payment later. They hit the income statement as an expense and the balance sheet as an increase to accounts payable. Expense items paid during the current period increase expenses on the income statement and reduce cash on the balance sheet.

We can trace the increases or decreases in cash as shown on the statement of cash flows to the change in cash on the balance sheet. Here's how:

Prior period ending cash on balance sheet

Plus or minus increase or decrease in cash from the statement of cash flows

Equals current period ending cash on balance sheet

Income Statement. The income statement summarizes all the income and expenses that took place during the period. The bottom line (profit or loss) then flows to the balance sheet adds (or subtracts) to (from) retained earnings in the case of a corporation. If the company is a partnership, profit or loss is added (or subtracted) to (from) partner's capital.

Note that the current-period income statement does not recognize cost of durable goods purchased by the firm and capitalized (depreciated over time). Instead, the income statement expenses only the amount of depreciation allocated to that period. The balance sheet shows an accumulated depreciation account which equals the sum of all depreciation reported for all periods on the income statement.

Here's an easy way to verify that depreciation is correctly related between the income statement and balance sheet: subtract current period accumulated depreciation (appearing on the balance sheet) from that of the prior period. The answer should equal depreciation expense as reported on the income statement.

Note that the same relationship exists for amortization expenses of things like goodwill, prepaid rent, and points paid on loans.

Statement of Cash Flows. The statement of cash flows (SCF) provides a link between the income statement and balance sheet. Since November 1987, Statement 95 of the Financial Accounting Standards Board (FASB) requires an SCF as part of a full set of financial statements.

The SCF provides information regarding:

- The potential to generate future positive cash flows
- The ability to meet financial obligations, pay dividends, and return partner's invested capital
- Ability to meet loan requirements and the firm's ability to attract future lenders
- Explanations for differences between net income and associated cash receipts and payments
- Changes in financial position resulting from both cash and noncash investing and financing transactions

Companies reporting financial results under AICPA guidelines must disclose the effects of investing and financing activities that influence their financial position but have no direct impact on cash flow during the period. FASB 95 guidelines also require a supplemental schedule with the SCF that reconciles net income to net cash provided by operations.

In case you're unfamiliar with the format, Figure 8-2 illustrates a sample SCF along with supplemental schedules.

Notice that the SCF combines cash flow information from both the balance sheet and income statement in:

- Operations
- Investments
- Financing

Maggie Corporation
Statement of Cash Flows (Direct Method)
For the Year Ended December 31, 19X1
Increase (Decrease) in Cash

Cash flows from operating activities:	
Cash received from customers	$1,500,000
Cash paid to suppliers and employees	(350,000)
Interest paid	(80,000)
Income taxes paid	(175,000)
Other receipts (payments)	25,000
Net cash provided by operating activities	$ 920,000
Cash flows from investing activities:	
Proceeds from sale of assets	300,000
Payments for purchase of equipment	(200,000)
Payments for purchase of real estate	(175,000)
Net cash used in investment activity	$ (75,000)
Cash flows from financing activities:	
Net increase in short-term credit	300,000
Proceeds from common stock issuance	150,000
Proceeds from bond issuance	75,000
Payment of long-term debt	(65,000)
Payment of dividends	(60,000)
Net cash provided by financing activities	$ 400,000
Effect of exchange rate changes on cash	10,000
Net increase in cash	$1,255,000
Cash at beginning of year	1,000,000
Cash at end of year	$2,255,000
Reconciliation of net income to net cash provided by operating activities:	
Net income	$ 475,000
Adjustments to reconcile net income to net cash provided by operating activities:	
Depreciation and amortization	75,000
(Gain) loss on asset sales	20,000
Exchange loss	(10,000)
Decrease in accounts receivable	350,000
Increase in inventory	(55,000)
Increase in accounts payable	70,000
Decrease in interest and taxes payable	(5,000)
Net cash provided by operating activities	$ 920,000

Figure 8-2. Statement of cash flows and supporting reports.

Computation of cash received from customers and cash paid to
* suppliers and employees:*
Cash received from customers:
  Revenues $1,150,000
  Decrease in accounts receivable   350,000

   Cash received from customers $1,500,000

Cash paid to suppliers and employees:
  Cost of sales $ 260,000
  Effect of exchange rate changes of cost of sales   3,000
  General and administrative changes   77,000

   Total operations requiring cash payments $ 340,000
  Increase in inventory   (55,000)
  Increase in accounts payable   70,000
  Decrease in interest and taxes payable   (5,000)

Cash paid to suppliers and employees $ 350,000

Figure 8-2. (*Continued*)

Reporting Foreign Currencies. Notice the line which reads "Effect of exchange rate changes on cash" in Figure 8-2. This has to do with foreign currency transactions the company may have made. When presenting the cash flows of foreign operations we usually translate the foreign currency into the currency being reported. We call this the *functional currency* of the parent company.

These foreign exchange rate changes are not cash receipts or payments. The SCF reports them as a separate item that reconciles beginning and ending cash balances. For further information on foreign currency translation rules, please see FASB Statement No. 52, *Foreign Currency Translation,* published by the Financial Accounting Standards Board.

Here is the cash reporting procedure to use when foreign subsidiaries report to the parent in their own local currency (their functional currency is not the U.S. dollar):

1. Foreign subs' cash flow reports are prepared in their own local currencies.

2. Translate local currency into the reporting currency using either:
   - The exchange rate in effect at the time of the cash flows
   - A weighted exchange rate for the period

   Either method is acceptable as long as the result is substantially the same.

3. Report the consolidated effects of the exchange rate changes as a single line on the statement of cash flows.

4. Reconcile the translated statement of cash flows to the increase or decrease in cash balances after translation to the reporting currency.

Computation of Exchange Rate Changes on Cash	
Effect on beginning cash balances:	
Beginning cash balance in local currency	LC 1000
Net change in exchange rate during the year	× .05
Effect on beginning cash balance	$ 50.00
Effect on operating activities during the year:	
Cash provided by operations in local currency	LC 500
Year-end exchange rate	× .25
Operating cash flow based on year-end exchange rate	$125.00
Operating cash flow from statement of cash flow	$100.00
Effect from operations during the year	25.00
Effect from investing activities during the year:	
Cash used in investing activities in local currency	LC 100
Year-end exchange rate	× .25
Investing cash flows based on year-end exchange rate	$25.00
Investing cash flows reported in statement of cash flows	30.00
Effect from investing activities during the year	(5.00)
Effect from financing activities during the year:	
Cash provided by financing activities in LC	LC 1000
Year-end exchange rate	× .25
Financing cash flows based on year-end exchange rate	$250.00
Financing cash flows reported in statement of cash flows	230.00
Effect on financing activities during the year	20.00
Effect of exchange rate changes on cash	$ 90.00

Figure 8-3. Computing exchange rate changes.

To see how to compute the effects of changes in foreign exchange rates for use on the statement of cash flows, study the sample format in Figure 8-3.

There's also an indirect method of computing the SCF. FASB Statement 104 provides details of this method. This is for companies that can't provide the detailed cash receipts and payments needed in the direct method. Financial institutions primarily use the indirect method. For detailed explanations of FASB 95 and its amendment statement, FASB 104, please see the Statement 95 and 104 pamphlets published by the Financial Accounting Standards Board (P.O. Box 3821, Stamford, CT 06905-0821).

Comparative Financial Statements

Monthly financial statements are of little use unless we can compare them with something. This gives readers a point of reference against which to judge current-period performance. Remember the difference between raw data and information? Comparative financials take a giant step toward converting data to usable information.

What should we compare? Here are the most common comparisons to give you some ideas of ways to configure your comparative financials:

- Current period
- Prior period
- Current better (worse) (B[W]) prior in $
- Current B(W) prior in %
- Current-period plan
- Current B(W) plan in $
- Current B(W) plan in %
- This month last year
- Current B(W) this month last year in $
- Current B(W) this month last year in %
- Current period year to date (YTD)
- Plan YTD
- Current YTD B(W) plan YTD in $
- Current YTD B(W) plan YTD in %
- This month last year YTD
- Current YTD B(W) this month last year YTD in $
- Current YTD B(W) this month last year YTD in %

Choose the most meaningful comparisons for your business. If, for example, management bases bonuses in part on achieving the plan, then comparison against plan is a necessity. Likewise, if improving results over last year is important, then present that comparison as well.

Some comparative financial reports may get fairly wide with all the columns required. This can make tracing the numbers across the page difficult. To lessen this burden on the reader, some reports show the row headings in the middle of the page. The columns then emanate to the right and to the left. Again, the emphasis is on making the report user-friendly.

Choosing Which Statements to Compare. Most companies present comparative income statements. Some present comparative statements of cash flow and changes in financial condition. Few do comparative balance sheets on a monthly basis. That's because balance sheets change only as a result of changes in the income statement and statement of cash flows. Therefore, if you have the comparison of income and cash, you have by definition the changes to the key balance sheet items that may have changed.

Year-end balance sheets prepared by your independent auditors are a different matter. There, they will always provide comparative balance sheets.

Working Capital Requirements

Simply stated, *working capital* is the money it takes to run the firm. The equation is equally as simple:

$$\text{Working capital} = \text{current assets} - \text{current liabilities}$$

When reporting working capital, treasurers like to see how the components change. Figure 8-4 shows a good example of a typical month-end working capital report. Notice how the statement shows the working capital composition. Readers quickly identify the reasons working capital requirements rose:

- Receivables and inventory rose
- Payables and accrued liabilities fell

Another way of reporting working capital changes is through the statement of changes in financial position—working capital basis. Figure 8-5 shows an example.

See where the money comes from and where it goes? Many controllers and treasurers include the statement of changes in financial position in their monthly reporting packages for just this purpose.

| | December 31 | | Working |
Capital Decrease	19X1	19X2	Increase
Current assets:			
Cash	$ 51,000	$ 45,000	$ 6,000
Accounts receivable	35,000	40,000	5,000
Inventory	30,000	40,000	10,000
Total current assets	$116,000	$125,000	$ 9,000
Current liabilities:			
Accounts payable	$ 20,000	$ 15,000	5,000
Accrued liabilities	9,000	5,000	4,000
Total current liabilities	$ 29,000	$ 20,000	$ 9,000
Working capital	$ 87,000	$105,000	$18,000

Riley Partners, Ltd.
Statement of Changes in Working Capital
For the Year Ended December 31, 199X

Figure 8-4. Changes in working capital.

Tobby Enterprises
Statement of Changes in Financial
Position—Working Capital Basis
For the Year Ended December 31, 199X

Financial resources provided:	
Working capital from operations:	
Net income	$20,000
Plus nonworking capital expenses:	
Depreciation	4,000
Total working capital from operations	$16,000
Issuance of common stock	45,000
Total financial resources provided	$61,000
Financial resources applied:	
Purchase of plant assets	$14,000
Dividends expenditure	29,000
	43,000
Increase in working capital	$18,000
Schedule of changes in working capital components:	
Increase (decrease) in current assets:	
Cash	$ (6,000)
Accounts receivable	5,000
Inventory	10,000
	$ 9,000

Increase (decrease) in current liabilities:		
Accounts payable	$5,000	
Accrued liabilities	4,000	9,000
Decrease in working capital		$18,000

Figure 8-5. Statement of changes in financial position—working capital basis.

Reporting Inventory

There are two things we want to get across when reporting inventory balances to management each month:

- Adequacy to cover demand
- Obsolete or slow-moving balances

Of course, there are many other inventory reports those responsible for the warehouse and production line need to see. Nevertheless, adequacy and slow-moving items are the main inventory issues concerning top management.

The following two equations help to assess these measurements.

Average Inventory Investment Period

This index illustrates the number of days we have of inventory on hand given current requirements. A rising investment period isn't good. It means the time to convert payment for inventory sales into collected customer payments has increased. It may be caused by poorly chosen inventory items or a buildup of obsolete inventory.

Conversely, the lower the investment period, the less the company has invested in inventory. This means that working capital requirements have dropped. Here's the equation to compute average investment period of inventory:

$$\text{Average investment period of inventory} = \frac{\text{present inventory balance}}{\left(\dfrac{\text{annual cost of goods sold}}{360}\right)}$$

Inventory Turnover Rate

Inventory turnover shows us how quickly our inventory investment converts into sales. We want a high turnover rate. This means our inventory is in high demand and doesn't sit around the warehouse, sucking up precious working capital.

Compute inventory turnover as follows:

$$\text{Inventory turnover rate} = \frac{\text{annual cost of goods sold}}{\text{average inventory balance}}$$

Reporting Fixed Assets

Management doesn't usually ask for a detailed list of fixed assets each month. These lists are extensive for most companies. However, the balance sheet usually reports fixed assets in these categories:

- Land
- Buildings
- Property, plant, and equipment
- Furniture and fixtures
- Leasehold improvements

The list goes on depending on the company. The point is, all the details are lumped into just a few categories. Periodically, the controller should verify that the detail does indeed tie with what's reported on the balance sheet. If your company undergoes a certified audit, the auditors will do this. However, it's embarrassing (to say the least) when an outsider tells you the fixed assets you've been reporting all year long are wrong.

Capital Expenditures

Companies with active capital expenditure programs usually report progress against the capital expenditure plan each month. This report lists each capital project, the actual spent to date, and compares it with the plan. Usually another column subtracts the two for the reader to better track the plan.

Treasurers concerned about cash flow often take this one step further. Each month they project cash outflow associated with the capital expenditure program. This report includes funds already committed, those coming due for payment, and those not yet committed but on the payout schedule for later in the year.

Reporting Compliance

Many of the compliance issues addressed by businesses relate to debt. Organized treasurers usually have monthly reports that analyze their chief concerns regarding debt. These include:

Debt Components

The balance sheet normally separates debt into the part due this year and that due long term. For each component of debt many treasurers report separately:

- End-of-month balance
- Lender
- Interest rate

Total the various components and tie them back to the balance sheet.

Compensating Balances

This is an expensive requirement of many lending agreements. It's wise to report each month the year-to-date balances kept in all compensating balance accounts. Match these with the bank's figures and the terms of the loan agreement.

The report probably won't go to senior management. However, they are valuable to a treasurer or controller responsible for financing costs.

Complying with Lending Covenants

Borrowers must meet specific lending covenants to avoid being in default. Many treasurers manage this with a comparison report that matches actual performance against each covenant and restriction. The treasurer can scan the report and

Maggie Corporation
Lending Covenant Compliance Report
For the Period Ending December 31, 199X

Lending covenant	Actual	Loan 1	Loan 2	Loan 3
Current ratio	2.3	2.0	2.0	2.1
Quick ratio	1.1	1.0	0.9	0.95
Times-interest-earned ratio	4.6	3.5	4.1	6.0
Debt-to-equity ratio (maximum)	4.0	4.0	4.5	4.5
Net income	$ 25,000	$ 20,000	$ 20,000	$15,000
Minimum working capital	$ 87,000	$ 60,000	$ 70,000	$75,000
Total cash and cash equivalents (minimum)	$155,000	$100,000	$125,000	$85,000
Average compensating balance	$123,000	$ 75,000	$ 25,000	0

Figure 8-6. Report of lending covenant compliance.

quickly note any breaches of lending terms. Figure 8-6 shows a typical format for this report.

A quick review of this report indicates there's a problem with the times-interest-earned ratio for loan 3.

Sample Month-End Reporting Package

The month-end reporting package shown in Figure 8-7 includes many of the reports discussed in this chapter.

Peaches Enterprises
Summary of Key Financial Information
For the Period Ending March 31, 199X

	March	February	March B(W) February	YTD Actual	YTD Plan	YTD Actl. B(W) YTD Plan
Total sales	$ 922,503	$ 926,075	($3,572)	$9,573,010	$9,079,206	$493,804
Cost of goods sold	110,563	115,567	5,004	4,207,674	3,994,014	(213,660)
Gross margin	$ 811,940	$ 810,508	$1,432	$5,365,336	$5,085,192	$280,144
Total expenses	506,909	541,876	34,967	1,635,872	1,547,452	(88,420)
Income before debt service	$ 305,031	$ 268,632	$36,399	$3,729,464	$3,537,740	$191,724
Debt service & other items	282,600	211,800	(70,800)	635,400	847,800	212,400
Net income before taxes	$ 22,431	$ 56,832	($34,401)	$3,094,064	$2,689,940	$404,124
Cash	$1,756,732	$1,207,016	$549,716	$1,756,732	$1,800,000	($43,268)
Accounts receivable	159,981	180,000	20,019	159,981	167,000	(7,019)
Weighted average aging of A/R	31	33	2	33	30	−3
Inventory	96,420	125,000	28,580	125,000	155,000	30,000
Days of inventory on hand	26	27	1	27	25	−2
Inventory turnover rate	13	10	3	10	13	−3
Accounts payable	136,060	155,000	(18,940)	155,000	135,000	20,000
A/P aging	59	62	−3	62	65	−3
A/P turnover rate	5	6	−1	5.6	6	−0.4

Figure 8-7 Sample month-end reporting package.

Peaches Enterprises Income Statement
For the Period Ending March 31, 199X

	March	February	March B(W) February	YTD Actual	YTD Plan	YTD Actl. B(W) YTD Plan
Sales						
Sales—product A	$775,082	$782,096	($7,014)	$9,156,782	$8,678,420	$478,362
Sales—product B	36,750	31,087	5,663	84,810	79,193	5,617
Sales—product C	110,671	112,892	(2,221)	331,418	321,593	9,825
Total sales	$922,503	$926,075	($3,572)	$9,573,010	$9,079,206	$493,804
Cost of goods sold	110,563	115,567	5,004	4,207,674	3,994,014	(213,660)
Gross margin	$811,940	$810,508	$1,432	$5,365,336	$5,085,192	$280,144
Operating expenses						
Advertising	2,911	3,057	146	9,170	8,733	(437)
Auto and truck exp.	39,845	42,893	3,048	126,783	119,535	(7,248)
Depreciation	12,985	12,985	0	38,956	38,956	0
Amort. of goodwill	55,392	44,344	(11,048)	133,032	133,032	0
Amort. of org. fees	40,000	40,000	0	121,687	120,000	(1,687)
Legal and accounting	26,489	27,813	1,324	83,440	73,456	(9,984)
Licenses	2,318	2,382	64	7,302	6,954	(348)
Office supplies	20,145	21,152	1,007	63,457	60,435	(3,022)
Sales salaries	39,809	41,799	1,990	127,932	119,427	(8,505)
Sales expense	4,230	4,442	212	13,325	14,681	1,357
Salaries—exec. & office	153,859	183,582	29,723	568,371	521,559	(46,812)
Payroll taxes	21,503	22,578	1,075	67,734	64,509	(3,225)
Rent	40,553	42,581	2,028	123,868	121,659	(2,209)
Entertainment	4,055	4,258	203	12,773	13,168	395
Travel	15,234	15,996	762	47,987	45,702	(2,285)
Telephone	19,876	23,924	4,048	65,785	63,467	(2,318)
Utilities	7,705	8,090	385	24,271	22,179	(2,092)
Total indirect expenses	$506,909	$541,876	$34,967	$1,635,872	$1,547,452	($88,420)
Income before debt service	$305,031	$268,632	$36,399	$3,729,464	$3,537,740	$191,724
Int. exp. from debt service	318,600	247,800	(70,800)	743,400	955,800	212,400
Net income from leasing co.	36,000	36,000	0	108,000	108,000	0
Profit before taxes	$ 22,431	$ 56,832	($34,401)	$3,094,064	$2,689,940	$404,124

Figure 8-7 (Continued)

Peaches Enterprises
Comparative Balance Sheet as of March 31, 199X

	March	February	Current B(W) Prior month
Current assets:			
Cash	$1,756,732	$1,207,016	$549,716
Accounts receivable	159,981	180,000	(20,019)
Interest receivable	559	0	559
Inventory	96,420	125,000	(28,580)
Total current assets	$2,013,692	$1,512,016	$501,676
Property, plant, & equipment:			
Machinery and equipment	1,380,600	1,380,600	0
Furniture and fixtures	140,000	40,000	100,000
Leasehold improvements	129,854	129,854	0
Subtotal PP&E	$1,650,454	$1,550,454	$100,000
Accumulated depreciation	(38,956)	(25,971)	(12,985)
Property, plant, & equipment	$1,611,498	$1,524,483	$87,015
Other assets:			
Deposits	18,826	18,826	0
Goodwill	773,760	773,760	0
Less accum. amortization goodwill	(133,032)	(88,688)	(44,344)
Organization fees	200,000	200,000	0
Less accum. amortization org. fees	(120,000)	(80,000)	(40,000)
Total other assets	$ 739,554	$ 823,898	($84,344)
Total assets	$4,364,744	$3,860,397	$504,347
Current liabilities:			
Accounts payable	$ 136,060	$ 155,000	$ 18,940
Accrued commission	28,355	0	(28,355)
Payroll taxes payable	217	0	(217)
Sales taxes payable	188	0	(188)
Total current liabilities	$ 164,820	$ 155,000	($9,820)
Bank note	960,000	720,000	(240,000)
Bonds payable	840,000	630,000	(210,000)
Shareholder's equity:			
Common stock	761,048	750,000	(11,048)
Retained earnings	1,638,876	1,605,397	(33,479)
Total shareholder's equity	$2,399,924	$2,355,397	($44,527)
Total liab. & S/H equity	$4,364,744	$3,860,397	($504,347)

Figure 8-7 (*Continued*)

Peaches Enterprises
Statement of Changes in Financial Position
For Period Ending March 31, 199X

	March
Sources of cash:	
Profit before taxes	$ 22,431
Add deprec. (indrct.)	12,985
Add amort. of goodwill	55,392
Add amort. of org. fees	40,000
Capital stock	11,048
Accounts receivable	20,019
Interest receivable	(559)
Inventory	28,580
Bank note	240,000
Bond issuance	210,000
Sources of working capital	$ 639,896
Uses of cash:	
Prop., plant, & equip.	100,000
Accounts payable	18,940
Accr. comm. payable	(28,355)
Payroll taxes payable	(217)
Sales taxes payable	(188)
Paydown of bank note	0
Bond retirement	0
Uses of working capital	$ 90,180
Incr (decr.) in cash	$ 549,716
Cash at beginning of year	$1,207,016
Plus cash sources	639,896
Less cash uses	90,180
Cash at end of period	$1,756,732

Figure 8-7   (*Continued*)

Peaches Enterprises
Statement of Cash Flows
For the Month Ended March 31, 199X
Increase (Decrease) in Cash

	March
Cash flows from operating activities:	
Cash received from customers	$ 942,522
Cash paid to suppliers and employees	(471,254)
Interest paid	(318,600)
Income taxes paid	0
Other receipts (payments)	36,000
Net cash provided by operating activities	$ 188,668
Cash flows from investing activities:	
Proceeds from sale of assets	0
Payments for purchase of equipment	(100,000)
Payments for purchase of real estate	0
Net cash used in investment activity	($100,000)
Cash flows from financing activities:	
Net increase in short-term credit	240,000
Proceeds from common stock issuance	11,048
Proceeds from bond issuance	210,000
Payment of long-term debt	0
Payment of dividends	0
Net cash provided by financing activities	$ 461,048
Effect of exchange rate changes on cash	0
Net increase in cash	$ 549,716
Cash at beginning of month	1,207,016
Cash at end of month	$1,756,732

Reconciliation of Net Income to Net Cash Provided
by Operating Activities

Net income	$ 22,431
Adjustments to reconcile net income to net cash provided by operating activities:	
Depreciation and amortization	108,377
Decrease in accounts receivable	20,019
Increase in interest receivable	(559)
Decrease in inventory	28,580
Decrease in accounts payable	(18,940)
Increase in accrued commissions	28,355
Increase in taxes payable	405
Net cash provided by operating activities	$ 188,668

Figure 8-7 (*Continued*)

Computation of Cash Received from Customers and Cash Paid to Suppliers and Employees

Cash received from customers:	
Revenues	$922,503
Decrease in accounts receivable	20,019
Cash received from customers	$942,522
Cash paid to suppliers and employees:	
Cost of sales	$110,563
General and administrative	398,532
Total operations requiring cash payments	509,095
Decrease in inventory	(28,580)
Decrease in accounts payable	18,940
Increase in accrued commissions	(28,355)
Increase in accrued interest receivable	559
Decrease in taxes payable	(405)
Cash paid to suppliers and employees	$471,254

Figure 8-7   (*Continued*)

Figure 8-7 (*Continued*)

Peaches Enterprises
Management Ratio Report
March 31, 199X

Asset ratios	Current month
1. Current ratio: Equation: current assets/current liabilities	
Current assets	$ 2,013,692
Current liabilities	164,820
Current ratio	12.22
2. Quick ratio: Equation: (cash + marketable securities	
Cash	$ 1,756,732
Marketable securities	0
Accounts receivable	159,981
Current liabilities	164,820
Quick ratio	11.63

Accounts receivable ratios	
1. Accounts receivable turnover rate: Equation: annual sales/average A/R balance	
Annual sales	11,070,036
Average A/R balances	169,991
A/R turnover rate	65.1
2. Average collection period: Equation: accounts receivable	
Accounts receivable	$ 159,981
Annual sales	11,070,036
Avg. collection period (days)	5

Figure 8-7   (*Continued*)

3. Aging of accounts receivable:
   Equation: sum of (weighted avercket*)

	Amount	Weighting % In bucket	Aging bucket weighting
A/R balances by aging bucket:			
Current	$ 50,000	31%	0 days
30 days	79,981	50%	15 days
60 days	10,000	6%	4 days
90 days	15,000	9%	8 days
120 days	5,000	3%	4 days
Total A/R	$ 159,981	100%	31 days

Inventory ratios

1. Average investment period of inventory:
   Equation: present inventory balance

Present inventory balance	$ 96,420
Annual cost of goods sold	1,326,756
Avg inv. period of inv. (days)	26

2. Inventory turnover rate:
   Equation: annual cost of goods

Annual cost of goods sold	$1,386,804
Average inventory balance	110,710
Inv. turnover rate (times per year)	13

Accounts payable

1. Aging of accounts payable:
   Equation: sum of (weighted avercket*)

	Amount	Weighting % in bucket	Aging bucket weighting
A/P balances by aging bucket:			
Current	$ 5,000	4%	0 days
30 days	25,000	18%	6 days
60 days	75,000	55%	33 days
90 days	31,060	23%	21 days
120 days	0	0%	0 days
Total A/P	$ 136,060	100%	59 days

* Average percentage of each aging bucket × number of days in each bucket.

Figure 8-7   (*Continued*)

2. Average payment period:	
Equation: accounts payable	
balance/(annual expenses/360)	
Accounts payable balance	$ 155,000
Annual expenses	419,600
Average payment period (days)	133
3. Accounts payable turnover rate:	
Equation: annual expenses/	
average A/P balance	
Annual expenses	$ 419,600
Average A/P balance	86,970
A/P turnover rate (times/year)	5

Figure 8-7 *(Continued)*

Peaches Enterprises
Management Performance Report
March 31, 199X

Cash and assets	Current month	Prior month	Current B(W) prior	Year to date	Current B(W) YTD	Target	Year to date B(W) target
Cash	$1,756,732	$1,207,016	$549,716	$1,756,732	$0	$500,000	$1,256,732
Marketable securities	0	0	0	0	0	0	0
All other cash items	0	0	0	0	0	0	0
Total cash	$1,756,732	$1,207,016	$549,716	$1,756,732	$0	$500,000	$1,256,732
Current ratio	17.78	9.75	8.02	17.78	0.00	15.00	2.78
Quick ratio	17.19	8.95	8.24	17.19	0.00	12.00	5.19
Accounts receivable							
Accounts receivable turnover rate	65.12	12.00	53.12	65.12	0.00	15.00	50.12
A/R receivable collection period	5.20	21.00	15.80	5.20	0.00	25.00	19.80
Weighted average A/R aging	30.94	33.00	2.06	30.94	0.00	41.00	10.06
Inventory							
Avg. investment period of inventory	26.16	4.00	−22.16	26.16	0.00	30.00	3.84
Inventory turnover rate	12.53	135.00	−122.47	12.53	0.00	12.00	0.53
Accounts payable							
Weighted average A/P aging	59.13	60.00	−0.87	59.13	0.00	11.00	48.13
Average payment period	132.98	3.00	129.98	132.98	0.00	11.00	121.98
A/P turnover rate	4.82	100.00	95.18	4.82	0.00	8.00	3.18

Manufacturing performance							
Material price variance	(45,000)	20,000	(65,000)	(10,000)	(35,000)	0	(10,000)
Labor price variance	10,000	(500)	10,500	5,000	5,000	0	5,000
Mfg. price variance	(20,000)	10,000	(30,000)	0	(20,000)	0	0
Safety stock	10,000	10,000	0	10,000	0	15,000	5,000
Stock out costs	0	500	500	1,000	1,000	5,000	4,000
Financial performance							
Working capital	2,793,717	1,357,016	1,848,872	2,793,717	N/A	2,500,000	293,717
Short-term borrowing	960,000	720,000	(240,000)	960,000	N/A	1,500,000	540,000
Long-term borrowing	840,000	630,000	(210,000)	840,000	N/A	2,000,000	1,160,000
Interest expense	318,600	247,800	(70,800)	700,000	381,400	35,000	(665,000)
Aggregate int. rate on investments	0.00%	0.00%	0.00%	0.00%	0.00%	0.00%	0.00%
Aggregate interest rate on debt	12.00%	11.95%	-0.05%		-12.00%	12.00%	12.00%
Lending covenants							
Debt coverage ratio	0.07	0.23	-0.16	4.16	-4.09	2.00	2.16
Ratio of debt to net worth	0.64	0.99	0.35	0.64	0.00	1.00	0.36
Minimum cash balance	$2,000,000	$2,000,000	$0	$2,000,000	N/A	$1,000,000	$1,000,000
Compensating balance	$ 100,000	$ 120,000	$20,000	$ 100,000	$0	$ 100,000	$0
Owner's equity	$2,399,924	$2,355,397	$44,527	$2,399,924	$0	$2,500,000	($100,076)
Owner's draw	$0	$0	$0	$0	$0	$ 500,000	($500,000)

Peaches Enterprises
Schedule of Receivables Aging as of March 31, 199X

	Current	30 days	60 days	90 days	120 days and over
Ford Motor Company	$ 25,398	$1,232	$ 848	$ 167	$ 33
Cohen Corp.	34,267	0	1,235	56	78
Dragon, Ltd.	10,596	0	2,135	200	66
IBM	5,432	506	468	0	0
Z, C & W, Inc.	4,498	232	1,568	23	133
Inacomp	8,006	768	0	0	0
Edison Co.	7,898	1,105	1,235	46	23
Traulson, Inc.	1,578	2,258	1,567	46	97
Honda of America	1,322	31	2,156	32	32
Ashton-Tate	3,393	268	3,158	101	21
S/T	$102,388	$6,400	$14,370	$ 671	$483
Others	25,597	1,600	6,428	1,730	315
Total receivables	$127,985	$8,000	$20,798	$2,401	$798

Peaches Enterprises
Schedule of Receivables Roll Rate as of March 31, 199X

	Current to 30 days	30 days to 60 days	60 days to 90 days	90 days to 120 days	120 days to W/O
Current	$28,978				
30 days		$1,200			
60 days			$4,160		
90 days				$1,201	
120 days					$600
Total receivables rolled	$28,978	$1,200	$4,160	$1,201	$600

Elapsed time from sale to invoice based on sample of 100 sales: 2.3 days

Invoice entry backlog averaged through the month: 26 invoices totaling $12,345

Internal deposit float from time of receipt to time of deposit: 1.75 days
Value of internal deposit float:
Receipts from customers:	$2,400,000
divided by 31 days =	77,419 /day
multiplied by internal deposit float	1.75 days

Value of internal deposit float | $ 135,483 |

Annual cost of internal deposit float at weighted average cost of funds of 8%: $10,839

Figure 8-7 (*Continued*)

Peaches Enterprises
Schedule of Payables Aging as of March 31, 199X

	Current	30 days	60 days	90 days	120 days and over	Total
Goodyear Tire Co.	$ 4,521	$ 596	$ 945	$ 325	$ 0	$ 6,387
Styro Cup Co.	5,657	500	1,538	23	0	7,718
So. Cal. Edison	6,536	5,688	1,357	1008	0	14,589
CA Service Corp.	15,656	2,135	466	0	0	18,257
Cussler Corp.	205	565	323	237	235	1,565
Compaq Computer Corp.	1,756	3,056	2,358	0	989	8,159
Morgan/Rather Partners	2,356	1,578	232	0	0	4,166
General Telephone	5,658	2,358	3,235	1235	0	12,486
Space Products Partners	11,568	4,566	1,638	0	1056	18,828
Art Dimensions	15,687	2,358	658	1,972	168	20,843
Top 10 payables	$69,600	$23,400	$12,750	$4,800	$2,448	$112,998
Other payables	17,400	1,600	2,250	1,200	612	23,062
	$87,000	$25,000	$15,000	$6,000	$3,060	$136,060

Discounts missed:	$ 5,677
Discounts taken advantage of:	$23,538

Figure 8-7   (*Continued*)

9
Financial Analysis and Support

Overview

Because of their proximity to financial information and their quantitative backgrounds, most controllers provide financial analyses and other support services to the rest of the firm. There are many analytical tools employed by controllers to interpret financial results. Most involve comparisons of different time periods or analysis of the relationship of two different numbers to form a ratio.

This chapter features five of the functions that compose the analytical and support duties of many controller's jobs:

- Financial analysis
- Period-ending procedures
- Inventory control
- Analysis of production costs
- Support functions provided by the controller

Additionally, the chapter presents some of the quantitative tools often used.

Financial Analysis

A financial background provides a unique combination of skills necessary for the analysis of quantitative information. The analyst's mission here is to draw conclusions about the company's performance from the period-ending financial reports. The most effective analytical reports don't try to sway the reader to the analyst's point of view. They simply provide the facts.

Skilled analysts package these facts using a combination of narrative explanation, financial statistics, charts, and graphs. The purpose is to quickly tell someone unfamiliar with the numbers what happened during the operating period.

The analyst's results provide decision makers with better information about the direction the firm is taking. From here, they can determine where the business is likely to go if left alone and how to bring it back on track if it has strayed.

Analyzing Monthly Financial Reports

The key questions each month are:

- How did we do compared to last month?
- Are we tracking against the plan?

Answers to these questions give some frame of reference regarding performance. The easiest way to communicate this is by presenting comparative financial statements. Chapter 8, "Financial Reporting," showed the most effective ways of comparing monthly financial performance information. This, coupled with a narrative explanation on specific issues that pop out of the financials, provides a good point at which to begin the financial review.

Many analysts begin their narrative with explanations regarding the things most important to management. If it's profit, then explain why profits are up or down compared to last month. Cash balance is often another concern. Tell readers why cash changed the way it did during the month. If future availability of cash is an issue, identify how much is needed, when, and where the funds are coming from.

Another issue is often inventory and production. Without enough of the right goods to sell (or too much of the wrong ones), profits drop. Many managers want to know where their inventory and production costs stand. Since these numbers aren't readily visible on standard financial statements, the narrative explanation is a good place to answer such questions.

Formatting the Narrative.   Narrative explanations must be brief. They are there only to supplement the numbers. Chapter 8 demonstrated the style of an explanation accompanying financial statements. Here's a format for narrative explanations that usually works:

- Identify the issue.
- Explain what problem the issue creates or solves.
- Use numbers to quantify and prove the reasoning.
- Trace the numbers back to the financial statements so readers don't have to hunt for them.

Tooling Up for Analysis

Accountants have certain shortcuts they use every day in their work. Most are very simple to employ. They can speed up the preparation and analysis of financial statements. Here are a few:

Balancing Debits and Credits

If something is out of balance, there's a chance that just one number is the culprit. That number may have been misentered as a debit (or credit) rather than a credit (or debit). To find it, divide the amount you're out of balance by two. Then check your list of entries to see if there's a debit or credit of that same amount that was entered on the wrong side of the ledger.

Grossing Up a Number

This is a simple mathematical exercise used to approximate a gross number from a net number. Here's how it works: Divide the percentage the net represents of the gross into the net number. For example, say we know that net income is usually about 2 percent of gross revenue. If our net is $50,000, how much should have been the gross revenue?

$$\frac{\$50,000}{.02} = \$2,500,000$$

The $2,500,000 is the grossed-up revenue. This is a quick analytical test frequently performed to establish the reasonableness of a number.

Annualizing a Number

A frequently asked question is, "At this rate, how will our year end look?" It's a fair question, and one that we can mathematically answer. Here's how: Use a simple proportion that employs a known result from the months elapsed to date. Say we're $25,000 over our planned costs after nine months. At this rate, how far over will we be by year end?

$$\frac{\$25,000}{9 \text{ months}} = \frac{x}{12 \text{ months}}$$

Solving for x, the answer is $33,333 ([$25,000 × 12]/9 = $33,333).

Mean, Median, and Mode

Large groups with homogenous characteristics—such as accounts receivable, payable, and customer purchasing habits—employ many analytical tools. Here are three simple statistics frequently used:

Mean.   The mean is a simple average. It tells what an average observation in the population will likely be. Here's the equation:

$$\text{Mean} = \frac{\text{sum of all observations}}{\text{number in the population}}$$

Median.   The median is the midpoint between the highest and lowest values of the population. You can find the median simply by taking the highest and lowest observations, subtracting them, and dividing the difference by two.

Mode.   The mode is the most frequently observed value in a population. This is particularly interesting when dealing with receivables. It answers the question, "How much do our customers usually make us finance for them?" Alternatively, it also answers the question, "How long do our customers usually make us carry them?"

Analyzing Ratios

Apart from the standard financial ratios used by bankers to assess the credit-worthiness of a company, many controllers employ specific ratios. These act as benchmarks by which to gauge the firm's performance from month to month. Here are a few:

Return on Assets

We want to find out how much our assets are earning. That number had better be higher than the rate we get by investing the same funds and undertaking the same amount of risk (or less). If not, there's no point in remaining in business. Here's the equation:

$$\frac{\text{income before interest and taxes}}{\text{total assets}} = \text{return on assets}$$

Income per Employee

It may sound callous, but there's only one reason for having employees: the income they bring in through the work they do exceeds their total compensation. Many firms measure this statistic regularly to ensure uniform productivity. Here's the equation:

$$\text{Income per employee} = \frac{\text{net income}}{\text{total number of employees}}$$

Turnover

Controllers talking about turnover really mean the velocity by which things are changing—usually into cash. Here are some of the more common turnover measurements:

Asset Turnover.   It makes no sense holding assets that don't help the company make money. The asset turnover ratio shows how many times a year sales replaces assets. We want this number to be as large as possible. The larger the turnover, the leaner and meaner is the company. Here's the ratio:

$$\text{Asset turnover} = \frac{\text{total revenue}}{\text{total assets}}$$

Receivables Turnover.   We can say the same thing about receivables. We want them to turn as fast as possible. That means we're financing less of our customer's business. Here's the equation:

$$\text{Receivable turnover} = \frac{\text{total revenue}}{\text{average accounts receivables}}$$

Inventory Turnover.   Similarly, inventory turnover tells us something about the demand for our product. Ideally, inventory stays in the warehouse just a short time before it's shipped to a customer. Only by shipping can we render an invoice, record the sale and the receivable, and hope that the customer pays us according to the terms of our sales agreement. Here's how to compute inventory turnover:

$$\text{Inventory turnover} = \frac{\text{cost of goods sold}}{\text{average inventory}}$$

Measuring Profit

Most people want to get to the bottom line. That's usually profit. However, we measure profits in different ways, depending on what most interests the audience.

Gross Margin.   Gross margin interests most production managers. That's the only component of profitability they control. Compute gross margin like this:

$$\text{Gross margin (\$)} = \text{sales} - \text{cost of goods sold}$$

The dollar amount is what goes to pay all other costs of running the firm. Alternatively, analysts often present the gross margin as a percentage:

$$\text{Gross margin (\%)} = \frac{(\text{sales} - \text{cost of goods sold})}{\text{sales}}$$

Net Income.   This has a particular meaning to accountants. Net income is what's left after all costs and expenses, including provision for taxes. It's the *bottom* bottom line. Alternatively, you may hear these terms tossed about:

- PBIT (profit before interest and taxes)
- PBT (profit before taxes)

These measure "profit" at different stages of the income statement. Since both interest and taxes must be paid, PBIT and PBT should not be confused with net income—the real bottom line.

Earnings Per Share (EPS).   EPS is a common index used by investors to determine how much a company earns for every share of stock—usually common stock—outstanding. Compute EPS like this:

$$EPS = \frac{net\ income - preferred\ stock\ dividends}{number\ of\ common\ shares\ outstanding}$$

Price/Earnings Ratio (P/E).   This is another common investor's index. Use it to measure the relationship between the market price of a share of stock and the earnings per share. Here's the equation:

$$P/E = \frac{stock\ price\ per\ share}{EPS}$$

Covering Interest

One common measurement used in assessing creditworthiness is the interest coverage ratio. It's computed like this:

$$Interest\ coverage = \frac{PBIT}{(interest + preferred\ dividends)}$$

One way to look at this is to think of it as a cushion. The question then becomes, How much could profits decline and still allow payment of interest and preferred dividends (if any)? Theoretically, the larger the coverage, the less risk to the lender.

Breaking Even

The breakeven point is something everyone wants to know. It's usually related to revenue. The breakeven is that point where:

Total revenue = total fixed costs + total variable costs

Here's how to find the breakeven point:

$$Breakeven = \frac{total\ fixed\ costs}{contribution\ margin\ per\ sales\ dollar}$$

Contribution Margin.   We find the contribution margin per sales dollar using the equation:

$$CM = 1 - \frac{variable\ costs\ per\ unit}{sales\ price\ per\ unit}$$

It is that portion of each sale that goes toward covering fixed costs. Many analysts equate contribution margin to gross margin (sales − cost of goods sold = gross margin).

A variety of things affect contribution margin. These include:

- Mix of products sold
- Price changes of products sold
- Amount and cost of labor used in production
- Amount and cost of materials used in production
- Downtime of production equipment

Here's an example of the breakeven computation using contribution margin in the denominator. Assume the following:

Sales revenue = $6,000,000

Fixed costs = $1,600,000

Variable costs = $3,600,000

Sales price/unit = $400

Variable costs/unit = $240

The breakeven point is a sales level of $4,000,000, found as follows:

$$\frac{\$1,600,000}{1} - (240/400) = \$4,000,000$$

Marketing Products

Marketing expenses are a significant part of the cost of running most businesses. Management needs to be sure the marketing dollars are promoting those products that make the firm the most profit. If we track these costs carefully, we can monitor the effectiveness of specific marketing programs.

Computing Return on Marketing Costs

One gauge many analysts use to track the effectiveness of marketing dollars spent is the return they get. Compute this like any other return on investment:

$$\text{Return on marketing costs} = \frac{\text{sales}}{\text{marketing costs}}$$

Our objective is to get some sort of multiple—certainly the return should exceed 100 percent of the costs or the expenditure isn't worthwhile. We can use this return as an index of performance. The absolute number may not be as important as the direction in which it moves over time.

Using this technique, we can assess which marketing methods work best on specific products. If one advertising campaign seems to have reached its saturation point (the return percentage has peaked and is now falling), cancel it and start a new program in its place.

Profiting from Market Analysis

Many controllers prepare separate profit and loss statements by sales territory. Using this technique, we can identify this information by sales territory:

- Product sales composition
- The most effective advertising campaigns
- Customer collection and bad-debt problems
- Product returns

For controllers with enough information, sales territory P&L's can also include useful details such as:

- Salesperson's salaries and commissions
- Travel expenses
- Product packing and shipping costs
- Amount of an average order

Each of these costs can affect gross margin for products and territories. After all, we don't want sales territories whose customers cost the company more to market to them than they provide in gross profits. Use this information also as the base for a territorial sales manager's bonus and incentive to hit a specific level of profit.

Analyzing Sales Price

Identifying what the market will bear is a quandary most marketing managers go through. Naturally, we want the highest price we can get for our products. Right?

Not necessarily. As price rises, demand usually falls. As sales fall, so may profit. There is a maximum price where units sold less fixed and variable costs yields the greatest profit. Prices below that point may sell more units, but overall profit is

Peaches Partners, Ltd. Analysis of Optimum Sales Prices					
Sales prices per unit	No. of units sold at each price	Total sales volume	Variable costs	Fixed costs	Profit (loss)
$20	20,000	$ 400,000	$ 160,000	$350,000	($110,000)
18	50,000	900,000	400,000	350,000	150,000
16	80,000	1,280,000	640,000	350,000	290,000
14	110,000	1,540,000	880,000	350,000	310,000
12	140,000	1,680,000	1,120,000	350,000	210,000
10	170,000	1,700,000	1,360,000	350,000	(10,000)

Figure 9-1. Maximizing profits through price changes.

lower. Prices exceeding that point will sell fewer units and yield lower overall profits. Figure 9-1 illustrates this analysis in tabular format.

The price that gets Peaches the largest profit is $14: $310,000 profit on 110,000 units sold. The graph in Figure 9-2 shows this relationship between price and profits.

Fixing Prices

Marketing managers should establish product prices during the development stage. That way they know the approximate level of profit a product should produce. Market research can predict the level of demand (units sold) at various pricing levels.

Financial analysts like to compute the return on capital a given price is likely to provide. If this doesn't meet the firm's criteria for capital investment, then drop the product. Here's how to compute prices based on return on capital employed:

$$\text{Price} = \frac{\text{total costs} + \text{desired rate of return} \times \text{capital requirement}}{\text{sales volume in units}}$$

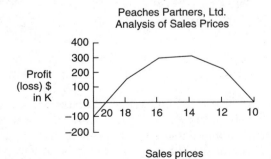

Figure 9-2. Analysis of sales prices.

For example, let's say that we want to find the product price that will give us a 20 percent return on our capital given:

Total cost of the product to produce is $300,000.

The capital requirement for production equipment is $275,000.

We expect to sell about 50,000 units.

The price is:

$$Price = \frac{\$300,000 + (20\% \times \$275,000)}{50,000} = \$7.10$$

This means that the marketing manager should establish a price of at least $7.10 for the product or it will fail to meet the firm's return on capital requirements. If the market won't absorb such a price, then the product is unprofitable.

Closing the Books

Part of most controllers' monthly routine is to close the books for that month and begin the new month. This usually requires a number of steps to complete. Following is a common month-end closing routine. Distribute the schedule so the accounting staff knows who is responsible for meeting each deadline.

Step 1: Cutting Off Transactions

Cutoff is important to maintain a credible accounting system. We want to know what happened *this* month. That doesn't include some transactions from last month and next month as well. Therefore, we stop entering new transactions into the accounting system as of the month-end cutoff date.

Step 2: Posting of Ledgers

Once all transactions for the month are in, the subledgers (A/R and A/P, for example) are all posted. Check these for accuracy. Then post all subledgers to the general ledger.

Step 3: Running the Trial Balance

The next step in closing the books is to run a trial balance of the general ledger. The purpose here is to check over each account balance to be sure it is correct. Fix any errors by adjusting journal entries. At this stage all subledgers should tie to the corresponding account in the general ledger.

Step 4: Printing the Financial Statements

Prepare the financial statements after reviewing and correcting (if necessary) the trial balance. This includes the balance sheet, income statement, and statement of cash flows. Again, management reviews all statements to be sure they are correct and the numbers tie to those they are supposed to.

Step 5: Analyzing Month-End Performance

The last step in month-end closing for most companies is to prepare the management reporting package. This contains all the financial statements as well as the narrative explanation and analytical support.

Reporting to Regulatory Bodies

Many businesses are in regulated industries that require monthly reports. These are prepared and submitted after producing the company's financial statements.

Special Projects

The finance department gets involved in many of the analytically intense projects around most companies. Not only does the financial staff have the necessary quantitative background, they have access to the numbers often required to do the work. Following are some of the types of special projects that frequently involve the controller and financial staff.

Capital Acquisitions

The controller's department frequently has total responsibility for evaluation of capital expenditure proposals. At the least, most controllers provide substantial input into these analyses. Chapter 17, "Capital Expenditures," focuses exclusively on the methods used for quantitative assessment of capital expenditures.

Acquisitions and Divestitures

Companies that look to acquire other firms, or divest themselves of entire divisions or major portions of their business, usually form project teams. The analysis and information that goes into these decisions require many of the resources available from the financial department.

The CFO and the controller are usually key members of the evaluation team. The board of directors looks to them for timely and accurate assessment of the financial impact of such far-reaching decisions. Here are some of the valuation methods employed for buy/sell decisions:

Liquidation Value. This is the value of the assets if the firm liquidated a division rather than selling it. Often, just shutting down and liquidating everything is a better option than taking a low offer.

Going-Concern Value. This is the opposite of the liquidation value. Computation of a business entity's value as a going concern deals with such intangibles as:

- Future discounted cash flow
- Strategic value to a specific buyer

Intrinsic Value. Buried in the going-concern value is a value supposedly independent of market forces—an intrinsic value. This value has to do with assets and their use, management abilities, earnings, dividends, and prospects for the future. Intrinsic value changes more slowly than market value.

Book Value. Be careful when evaluating an asset, business, or stock using the value as stated on the books. The original cost includes adjustment for depreciation, amortization, and depletion using generally accepted accounting principles. There is a difference (usually a big one) between market value and book value. Real estate is an example. Buildings are depreciated on the firm's books, yet the market value of these buildings can still be greater than the book value.

Capitalizing Income. This method of business valuation assumes that there is a rate of return that might induce a prudent investor to buy the firm. Net income divided by this rate of return yields a purchase price. This is more commonly called the *capitalization method*. It's often used in valuing commercial real estate.

Floating a Private
Placement of Debt or Equity

Private placement refers to a limited offering not available to the general public. These often are called Reg. D. Transactions or Rule 505 Placements after the section of SEC code that governs limited offerings.

Companies go for a private placement rather than attempt to access the public funds markets in the following situations:

- Their story is complex.
- The offering amount is small.
- The full disclosure is not possible.

Offerings that exceed $500,000 must have a private placement memorandum provided to the SEC and offerees. This document is less extensive than those filed for public offerings. Nevertheless, it provides disclosure of all the material information necessary to make an informed investment decision. The financial staff usually spearheads the filing and placement of bonds or stock.

Going Public

Public stock and bond offerings require huge amounts of work before the public ever puts up its money. This is a massive undertaking. Usually the company assembles an offering team to conduct the work. Most public offering teams include:

- Key executives of the offering company
- Outside legal counsel
- Underwriters
- Independent auditors
- Financial printer and bank note company
- Transfer agent and registrar

Along with involvement on the offering team, the financial staff usually takes responsibility for:

Authorization. The board of directors must issue a resolution specifically authorizing management to execute a securities offering. Additionally, the company must amend its Certificate of Incorporation to increase the number of authorized shares. By law, existing shareholders get the opportunity to sell a portion of their shares in the offering.

Regulators. In this case, the NASD must receive the following information:

- Registration documents.
- Filing documents that request listing on the exchange that trades the company's stock.
- Request for the ticker symbol the company wishes to use.
- Final public-issue documents.
- Selling shareholders. The shareholders who wish to sell stock in the offering appoint an attorney in fact as well as a transfer agent.

With all of the financial data required and since the money obtained from a public securities offering is used by the finance department, it makes sense to involve the controller.

10

Cash Management

Overview

Responsibility for cash management falls to different people depending on the size of the firm. At very large companies, there may be a cash management specialist who works for the treasurer. Sometimes there are several, including one or more who are experts in international cash management. Smaller companies may have the treasurer manage the firm's cash on a daily basis. For companies too small to employ a treasurer, cash management responsibilities often fall on the controller or a member of the accounting staff.

Certainly the more diverse someone's duties, the less attention he or she is likely to pay to cash management. At small companies without much money flowing through the firm each day, this may not be a problem. However, most companies with a sizable cash flow or with problems in that area can benefit from understanding the basics of this technical discipline.

That's what Chapter 10 demonstrates—the basics of cash management as practiced by the experts. It doesn't matter how big your company is. The theories are applicable to everyone. Although the benefits may not always repay the extra work involved at very small firms, not practicing some of these standard cash management techniques is symptomatic of a sloppy financial operation.

Cash Management Responsibilities

There are many different things to watch when you're responsible for managing your company's cash. Here are a few of the more important ones:

Managing Cash Flows

This means that the cash manager (or whoever does this critical function) is responsible for having enough cash in the checking account to clear the company's checks on demand. If cash is there too far ahead of time, it increases working capital requirements and may cause unnecessary borrowing. If it arrives after the check is presented for clearing, the company's creditworthiness may be questioned. Neither situation is acceptable.

Collecting Money

A major part of cash management deals with the credit approval process and management of accounts receivable. Though the person responsible for cash management is not always directly involved in credit or collections, the results of these two areas impact the amount and timing of funds coming into the company. This influences cash flow.

Therefore, the cash manager should insist on at least understanding (if not assisting in) the management of trade credit and collections. Before changing these areas, the cash manager must grasp the impact they will have on cash flow.

Disbursing Money

Cash managers don't usually physically write the checks. However, they are responsible for controlling funds outflow. The payables aging policy established by the cash manager depends on the company's relationship with its vendors and its working capital position.

Additionally, the way a company pays certain of its obligations has a great influence on daily cash balances and float. The cash manager should be responsible for choosing the various methods of payment.

Investment Maturities

The cash manager is the one closest to the firm's upcoming funds requirements. When the person investing the firm's short-term excess cash takes a position, the maturity of that investment must match the cash manager's funds requirements. In this sense, the cash manager has something important to say about investment policy.

Forecasting Cash

Anticipating future balances is one of the cash manager's most important duties. Certainly, early prediction of funds shortfall assists the treasurer in determining the most advantageous way to meet it. Conversely, when the cash manager knows of a cash surplus, the investment officer can safely change the maturity schedule of the firm's investments. The farther out on a positively sloping yield curve we invest, the better the yield.

Tools of the Trade

Cash management is part science with a little bit of art mixed in. There are some specific indicators, mechanisms, and shortcuts many cash managers use to make their job easier and more precise. Here are a few.

Monitoring Cash Performance

An accurate assessment of the company's current position is essential. The report in Figure 10-1 quickly tells cash managers where they stand. It first appeared in *The Cash Management Handbook* by Christopher R. Malburg, copyright 1992, and is reprinted by permission of the publisher, Prentice-Hall, a division of Simon & Schuster, New York.

Computing the Cost of Excess Cash

Don't make the mistake of thinking the more cash held by a company the better off they are. Modern cash managers can precisely compute the cash required to run the company. Beyond that level, excess cash is usually put to use in three ways:

- Funds working capital requirements
- Repays debt
- Pays dividends to investors

Keeping more cash on hand than is truly needed is costly to the company. As a rule:

The level of disposable cash should not exceed that absolutely necessary to run the company.

Beyond that level, the return on invested excess cash is less than what could be had by plowing it back into the company. If it is not, then management should sell the firm and just invest the proceeds. Therefore, income from invested cash is merely an *offset* to the cost of carrying it. Figure 10-2 shows how to compute the cost of keeping too much cash on hand.

You can see that this cash manager's imprecise way of identifying the firm's cash needs has cost the company $25,000 in interest expense on working capital borrowings that were never needed in the first place.

Computing Disposable Cash

Net income as shown on the income statement is not the amount of cash available for spending. We must remove the items contained in net income that don't affect

Figure 10-1. Cash management performance report.

Cash Management Performance Report
08-Dec-9X

Cash and assets	Current month	Prior month	Current B(W) prior	Year to date	Current B(W) YTD	Target	Year to date B(W) target
Cash	$ ___	$ ___	$ ___	$ ___	$ ___	$ ___	$ ___
Marketable securities	___	___	___	___	___	___	___
All other cash items	___	___	___	___	___	___	___
Total cash	$ ___	$ ___	$ ___	$ ___	$ ___	$ ___	$ ___
Current ratio	___	___	___	___	___	___	___
Quick ratio	___	___	___	___	___	___	___
Accounts receivable							
Accounts receivable turnover rate	___	___	___	___	___	___	___
A/R receivable collection period	___	___	___	___	___	___	___
Weighted average A/R aging	___	___	___	___	___	___	___
Inventory							
Avg. investment period of inventory	___	___	___	___	___	___	___
Inventory turnover rate	___	___	___	___	___	___	___
Accounts payable							
Weighted average A/P aging	___	___	___	___	___	___	___
Average payment period	___	___	___	___	___	___	___
A/P turnover rate	___	___	___	___	___	___	___

Manufacturing performance

Material price variance						
Labor price variance						
Mfg. price variance						
Safety stock						
Stock out costs						

Financial performance

Working capital		N/A				
Short-term borrowing		N/A				
Long-term borrowing		N/A				
Interest expense		$				
Aggregate int. rate on investments	%	%	%	%		
Aggregate interest rate on debt	%	%	%	%		

Lending covenants

Debt coverage ratio						
Ratio of debt to net worth						
Minimum cash balance	$	N/A	$			
Compensating balance	$	$	$			
Owner's equity	$	$	$			
Owner's draw	$	$	$			

Computation of the Cost of Excess Cash	
Excess disposable cash held for one year:	$500,000
Alternative use of cash: repay line of credit:	
Interest rate	12%
Cost of not repaying line of credit	(60,000)
Interest income from short-term repurchase agreement rolled over for 12 months at 7%:	35,000
Net costs of carrying excess disposable cash	$ (25,000)

Figure 10-2. Computation of excess cash.

cash. From that point, net out already committed cash outflows according to their priority of payment. What's left is disposable cash. This is "pure" cash—cash not earmarked for anything. Figure 10-3 shows the computation of disposable cash.

Notice that disposable cash does not equal the projected ending cash balance. The ending cash balance from the reconciliation should, however, tie to the cash balance on the balance sheet for that period of time.

Computing Leverage

There are three kinds of leverage we're going to talk about:

- Operating
- Financial
- Combined

Operating Leverage.   Cash managers use operating leverage to quickly assess the impact of changes in sales on operating profit and, therefore, on cash generated from operations. The equation to compute operating leverage is:

$$\text{Operating leverage} = \frac{\text{sales} - \text{variable costs}}{\text{EBIT}}$$

Therefore, if sales were $1,000,000, variable costs were $500,000, and EBIT was $150,000, operating leverage would be 3.3, computed as follows:

$$\frac{\$1,000,000 - \$500,000}{\$150,000} = 3.3$$

This means that for every $1 sales moves, EBIT moves 3.3 times what it was before. So a decrease in sales of just 10 percent would decrease EBIT over 30 percent.

Financial Leverage.   This represents the change to income before tax as sales changes. The equation to compute financial leverage is:

Tobby Corporation
Computation of Disposable Cash
For the Month Ended July 30, 199X

Cash provided by operations	$25,000
Cash outflows in order of priority:	
Current principal on debt payable	(11,200)
Tax payments (not included in operating cash)	(1,800)
Lease payments (not included in operating cash)	(950)
Subtotal priority outflows	($11,050)
Discretionary outflows:	
Capital expenditure program	(6,000)
Research and development expenditures	(2,200)
Preferred stock dividends	(4,500)
Subtotal discretionary outflows	$ (1,650)
Cash inflows:	
Term loan	3,000
Working capital loan	2,000
Subtotal cash inflows	$ 5,000
Disposable cash	$ 3,350
Cash balance reconciliation:	
Beginning cash balance	$ 5,000
Plus cash provided by operations	25,000
Less priority outflows	(13,950)
Less discretionary outflows	(12,700)
Plus cash inflows	5,000
Projected ending cash balance	$ 8,350

Figure 10-3. Computation of disposable cash.

$$\text{Financial leverage} = \frac{\text{EBIT}}{\text{EBIT} - \text{fixed financial costs}}$$

For example, if EBIT were $350,000 and interest expense was $235,000, financial leverage would be computed as:

$$\frac{\$350,000}{\$350,000 - \$235,000} = 3.04$$

This means that a 10 percent rise in EBIT gives us about a 30 percent rise in net income. Note also that for companies with no debt, their financial leverage is 1.0.

Combined Leverage.   There's a quick way cash managers compute the leverage derived from both operations and financing. The method is simple. Multiply operational leverage by financial leverage. Using the preceding examples, here's what we get:

Operational leverage	3.30
× financial leverage	3.04
Combined leverage	10.04

This means that combined leverage multiplies any percentage change in sales by 100.4 percent of the old net income before tax.

Compliance with Lending Covenants

Treasurers and cash managers need ready access to the credit markets. This requires that the firm maintain its compliance with existing loan covenants. Frequently they are numerous and complex.

An easy way to make sure the firm is in compliance each month is to create a spreadsheet that illustrates every covenant on every loan agreement and compares it with the company's actual performance for that period. Figure 8-5 in Chapter 8 shows a sample loan compliance report.

What to do if the company breaches a loan covenant? Astute treasurers have a system that tells them in advance of a breach in a loan covenant. They notify the banker and ask for a written waiver of the breach. They then take steps to correct the problem and ensure it doesn't happen again.

Tracking Float

Float is the time it takes between actually sending someone a payment and the point at which it clears the issuer's bank. Components of cash management float include:

- Mail time
- Internal processing
- Bank deposits
- Bank processing time
- Clearing through the Federal Reserve System

All these things take time. They can amount to an interest-free loan for a savvy cash manager who knows how to track float. Figure 10-4 shows a simple float-tracking system. It assumes the cash manager knows how long it takes to clear items and that no major changes have occurred such as:

- New electronic funds transfers
- Change of major payees

Assume that TDO Excavators, Inc., enjoys a weighted average float of four days from check disbursement to check clearing. The company tracks the float in its disbursements system along with the bank balance. Eventually, TDO incurs negative balances in its general ledger cash account. However, its bank balance is always positive. The following table shows how TDO's treasurer tracks the firm's float.

TDO Excavators, Inc.
Float-Tracking System
($ in thousands)

Date	Begin book bal.	Check mail	Deposits	End book bal.	Check clear	Act'l. bank bal.	Total float	Pymt. capacity
9-1	$200	$0	$0	$200	$0	$200	$0	$200
9-2	200	50	0	150	0	200	50	250
9-3	150	75	0	75	0	200	125	325
9-4	75	0	0	75	50	150	75	225
9-5	75	95	0	−20	0	150	170	320
9-6	−20	50	0	−70	75	75	145	220
9-7	−70	0	0	−70	0	75	145	220
9-8	−70	75	125	−20	95	105	125	230
9-9	−20	90	0	−110	50	55	165	220
9-10	−110	25	0	−135	0	55	190	245

Figure 10-4. Float-tracking spreadsheet.

- New customer collection facilities such as lockboxes
- Change of banks

The book balance first goes negative on September 5 while the bank balance remains positive. The payment capacity continues to be the sum of the actual bank balance and the total float.

TDO's cash manager has $75,000 in checks written on September 8 presented for clearing on September 11, thus producing an overdraft of $20,000. However, the cash manager knows that there will be a $200,000 electronic funds debit to the checking account that day from the firm's largest customer. All electronic fund direct debits are done first thing in the morning. There will be no overdraft. In fact, TDO's bank balance at the end of business that day will be $180,000.

Working Capital

Working capital requirements drive up the cash manager's interest expense. The more money it takes to run the firm, the more borrowing it needs or the less return it can give investors. Therefore, astute cash managers are constantly looking for ways to reduce working capital requirements.

Computing Working Capital

Think of working capital as simply the money the company must have on hand to operate. It's the difference between current assets and current liabilities. Figure 10-5 shows an example. Notice how working capital requirements decreased between the two years. The company aggressively pursued three avenues to accomplish that goal:

1. The cash on hand that used to be required was reduced by $11,000.

2. Accounts receivable were collected and not allowed to go back up. This withdrew another $10,000 from working capital.

3. Accounts payable rose by $5000. Presumably, Tyler did this without impugning its creditworthiness.

Unfortunately, both inventory and accrued liabilities rose. This offset some of the progress Tyler made.

The question most often asked by astute cash managers is: What can we do to reduce every component of working capital? They never stop trying to improve on already-low working capital requirements.

Accelerating Cash Inflow

Too many financial people disavow responsibility for maintaining and improving cash inflow. There are lots of things an aggressive manager can do to accelerate cash inflow.

	March 31		Working capital	
Tyler Enterprises Statement of Changes in Working Capital For the Year Ended March 31, 19X2				
	19X1	19X2	Increase	Decrease
Current assets:				
Cash	$21,000	$10,000		$11,000
Accounts receivable	30,000	20,000		10,000
Inventory	26,000	30,000	$4,000	
Total current assets	$77,000	$60,000		$17,000
Current liabilities:				
Accounts payable	$10,000	$15,000		5,000
Accrued liabilities	2,000	0		2,000
Total current liabilities	$12,000	$15,000		$3,000
Working capital	$65,000	$45,000		$20,000

Figure 10-5. Statement of changes in working capital.

Managing Terms of Sale

The terms of sale are a negotiable part of the entire sales package. Of course, every company needs to stay competitive. However, if we can shorten something so fundamental as the payment due date without giving away market share, it will certainly accelerate cash inflow.

Additionally, the purchasing manager negotiates the method of payment. For certain customers with frequent and very large purchases it may help to negotiate electronic funds transfer payments directly into the cash concentration checking account.

Invoicing

It makes absolutely no sense to do a great job negotiating a favorable sales contract only to have it negated by failing to render an invoice promptly. Invoices should go out on the day of sale.

Many astute managers carefully watch the invoicing backlog. They know the cost in additional working capital by day. When that cost reaches the additional expenditure needed to reduce an invoicing backlog (such as using temporary help or overtime), they gladly pay it.

Reducing Accounts Receivable

Chapter 11 details the various aspects of managing receivables. However, strict control over this area prevents it from quickly getting out of hand and gobbling up working capital that could be more profitably employed elsewhere within the firm.

Some cash managers think they can accelerate collections by offering trade discounts for early payment. Sometimes this works. However, it almost always costs more than borrowing the additional working capital would. Here's how to compute the cost of a trade discount:

$$\frac{\text{discount \%}}{\text{due date} - \text{discount date}} \times 360 \text{ days} = \frac{\text{annualized interest expense}}{\text{from offering a trade discount}}$$

Let's assume a $10,000 invoice whose terms are 1/10, net 30. That is, if the invoice is paid within 10 days, the buyer is entitled to a 1 percent discount. Otherwise the full amount is due within 30 days. In this case the cost to the company for offering the 1 percent discount is a whopping 18 percent ([.01/(30–10)] × 360 = 18%). Almost certainly the company can borrow the funds at a lower rate. Offering such a discount accelerates cash inflow but reduces profits.

Use this rule to determine when it's wise to offer a trade discount to accelerate cash inflow:

If the company's aggregate borrowing rate is less than the cost of the discount, then don't offer a discount.

Processing Payment Receipts

Once again, it makes no sense working to collect receivables and accelerate cash inflow only to have it stopped due to a backlog in processing the receipts. This isn't a complicated process. However, it often takes more time than necessary. Here are the steps of payment processing:

- Opening the mail
- Distributing payment checks to the A/R staff
- Recording a credit to the customer's account
- Posting the A/R subledger to the receivables account in the general ledger
- Depositing checks in the bank
- Clearing checks through the banking system and making the funds available for use

Any point along this process can create a bottleneck. Ideally, checks get deposited the same day as received. The banking agreement should allow for same-day availability on checks received prior to 2 p.m. drawn on nearby banks.

Slowing Cash Outflow

The opposite side of the same coin is to slow cash outflow. We want to keep the money in house as long as possible before paying it out. There are generally two large channels that siphon cash out of the firm:

- Accounts payable
- Payroll

Accounts Payable

The objective for A/P is opposite that of receivables. We want to keep payables as high as possible without impugning the creditworthiness of the company. Further, we don't want to risk our vendors revoking favorable terms because we've become slow payers. Nevertheless, the more trade credit we can get from our vendors, the lower our own working capital requirements.

Ideally, we collect our receivables before the payables necessary to create those same receivables are due. In that way, our vendors finance our cash requirements.

Chapter 12 deals exclusively with payables management. Therefore, the last we'll say about it here has to do with trade discounts for early payment. Usually it makes good business sense to take the discount and pay early. This is true even though it accelerates cash outflow. The equation to compute the percentage saved is the same as the one used previously in receivables:

$$\frac{\text{discount \%}}{\text{due date} - \text{discount date}} \times 360 = \frac{\text{annualized interest savings}}{\text{from taking a trade discount}}$$

As long as this is greater than the company's aggregate cost of funds, and the funds are available, taking the trade discount is beneficial.

Forecasting Cash Flow

The objective of cash flow forecasting is twofold:

- To project ending cash balances
- To track specific cash inflows and outflows

The ending balances are important so we know when and how much we'll need to borrow in the event of a cash shortfall. Conversely, we also need to know when we'll have excess cash so we can plan our investment strategy and adjust the terms of current investments.

Timing the Cash Forecast

Cash forecasts don't have to be huge, elaborate affairs. Indeed, the simpler the better since they must be easily updated. Many cash managers and treasurers use a three-month timing horizon for their cash forecasts. The time frames in columns across the forecast spreadsheet are often something like this:

- Today
- End of this week
- End of this month
- End of two months
- End of three months

If your own cash isn't so volatile, maybe you'll want to omit the daily forecast computation.

Forecasting Cash Inflows

Our objective is simply to identify all inflows over the forecast period and match them against all outflows. The difference is either excess cash or a deficit that requires funding.

Here are most of the common cash inflows you're likely to encounter:

Beginning Cash Balance.   Though not precisely a cash inflow, the beginning cash balance rolls into the forecast from the ending cash balance of the prior period. Therefore, the ending forecast cash balance for this month becomes the beginning cash balance for next month.

Sales.   Separate sales into its component parts such as cash, on account, credit card. That way you can put the various parts where they belong in the cash forecast.

Collections from Accounts Receivable.   This is often the largest inflow of cash. Show changes to the collection effort in the cash forecast. These might include:

- More collections staff
- Offering trade discounts for early payment
- Changes in credit policy

Insurance and Lawsuit Settlements.   Including expected major settlements in the cash flow plan signals the expectation that the funds will arrive. If they don't, it prompts action from the cash management staff. Further, watching for the payment inflow provides a further deterrent against employees misappropriating a large unscheduled cash receipt.

Additionally, take care to ensure the proper accounting of these unusual cash receipts. Some cash managers ask to see a copy of the journal entry recording the settlement receipt just to make sure.

Maturing Investments.   This schedule tells when specific investment securities (maturing principal and interest) should return to the company's cash concentration account. Including this item in the cash forecast ensures that staff is aware of specific investments maturing and knows what to do with the money when it arrives. This provides less chance of underemploying excess funds (or worse, leaving them idle) for any longer than absolutely necessary. Further, compare interest income as computed by the company with what was actually received on the investment. Identify any mistakes and correct them promptly.

Additionally, if the company owns stock in other corporations, forecast dividends declared by these companies as a cash inflow.

Receipts from Sale of Assets and Loan Payments.   Here's another nonroutine cash inflow. Most companies don't make a habit of selling their assets. They don't usually lend money either. Monitoring receipt of these items is especially critical for long-term installment sales contracts and multiyear loans. Include both principal and interest payment inflows in the cash forecast.

Forecasting Cash Outflows

The key to controlling cash outflows comes from knowing the disbursement schedule and managing it. The company has the ability to slow down or turn off completely the money spigot when necessary. Here are the most common cash outflows to include in the cash forecast:

Accounts Payable.   This is usually the largest routine cash outflow for most companies. If you are using one of the modern A/P computer systems, chances are it will tell you the cash requirements needed to keep all invoices current for the periods in your forecast.

Additionally, be sure that any changes in the company's payment policies get reflected in the cash forecast.

Outflow Float.   Smart managers compute and use the float associated with their payments system. Sources of this float include:

- Mail float
- Payee's internal float
- Bank float

Note that on the disbursement side, bank float comes from both the vendor's bank and your own disbursement bank.

Debt Payment.   Be sure to include both the principal and interest owed on outstanding debt in the cash forecast. Sometimes we don't know the interest owed on variable-rate debt until just before the payment date. Even so, a projection is better than nothing. Further, banks have been known to be wrong in their computations of variable-rate interest. It's not a bad idea to verify their calculations.

Include in the cash forecast any balloon payments or annual cleanup provisions for lines of credit.

If your company has outstanding bonds, these usually require interest payments twice a year. "Good" funds must be at the disbursing agent's on the appointed date or the company is in default.

Taxes.   These include outlays for federal and state income taxes, city and local taxes, and property taxes.

Payroll.   This is usually a large, single disbursement on a regular basis. Be sure to include not only the payroll expense, but also the payroll tax liability.

Capital Expenditures.   Here's another source of potentially large cash outflows. Include not only the actual payments, but any deposits or down payments too. For payments based on percentage of construction completion, make sure the cash forecast includes any changes to the construction schedule.

Dividends.   When the board declares dividends, they'll usually determine the payment date at the same time. Cash required to pay dividends must be at the disbursing agent's in the form of "good" funds no later than the day of disbursement.

Arranging Capital Structure

A company's capital structure consists of the funds invested in the firm either by partners, shareholders, bondholders, or private investors. Once in place, the capital structure doesn't often change much. When it does, however, it is usually a major undertaking. Changing a firm from a publicly held corporation to a private enterprise (taking it private) is one example. Another would be when a firm holds an initial public offering for its stock on a publicly traded exchange.

The capital structure should be such that it provides the firm access to the type and amount of capital it requires. Often the person managing the cash is one of the first to realize that a change should take place. Symptoms may include:

- Existing credit facilities have been exhausted.
- The cost of funds has risen above acceptable levels.
- Interest rate risk is more than it need be.
- Investors demand a return of their capital.

11

Accounts Receivable

Overview

The controller runs the accounts receivable system. However, receivables relies on accurate information coming in from parts of the company such as:

- Sales
- Payments processing
- Collections

Further, controllers use the information going out of A/R to make credit decisions as well as manage cash flow and keep straight who owes the company what.

Chapter 11 details the receivables management responsibilities and techniques most beneficial to controllers. I'll show you how to:

- Identify and report receivables balances
- Pinpoint problem accounts
- Measure collections efficiency
- Project future write-offs
- Integrate automated order entry with A/R
- Use dunning letters
- Finance accounts receivable

Sources of A/R Information

Credit sales or payments accepted for a sale affect receivables. Those are the obvious things that prompt an entry to the accounts receivable subledger. The controller makes the following routine entries:

	Debit	Credit
Record sale:		
Accounts receivable	X	
Sales		X
Record payment received:		
Cash	X	
Accounts receivable		X

Recording Sales

Credit sales are the most common entries into accounts receivable. Record a sale into A/R when giving an invoice to a customer who has promised to pay by a date specified in the sales agreement. There should be some mechanism in your company to ensure the entry of all credit sales invoices into the A/R system. Without that assurance, you risk sending goods out the door without guarantee of future payment.

One way to watch for unrecorded receivables is to balance each day the sum of cash received plus debits to accounts receivable to sales. There may be reconciling items such as interest charges, but the balance should match the daily sales number.

Much of the information required comes from the order entry department. It gathers the following data for A/R:

- Customer name and account number
- Amount of purchase
- Terms of purchase—payment due date

Recording Payments

The flip side of sales in the A/R system is recording a payment received. Generally, this information comes from the treasurer's department or whoever opens the mail and records cash receipts. The cash (checks, currency, and credit card slips) goes to the bank for deposit. Forward the accompanying documentation—such as copies of invoices—to accounts receivable for entry into the system. Once again, there should be some balancing mechanism to ensure that cash receipts tie to the amount of credits entered into the A/R system. Without such control, there can be no assurance that receivables balances are being properly credited.

Recognizing Returns and Credit Memos

This amounts to another payment as far as the A/R system is concerned. The entry to the receivable system to record a credit or return of merchandise is:

	Debit	Credit
Record credit memo or return of merchandise:		
Accounts receivable	X	
Sales		X

Sometimes the firm issues credit memos for things other than merchandise returns. A good example is leniency given by the company to retain a customer's goodwill. Say that the A/R system assesses and debits interest charges to the individual customer accounts. This increases the balance owed. However, a long-standing customer argues that the payment was made. The company just failed to process and post (credit) it to their A/R account before the interest deadline. In this case it might make good business sense to issue a credit memo, wiping out the interest charge.

Using A/R Information

Information from A/R goes out to different departments in the company that use it to make critical decisions regarding:

- Cash flow
- Credit
- Customer service
- Collections
- Banking relationships

Cashing In on A/R Information

From the treasurer's point of view, information coming out of the A/R system is among the most important of any in the company. Treasurers base part of their cash flow projections on payment history of the receivables portfolio. The more reliable and timely this information, the more accurately the treasurer can estimate future cash inflows from current sales.

At a minimum, the A/R system should be able to provide:

- Balances owed by each customer
- Balances owed in each aging bucket
- Percentage of customers who pay within each aging bucket

Customer Statements

What customer is going to pay based on an inaccurate statement of account? Few, if any. That's why the customer statements mailed at the end of each month must accurately reflect the balance owed as of the date of printing (or a date appearing on the statement face).

Many firms utilize a random audit of customer statements to make certain the balances are correct and that the right customers are receiving their statements. They do this by selecting a sample of statements and requesting a confirmation of the balance. Differences must be explained. Pursue those customers who don't respond to ensure no sales were made to fictitious persons.

Collateralizing Loans

Many banks secure their commercial loans with accounts receivable. Knowingly providing inaccurate (usually inflated) receivables balances is fraud. However, unknowingly providing the same inaccurate information is negligence. Either way, that's not the position in which we want to be.

Many loan agreements require reports on the receivables balance periodically. A statement from the firm's officers attesting to the accuracy often accompanies these reports. That's just one reason for the necessity of accurate A/R information.

Making Credit Decisions

The credit department needs an accurate payment history for each customer in order to evaluate requests for increased credit limits. Usually such information consists of:

- Amount purchased year to date
- High credit extended
- Amount currently outstanding
- Payment history

Collecting Receivables

Many companies have a separate department assigned the responsibility of collections. This task focuses on taking in the most money as fast as possible. They rely on accurate information from the receivables system with regard to:

- Balance owed
- Aging
- Name, address, and phone number of customer

Many companies allocate their collection resources based on payment history of various aging buckets. The A/R system provides this critical information.

Reporting Receivables

Receivables reports can be extensive. They generally don't find their way to senior executives—unless there's a problem. Then you may be called on to provide many of the reports used to manage both accounts receivable and collections and credit.

Let's take a look at some of the reports and statistics you can use to put receivables into perspective.

Aging Receivables

Most companies produce an aging schedule for their receivables. It shows the entire receivables portfolio in these aging buckets (that's the term used):

- Current
- 30 days
- 60 days
- 90 days
- 120+ days

Managers use this report to keep an eye on the control they have over collections. The less money in the older aging buckets, the more valuable the portfolio. This goes on the theory that the older a receivable gets, the less likely its collection.

However, many managers use the aging report as a forecasting tool. That's right. An accurate aging report can tell us when sales made today will likely be collected. This assumes that nothing has changed in the variables that affect collections, such as:

- Customer mix
- Credit policies
- Location of the customer base
- The economy

Figure 11.1 shows an example of what the receivables collection schedule looks like. Using this schedule, we can forecast cash inflow from collections for the upcoming months. There are three additional things you may want to include in this schedule:

1. Notice it begins in January. However, in practice, sales coming in from previous months—in this case, from October, November, and December of the previous year.
2. Most cash inflow forecasts provide a cushion for contingencies. You can put this at the bottom of the schedule before the total.
3. Every business has bad debts. You may wish to add this to your schedule after the last aging bucket used.

One last point: things change with collections. To be safe, you should compute the percentages of the portfolio in each aging bucket at the end of each month. If the percentages have changed, then recompute the projected collections.

Assume that we draw these conclusions about which percentage of each aging bucket is collected:

Current:	20%
30–60 days:	40%
60–90 days:	25%
90–120 days:	15%
	100%

T-D-O Partners, Ltd.
Schedule of Receivables Aging

Sales month	Total sales	January Current	February 30 days	March 60 days	April 90 days
January	$ 20,000	$4,000	$ 8,000	$ 5,000	$ 3,000
February	30,000	0	6,000	12,000	7,500
March	40,000	0	0	8,000	16,000
April	50,000	0	0	0	10,000
Total	$140,000	$4,000	$14,000	$25,000	$36,500

Figure 11-1. Schedule of receivables aging composition.

Analyzing the Receivables Roll Rate

Uncollected receivables roll from one aging bucket into the next. We can measure the propensity for receivables to roll from bucket to bucket. Using roll-rate analysis, we can determine three important things:

- Estimated collections
- Projected balance for any given receivable aging bucket
- Estimated loss from bad debts

Roll rate is nothing more than the percentage of receivables in each aging bucket that moves to the next bucket without being collected. Funds in a bucket that don't move either got collected or written off. Like aging, performing the analysis over a long enough period of time familiarizes you with the company's receivable roll rate. Figure 11-2 shows a roll-rate analysis.

The table in Figure 11-2 derived the estimated amounts rolling into each succeeding aging bucket by multiplying the balance in the prior bucket by the roll-rate percentage of that bucket. The table found the amount collected by subtracting the amount rolling into the next aging bucket from the amount

Assume that the spring promotion should add $1 million in credit sales.

Research of past receivables records indicated the roll rate from one aging bucket to the next is:

- Current to 30–60:   50%
- 30 to 60–90:   25%
- 60 to 90–120:   30%
- 120 to write-off: 35%

Using this table, here's how Waffles Enterprises expects to collect its spring credit sales:

Waffles Enterprises
Analysis of Receivables
Roll Rates—Spring Promotion

Month	Current	Current to 30–60	30–60 to 60–90	60–90 to 90–120	90–120 to write-off
April	$1,000,000				
May		$500,000			
June			$125,000		
July				$37,500	
August					$13,125
Total	$1,000,000	$500,000	$125,000	$37,500	$13,125
Collection	$ 500,000	$375,000	$ 87,500	$24,375	$ 0

Figure 11-2. Receivables roll-rate analysis.

originally in that bucket. Waffles expects to collect about $986,875 within 120 days after the spring promotion. The remainder will likely prove uncollectible and be written off.

Notice how the percentage rolling from one bucket to the next increases the farther from current we get? That's a reflection on the relative "quality" of an aged receivable. Once again, the older a debt, the less likely its collection.

Computing Receivables Return on Investment

Not only is accounts receivable an asset, but it's also an investment in working capital. We need to achieve an acceptable return on that investment or we shouldn't make it. Here are the two items needed to compute return on receivables investment:

1. The expected increase in sales and net income as the result of additional investment in receivables

2. The average receivables balance

Let's say that by easing credit terms (increasing receivables), you knew that sales would rise by $500,000 and net income would increase by $100,000. From the aging and roll-rate analyses, we expect a rise in receivables of $300,000. The return on this additional investment of working capital would be 33 percent ($100,000/$300,000 = 33%). We'd most likely make this investment.

That was easy. However, the technique gets further complicated if the firm requires additional capital investments to achieve additional sales. Then we must include cost of the fixed assets in the ROI equation.

Competition isn't likely to sit still either. Sales projections may not behave as you expected. They may stay flat or may even fall as the result of a change in credit policy by the market leader.

Finally, don't overlook the risk of bad debt. Changes in credit policy may alter the composition of the receivable portfolio. Make sure you include such variables in your analysis.

Identifying Problem Accounts

For many companies, accounts receivable represent a significant asset. They monitor the A/R portfolio closely, trying to identify potential problem accounts before they become uncollectible. Probably the best sources for this information are the reports we've already identified:

- Roll rate
- Aging
- Largest balance
- Highest balance
- Balance exceeds credit limit

The last two pieces of information—highest balance and balance exceeds credit limit—provide a measure of credit risk the company has elected to take from its customers. They tell which customers' accounts now exceed their previous highs and which the firm has continued to sell to even though their balance now exceeds their credit limit. Either way, we now know who is a potential risk. Perhaps the credit manager needs an updated credit application or a new balance sheet on the customer. Perhaps the firm should refuse further orders until they clear up the balance owed.

Measuring Collection Performance

The most obvious way to monitor collections performance is to see how much A/R increased over the prior month. If sales were flat, but A/R rose, then the collections rate declined during the month.

Another method uses the roll-rate report introduced above. Using this analysis, we can see what percentage of each aging bucket moved from one aging category to the next during the month. If the percentages are increasing for one or more buckets, we can pinpoint where the problem lies in the collection effort. Larger companies have one or more collectors who handle a specific aging bucket. Assessing roll-rate performance is really a way of judging the collectors running each aging bucket.

Rising Sales

How do we judge collections performance when sales rise? After all, shouldn't receivables rise as well? Yes. However, a good index to use is the *percentage* of A/R that current sales make up. Using this as a gauge, even as sales rise, the percentage should remain constant (or better yet, drop). However, if it rises we know that something has happened to cause receivables to grow beyond what we'd normally expect.

Projection Write-offs

Once again the roll-rate analysis helps predict when accounts will go to write-off. When used properly, we can project likely losses for a group of accounts as soon as they enter the A/R system. The method uses the experience learned from the receivable balances that roll from current to 30 days, 60, 90, 120, and finally write-off. Divide the percentage rolling out of the 120-day bucket to write-off by the balances newly entering the system. The result is the predicted percentage lost as uncollectible.

Note that the percentage changes every month as the roll-rate analysis changes.

Interfacing with Other Departments

The most important departments using A/R information include:

- Order entry
- Treasury
- Credit extension

Order Entry

The order takers must have some way to determine if the person placing an order (often on the telephone) is someone to whom the company wishes to extend credit. A good way to do this is to have an automated *interface* between the A/R system and the company's order entry system. This provides such information as:

- Past customer purchases
- High balance
- Current balance
- Credit limit
- Date of last credit assessment
- Annotated comments from the credit manager

With this kind of information instantly available before taking the order, the company can make a more informed credit decision. We can stop credit problems before they start.

Treasury

The treasury department uses information coming out of A/R to project cash inflow. If the A/R reports are accurate and consistent, they provide a solid indicator of the money coming in as a result of collection efforts. Further, using historical receivable information, the treasurer can predict how changes—such as different credit criteria or new products—will impact the need for working capital resulting from altered receivable balances.

Credit Extension

The risk of the customer not complying with the terms of sale dictates granting of trade credit. Requests by existing customers for a larger credit limit use the same type of information needed by the order entry person(s) to approve a sale.

Additionally, the credit manager usually considers such variables as the customer's:

- Financial stability
- Industry trend
- Collateral and security of the debt
- Cash flow

Dunning Customers

Dunning is simply a request for payment. It comes in the form of letters, phone calls, and legal action. Often, having to resort to dunning devices is as embarrassing for the company as it is for the customer—especially if it's a long-standing customer. Nevertheless, dunning works. Customers strapped for cash won't pay unless specifically asked for payment.

More sophisticated companies send out different dunning letters for various stages of A/R delinquency. These range in potency from *maybe you forgot* to the more harsh, *pay up or else.*

The important thing to know is that you should never make a hollow threat to a customer. If the company expects to take further action for as yet unpaid balances, simply lay out the sequence of events the customer can expect. Then be sure to follow through with these actions. The best collecting companies are those that have a reputation for being serious about collecting their receivables.

Many of the more popular accounts receivable computer systems have dunning packages. The more sophisticated ones allow for different letters, depending on aging and balance owed.

Financing Receivables

Accounts receivable can be a source of cash when used as collateral. *Factoring* is the most common method. A bank or finance company acts as the factor. They purchase the receivables portfolio (or a portion) from the company. The factor advances funds based on the receivables purchased—always at a discount to their face value.

When using receivables factoring, the finance company may or may not elect to collect the accounts themselves. Usually factoring *with recourse* allows the factor to make the company liable for bad debts acquired in the portfolio. Those deals *without recourse* make the factor liable.

12
Accounts Payable

Overview

Companies without an emphasis on strong management policies often don't pay much attention to payables. Their main concern is that vendors don't complain about late payments. Chapter 12 shows how to manage the accounts payable system from an operational standpoint. We'll focus on the ways top professionals use the A/P system to control cash outflow and manage vendors' payment terms.

The controller and treasurer often work as a team in managing their company's payables. The treasurer helps establish payment policies. Such issues as aging before payment, acceptable purchase terms, and use of trade discounts for early payments fall under this topic.

The controller, on the other hand, deals mostly with the daily operation of the payables system. This includes such things as:

- Writing checks
- Maintaining balance consistency between A/P subledger and the general ledger
- Tracking invoice payment dates
- Maintaining system of internal accounting controls

Payables Responsibilities

Figure 12-1 clarifies the separation of duties in accounts payable between the controller and treasurer. See how the controller and treasurer divide the A/P responsibilities? Neither has complete control over the entire disbursement function. Both are in positions to check each other's work. That's part of the system of internal accounting controls.

Controller	Treasurer
Verifies accuracy of invoices	Prepares A/P performance statistics
Invoice entry	Controls acceptance of payment discounts
Custodian of check stock	Custodian of signature plate or is authorized signatory
Controls check register	Administers payables aging policy
Prints payment checks and executes payment by other methods	Authorizes payment method
Releases signed checks	Manages bank account balances and controls float
Reconciles accounts payable subledger and ties it to the general ledger	Reviews and approves reconciliations and reconciles checking accounts
	Conducts audits of A/P portfolio to ensure existence of authorized payees

Figure 12-1. Accounts payable responsibilities.

Tracking Invoice Payment Date

It's important that the A/P system have some sort of mechanism that tells the due date for each invoice. Without it, there's danger of missing (or not being able to control) invoice aging policy and acceptance of trade discounts. The result can be:

- Damage to the firm's reputation and creditworthiness
- Failure to take advantage of lower vendor prices

Tracking by a Manual System

Many controllers use a manual tickler method to tell them when particular invoices are due for payment. In many cases it's nothing more sophisticated than a card file for each day of the month. On each card is the name of the vendor whose invoice is due for payment on that day. The payment date can be either the date needed to take advantage of a trade discount or it can be the normal payment date in line with company invoice aging policies. Other companies use a master payables calendar that schedules the payment date for each invoice.

Regardless of the manual method used, the payment dates entered from the invoices are the dates when the company pays its vendors.

Automated Tracking Mechanism

Many of the popular accounts payable software systems have a built-in mechanism that tells when each invoice is due. They key in the due date the menu asks for when the invoice is first entered into the system. If there's a trade discount involved, they'll usually ask for the payment date required to qualify for the early payment discount.

With that information, the system produces reports that tell exactly which invoices to pay on any given day. Additionally, they can report cash required to keep the A/P system current on any given day and often for a specified period in the future.

When to Pay

Many companies establish an arbitrary payment policy they think helps them manage cash. Some companies pay on the last day of the month. Others pay on the 15th and the last day. Here's what such an arbitrary policy does:

- Guarantees the invoice won't be paid according to the purchase terms
- Ensures payment before or after the trade discount due date
- Risks impugning the creditworthiness of the company
- Irritates vendors who are chronically paid late
- Gets little notice by vendors who are paid early

Arbitrary payment policies are a bad idea. Instead, it's much better to pay the invoice on the day it's due. This does mean that the company must write checks every day. However, the time spent evens out over time. Further, use of the cash by stretching each invoice to the properly aged time according to company policy makes up for the added effort.

Accepting Trade Discounts

Except in cases where a company's aggregate cost of funds is very high, it makes sense to take advantage of trade discounts when offered. Here's the equation for determining the annualized income from taking advantage of a trade discount:

$$\frac{\text{discount \%}}{\text{due date} - \text{discount date}} \times 360 \text{ days} = \text{income from taking advantage of a trade discount}$$

For example, say the payment terms were 1/10, net 30. The income from taking advantage of the trade discount is 18 percent and was computed as follows:

$$\frac{1\%}{30 - 10} \times 360 = 18\%$$

Therefore, unless the firm's cost of funds is over 18 percent it doesn't make economic sense to pass up the discount offer.

Implementing Payables Aging Policy

What do you do when an invoice has no trade discount? Instead, the terms of purchase are, say, net 30. The answer depends. Many astute treasurers know their vendors very well from having dealt with them for years. They know which charge interest on a balance still unpaid after the due date. *More importantly, they know which do not.* They also know those vendors over which the company has some leverage—perhaps the firm is a large customer. Additionally, some vendors don't have a tracking mechanism that tells them which customers don't adhere to their payment terms.

It's these types of vendors for which the company can institute its own payables aging policy. We don't intend for this to be abusive. Additionally, we aren't willing to impugn the company's creditworthiness for the sake of holding onto our disbursements for an extra week or two. However, if the opportunity knocks—and it won't harm the firm—there's no reason not to take it.

Stretching Payables

The question is really, *how far can I go within the bounds of normal industry practice?* An abusive payment stretching policy, on the other hand, tries to stretch vendors until just before they cut your company off from further purchases.

If most companies in your industry hold payments for at least 45 days and you are paying within 30, then you are excessively benevolent. Probably needlessly so. Vendors may not expect payment for at least 45 days.

Take for example the garment industry. Clothing shops routinely withhold payment for 60 days and more to the manufacturers. It would be unusual to receive payment before then. A vendor may thank you for your "early" payment but they probably won't give you anything because they never asked for the favor in the first place.

The trick is to find the balance between an aging policy that's expected and that won't damage the firm's reputation or access to future needed goods and services.

Getting Something in Exchange

If you choose to pay before industry custom to particular vendors make sure they know this is a conscious decision of yours. Perhaps they're in a cash crunch themselves. Maybe the treasurer called you and requested payment by a certain date. Let them know that this is a favor you are doing and that there is a quid pro quo.

Some controllers lay it right out on the table and negotiate a purchase discount for the next shipment. Others request more lenient payment terms in the future.

Regardless, your company should receive compensation in some way for payment before standard industry practices.

Payment After the Due Date

Some companies have already experienced a cash crunch. Those that have not, probably will at some time in the future. Under circumstances where the company cannot keep its payable portfolio current or at least within normal industry practices, the controller and/or treasurer really earn their pay. They face the task of keeping the wolf away from the door.

The controller must allocate cash available for disbursement to those vendors who can do the company the most good (and often to those who can do it the most damage). Generally, the company pays those vendors who furnish items that the company absolutely cannot do without. Next come the vendors who are threatening to take serious action—such as a lawsuit—against the company.

Managing Late Payments.   There's a professional way to manage vendors your company must pay later than the agreed-upon terms. It's the way you would like to be treated by your own customers if (and when) you face the same situation. An astute controller or treasurer will contact vendors they cannot pay on time.

If you wait for them to call you, you're creating a problem just by making them wonder about the financial stability of your company. Instead, confront the issue honestly and with candor. Explain the nature of the cash flow problem your company is currently undergoing. Let them know what steps your firm is taking to solve the problem.

The most important piece of information to the vendor is *when* they can expect payment. Controllers and treasurers who are doing a good job of forecasting their company's cash flow should be able to answer that question. Many vendors are willing (grudgingly, but willing nevertheless when the alternatives are explained to them) to accept a payment schedule.

If you use special vendor payment schedules be sure to stick to them. The company has already missed one deadline. Its credibility and that of its financial executives is now suspect. Vendors may be willing to grant the benefit of the doubt—once. If the customer misses a second payment deadline, whatever amount of trust that remained in the relationship dissolves immediately.

Controlling Financial Impact of Purchase Terms

The controller or treasurer usually works with the purchasing department in establishing some of the purchase terms. Those most relevant to management of the A/P system include:

- Payment date
- Discount terms, including date and percentage

- Type of payment
- Place of payment

Often purchasing agents are more focused on the purchase price of the products they're buying. That's important. However, by ignoring the financial issues they may place the company in the position of giving back whatever price concessions they worked so hard to win in the first place.

It's up to the treasurer to educate the company's purchasers on the impact of certain contractual concessions regarding payment terms. Once understood, we can compute the *complete* purchase price. If they give something away, such as payment by electronic funds transfer instead of a check, we can compute the cost. Armed with this type of information, the firm is in a position to extract a concession to offset what was just given away.

Dealing Directly with Vendors

Some purchasing agents want to be the vendor's best friend. They play the good cop and turn irate vendors over to the A/P department who plays the bad cop. The transfer often takes place with the purchasing agent saying, "I don't know what's wrong with our payables department. Why don't *you* talk with them?"

If your firm allows this sort of game playing, make sure the transfer goes to someone with authority to make a decision—either the controller, cash manager, or treasurer. Additionally, if the purchasing department is going to get the financial people involved, it must supply them with the information they need to make an informed decision on payment terms. This information should include:

- Importance of the supplier to the company
- Competition for your business
- What kind of a customer you've been in the past
- Future needs for this vendor

Armed with this information, we can make accurate payment decisions without risk of adverse consequences to the company if the vendor still goes away unhappy.

Managing the Payables Portfolio

The techniques for measuring the age of the payables portfolio are the same as those used for the receivables portfolio. Most companies keep track of the payables performance in order to make sure company payment policies are being followed. It makes no sense to install and count on a disbursement schedule only to discover the staff ignored it.

Weighted-Average Aging

The weighted-average aging of the A/P portfolio tells us how long we age our payables before payment. It provides a good gauge to compare with the industry average. Further, whether your firm uses an automated A/P system or manual, there needs to be a conscious effort to identify the payment due date and make it comply with the company's A/P aging policy.

Of course, we can always circumvent the policy if a particular vendor demands payment or for any number of other reasons. The point is that the weighted-average aging computation identifies how closely the actual payment-aging practices conform to the firm's policy.

Here's the equation to compute the weighted average aging of A/P:

Weighted-average age of accounts payable = sum of (weighted-average percent of each aging bucket × no. of days in each aging bucket)

Figure 12-2 shows a practical example of one company's weighted-average payables aging.

The result illustrates an elapsed time for which the company pays its obligations of 60 days. The longer payables age, the more leverage the company derives from its vendors. Compare this with company policy and industry standard. Some industries do not consider this a slow-paying company.

Computing the Average Payment Period

The average payment period tells how many days of average expenses vendors have invested in the firm's accounts payable. The higher the average payment period, the greater the company's use of trade credit. Treasurers want this number to be as high as possible without impugning the creditworthiness of the company. Here's the equation:

Average payment period = average accounts payable balance/(annual expenses/360)

A/P balances by aging bucket	Amount owed the company	Weighting % in aging bucket	Weighting factor in days
Current	$ 5,000	4%	0 days
30 days	25,000	18%	6 days
60 days	75,000	55%	33 days
90 days	31,060	23%	21 days
120 days	0	0%	0 days
Total A/P	$136,060	100%	60 days

Figure 12-2. Weighted-average payables.

Let's run the equation to see just how large the payables balance must be in order to take advantage of vendor's trade credit:

Average A/P balance: $1,000,000

Annual expenses: $20,000,000

Average payment period = $1,000,000/($20,000,000/360)

Average payment period = 18 days

For some firms 18 days is too low. They may compare this with the average collection period from the accounts receivable system. Chances are the A/R collection period exceeds 30 days. The trick is to get both numbers as close as possible.

Many companies use a report that identifies those vendors paid either before or after the average payment period. Using this mechanism, vendors paid prior to the average "owe" you something. Likewise, we can track tardy payments jeopardizing a valued relationship and correct them if need be. Remember, the cost of a terminated relationship probably far outweighs any benefit derived from holding on to the cash owed.

In any case, this statistic provides control over compliance of payment practices compared to management policy. It allows for a closer tie with the payment custom in the industry.

Turning Over Accounts Payable

Another indication of how well a company is utilizing its trade credit is by measuring A/P turnover. The higher the A/P turnover rate, the faster cash leaves the firm. This creates more demand for working capital. Here's the A/P turnover equation:

$$A/P \text{ turnover} = \text{annual expenses}/\text{average A/P balance}$$

As we saw above, the turnover of your receivables ideally should match A/P turnover. Let's say, for example, the average collection time for receivables is 45 days. If payables also turn every 45 days (or more), then you are in the enviable position of having your vendors finance your inventory. In other words, the firm uses none of its own working capital to pay for inventory.

Specifying Payment Type

This is an issue more relevant to larger companies. On the payment side, companies are concerned with slowing down the outflow of cash from the company. They want to extend the payment float as much as possible. This means the preferable method of payment through the A/P system is by a paper check that has to run through the banking system before it's cleared at the issuer's bank.

Some purchase contracts negotiated by savvy vendors specify the method of payment, say electronic funds transfer. Of course, that will accelerate the flow of funds out of the company. That's not necessarily bad as long as you compensate the payee for loss of float. Often the trade-off comes in the form of:

- Discount period extension
- Larger discount percentage
- Accelerated delivery schedule

Generally, anything that adequately compensates the company for the premature loss of its cash float will do. Additionally, in the case of EFT payments, there can be an added bonus. If the firm negotiated its float loss with some sort of compensation, chances are it broke even. Since an EFT system is less expensive to run than a paper check system, we could argue that the company actually made a profit on the deal.

Wire Transfers

Plain wire transfer of funds has been around a long time. They're used frequently to pay large sums. However, the process is costly and inefficient for both the customer (payer) and vendor (payee). The only thing really electronic in a wire transfer is the actual movement of money. None of the information about the invoice that's being paid goes over the wire and through the bank—that remains manual.

Since wires are cumbersome and expensive, most companies don't use them to pay routine invoices. When they do, it's usually as a special favor to a vendor or because they have extracted some compensating benefit.

Advantages of EFT

Since electronic funds transfers eliminate some of the paper involved in payments, they provide some significant advantages. Companies generally need to be large enough and have payment volume of a size to provide for these economies. However, for those that meet the qualifications, EFT presents these advantages over a paper check disbursement system:

- Less cumbersome internal controls.
- Reduced time spent on disbursements.
- Costs, such as postage, are eliminated.
- Cost savings are partially offset by EFT transaction fees.
- Precise knowledge of when funds will clear.

Electronic Data Interchange (EDI).   A component of the EFT system is electronic data interchange. This is the electronic communication of the invoice data that goes with a payment. This provides vendors who receive an EFT payment all the information to *electronically* post the payment information directly to their accounts receivable system.

The National Automated Clearing House offers EDI in a service it calls Corporate Trade Exchange (CTX). Using this information conduit as well as the electronic payment facility, we accelerate both the payment *and* the recording processes. This presents a great advantage to vendors—one they're often willing to negotiate better terms to their customers to get.

Preauthorized Debits (PADs)

It takes a special (and often unusual) business relationship to make profitable use of preauthorized debits. We need two ingredients to make it successful:

- Mutual trust
- A large number of small purchases

PADs work like this: One company authorizes another to debit their bank account each month with the amount of the purchases the firm has made. This preauthorized debit can be either in the form of a check or (if the company is *really* trusting) a standing EFT order. Usually there are maximums placed on the amount of each debit. The vendor provides the supporting paperwork each month to its customer that documents every transaction.

PADs save everyone a lot of time and processing expense associated with many small transactions. Vendors are happy because they get paid promptly. The customers are happy because their payables system isn't inundated with many small bills.

Internal Accounting Controls

The accounts payable system requires close attention to internal controls. Potential exists for the insertion of nonexistent vendors, then submitting false invoices for payment. Additionally, vendors' invoices could be doctored to reflect a larger balance than what is actually due. The company issues a check to an intermediary who cashes it, pays the vendor what it is actually owed, and pockets the difference.

The best way to maintain proper internal controls in the payables department is to separate the responsibilities for:

- Payment authorization
- Disbursement
- Accounting

That way it would take collusion between unrelated parties to defraud the company.

Accounts Payable Responsibilities

Here are the duties of the financial staff as related to accounts payable. Notice how no single person has complete control over the authorization, disbursement, or accounting.

Accounting.   Responsible for entering invoices into the A/P system. Reviews the receiving document and purchase order to determine accuracy of invoice. Additionally, some firms require an authorized signatory to sign the receiver and invoice prior to entry into the A/P system.

Treasurer.   This person is the authorized signatory on the checks. The treasurer reviews and approves the invoice package with check prior to disbursement. Often approval comes in the form of a signature on the check. Additionally, the treasurer maintains custody of the signature plate but not the check stock.

Payment officer.   Maintains custody of both the prenumbered check stock and the check register. Cancels invoices with a PAID stamp or perforates them to prevent further use. Mails checks after signature. Provides accounting for all prenumbered checks. The check register records all voids or damaged checks. The treasurer places the actual check stock in safekeeping. Alternatively, the payment officer might destroy it.

Additional Accounts Payable Controls

Along with adequate separation of duties, there are several other features that help control the A/P system:

Independence.   Separate the purchasing process from disbursements either through accounts payable or anywhere else in the company.

Prenumbered receivers.   All receiving documents used in confirming receipt of goods and authorizing entry of an invoice into the A/P system are prenumbered. Someone independent of the receiving function controls and issues them. Account for all gaps in numbering sequence. This ensures that items entered into the A/P system were indeed received.

Prenumbered purchase orders.   Someone independent of the purchasing function maintains all prenumbered POs. Account for gaps in the numbering sequence.

A/P performance statistics.   The controller and treasurer receive each month all computations associated with the payables aging, turnover, and average payment period. They correct deviations from company policy.

Account reconciliation.   Two different people independent of the disbursement function reconcile and review all disbursement bank accounts each month. Someone in authority follows up and resolves all open items. The process also includes balancing the A/P subledger with the accounts payable account in the general ledger.

Trade discounts. The company policy should normally be to take advantage of trade discount terms. When performed periodically, the computation of the discount savings compared against cost of funds verifies appropriateness of this policy.

Management review. Qualified and independent personnel should perform regular audits and review of the A/P system. The review should focus on compliance with the system of internal accounting controls and with management policy toward accounts payable.

Float

Management of disbursement float can mean an interest-free loan to a company. If done correctly, there's little danger of overdrawing the checking account. Disbursement float consists of three main areas:

- Mail float between the disbursing firm and the vendor
- Internal float while the vendor processes customers' payments
- Bank float—the time a check takes to clear disburser's bank

The first two, mail float and internal float, don't offer much opportunity. Despite complaints, our mail system is fairly efficient. Many treasurers count on between one and three days of float. Vendor's internal float isn't manageable either. Few companies try not dating or signing their payment checks. Fewer still attempt the old trick of making the number amount disagree with the written amount. These ploys are transparent and just irritate vendors. Figure 10-4 in Chapter 10 demonstrates how to compute and track float.

Controlling Disbursements

Part of the payment system of most companies includes attention to the funds leaving the firm. The objective is to maintain control of these funds for as long as possible. Additionally, astute controllers consider the *information* surrounding their disbursement operation of almost equal value as the funds. The reason is that information—especially early information—provides the amount of investable funds available without danger of overdrawing the checking account.

Banks offer three types of disbursement control devices:

- Presentment reporting
- Sweep accounts
- Balance reporting

Presentment Reporting

The biggest unknown when managing the disbursement float of any company is the amount of checks presented at your bank for clearing each day. Presentment reporting services eliminate the guesswork. Here's how:

1. *Separate disbursement account.*   The company establishes a separate checking account designated as the disbursement account. This is the account that pays checks presented for clearing.

2. *Bank reporting services.*   This is simply a notification to the company early in the morning (before 11:00 a.m.) of the amount of checks presented for clearing that day through the customer's disbursement account. With this information, the payment officer of the company knows what the account's excess balance will be at the end of the day. However, they know this number early in the morning while there's still time to use the excess money.

3. *Investment.*   Overnight repurchase agreements provide the usual investment vehicle of choice. They mature the next morning and the presentment reporting process begins again.

Sweep Accounts

This is an additional service that further enhances the value of presentment services. The bank automatically scans all disbursement accounts and *sweeps* any excess funds not needed for clearing checks that day into an interest-bearing account such as a money-market fund.

If your company has several divisions, each with their own checking accounts, the bank can automatically perform the presentment and investment function for the corporate controller. The bank determines the amount presented for clearing that day against each account. Early in the morning the bank subtracts the available balance from the amount scheduled for clearing and sweeps the excess into a corporate investment account.

Alternatively, if the firm has an outstanding line of credit, the sweep funds might pay down the LOC rather than go to an investment.

Automated Balance Reporting

If information is the name of the game in controlling disbursements, then *timeliness and convenience* are the standards of excellence. Many banks offer their corporate customers on-line computer access to their accounts using nothing more than a desktop personal computer.

Right from his or her office the controller or treasurer can do most of the firm's banking through the computer without ever having to speak with a banker. The information and transactions most commonly offered include:

- Line of credit draws and pay-downs
- Transfer of lockbox deposits to a concentration account
- Account balance reporting and availability schedule
- Automated clearinghouse transactions

Additionally, if the company is international, some major money center banks offer worldwide account access from the same computer system.

The most significant disbursement of many payables systems is the amount paid for inventory. Sometimes it's in the form of raw materials or subassemblies. Nevertheless, inventory control is one part of the company that presents profit risk if it's handled poorly or a real opportunity if it's worked professionally. Chapter 13 shows you how.

13
Inventory Control

Overview

Inventory is often the single largest component of working capital. For many controllers this is the most dynamic of the many moving targets they must manage. Often the objectives for the inventory are at cross-purposes among different departments. Chapter 13 discusses the different agendas regarding inventory management. Often the strongest voice wins. However, the decision isn't always what's best for the firm.

That's why we'll spend some time identifying the most advantageous quantity of inventory items to order and the best level of safety stock to have on hand. Additionally, Chapter 13 demonstrates the various control mechanisms and performance measurement procedures a modern controller establishes over inventory.

Identifying the Agenda

Different departments within the company exert influence over inventory-control policies. They all have their own agendas. However, the goals that benefit one department may not be as good to another.

An example is the production group. Generally, production wants a large inventory. This guarantees long cost-effective production runs without risk of running short, which allows purchase of raw materials and subassemblies in larger quantities. The company benefits from bulk discounts.

The sales group also likes the idea of large inventories. After all, sales commissions depend on the company having products to ship. Few companies pay commissions on backordered goods.

So, most firms have at least two powerful departments pulling for a large inventory. Some of the arguments they promote include:

- Unknown customer demand
- Need for a full line of items—even those that are slow movers

- Stockpiling in a market where prices are rising
- Avoidance of loss from recognition of obsolete items
- Disbelief and disregard of control measures

The finance group, on the other hand, wants a low inventory that turns over quickly. This reduces the amount of working capital tied up in slow-moving assets. Additionally, this cash-conscious department is very aware of inventory items that don't sell quickly. However, the politics of business usually identifies the finance group as just an overhead cost center. Consequently, it rarely exerts the power and influence that sales or manufacturing can over inventory policy.

Nevertheless, there are some convincing arguments for sensible inventory control procedures an astute controller or treasurer can provide. Further, the information derived from the accounting and financial information systems can make better managers out of those with the power to control inventory purchase and quantity policies.

Interfacing with Order Entry

Many companies have a separate order entry department that uses an automated O/E system. Smaller firms employ an order entry desk that processes sales orders. Still other firms have their sales force act as order processors.

Regardless of the method used to take in and process orders, there must be some way to tell if the goods just purchased are indeed in the warehouse and ready to ship.

Sophisticated O/E systems link directly to the inventory control system. At the point of order there's an updated list showing the availability status for each inventory item.

This linkage provides information about possible delays in delivery or projected shipping dates directly to the order taker. For customers, this system interface takes the guesswork out of buying from the company.

Backordering is also an issue in the order entry department. Often the O/E person is the first to know when an item is out of stock. Who better to flag the item to the company's purchaser?

Substituting Goods

Another benefit of having a computer link between order entry and the inventory system is the potential for *substitutability*. Often, currently out-of-stock goods can be substituted for those that are available. Additionally, the O/E clerks may not be familiar enough with the technical aspects of the company's inventory to know by themselves which goods provide an acceptable substitute. The computer's suggestions can save a sale that might otherwise have gone to a competitor. This satisfies the customer's needs and the company makes a friend.

Inventory control systems having the ability to interface with order entry and provide a list of substitutes generally ask for them as an input field when the inventory item is being entered. A data entry person familiar with the company's inventory enhances accuracy of the substitution list.

Of course this prolongs setup of the inventory control system. Further, it makes errors possible if the data entry person is unfamiliar with the company's inventory. Inventory interface with order entry and substitutions can be powerful tools.

Internal Controls for Inventory

Inventory isn't as liquid an asset as some of the cash or cash equivalents a company may have. However, as one of the firm's largest investments, it needs attention. Often those involved with inventory aren't conscious of the need for internal control procedures. Frequently they're not trained in the ways inventory can be misappropriated.

The polite term is *inventory shrinkage.* This is an expense that usually goes without explanation. Somehow the inventory just got up and walked out of the warehouse. Here are the control procedures most often used to keep track of valuable inventory:

Counting Inventory

A good deterrent against unexplained inventory losses is to do periodic (and sometimes surprise) physical inventory counts. Match the resulting physical inventory against that which is on the books. Inventory control staff explains the differences.

Accountability for Shrinkage

Another way to increase effectiveness of the deterrent is to make the warehouse manager responsible for losses to inventory.

Additionally, maintain records of the inventory results. Spot trends quickly and correct them. Sometimes this results in personnel leaving the firm. In some cases, criminal prosecutions result.

Uncomplementary Duties

There are certain jobs in the warehouse that the same person or two people deemed related parties should not do. For example, the person responsible for receiving inventory into the warehouse should not be the same person who makes the accounting entry into the inventory control system. Nor should the person who does the physical count of inventory be the same person who checks it into the warehouse.

The purpose is to have at least two independent people oversee the inventory as it comes into the company; as it sits in the warehouse waiting processing or sale; and as it leaves. As we pointed out in Chapter 5, "Internal Controls," the objective is to make collusion necessary for a misappropriation to occur.

Securing Inventory

Some companies use the same warehouse security measures even after the value of their inventory has increased. For example, say a company's security is fine for its inventory of chassis boxes that house computers. However, lately they've begun assembling entire computers. Now they inventory chips and circuit boards. The inventory value has jumped. Suddenly the company presents a more profitable target.

Often insurance companies have specialists on staff or can recommend a consultant who specializes in physical plant security. The solution may be as simple as placing a deadbolt lock on the back door. Alternatively, it may require a specialized alarm system for certain parts of the warehouse.

Regardless, the physical security of inventory is usually far less expensive than regular losses due to unexplained shrinkage.

Computing Inventory Performance

There are many computations used to monitor inventory. Depending on a company's concern, it may use some or all of them. Most of these measurements have at least something to do with the speed inventory moves through the company. It seems that accelerated *throughput* of inventory usually benefits most companies. Here are the most useful measurements for inventory performance:

Cost of Goods Sold

For most companies cost of goods sold (CGS) is the largest expense. Compute the firm's gross margin by subtracting CGS from sales revenue.

There are two different ways to value inventory. Both affect the result of cost of goods sold.

Periodic Inventory. This requires a physical count of inventory at the end of the accounting period. Compute cost of goods sold as follows:

$$CGS = \text{beginning inventory} + \text{purchases} - \text{ending inventory}$$

The drawback to this method is that both inventory and CGS computations must usually wait until the end of the accounting period. Also, for large companies, a physical inventory can be a costly and time-consuming effort.

Perpetual Inventory.   This method is more accurate since it computes costs of the inventory actually produced (or received). When sold, the costs come out of inventory and are debited to cost of goods sold. That way the company has a running balance at any point in time, not only of its inventory value, but of the cost of goods sold.

Compute ending inventory using the perpetual inventory method as follows:

$$\text{Ending inventory} = \text{beginning inventory} + \text{purchases} - \text{CGS}$$

Barring error or unexplained shrinkage, the ending inventory balance on the books should always equal the inventory arrived at by physical count.

Inventory Turnover

The speed with which a company converts its investment in inventory into sales interests everyone. The turnover computation tells us that. Here's the equation:

$$\text{Inventory turnover} = \frac{\text{annual CGS}}{\text{average inventory balance}}$$

The more inventory turns over, the faster it flows out to customers and the less working capital is tied up in slow-moving stock. If you see inventory turnover slow, then inventory is building. Alternatively, an accelerating turnover rate indicates that stockpiles of inventory are falling.

Smart controllers and treasurers try to *anticipate* changes in inventory turnover. They adjust the firm's purchase of raw materials accordingly. By waiting until the turnover rate actually changes, it's too late. Purchases have already been made for goods that won't be sold at the pace assumed by the order size.

Gross Margin per Inventory Turn.   Fast inventory turnover provides liquidity in the sense that the investment in inventory turns into sales and, eventually, cash. However, it does little good to turn inventory quickly but at a decreasing *profit margin*. The way many firms track that is by computing gross margin per inventory turn. Figure 13-1 illustrates this concept.

Notice how fast inventory turned in the second year—11 times compared to just 7 times the year before. Additionally, the days of sales tied up in inventory has also fallen from 51 to just 33 days. Both changes are good for liquidity. Everybody is working harder in the production area. *However, Harvey is working harder for less profit.* Gross margin per inventory turn has dropped by almost 50 percent. Maybe they suffered a price discount. Perhaps production costs jumped. Whatever the cause, Harvey has sacrificed profit for cash flow and liquidity.

Harvey Production Corporation For the Year Ended December 31, 19X2		
	19X1	19X2
Cost of goods sold	$20,000,000	$20,000,000
Average inventory of finished goods	4,000,000	2,000,000
Inventory turnover	5 times	10 times
Days of sales in inventory (360 days/turnover)	51 days	33 days
Gross margin	$12,000,000	$ 9,500,000
Gross margin per turnover	$ 2,400,000	$ 950,000

Figure 13-1. Gross margin per inventory turn.

Average Investment Period

Employ this index to tell how many days of inventory are on hand at the current sales level. As the average investment period rises, inventory builds and the turnover slows down. The amount of working capital invested in inventory also builds. The equation for computing average investment period is:

$$\text{Average investment period} = \frac{\text{present inventory balance}}{(\text{annual cost of goods sold}/360)}$$

Days of Inventory on Hand

A quick way to tell the status of inventory is to compare it with demand. The equation is:

$$\text{Days of inventory} = \frac{\text{total inventory}}{\text{daily demand}}$$

The objective is to have enough inventory to meet the daily demand—not just for today, but to last until the next delivery. Many controllers also add a reserve for delayed delivery and a safety stock in the event demand increases. Figure 13-1 used days of inventory as a reference point. As inventory turnover increased, the number of sales days of inventory on hand fell.

Estimating Ending Inventory

There are two quick computations that provide an estimate of the ending inventory. Controllers use these to test the reasonableness of ending inventory numbers. Additionally, they help in forecasting profits and, therefore, cash flows. There are two ways of estimating ending inventory:

- Gross margin method
- Retail method

Poncho Enterprises
Estimated Ending Inventory
Gross Margin Method
December 31, 199X

Beginning inventory balance at cost		$10,000,000
Plus inventory purchases at cost		30,000,000
Cost of inventory available for sale		$40,000,000
Less computation of estimated CGS:		
Sales:	$50,000,000	
Gross margin @ 35%	17,500,000	
Estimated cost of goods sold		(32,500,000)
Estimated ending inventory as of December 31, 199X		$ 7,500,000

Figure 13-2. Estimation of ending inventory—gross margin method.

Gross Margin Method.   Manufacturing companies that either produce or assemble finished-goods inventory use this method. Figure 13-2 shows how it works.

For retail companies, there's a similar method for estimating ending inventory, as shown in Figure 13-3.

Economic Order Quantity

Inventory purchase that exceeds what is really needed concerns controllers and treasurers. That only eats up precious working capital. However, it's still true that bulk purchases give the firm price breaks which increase gross margins. There's a way to compute the optimum order quantity that considers both needs. We call it

Autumn Garden Shops, Inc.
Estimated Ending Inventory
Retail Method
December 31, 199X

	Cost	Retail price
Beginning inventory balance	$10,000,000	$17,000,000
Purchases	5,000,000	8,500,000
Freight in	1,000,000	0
Cost of goods sold @ 40% gross margin	5,000,000	8,500,000
Estimated ending inventory	$11,000,000	$17,000,000

Figure 13-3. Estimation of ending inventory—retail method.

the *economic order quantity*. It represents an order size that provides the lowest possible overall cost to the company. The EOQ equation is:

$$EOQ = \sqrt{\left\{\frac{2ap}{sz}\right\}}$$

where a = the annual quantity of the item used in units
p = the purchase order cost
s = the annual direct and indirect carrying cost of a unit of inventory
z = the purchase price of the inventory item

Assume the following:

- Annual demand is 100,000 units.
- Cost to issue a purchase order, receive the goods, and stock the warehouse is $100.
- Annual cost of carrying inventory is 12 percent.
- The cost of each item in quantities between 5000 and 10,000 is $2.00.

Plugging these numbers into the EOQ equation, we get:

$$EOQ = \sqrt{[2 \times (100,000 \times \$100)] / (12\% \times \$2.00)}$$

$$EOQ = 9,129 \text{ units per order}$$

If the company needs 100,000 units annually, it will issue about 11 orders (100,000 / 9,129 = 10.95) during the year.

Safety Stock

Safety stock is really the cushion production managers insist on to avoid running out. Stock-outs can cause costly disruptions to production runs. Along with the production managers, the sales staff support the idea of large safety stocks. Their livelihoods depend on there being sufficient finished goods inventory to fill their orders.

However, unnecessarily large safety stocks are contrary to the controller's objective—to have as little inventory on hand as possible and to keep it turning quickly. Fortunately there's a way to compute the optimum safety stock.

The objective is to carry a level of safety stock that's the most cost-effective. Here's the safety stock equation:

Probability of stock-out at a given level of safety stock × stock-out cost × number of orders per year (demand/EOQ) = expected stock-out cost + carrying cost of safety stock = total inventory carrying cost

Units of safety stock	Probability of stock-out	Cost of stock-out	No. of orders per year	Stock-out cost (A)	Carry cost (B)	Total cost (C)
60	60%	$100	15	$900	$300	$1200
70	40%	100	15	600	350	950
80	35%	100	15	525	400	925
90	33%	100	15	495	450	945

Figure 13-4. Computation of inventory safety stock.

Set up the safety stock computation in tabular form. Then compute the cost of various levels of safety stock. The lowest total cost is the best answer. Figure 13-4 provides an example.

1. Compute stock-out cost as the probability of stock-out × cost of stock-out multiplied by number of orders per year (EOQ).

2. Compute carrying cost as the cost of holding one unit per year (assumed to be $5.00) × safety stock. Carrying costs include things such as financing, space, handling, security, and insurance. All are associated with the costs to keep an item of inventory on the warehouse floor. Often carrying costs run as high as 25%–35% of an item's acquisition cost.

3. Compute total cost as stock-out cost + carrying cost.

In this example, the optimum level of safety stock is 80 units. Notice that safety stock is one of those rare things in life where more is not necessarily better. The controller or treasurer can argue a case for maintaining the safety stock at this level.

As often happens, though, there may be other circumstances involved. Perhaps the manufacturing department knows of a risk to the firm's steady supplier. That case justifies increased inventory well beyond any levels required by safety stock considerations. Alternatively, perhaps there's an anticipated cost increase. The production department wants to maintain its cost budget. So again, more inventory is stockpiled. The company has become a commodity futures trader. Instead of just buying an option to hedge against a possible price increase, they've taken delivery—a very risky enterprise.

Accounting Policies

The *Accounting Research Bulletin* (ARB) 43, chapter 4, identifies many of the valuation rules regarding inventory. By definition, inventory from an accounting standpoint is:

> Items of tangible personal property that are: (1) held for sale in the ordinary course of operations as finished goods, (2) goods in the process of production as work-in-process, or (3) raw materials and

supplies which are to be currently consumed directly or indirectly in the manufacturing process.

Process Contracts

Some firms have inventory in process for specific customers already under contract. In this case, record the production costs incurred for a particular accounting period in a process inventory account *by contract*. Additionally, the firm may accrue annually earnings for the progress made on completion of that contract. This amounts to the estimated earnings applicable to undelivered items on a fixed-price contract. The income and expenses most often attached to such process contracts include:

- Accrued earnings
- Labor by contract
- Material
- Variable manufacturing
- Fixed manufacturing
- Delivery

Inventory Costing Methods

There are several common inventory costing methods in use. Choosing one usually depends on the nature of your business. Generally, the controller recommends the most appropriate method for reporting purposes.

There are four questions financial professionals usually ask before selecting an inventory costing method:

1. Which will maximize the firm's net income?
2. Which will minimize the firm's income tax liability?
3. Which provides the most information considering the nature of the company?
4. Which method is least likely to be abused?

Regardless of the inventory costing method used, it's imperative that it be *consistently* applied. Companies don't switch from one method to another without good reason. Additionally, they certainly don't change in the middle of an accounting period, regardless of the reason. The different inventory costing methods include:

- Last in, first out (LIFO)
- First in, first out (FIFO)
- Lower of cost or market (LCM)
- Average costing

LIFO.   Under this costing convention, goods enter cost of goods sold in the reverse order of their entry into inventory. This method assumes sale of the newest goods first. Therefore, what's left in inventory is older.

During periods of rising prices, the LIFO method increases cost of goods sold since the higher-priced goods are the ones going out to customers and the lower-priced goods are what's left. This can be advantageous taxwise since net income is lower than under the other inventory costing methods.

Conversely, during periods of falling prices, LIFO gives a higher current ratio than valuing the inventory using the other two methods. Too large a current ratio can mean that current assets are being financed using long-term liabilities such as debt or owner's equity. If the yield curve is positively sloping, that means that longer-term financing is more expensive than short-term. The practice of financing less expensive short-term assets with more expensive long-term liabilities can cut into profit margins.

FIFO.   The first in, first out costing method assumes sale of the oldest goods first. This is true of many industries—particularly those concerned with spoilage or obsolescence. They want to sell the oldest goods first.

During periods of rising prices, FIFO provides a lower cost of goods sold, thus increasing net income and the consequent income tax liability.

Lower of Cost or Market (LCM).   This is one of the more conservative approaches to inventory valuation. The results usually come close to FIFO except in periods of rapid price change. The controller simply values ending inventory at the lower of either what the company purchased (or produced) the goods for or their current market value.

Some accountants argue that this method more closely approximates the true value of inventory and that it's less likely to overstate this major asset. Items best valued using LCM costing include:

- Precious metals
- Publicly traded securities with a ready market
- Commodities

Notice that the values of these types of items can change rapidly. Additionally, we can easily ascertain and verify the current value.

Average Costing.   This valuation method attempts to remove the peaks and valleys of inventory costs throughout the year. It does this by recomputing inventory costs after each purchase or production run. That way there's always a fairly constant average cost per unit that reflects pricing *trends* rather than actual changes.

Influences on Inventory Valuation

Along with changing prices, there are three other factors that can influence the income effects of inventory valuation. They include:

1. Year-to-year changes in inventory quantity.
2. If there was a liquidation, how much was actually liquidated relative to the quantity of goods sold?
3. If there was a liquidation, was the spread between inventory cost and average LIFO layers greater than the increase in price from the preceding year?

Figure 13-5 summarizes how each factor influences income under various pricing trends.

Income Tax Effects

Seek professional advice from a qualified expert when selecting an inventory costing method. Companies that elect a LIFO method of tax determination must also use LIFO for financial reporting. In other words, you can't have the best of both worlds—high income reporting and low tax liability.

Under FIFO, during inflationary times, net income will be greater and so will be the tax liability. The reverse is true of the LIFO method.

Companies that do switch from one method to another should time the change to reduce tax expense for that year.

Just-in-Time Inventory

There's a popular method of reducing the amount of working capital tied up in inventory. It's called *just-in-time* inventory management. Under this theory, goods

Ending inventory is:	If prices are rising:	If prices are stable:	If prices are falling:
> beginning inventory	LIFO income < FIFO income	LIFO income = FIFO income	LIFO income > FIFO income
= beginning inventory	LIFO income < FIFO income	LIFO income = FIFO income	LIFO income > FIFO income
< beginning inventory	LIFO income > FIFO income	LIFO income > FIFO income if liquidated LIFO layers have costs < current unit costs	LIFO income > FIFO income if liquidated LIFO layers have costs < current unit costs

Figure 13-5. Inventory value under price changes.

come into the warehouse or onto the shop floor just in the nick of time. This removes costly storage of inventory items in the warehouse or raw materials inventory waiting for usage.

Naturally, this concept requires a larger number of smaller inventory deliveries. However, goods don't sit around waiting to be used (or damaged, spoiled, or stolen). Instead they arrive and are immediately used.

Often, there's a quid pro quo given vendors in the form of immediate payment. This helps compensate them for the added effort of more deliveries.

Matching Inventory Purchases with the Business Plan

Treasurers have a vested interest in making sure that planned inventory purchases match both the sales and production plans. If they don't, cash outflow to inventory vendors is likely to exceed cash inflow from paying customers.

Balancing Inventory

To reduce the risk of having too much or too little inventory, many treasurers try balancing inventory. The intent is not for the finance department to stick its nose into the inventory decision-making apparatus. That's not the controller's or treasurer's job. However, these tools do assist in understanding *approximately* what's going on. The two inventory-balancing equations most often used are:

1. Beginning inventory + planned production = projected sales + targeted ending inventory

2. Target inventory = normal inventory + growth stock (if any) + safety stock

These tools provide an approximation of how the inventory purchasing, production, and sales plans balance one another. For example, say that cost of goods sold runs about 60 percent of retail sales price (a 40 percent gross margin). Also, the firm thinks it needs a month and a half of inventory on hand to avoid stock-outs. Monthly sales planned for $500,000 require an approximate level of finished goods inventory of $450,000, computed as follows:

$$(\$500,000 \times 60\%) \times 1.5 = \$450,000$$

If inventory is materially different from that number, there should be a good reason. The production and sales departments won't complain—large inventories are to their best interest. However, the treasurer should be aware of the impact an unbalanced inventory will have on the cash plan.

Features of Modern Inventory Control

Automated inventory control systems now available on the market have become extremely sophisticated—especially those available on desktop computers. Now more than ever before, businesses—regardless of their size—can have the pinpoint control over their inventory that once was available only to large companies willing to pay the exorbitant price.

The following is a list of the features you may find useful in assessing the value of your current method of inventory management.

Multiple Warehouses

Many companies maintain inventory at more than one location. A modern inventory control (I/C) system allows several locations, but each warehouse can order separately and transfer items between locations. Inventory reports indicate which warehouse has what goods.

Separating Goods by Product Line

Inventory items in the same product line often have similar information such as:

- General ledger posting data
- Method of valuation
- Sales commission structure
- Price code

Up-to-date I/C systems allow for product-line groupings. This greatly facilitates setup of the system to begin with and new items as they arrive.

Pricing Inventory Items

Companies don't always sell items to different customers at the same price. The state-of-the-art I/C systems provide for discounts and markups on items based on a standard cost. Access this information straight through the order-entry system.

Costing Methods

Flexibility in item-costing methods provides an advantage. Modern I/C systems allow the four standard methods discussed earlier.

Measuring Units

Some companies use different measuring units for inventory, depending on whether they are purchases, sales, or stock. The more sophisticated systems automatically convert between units of measure if they are different for the same item, depending on the item's status.

Vendor Information

Often it's necessary to know which vendors furnished the last batch of purchases—maybe there was a problem. I/C should provide information on the primary and secondary vendor for each item. Some even provide additional information such as lead time and backlog at a vendor's warehouse.

Reordering

Many systems prompt for a reorder point during entry of inventory items—that is, the level of stock where management has determined it needs to reorder. The more sophisticated systems suggest reorder quantities based on economic order quantity, maximum stock quantity, or simply a management-entered stock reorder point. Most systems with this feature also provide reports listing all the items that require reorder.

Inquiring About an Item

Most of the sophisticated systems allow for various types of item inquiries. The reports most often asked for include:

- Quantity on hand
- Items that are on purchase order
- Sales orders (and therefore, items already spoken for)
- Items on backorder (and already allocated to customers when they arrive)

Substitutions

We've already talked about the benefits of having the I/C suggest possible substitute goods through the order-entry system. Many systems ask for alternate goods as part of the item input menu.

History of Sales

Among the most useful features of any I/C system is its ability to tell what's hot and what's not. Sales history features often tell such things as:

- Quantity sold at various points in time
- Items returned
- Dollars of an item sold
- Cost of goods sold for each warehouse location
- Best-sellers and worst-sellers
- Goods that haven't sold more than _____

This information is of most benefit if it's available for the current period, year to date, and for the prior year.

Price Lists

Along with the current listed sales price, the cost of goods sold and gross margin are usually available as well. Additionally, it's often helpful for the I/C system to display specific customer price levels and the firm's policy on quantity price breaks. Often the sales staff uses this kind of information in formulating bids.

Filling Backorders

For some companies it's a chore to remember which orders require filling from goods just received into inventory. Several automated I/C systems display a complete list of orders that had goods backordered, but for which the missing items have just arrived. This enhances greatly the processing speed and accuracy of these backordered sales.

Changing Prices

Often manufacturing operations use the same component in several products. What happens to inventory costs and sales prices when that component experiences a price increase? The best I/C systems allow for automatic cost and sales price updates over the entire inventory.

14
Cost Accounting

Overview

Cost accounting isn't just for manufacturing operations. Many different types of companies—even service providers—use cost accounting methods to monitor and control their profit-making process. Chapter 14 describes components of the cost accounting system most relevant to treasurers and controllers. This section explains the mechanics of transferring inventory during the various stages of production. Additionally, we'll demonstrate how the cost accounting system enters labor into the product manufacturing equation.

Equally important is how controllers use cost accounting information to control profit. Chapter 14 identifies the various ways cost information assists in monitoring profitability and identifying problem areas.

Designing Cost Accounting Systems

Cost accounting has one mission: *to gather the costs of production and assign them to the items produced.* We use this information to identify production problems and correct them before they get out of control. From an accounting standpoint, the cost system accumulates information for reporting on the income statement.

Cost accounting benefits most companies with a manufacturing process. The system monitors the combination of different materials and some already partially assembled components on the production line. Manufacturing requires production-floor labor. Materials and manufacturing labor comprise the *direct costs* associated with making a product.

There are two other types of costs identified by the cost accounting system:

- Indirect costs
- Costs arbitrarily allocated

Such costs don't specifically originate from the manufacturing process. However, the product benefited from them. Therefore, the cost accounting system allocates portions of these costs to each item produced.

The cost accounting system traces all these costs from their source. Then it determines the method of allocation to each of the products benefiting from them. Some products benefit more than others simply because the company produced more of them. Just like direct costs, these indirect costs accumulate in the cost of goods account for each product. Once the manufacturing process is completed, all production costs sit in the work-in-process inventory account for each product. That's how we compute *cost of goods sold*. Indeed, that's the purpose of the cost accounting system—to maintain a running tally of production costs.

The cost accounting system controls production costs. It does this by identifying the standard production costs. Then the system accumulates all *actual* production costs. With these two pieces of information—the standard costs and actual costs—the cost accounting system identifies both favorable and unfavorable production cost variances.

Tracing Inventory and Other Costs

The cost accounting system tracks the flow of inventory as it moves from raw materials to work in process and finally into finished goods inventory. The cost accounting system executes that transfer of information. Figure 14-1 shows how the cost accounting system tracks production costs.

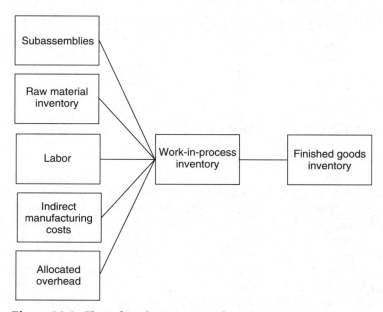

Figure 14-1. Flow of production cost information.

The five sources shown in Figure 14-1 comprise the primary information sources for the cost accounting system. It accumulates this information in the work-in-process inventory accounts as items proceed through production. On completion of production, all costs transfer to the finished goods inventory. At that point we know the cost of goods sold.

Tracking Service Costs

Can businesses without inventory benefit from cost accounting? Yes. Auto repair garages, professional businesses, and real estate operators are good examples of companies that profit from knowing the costs of delivering their services. They use cost accounting information to establish their prices.

For example, the service technicians of on-site computer repair companies have sophisticated knowledge. Their employers pay them well and provide employee benefits competitive in their industry. The cost accounting system tells the company what it costs for each hour these highly skilled professionals are on the job.

Further, they carry expensive equipment with them to each job site. The company also knows the cost of that equipment and how much it needs to charge customers for its use. All these costs go into the hourly service rate. There's one more thing they include—profit. The company not only needs to cover its basic costs, it must make a profit. The cost system boils that into the hourly rate as well.

Categorizing Cost Systems

Cost accounting methods differ, depending on your business. The most common cost systems are:

- Full cost
- Process
- Job order
- Costing joint products and by-products

Full-Cost Systems

Full-cost accounting systems allocate every manufacturing cost associated with production. That includes all costs *directly* traceable to each item as well as those *indirectly* related. Whether large or small, businesses that fail to carefully allocate costs in their accounting systems get their lunch eaten.

Overhead and other costs not directly traceable to production can quickly get out of hand. Most companies plan for inclusion of these direct and indirect costs by determining a standard (planned) cost for each product. That's what the cost accounting system uses to track against actual production costs. Excess costs show up as unfavorable variances that the controller follows up and corrects.

Process Cost Systems

Process cost systems work best in businesses producing large quantities of identical products. The cost system accumulates costs for the entire production run. We compute unit costs by dividing the total production cost by the number of units produced.

Process cost focuses on producing an entire batch of similar goods. Contrast this with the job order cost system (described below) that focuses on a single unit. Process costing goes through a series of steps to produce the final product. Each process is costed separately. Often different products branch off the same process. The cost accounting system identifies the separate costs associated with each branch product.

The petrochemical industry uses the process cost accounting system. As the plant refines the feedstock crude oil it branches off into different products—automotive gasoline, aviation fuel, kerosene, and alcohol—to name a few.

Designating Production Costs.   A process system reports costs for each stage of production. It then averages them over the equivalent units produced for a given period of time. Process reporting usually consists of these five steps:

1. Record total units transferred from one process department to the next.
2. Add material, labor, and overhead contributed by each process department.
3. Accumulate all costs in the various stages of work in process.
4. Convert total costs at the end of the production process to unit or equivalent unit costs.
5. Transfer to finished goods inventory.

Inventory Valuation.   Each process accumulates costs. The ending costs for one process become the beginning costs for the next. Most firms use either average cost or FIFO costing when transferring inventory from one production process to the next.

Average costing uses costs of the inventory at the beginning of the period, then adds the costs during production. Determine unit costs simply by dividing total costs for the period by the number of units produced. Ending inventory transfers to the next process step as one cumulative number.

FIFO, on the other hand, separates beginning work-in-process inventory from those products started and finished in the same accounting period. FIFO first takes WIP at the beginning of the period and completes their production process.

Next FIFO begins and completes the process for items started in the current accounting period. It transfers these to the next step at a cost separate from those that included the beginning inventory.

A drawback of the FIFO method is that the next department averages out these inventory costs. This loses much of the value given by FIFO accounting.

Job Order Cost Systems

Businesses that manufacture custom-made products use a job order cost accounting system. Unlike a process system, job order cost attaches specific costs of production for *each* unit produced. Custom cabinet shops and custom home builders use job order cost systems. Additionally, certain service providers such as engineers, architects, and consultants use some of the job order techniques to track the specific costs in each project.

Job order costing works best when each product is unique and allows specific costs allocated to it.

Job Order by Lots.   Job order by lots assumes the company produces a line of identical products for a particular customer. Private-label manufacturers cost jobs for their customers by the lot. For example, a production run of shoes manufactured for a private-label retailer lends itself to job order costing.

As the job goes through the firm's production line, the cost system compares actual costs with those estimated when the contract was originally bid. The controller identifies variances and corrects them while there's still time. That's the real benefit of any cost accounting system—control.

Joint Product Costing

Often process manufacturers create several products from the same process. For example, a dairy processes raw milk. From this process come the joint products of whole milk, skim milk, low-fat, and buttermilk. However, these *joint products* all emanated from the original process. The cost system needs to allocate costs from the original process to the joint products.

The usual method is similar to the way we allocate some overhead items—by volume.

Figure 14-2 shows the joint costs shared by processing three of the dairy's joint products—whole milk, skim milk, and low-fat. This diagram shows allocation of the $180,000 for homogenizing to each joint product emanating from the original 100,000 gallons of raw milk. The allocation process isn't complicated. If you use a process cost system, the entry that records these costs is similar to that of every other production cost.

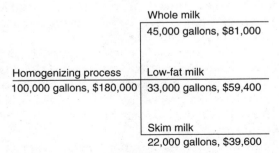

Figure 14-2. Allocating costs to joint products.

However, controllers often want to know *when* to record the joint product cost. The answer is, *at the split-off point*. This is the point at which joint products become separately identifiable from their originator.

Costing By-Products

Many manufacturing processes actually create a secondary product that has some value. We call these *by-products*. Take, for example, the production of applesauce. The process cores and seeds the apples. These by-products (cores and seeds) have several ready markets.

Some by-products sell in their original form. Others require additional work. Manufacturers of leather goods provide an example. They produce many by-products during the production process. These may include scraps and secondary items not meeting the firm's primary quality criteria. Each presents a cost allocation issue.

Most cost accountants use one of three methods to record the income from by-products.

1. Recognize by-product revenue in a separate category such as *other income.*
2. Deduct by-product revenue (less costs for any additional work) from costs of the main product.
3. Treat the by-product as if it were a normal production item and allocate all joint production costs.

Adding Accounts to the General Ledger

The controller identifies movement of inventory, labor, and indirect costs associated with the production process. Further, areas of responsibility receive cost accumulations. All these items go into specific general ledger accounts. Figure 14-3 shows the list of new accounts the G/L needs for the cost accounting system. Include an account for all the critical costs associated with the production area you want to track. We've identified most of the important ones in Figure 14-3—materials, labor, overhead, and maintenance. Be sure to include the others your company has.

Numbering the General Ledger

Adding cost centers quickly increases the number of accounts in a general ledger. When adding accounts for a cost system, first identify the method of reporting for each cost. Most companies associate particular costs with each item they manufacture. If that's your choice, create one main G/L account for each type of cost and add a suffix to identify the item manufactured. The account number looks like this:

XXX-XX

G/L Accounts Used by the Cost System

Raw materials inventory
Work-in-process inventory
Finished goods inventory
Labor:
    Direct labor
    Indirect labor
    Supervisory labor
    Idle labor
    Manufacturing overtime
Indirect materials
Spoilage expense
Supplies
Specific manufacturing department expenses
Overhead allocations to manufacturing costs:
    Depreciation of manufacturing machinery
    Supplies
    Utilities
    Supervisory costs
    Equipment repair
    Repair parts
    Repair labor
    Production department's share of general administrative expense

---

Figure 14-3. G/L accounts used by the cost system.

where the first three characters are the account number and the second two (the suffix) identify the cost center. Using this method, the accounting system reports in four ways:

- All the manufacturing costs for all products
- One manufacturing cost for all products
- All manufacturing costs for a particular product
- One manufacturing cost for particular product

For example, identify the following manufacturing costs:

Material	100
Labor	200
Overhead	300

Next, identify the products (cost centers) for which the accounting system accumulates these production costs. For example, assemblers of computer equipment might number their products like this:

Printer toner	10
Keyboard	20
Screen	30

Entries in the cost system to record labor for the keyboard go to account number 200-20.

Managing Cost Centers

Cost accounting systems assign responsibility for production costs to those in a position to control it. This requires separating costs between areas of responsibility. For example, many companies form cost centers for each distinct area of the manufacturing process. In the example used earlier, cost centers for the production process of the dairy may have included:

- Shipping
- Receiving
- Vat cleaning and sterilization department
- Homogenizing department
- Testing and quality control
- Container filling

Each cost center has its own suffix number attached to the G/L number. That allows identification of *all* costs associated with each cost center. The account number now looks like this:

XXX-XX-XXX

The first three characters identify the cost, the next two designate the product, and the last three show the cost center.

Continuing with the computer producer example, say we want to record costs of the shrink-wrapping used in the printer toner by the packing department (cost center 300). The entry goes to account 100-10-300.

Using this account numbering scheme, the cost system identifies and tracks each individual cost added by each production department to each product.

Integrating Cost with Other Accounting Systems

The cost accounting system sends and receives information to and from several accounting modules. Automated accounting systems do much of the information transfer electronically. Here are the accounting systems that trade data back and forth with the cost accounting system:

General Ledger.   The cost accounting system sends all inventory transfers and production costs to the G/L system. The more frequently the G/L receives and posts cost information, the more accurate the cost reporting at any point in time. That's the point of using a cost accounting system—providing up-to-date actual costs while there's still time during the month to fix any problems identified.

Accounts Payable.   The payables system records and allocates expenses from invoices to the cost accounting system. Invoice information moves from the A/P system to the various jobs, processes, or products for tracking by the cost system. Often these include not only raw materials purchased, but subassemblies and subcontractor fees as well.

Accounts Receivable.   Many firms that manufacture custom products on a fixed contract do progress billing. As the project moves along, the manufacturer bills its customer based on the portion completed. Often this includes time and materials, direct costs, allocation of indirect costs, and a percentage of the profit. The cost accounting system accumulates them all in work in process.

When billed, the cost system records these invoices against the products or projects in WIP. Then the amount billed transfers over to the A/R system for tracking and collection.

Inventory Control.   The cost accounting system transfers inventory throughout the production process. The entries move raw materials to work in process and into finished goods upon completion. These transactions flow directly into the inventory control system. Entries in the more sophisticated automated cost accounting systems automatically make their way to inventory control.

Purchasing.   Purchase orders often belong to specific projects tracked by the cost system. Many companies record both the receipt of goods and receipt of the vendor's invoice to the cost accounting system. This allocates the direct expenses to the job being controlled by the cost system.

Further, some companies record open purchase orders and trace them to particular jobs on the production floor. That way the cost system identifies the purchase commitments outstanding for any given production job.

Payroll.   The cost accounting system receives the labor expense allocation from payroll. Often the time and cost of one employee get allocated to several projects or products in process. This can often be a complex procedure. Nevertheless, the cost accounting system takes this information and distributes it among the various products manufactured.

Journal Entries

Cost accounting systems require up-to-date information to do their job. Without frequent recording of cost information, controllers don't know what it costs to produce their products. This makes for fuzzy profit margins.

The most frequently entered costs record:

- Raw material transferred into work-in-process inventory
- Direct labor added to WIP
- Overhead and indirect costs entered into WIP
- Finished goods inventory receiving transfer of completed WIP inventory

Here's how each of these entries appears on the general ledger:

Record transfer of raw material to WIP:

Work-in-process inventory	$3,000	
Raw material inventory		$3,000

Add direct labor to WIP:
Step 1: Record labor costs:

Direct labor expense	1,000	
Wages payable		1,000

Step 2: Transfer labor costs to WIP:

Work-in-process inventory	1,000	
Direct labor expense		1,000

Allocate indirect expense to WIP:
Step 1: Allocate overhead to the particular WIP inventory in question. Say the overhead item in question is the production shop's natural gas expense of $2000. Also say that the production item we're allocating accounts for 25 percent of total production. The allocation of electrical expense is $500 ($2000 × 25% = $500). Record the total gas expense:

Gas expense	$2,000	
Accounts payable		$2,000

Step 2: Transfer gas costs to WIP:

Work-in-process inventory:	$500	
Natural gas expense		$500

Transfer completed production items from WIP to finished goods inventory:

Finished goods inventory	$4,500	
Work-in-process inventory		$4,500

The WIP account accumulated production costs throughout the manufacturing process. Upon completion, the item included these costs:

Raw materials	$3,000
Direct labor	1,000
Electricity allocation	500
Total costs transferred	$4,500

The entries illustrate the theory supporting most cost accounting transactions. Allocations of indirect costs, joint costs, identification of split-off points, by-products, and layering of FIFO costs make some more complicated. However, every entry comes down to recording the debits and credits shown above.

Recording Cost Information

The cost accounting system records production costs for each unit or batch of units on the production line. Most cost systems accomplish this using a detailed cost record. This record identifies everything that's put into the goods produced. Most detailed cost records are preprinted sheets showing all the materials and labor that *should* go into the product. As the manufacturing process progresses, enter all costs associated with production of each particular item on the detailed cost record.

From the detailed cost record, account for all the costs via journal entry. These accumulate in work-in-process inventory.

Detailed Cost Record. The best detailed cost records show all the costs and the general ledger account numbers to which they're posted. They make transfer of cost data as simple as possible. Often cost information comes in units, pounds, or hours worked—not in dollars. Therefore, the detailed cost record translates them into dollars. It does this by extending the various units of measure by their unit costs. Figure 14-4 shows a sample detailed cost record.

Note the *raw materials* all contain the same general ledger account number. This makes it easy to remove them from raw materials inventory and transfer them to WIP for this product.

Additionally, notice that all the G/L account numbers end with the suffix 45. That designates the particular inventory item—the plastic-fruit lug #5786. Using

Dubonet Baskets, Inc.
Cost Record Detail

Product: Plastic-fruit lug #5786

Cost description	G/L acct. no.	Units	No. of units	Cost per unit	Extension	Date entered	Person
Polypropylene	100-45	lbs.	3	$ .25	$ .75	4-6-9X	RJ
Plastic handles	100-45	ea.	2	1.50	3.00	4-7-9X	BS
Metal feet	100-45	ea.	4	.25	.25	4-7-9X	CR
Direct labor	200-45	hour	1	15.00	15.00	4-8-9X	JB
Indirect labor	300-45	hour	.25	20.00	4.00	4-8-9X	SC
Screw assembly machine	400-45	hour	.25	10.00	2.50	4-9-9X	MC
Overhead allocation	500-45	units	2	$10.00	$20.00	4-9-9X	CR
Total cost					$45.50		

Figure 14-4. Detailed cost record.

such a G/L suffix designation, controllers identify all the costs associated with an item throughout its manufacturing process.

Summarizing the Detailed Cost Record. Most production businesses have detailed cost records accompanying each job or production run as they make their way through the manufacturing process. People on the production floor record the items added to each cost record. Then the cost accounting department periodically extends the costs, summarizes the changes, and prepares the journal entry for the general ledger.

Some companies summarize the detailed cost records once a month—usually at the end to record inventory and cost changes that occurred since the last financial reporting period. Others do it at the end of each production run or when an item has completed its manufacturing process. The more often the cost system receives updated information, the more help it provides in controlling production costs.

Summarizing production costs from the detailed cost record accomplishes two things:

- Provides a journal entry form for recording cost changes in the general ledger
- Provides a comparative report for tracking actual costs against standard costs

Figure 14-5 shows a sample cost summary record. Each product has its own detailed cost records. Using this summary record you can use the journal entry to record production costs into WIP inventory. Additionally, the cost record maintains a tally of actual production costs compared to standard costs. The difference—a negative cost variance in Figure 14-5—shows up on the summary as well. If management has enough advance warning, it can take action to correct production problems. *That's* the value of maintaining a cost accounting system.

Dubonet Baskets, Inc.
Summary Cost Record

Product: Plastic-fruit lug #5786

Description	G/L acct. no.	Debit	Credit	Standard costs	Variance
Polypropylene	100-45		$ .75	$ .80	$ .05
Plastic handles	100-45		3.00	3.10	.10
Metal feet	100-45		.25	.20	−.05
Direct labor	200-45		15.00	13.00	−2.00
Indirect labor	300-45		4.00	5.00	1.00
Screw assembly machine	400-45		2.50	2.50	—
Overhead allocation	500-45		20.00	20.00	—
Work-in-process inventory	150-45	$45.50			
Total entry		$45.50	$45.50	$44.60	−$ .90

Figure 14-5. Summary cost record.

Costing Payroll Expenses

Production payroll includes three labor categories:

- Direct manufacturing labor
- Indirect labor (production supervision)
- Overhead (allocation of executive salaries)

Companies disburse payroll on a fixed salary, by the hour, or by the unit produced (piece work). The payroll system records payroll expense. Then the cost accounting department allocates production labor expense from salary and wage expense to cost of goods sold.

Recording Labor Costs

The payroll system treats all salaries and wages the same regardless of use by the production operation. At the payroll level there's no allocation to production labor. The cost accounting department does that. Figure 14-6 shows the flow of labor cost information.

Allocating Indirect Labor and Overhead

Allocate indirect labor and overhead salaries just like any other overhead cost. We can't allocate the production supervisor's salary to any particular item manufactured. All items benefit from this person's involvement. Therefore, many firms just allocate that salary pro rata among the items produced. Many firms base the allocation on percentage of total production for each item manufactured. Regardless of the allocation method, make sure it's consistently applied.

Vacation time for production personnel is an overhead expense too. It still gets allocated to work in process as one of the normal costs associated with production.

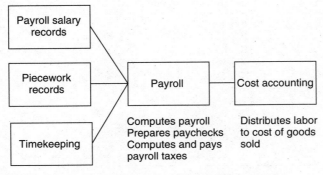

Figure 14-6. Capture and distribution of labor costs.

Identifying Standard Costs

Standard costs provide a benchmark for what each item *should* cost to produce. We use standard costs to control profit margins. Once we know the cost of planned finished goods inventory, the cost accounting system compares it with the actual costs as in Figure 14-5. We use standard costs for:

- Reporting cost of goods sold
- Cost control
- Budgeting
- Establishing sales prices and formulating bids
- Assigning standard costs to raw material, work in process, and finished goods inventory

Many companies perform time-and-motion studies to determine labor production standards. Along with this information they include the exact amount of raw materials and subassemblies for each item. Results from standard cost studies go to a document similar to the detailed cost record shown in Figure 14-5.

Standard costing works best in companies that manufacture similar items using a stable production technology. Standard costs are less useful in more rapidly changing environments where each item made is unique.

Establishing Standard Costs

As a company's cost accounting system becomes more useful, the effort expended gathering accurate standard costs increases. Determination of standard costs requires nothing more than common sense. Here are the steps most firms take to approximate their standard costs for one item of production:

1. List all the raw materials that go into *one* unit.

2. List all the subassemblies that go into *one* unit.

3. List the amount of labor time that goes into each unit. Frequently labor rates change between production stages. When they do, separate each stage having a different rate.

4. List all the shop machinery and equipment used in the production of each unit. Separate the time for each machine used in the production process into *machinery usage hours.*

5. Assign a cost to each of the preceding steps and extend by the number of units, labor hours, and machinery usage hours (or fractions).

6. Determine the overhead costs associated with manufacturing but not assigned to any particular production item. Assign a proportionate percentage for overhead allocation. Many companies simply use the proportion of the product being costed to the whole. For example, if item A usually comprises 20 percent

of total production, allocate 20 percent of the manufacturing overhead. If that normally amounts to $6000 and production for item A was 10,000 units, then allocate $.60 for standard overhead to each unit of item A produced.

7. Add up all the standard costs. The sum equals the standard cost to produce one item.

Tracking Variances

Many companies rely on their standard costs to compute cost of goods sold. They track actual costs and compare them with the standards. The cost system adjusts cost of goods sold to account for variances from standard costs in the materials, labor, machinery, and overhead used in the production process. The entries to record these variances are:

Cost of goods sold	X	
Materials price variance		X
Materials usage variance		X
Machine usage variance		X
Machine rate variance		X
Labor price variance		X
Labor usage variance		X
Overhead		X

Comparison of standard costs with actuals quickly identifies production problems. Notice these entries treat all variances as negative (a debit to cost of goods sold *increases* production costs). However, they just as easily could have gone the other way (credited CGS and debited the variance account), thus showing a favorable variance.

Allocating Overhead

Production department heads bristle at overhead allocations. They often see this expense as an unwanted intrusion. Allocating part of the costs for this intrusion just adds insult to injury.

Nevertheless, most cost accounting systems allocate overhead associated with nonproducing entities (such as finance or the accounting department) to the manufacturing area. From a cash flow standpoint, this allocation simply transfers funds from one pocket to another. Still, it does affect the profit of a division receiving, say, an allocated share of the corporate executive's salaries.

Allocate indirect costs and overhead using the same pro rata formula identified earlier. Some of the overhead items commonly allocated include:

- Employee overhead such as health insurance
- Rent

- Power
- Repairs
- Purchasing department
- Utilities
- Executive and officer salaries
- Warehouse operations

Making Cost
Information Profitable

Cost accounting information becomes valuable when it's used in identifying production problems. Use the variance reports that track actual costs with standard or planned costs. Companies that maintain up-to-date work-in-process records at various stages throughout the production process correct manufacturing problems while there's still time.

For example, say the quality control declines at the manufacturer of a subassembly. This causes rework or negative material usage variances for customers using the subassembly in *their* manufacturing operations. The cost accounting system catches these types of problems in their cost variance reports.

Many businesses capture and compute cost data at various stages of the production process. Often these correspond to:

- Split-off point for joint products and by-products
- Breaks in the type of labor used
- Critical inspection points
- Changeover to a different production line or machine

Regardless of where you accumulate production costs, be sure to review them at various stages of the process.

Cost-Volume-Profit Analysis

How much do we need to sell in order to break even? The cost accounting system answers this question. Three basic computations that provide the solution include:

- Contribution margin
- Breakeven point in units and dollars
- Sales to achieve a targeted profit

Contribution Margin.   Contribution margin computes the portion of sales that *contributes* to the coverage of fixed costs and profits. We measure contribution margin either in units sold or in sales dollar revenues. We express contribution margin as a percentage. Here's the equation:

$$\text{Contribution margin} = \frac{\text{total sales} - \text{total variable costs}}{\text{total sales}}$$

Say that Maggie Corporation sells each dog leash it makes for $10.00. Variable costs for each unit of production are $4.25. Contribution margin for each unit is 58 percent ($10.00 − $4.25)/$10.00 = 58%). Therefore, each leash sold at $10 contributes $5.80 to fixed costs and profits.

Breakeven Point.   With the contribution margin already computed, we're ready to calculate the breakeven point. Again, compute breakeven either in units sold or in sales revenue. Use this equation:

$$\text{Breakeven} = \frac{\text{fixed costs}}{\text{contribution margin}}$$

Figure 14-7 shows the breakeven point in a graph. The horizontal line shows Maggie's fixed costs. The line running through it is the unit sales. For Maggie Corporation, the breakeven point of 3478 units assumes fixed costs of $20,000 per month. We computed this as:

$$\text{Breakeven} = \$20,000 \ / \ (\$10.00 - \$4.25)$$

$$\text{Breakeven} = 3,478 \text{ units sold}$$

We can also compute the *revenue* breakeven using the contribution margin percentage:

$$\text{Breakeven} = \$20,000 \ / \ [(\$10.00 - \$4.25) \ / \ \$10.00]$$

$$\text{Breakeven} = \$34,783$$

Prove the answer by multiplying the breakeven units sold by the sales price:

$$3,478 \times \$10.00 = \$34,783$$

The result is the breakeven sales revenue.

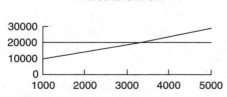

Figure 14-7. Breakeven point.

Sales to Achieve Specific Profit Levels. If you're after a particular profit level over the fixed costs to count as your breakeven point, simply add the desired profit to the numerator. Say Maggie wants a $5000 profit *over* fixed costs. Find the level of sales revenue that earns that profit:

Required sales revenue = ($20,000 + $5,000) / [($10.00 − $4.25) / $10.00]

Required sales revenue = $43,478

15
Tax Preparation, Management, and Planning

Overview

Chapter 15 does something far more important than teach you how to prepare a tax return. It demonstrates the best techniques to minimize the business' tax liability and that of its owners as well.

Additionally, Chapter 15 identifies the information required to prepare a business tax return. Some business structures provide a better vehicle to limit tax liabilities than others. This chapter describes the tax obligations under the various types of business structures.

Compliance with Tax Laws

Treasurers and controllers assume the responsibility of keeping their companies out of tax trouble. Most large companies have complicated tax issues. They maintain a staff of professionals whose job it is to ensure the firm's compliance with current tax law and to prepare its returns.

Alternatively, many companies hire their CPA firms to prepare their tax returns. There is a natural flow of information from the CPA's compilation or audit of the firm's financial statements to its tax return. In most cases the numbers come directly from the firm's income statement and balance sheet.

Issues of taxation most often arise from nonroutine transactions the company has during the year. Some of these include:

- Acquisition of another firm
- Issue of discount bonds

- Purchase of investment securities

- Recognition of foreign exchange losses

- Recognition of commodities gains and losses resulting from hedging operations

- Change in accounting principles for tax purposes

- Establishing defined employee benefit plans

- Discharge of indebtedness

- Energy credits

- Liquidation distributions

Filing Dates

Missed filing dates can get controllers into trouble quickly. Unlike the tax returns of individuals, due on April 15 or the 15th day of the fourth month following the close of the fiscal year, corporations have less time. The deadline for corporate tax returns is March 15 for calendar-year corporations. For corporations on a fiscal year, it's the 15th day of the third month following the close of the fiscal year.

Partnerships.   The tax year of a partnership takes on the same tax year as the majority of its partners. Most of these follow the calendar year. However, if a partnership's majority partner was a corporation whose fiscal year was not the calendar year, the partnership could have the same tax year as the corporate partner.

Partnerships have until April 15 or the 15th day following the fourth month after the close of their fiscal year to file their tax returns. Be aware, however, the partners must also file their personal tax returns. Therefore, the partnership must provide the Forms K-1 to their partner's in sufficient time for the individuals to file. Preparation of the K-1's usually requires closing the partnership's books. That completed, there's no reason why the firm can't file its own tax return on time.

Extensions.   Sometimes companies require additional time to file their tax returns. Corporations get an automatic extension of three months simply by filing the proper form. However, they also have to properly file their estimated tax. Additionally, the Secretary of Internal Revenue may grant an extension of no more than six months for sufficient reason as documented by the corporation.

Estimated Tax Payments.   Estimated tax payments are a big deal. Corporations estimating a tax liability greater than $500 for the year must pay four quarterly estimated tax installments. Failure of estimated payments to equal the statutory minimum results in penalties and interest.

For calendar-year corporate taxpayers, the IRS requires estimated payments due on:

- April 15
- June 15
- September 15
- December 15

Each installment must equal 25 percent of the lesser of:

- 90 percent of the current year's tax liability
- 100 percent of the prior year's tax liability

However, large corporations (defined as having taxable income of $1 million or more) cannot use the prior year's tax liability in their estimates.

Estimating S-Corporation Tax Payments.   S-corporations don't pay income taxes. However, they must still estimate and pay:

- Net passive income tax
- Built-in gains tax
- Capital gains tax
- Investment recapture tax

Underpayment results in a penalty equal to the amount of the underpayment added to the overall tax liability.

Information Required
to Prepare a Tax Return

The tax return requires identification of the various categories of income and expense. It also wants to know what tax payments the firm made during the year. Generally, this requires nothing more sophisticated than the year-end balance sheet and income statements of the company.

Computing Total Income

The first part of a corporate tax return computes total income. It not only requires the numbers, but your accounting system should substantiate the following income items:

- Gross receipts
- Less returns and allowances
- Less cost of goods sold (be prepared to compute CGS on Schedule A of Form 1120)
- Plus dividends

- Plus interest, rents, and royalties
- Plus capital gains (be prepared to identify each transaction including purchase date and cost as well as sale date and price)
- Plus any other income flowing into the company

Total income appearing on the tax return must reconcile to the year-end income statement produced by the accounting system.

Computing Deductions

Deductions come from the expense section of the income statement. Form 1120 lists 18 different expenses legitimately deductible by businesses. Make sure your accounting system provides at least these expense items:

- Compensation of officers (making sure to include officers' social security numbers, percent of their time devoted to the business, percent of the company's common stock each owns, and the total compensation paid to each by the company)
- Salaries and wages of employees
- Repairs and maintenance expense
- Bad debts
- Rent
- Taxes paid (not income tax, but property taxes and others)
- Interest
- Charitable contributions
- Depreciation and amortization
- Advertising expense
- Pension and profit-sharing plans
- Employee benefits
- Any other deductions in the normal course of business (be prepared to supply a schedule showing these items)

The total expenses must reconcile to the expense items shown on the corporation's year-end income statement.

Computing Tax and Payments

Compute total tax using the income and expense information already generated. From this, subtract:

- Estimated tax payments made during the year
- Any refunds from prior years applied to this year

- Any taxes already deposited by estimated payments or other means
- Any tax credits due the company from such things as fuels or regulated investment companies

Structuring the Company

Structure refers to the type of business entity your company uses. The most common forms include:

- Proprietorship
- Partnership
- C-corporation
- S-corporation
- Personal holding company

Proprietorship

This form of business interest restricts ownership to a single individual. Proprietorships do not file tax returns. Instead, all profits and losses flow directly to the owner's individual tax return (Schedule C, Form 1040). Tax liability for the business (including self-employment tax) is paid on April 15 along with the individual's personal return. Estimated tax payments come from the individual's own income tax obligations.

Profits flow from proprietorships as earned income. It doesn't matter that the money remained in the company rather than going to the owner. Such deferral techniques don't disguise earnings since the business' revenue posts to the individual's tax return anyway. Essentially, the IRS does not distinguish between the company's money and that of its owner. Further, the IRS considers any benefits the owner accrues from the business for personal purposes as taxable income.

Tax Benefits of a Proprietorship.   Many small businesses incur losses during the first year of start-up. These losses flow directly to the owner. From a tax planning standpoint, this is a big advantage proprietorships enjoy over corporations. Owners with business income from other sources to offset the proprietorship's losses effectively shelter income.

Along with losses, profits also flow to the owner. This eliminates the double taxation on dividends paid to shareholders of corporate stock. Rather than tax the company's earnings first at the corporate level as income to the corporation and then to the individual as dividends, a proprietorship's income gets taxed only once.

Disadvantages of a Proprietorship.   Proprietors personally bear 100 percent of the business' liabilities. Those with substantial net worth risk it all by forming a proprietorship. Financing can also be a problem. Few banks loan to proprietorships without the personal guarantee of the owner as well.

Many firms use the carrot of ownership as an incentive for their employees. That's not possible with a proprietorship. The entity would have to reorganize itself under a different structure to admit additional owners. Finally, there's no continuity to the business. Its existence depends on the longevity of the owner. It ceases to exist upon death of the owner. The firm's assets flow to the owner's estate.

Partnerships

Partnerships comprise one of the most popular business structures. All it takes to start a general partnership is a partnership agreement and a fictitious name filing. Some states have particular filing requirements for limited partnerships. This makes LPs only slightly more complicated. Firms failing to comply with their state's filing requirements risk counting all their partners as general partners. Further, the *actions* of limited partners themselves can sometimes make them appear as general partners.

Tax Advantages of a Partnership.   Unlike proprietorships, partnerships file tax returns (federal income tax form 1065). However, since partnerships pay no taxes, they file the returns for information purposes. The profits and losses flow through the firm to the partners (on federal tax form K-1). From there, the individual partners report their share of the firm's profits or losses on their own tax returns.

Partners must characterize the *type* of profits or losses flowing to them from the partnership entity. Under certain circumstances, this flow-through of profits and losses can create a tax advantage, depending on the partner's individual circumstances.

General partners bear joint and several liability for the partnership's losses. This satisfies the IRS' *at risk* requirement. It also allows general partners to treat their share of partnership operating profits and losses (not interest income or losses from real estate operations) as earned income. For firms just starting out with losses in the early years, this creates an income shelter for general partners having other sources of ordinary income.

The IRS treats limited partners differently. The profits and losses flowing from the firm to limited partners is *passive*. That's because the limiteds don't play an active role in management of the company as do the general partners. However, they don't have the unlimited exposure either.

Limited partnership interests shelter the LP's other passive gains *only to the extent they provide offsetting passive losses*. For those LPs in this tax situation, such an investment might make sense—especially if there's a good chance for the LP interest to generate future positive cash flow.

Tax Disadvantages of a Partnership.   Partners can't deduct losses greater than their ownership in the firm. Tax law restricts deductibility of the loss to that partner's *basis* in the firm. Further, all partners must characterize the losses flowing to them from the firm. The general partners may deduct only certain losses as ordinary income, depending on their character.

Limited partners may deduct the losses flowing to them from their interest in the partnership *only to the extent they have passive income to offset it.* Absent offsetting passive income, the partner cannot deduct the loss. Instead it waits, suspended, until eventual disposition of the partnership interest.

This restriction substantially limits any tax advantages limited partnerships used to have. As the partnership incurs losses, the capital account (and therefore the basis) of each partner decreases. This creates a larger capital gain when the partner sells the interest.

Dual-Capacity Partners.   Some partners own both a general and a limited partnership interest in their firms. We call this individual a *dual-capacity* partner. The IRS treats these two different interests owned by the same individual as a *single unified interest.* They combine the interests in order to determine basis for allocation of the firm's profits and losses. If the distribution by the firm to the dual-capacity partner exceeds basis of the aggregate unified interest, the difference counts as a capital gain.

This rule allows dual-capacity partners to present a larger basis to the IRS when counting partnership distributions as a nontaxable return of capital.

Shielding the Partnership's Decision Maker.   There's a way to limit the joint and several liability of a general partner. Take the following three steps:

1. Create a corporation with few assets, one of which is its nominal general partnership interest in the limited partnership. The *corporation* acts as the partnership's general partner.

2. The person who actually runs the partnership either owns the general partner corporation or works for it. Additionally, this person may own a *limited* partnership interest in the firm. That way they benefit from the fruits of their labor without incurring the unlimited liability of a general partner.

3. This person makes all partnership decisions on behalf of the general partner corporation. Documents requiring signature bear the name of the person with authority of the general partnership corporation to act on its behalf as the general partner of the limited partnership.

This may sound complicated. However, maintaining the limited liability of a substitute general partner requires strict adherence to the policy of having the GP corporation make all decisions.

Basis of Partnership Interest.   Capital contributions create the basis of each partner's interest in the firm. Cash contributions take on the basis of the amount of money contributed. There's never any question of a partner's basis when contributing cash. However, a partner's interest resulting from contributed property takes on the basis of the property *in the partner's hands* at the time of contribution.

This sometimes confuses people. Basis or amount of a capital contribution and the percentage of the partnership it buys often differs from the partner's profit/loss participation percentage. The partnership agreement identifies the profit participation percentage. That way a partner who contributed land with a basis of $100,000 but a fair market value of $200,000 has a basis in the partnership of only $100,000. Another partner who contributed $200,000 cash has a basis of $200,000. However, their *profit participation* still remains as specified in the partnership agreement—probably 50/50. This makes sense since both partners contributed needed capital equivalent in value.

Over time the partner's basis changes with the profits and losses of the firm. The partners receive an allocation according to their profit participation percentage stipulated in the partnership agreement.

Distributions made by the firm to its partners reduce basis. There's no tax liability since it's actually a return of capital—the partner's own money originally contributed. However, once a partner's basis drops to zero (never below), further distributions become capital gains.

Conversely, undistributed profits of the firm *increase* the partner's basis. This gives the partner a larger amount to count as return of capital once the firm distributes its profits to the partners.

Exchanging and Transferring Partnership Interests.   Say a general partner wishes limited exposure to the firm's liabilities. One solution is to exchange the general partnership interest for a limited interest. Conversely, a limited partner may decide it's time to exert more control over the firm even though it increases exposure to the firm's liabilities. That requires converting the limited partnership interest to a general partnership interest.

The IRS is ambiguous on whether such exchanges represent taxable transactions. In the simplest form of exchange:

- Profit/loss participation remains the same.
- Each partner's percentage of interest in the firm remains unchanged.
- Capital remains unchanged.

Such simple exchanges don't generally give rise to a taxable event. However, if any or all of these things change, the partner likely sold one interest and purchased another. Such a transaction could trigger a capital gain.

Some analysts try invoking Section 1031 of the Internal Revenue Code for tax-deferred exchanges of like-kind property when exchanging partnership interests. Forget it. Section 1031(a)(2)(D) specifically *excludes* partnership interests from tax-deferred exchanges.

A change in obligation for the firm's liabilities can further complicate an exchange of partnership interests. Often such a change results when a general partner swaps a general interest for a limited interest. Partners who increase or decrease their pro rata responsibility for the firm's liabilities also change their basis. For example, if the exchange reduced a partner's responsibility for the firm's liabilities and the reduction exceeds the partner's basis, a taxable gain may result.

Terminating a Partnership.   Many people confuse any disturbance in the members of a partnership with dissolution of the entity. The death or withdrawal of a partner, or the sale of an interest, or additions of partners *by themselves* does not terminate a partnership. Partnership agreements usually stipulate a termination date. Alternatively, the partners may elect to dissolve and wind up the business of the partnership. Regardless of method, once terminated, the partnership's tax year closes and it has 3½ months to file its tax return.

Death of a partner does not terminate a partnership. Instead, the deceased's estate stands in the former partner's place as the successor in interest. In that capacity the estate shares in the firm's profits and losses as the deceased partner would have.

Figure 15-1 shows a list of the things you should watch for when assessing the impact of terminating a partnership.

Family Partnerships.   If you run a family partnership, be aware that the IRS looks at this form of ownership closely. In the past, family partnerships transferred income from one family member in a high tax bracket to another family member with a lower tax rate—say, from parents to children. The intent was to abuse the tax law.

---

1. If the owners collapsed the old partnership, then all of its tax elections collapsed as well. They don't transfer to any new entity the partners might form. Each election needs to be refiled with the IRS.

2. The terminated partnership does not recognize a gain or loss. Instead it flows to the individual partners.

3. If the same partners formed a new partnership such that it appears the old one actually continues, the law may view the partnership as ongoing.

4. If the terminated partnership owned installment obligations receivable, distribute them pro rata to the partners. Alternatively, place them in a liquidation trust with the proceeds distributed to the partners pro rata. The IRS may construe failure to distribute notes receivable as a sale of the note.

5. Each partner's capital account should record the change in liabilities on termination of the firm.

Figure 15-1. Partnership termination checklist.

Under the tax code, income is taxed to the person who earned it through his or her own labor, skill, or capital regardless of any legal partnership interest. The law now provides for tracing income from a partnership whose interest transferred among family members through purchase, sale, or gift. Where capital is a substantial income-producing factor, the *donor* partner must include in his or her gross income the distributive share of the partnership's income up to the date of transfer.

Additionally, the IRS has deemed even the outward sale of a partnership interest among family members a gift. The IRS considers fair market value of the transferred interest *donated capital*.

If you're considering a sale or gift of a family partnership interest, make sure the IRS considers it a bona fide transaction. You want the IRS to recognize the new partners. Follow these three rules:

1. The donor must relinquish *all* control and ownership benefits of the interest. In other words, a father could not transfer the partnership interest to his three-year-old son's trust of which the father is trustee. The father in this case still retains control of the partnership interest.

2. The elements of an arm's-length transaction must exist both before and after completion of the transaction. The parties must be independent and act for their own interests. Money or other valuable consideration must exchange between the parties. The parties must exhibit capacity to transact the sale.

3. The transaction must vest complete control of the partnership interest to the donee.

Types of Partnership Interests.   The two most common partnership interests are:

- Capital interest
- Profit interest

A capital interest holds the full status of a partner. The holder participates in the profits and losses of the firm as well as its liabilities. The partner's capital account changes according to the firm's profits and losses.

A profit interest differs in that the holder has unlimited upside profit potential with no downside risk. Holders of profit interests don't participate in making good the firm's liabilities. Often partnerships pay profit interests instead of a salary.

However, the tax law requires recognition of income at the time a profit interest is granted as compensation—*not at the time of payment*. Therefore, the taxpayer may face the worst of all possibilities—owing taxes on money not yet received.

Alternatively, some astute partnerships carefully structure the commitment of an interest in the firm's future profits to avoid taxation at time of grant. To avoid this recognition problem, they establish an *unfunded account payable* rather than a profit interest. This forgoes the payee's recognition of the income until payment. It also forces both parties to stipulate a fair market value for the services rendered.

Put this in writing and make sure the value is reasonable in relation to the services performed.

Do not create a contract that in any way parallels that of a profit interest agreement for services rendered. Even though the partnership established a payable based on the future profit performance of the firm, the IRS could interpret such a contract as a profit interest. They then tax the individual and disallow the expense on the partnership's books at the time of granting.

C-Corporations

The Internal Revenue Code identifies corporations by the different subchapters describing them. It defines regular stock corporations in subchapter C. C-corporations protect investors from the unlimited liability accompanying proprietorships and general partnerships.

Owners of closely held corporations enjoy full control over the firms' operations and a shield from unlimited liability. Income of shareholders in closely held corporations derives from four sources:

- Salary and wages
- Bonuses
- Directors' fees
- Dividends paid to stockholders

Tax Advantages of C-Corporations.   Owners of C-corporations enjoy few tax advantages. Limited liability of the shareholders provides the major enticement. However, C-corporations can and do establish employee benefits such as:

- Group life insurance plans
- Group health plans
- Pension and profit-sharing plans
- Employee stock purchase plans
- 401(K) plans

This allows management to spread some of the firm's profits among those who made it happen without incurring large tax liabilities. The beneficiaries avoid taxation until distribution and the corporation enjoys a deduction for their contribution to defined plans.

Corporations may also have a fiscal year different from the calendar year. From a tax-planning standpoint this could help the firm and its investors defer dividends to a more advantageous time period.

Corporations also enjoy the dividends-received deduction on stock they hold for investment in *other* taxable corporations. Sections 243 through 246 of the Internal Revenue Code limit the amount of double taxation one corporation must pay on the dividends it receives from other corporations. If this were not the case, the shareholder *individuals* eventually receiving dividends from their company would pay *triple* taxes on the earnings of the original corporation whose stock their company owned.

The dividends-received deduction varies depending on the amount of a corporation's stock another corporation holds. Figure 15-2 shows how Section 243(a) of the IRC identifies these percentages.

There's another restriction. The IRC limits the amount of the total dividends-received deduction to the same percentage of the dividend deductible multiplied by the recipient's taxable income. For example, say MTH Corp. owned 15 percent of the common stock outstanding of TDO Excavators, Inc. MTH received a $70,000 dividend from TDO. TDO had taxable income of only $50,000. The amount of dividend MTH may *potentially* deduct is $49,000 ($70,000 × 70% = $49,000). However, the amount *actually* deductible is less because it's limited to the statutory percentage of taxable income. In this case the dividends-received deduction actually allowed is only $35,000 ($50,000 × 70% = $35,000).

Tax Disadvantages of C-Corporations.   Shareholders of corporate stock suffer double taxation of dividends paid them. Think of the shareholders as owners of the company. The firm's earnings belong to them as well. However, the company pays taxes on its earnings—just like any other taxpayer. When the corporation pays dividends, its shareholders pay personal income tax on the proceeds. That's taxation twice: once at the corporate level and again at the personal income tax level.

If a few shareholders own a small, closely held incorporated business, they should not elect to take most of their earnings in the form of dividends—especially if they work for the company as employees. It's better to take their income as salaries, bonus, and benefits. Then pay out the remaining earnings not needed for ongoing operations in the form of dividends.

Accumulated Earnings Tax.   Failure to pay out dividends exposes corporations to the *accumulated earnings tax*. Some corporations attempt to limit the tax liability of their shareholders simply by failing to distribute earnings. Instead, retained earnings simply builds and builds. The IRS wants the tax money from

Percent of common stock owned	Percent of dividend deductible
Less than 20%	70%
Between 20 and 80%	80%
More than 80%	100%
If the corporation is classified as a small business investment company	100%

Figure 15-2. Dividends-received deduction for corporate shareholders (Section 243(a) of IRC).

dividends paid to the individual shareholders. They won't allow the corporation to accumulate retained earnings beyond "the reasonable needs of the business." To prevent this, Congress enacted the accumulated earnings tax.

Reasonable needs is the operable expression in avoiding accumulated earnings tax. Instances that attract IRS attention and suggest possible accumulated earnings violations include:

1. The corporation has a high current ratio.

2. High-net-worth individuals hold the corporation's stock.

3. The corporation made no attempt to avoid application of the accumulated earnings tax.

4. No projects such as joint ventures or plans for new businesses appear to justify accumulation of the excess earnings.

5. The corporation has no debt.

6. Current operations provide the firm's working-capital needs without requiring excess accumulation of retained earnings.

7. No definition of the firm's "reasonable needs" for retained earnings exists.

8. The corporation made loans to officers, shareholders, and companies owned by shareholders.

The IRS levies accumulated earnings tax in the form of a penalty. The rate of accumulated earnings tax is a flat percentage for all corporations on the amount judged as accumulated excess earnings. Wait—it gets worse. The tax code provides *negligence penalties* for failure to pay. This amounts to a significant percentage of the accumulated excess earnings. Then, of course, there's interest due on the taxes owed that accumulate from the date the corporation's tax was originally due (without regard to extensions). Corporations caught in this web could pay out 50 percent and more of their excess accumulated earnings in taxes, penalties, and interest.

S-Corporations

S-corporations provide the benefits of corporate ownership along with the tax advantages of a partnership. S-corporations file tax returns (federal form 1120S). However, unlike a C-corporation, they don't pay taxes. Instead the firm's profits and losses flow through to the shareholders pro rata according to the number of shares owned—similar to that of a partnership.

Tax Advantages of S-Corporations.   Advantages of S-corporations parallel those of a partnership. The income from the corporation transfers its character to the shareholders. Categories of the character for S-corporation income items include:

- Ordinary income from the business' activities
- Net income from real estate activities
- Net income from rental activities
- Investment portfolio income
- Interest
- Dividends
- Capital gains
- Net gain or loss from Section 1231 assets
- Other types of income

This all flows to the individual shareholder's tax return. It retains the character it had at the corporate level.

Another advantage of S-corporations is the lack of excess accumulated earnings tax. By law, S-corporation shareholders recognize all the company's profits anyway. The fact that the firm may not actually distribute the income to its shareholders makes no difference.

Personal Holding Companies

Personal holding companies (PHCs) happen by default. They come as an unwelcome surprise. The laws governing PHCs limit the use of companies to hide passive income of the shareholders from taxation. Since 1934 the United States has had a special tax on undistributed personal holding company income.

The law defines PHCs using two general criteria:

- If 60 percent of the firm's income includes things such as royalties, income from the performance of personal services, rents, and investment income
- If five or fewer individuals own at least 50 percent of the stock

The tax on PHCs works in a manner similar to the accumulated earnings tax on corporations. The IRS defines PHC undistributed income as the company's:

- Taxable income
- Less its federal income tax liability
- Less the amount of dividends distributed

The tax rate to the shareholders is their personal rate. Further, they're subject to the same stiff penalty and interest rules as accumulated earnings tax.

Since the law requires distribution of all PHC income to its shareholders, there's really no tax advantage to owning one. However, there may be some benefit to limiting the individual's liability. Employees of a PHC may have less exposure to liability if the firm's clients hire the corporation rather than the individuals themselves.

Corporate Stock

Often corporate executives ask controllers and treasurers about the tax implications of their personal stock transactions. Corporate stock is a capital asset in the hands of its shareholders. As with all capital transactions, stock sale is subject to capital gain and loss treatment. Dividends paid shareholders generally come from earnings and profits of the current year. Form 1099-DIV goes to the shareholders receiving dividends. This form contains both dividends and distributed funds deemed *return of capital.* There's a big difference between the tax treatment of dividends and return of capital.

Dividends

Dividends count as ordinary income to the individual shareholders. They pay taxes on dividend income just as they do on earnings from their jobs.

Return of Capital

When corporations declare a distribution during years when they had no earnings, it's called a return of capital, not a dividend. The distinction is important. Return of capital returns the shareholder's own money back—*it's not taxable.* Companies often pay out dividends that exceed their earnings to maintain a flawless dividend record despite an absence of earnings for a given year. They won't let a little red ink spoil that record and possibly lower the market price of the stock.

Return of capital carries no immediate tax consequences. However, it does lower the shareholder's *basis* in the stock. On sale, the profit is larger and so is the tax liability for the resulting capital gain. This is the IRS' way of saying, *"Pay me now or pay me later—but you will pay."*

Sometimes corporations continue paying out dividends classified as returns of capital until the shareholder's basis reaches zero. Essentially, the shareholder receives more from the stock than the amount originally paid. The IRS treats distributions beyond a zero basis in the stock as capital gains.

Stock Dividends

Some companies pay dividends to their shareholders in stock rather than in cash. The IRS doesn't currently tax stock dividends until sale of the stock. However, stock dividends dilute the basis in the original stock held. Allocate the basis proportionately to the newly issued stock received as a dividend. Therefore, the overall basis for the entire stock position remains unchanged; only the basis in each individual share gets reduced.

For some individuals—those concerned about matching long-term and short-term gains and losses, for instance—keeping track of the long- or short-term nature of their stock holdings is important. Follow these four rules to maintain differentiation of the specific stock received and sold:

1. Maintain accurate records of the acquisition date for each stock certificate *by serial number.*

2. Hold all stock in the name of the individual owner—not a nominee.

3. Instruct the broker that the sale confirmation should read: "Sold XYZ at $___ , versus purchase on (*trade date*) for $___."

4. Match the sale date of each stock certificate—again by serial numbers.

This documentation assists in presentation of a case for differentiation of specific stock certificates received and sold.

Constructive Dividends

Constructive dividends come as an unwelcome surprise to unwary shareholders. The IRS views attempts at transferring corporate assets to shareholders tax-free as *constructive receipt of dividends.* The shareholders don't plan on being taxed for whatever the company gave them. The most common constructive dividends include:

- Selling or renting corporate assets to shareholders at bargain prices. The dividend is the difference between the fair market value and the bargain price.

- Lending shareholders money with no intent of repaying principal or interest.

- Shareholders claiming personal expenses as corporate expenses. Individuals holding most of the corporate stock get whipsawed in this event. The tax law first denies the corporation's deduction as a necessary business expense. Then it requires the shareholder to include the asset transfer as a dividend and, therefore, as ordinary income.

- Payment to shareholders as if they were employees when no work was done or the payment doesn't match the value of the work done.

Dividends in Kind

Sometimes small, closely held companies elect to pay shareholders their dividends in property held by the corporation. There's nothing wrong with this. However, shareholders receiving corporate property must treat it just like any other dividend—as ordinary income.

The amount of the dividend to the shareholder is the fair market value of the asset at the time of distribution. That also becomes the shareholder's new basis in the property.

If the fair market value of the property distributed has an adjusted basis greater than the company's earnings, then the firm recognizes dividends to the extent of its earnings. The shareholder recognizes a dividend in the amount of the firm's earnings. For distributions beyond the firm's current earnings, the shareholder recognizes a return of capital (and a reduction in basis of the stock held) in the amount of the difference between the fair market value of distributed property and earnings.

Sometimes companies transfer property to shareholders along with liabilities attached to the property. Real estate and motor vehicles fall into this category. In this case, the company recognizes earnings to the extent of the liability transferred to the shareholder. The shareholder's basis in the property becomes its fair market value *less* the amount of the liability assumed.

Reorganizing a Corporation

The IRS looks closely at reorganizations and recapitalizations. Shareholders of closely held corporations in the past used corporate reorganizations to bail their capital out of companies having financial difficulties. Reorganizations done correctly exchange one class of stock for a new class of stock. There's no recognition of a gain or loss. There exists a formal plan for reorganization approved by the board and ratified by the shareholders.

Under reorganization, the old corporation collapses and the new corporation (now a *party* to the reorganization) issues its own stock. Consider this *like-kind stock* as long as the same individuals continue to control the new corporation. Problems arise when the transaction takes on the character of a stock sale—a taxable event.

Worthless Stock

As a controller or treasurer, let's hope you don't face this prospect for your firm's stock. However, should the issue arise, your shareholders probably at least want a capital loss out of it. However, the stock must be *completely* worthless. The tax law treats cases of completely worthless stock as if it sold for zero on the last day of the tax year. That way the owner declares a capital loss equal to the basis in the stock.

However, there's often an argument with the IRS as to what constitutes completely worthless stock. Lack of a ready market doesn't necessarily make a stock completely worthless. The IRS takes the position that you just haven't found a buyer *yet*. A later reorganization may yet make the stock worth something. Even if the individual can prove a stock is completely worthless, the IRS often disputes the *year* in which it became completely worthless.

Consider these two strategies when dealing with worthless stock of your company:

1. Don't argue with the IRS as to the worth of a stock and the timing of its worthlessness—it's a losing proposition. Instead, sell it for a nominal amount to a third party. Then declare the capital loss just as if it were any other sale of stock.

2. Investors sometimes short the stock of a company just before it becomes completely worthless. They probably won't ever have to make delivery to close the short position. Since the short position is theoretically permanently open, no taxable event occurred. In that case, they don't pay taxes on profits from the short sale.

Taxation of Stock Splits

Stock splits by themselves do not constitute a taxable event. The shareholder's basis in each share of stock declines proportionately—just as in a stock dividend. However, the overall basis in the stock position remains the same. Shareholders pay capital gains only when selling their shares of stock.

Bonds

Bonds require the company to pay a fixed amount of interest, usually twice a year. Failure to meet a scheduled interest payment throws the company into default. Since bondholders have the status of a creditor rather than just an investor, many consider bonds less risky than stocks. Actually, that's not the case. Bonds have not only the creditworthiness of the underlying company to drive their price, but overall interest rates as well.

Worthless Bonds

The same rules apply to completely worthless bonds as were discussed earlier for completely worthless stock. Unless there's incontrovertible proof of zero value, you may have to fight the IRS. It's so much easier just to sell the bonds and take the loss.

Premium Amortization

Bonds purchased above par (for more than $1000) carry a premium. Bondholders amortize that premium over the remaining life of the bond for as long as they hold it. Issuing companies amortize it over the life of the bond. Bondholders amortize the premium as an interest expense; bond issuers, as interest income.

Further, the premium amortization reduces the bondholder's basis in the bond. By the way, though it's not applicable for taxable bonds, holders of municipal bonds can't write off the interest deductions, since their bonds are tax-exempt. However, they still must reduce their basis in the bond by the annual amount of premium amortization.

The easiest way of amortizing bond premium is the straight-line method. Follow these three steps:

1. Compute the portion of the premium amortized for each bond interest payment. This is the amount paid for the bond less its face value, divided by the number of coupon payments remaining in the life of the bond.

2. Subtract the amount of the premium amortized from the issue price of the bond (its book value) to arrive at the adjusted book value net of that year's premium amortization.

3. In the hands of the bondholder, the purchase price less accumulated amortization of premium yields the adjusted basis of the bond after each interest payment amortization.

Figure 15-3 shows how to amortize a bond premium using the straight-line method.

Original Issue Discount Bonds

Firms issuing debt (bonds) often can't sell the issue at par. Instead, they must discount the bonds below their face value. The difference between face value and sale price is the *original issue discount* (OID). The issuing company treats that as an interest expense. They're obligated to repay the full face value of the bond even though they sold it for something less. Many OID bonds pay no coupon interest. We call these zero-coupon bonds.

Assume:

Face value	$1,000,000.00
Purchase price	1,069.69
Coupon rate	12%
Yield to maturity	10%
Life of the bond	4 years

Year	Payment no.	Premium amortization of payment	Accumulated premium amortization	Basis
				$1,069.69
1	1	$8.71	$ 8.71	1,060.97
	2	8.71	17.42	1,052.26
2	3	8.71	26.13	1,043.55
	4	8.71	34.84	1,034.84
3	5	8.71	43.55	1,026.13
	6	8.71	52.26	1,017.42
4	7	8.71	60.97	1,008.71
	8	8.71	69.69	1,000.00

Figure 15-3. Amortization of bond premium using the straight-line method.

Bond issuers and purchasers amortize OID discounts in much the same way they do bond premiums. The issuer treats the amortized discount as interest expense. The purchaser treats it as interest income. Follow these three steps to amortize original issue discount:

1. *Compute the discount.*   OID is simply the difference between issue price and the bond's face value. A bond issue of $1 million that sold for $850,000 carries a $150,000 original issue discount.

2. *Identify the daily discount.*   Bonds get issued at different times during the year. Therefore, we must compute the daily discount amortization. Divide the total discount by the total number of days in the life of the bond. A bond issued on January 3 that matures on December 31 five years from now has a life of 1824 days. Continuing with our example, the daily discount amortization is $82.24 ($150,000/1824 = $82.24).

3. *Compute the discount for the year.*   Multiply the daily discount by the number of days in the year. The first year, the company had the bonds outstanding for only 362 days. Therefore, interest expense recognized on the OID bond is $29,771 ($82.24 × 362 = $29,771).

The bondholders' basis in OID bonds *increases* as the discount amortizes and they recognize interest income.

Retirement Plans

Retirement plans provide companies the ability to set aside funds for employees on a tax-deferred basis. The income generated by these plans is often free of taxes until distribution. Further, the employer's contribution counts as a deduction. The most popular plans include:

- Keoghs
- Profit-sharing
- 401(K) plans

Keogh Plans

Keogh plans work best for those who exert substantial control over the company—such as partners or proprietors. These plans fall under the heading of *defined contribution plans* and *defined benefit plans*. As such, the tax law places specific contribution limitations on the owner. Specifically, these include:

- For defined contribution plans, the lesser of 25 percent of earnings from self-employment or $30,000. The deduction cap on profit-sharing contributions is 15 percent of compensation.

- For defined benefit plans, the limit is an annual retirement benefit of 100 percent of compensation for the high-three-years salary.
- Owners controlling more than one business must have a plan that covers all employees of all the businesses.
- A fiduciary must administer the plan.

If you are self-employed, don't forget to deduct half of the self-employment taxes you pay. Many people neglect this deduction since it appears on a different form (1040) than where they computed self-employment tax (Schedule SE). Additionally, don't attempt to deduct the owner's Keogh contribution as an ordinary business expense—it's not. However, contributions for employees are deductible.

Profit-Sharing Plans

The tax law defines a profit-sharing plan as one whose employer contributions depend on the earned income of the self-employed owner. The firm need not contribute a set amount or percentage of its profits to the plan. However, the law requires contributions to be "substantial and recurring." Further, it must have a definite and written formula for allocating profits to the accounts maintained for the benefit of the participants.

Stock bonus and employee stock purchase plans (ESOPs) work in a manner similar to profit-sharing plans. All such plans intend to give the employees a financial stake in the firm's success.

Pension Plans

Pension plans provide for payment of a specified percentage of the employee's income into the plan. The contribution isn't dependent on the earnings of the firm—that's what makes it different from a profit-sharing plan. However, in practice, the purpose of pension and profit-sharing plans is the same.

Many such plans have a vesting requirement. This allows gradations of the employee's accrued benefit to grow during the course of employment. As with profit-sharing plans, the employer's contribution to a pension plan is tax deductible.

401(K) Plans

This plan carries the section heading of the IRS code that governs it. It provides for employers and employees contributing to a qualified pension or profit-sharing plan. The employee's ordinary income excludes the employer's contributions on behalf of the employee. Many such plans allow for the employee to contribute to the plan above and beyond the employer's contributions.

The tax law treats this excess contribution as ordinary income when earned. However, the interest income on the entire plan continues on a tax-deferred basis until distribution.

Employer-Sponsored Annuities

Annuities shelter investment income, allowing interest to compound tax-free until distribution. The employee's basis in the annuity plan is his or her nondeductible contribution to the plan. It makes no difference if the employer took a payroll deduction for the employee and put it into the plan or if the employee paid the plan directly. Unlike a 401(K), the contribution is not tax deductible.

16
Banking Relationships

Overview

Treasurers and controllers supervise their company's banking relationships. Services offered by competent banks greatly improve financial executives' performance. Chapter 16 deals specifically with banks—what they can do for you, how to use them, the services they offer and how to pay for them. The chapter describes various types of financial institutions and the strengths of each. It explains how to integrate bank services into your financial system. Selecting a bank with the requisite personnel and resources your company needs isn't always easy. Chapter 16 shows you how to determine which banks are for you.

Types of Financial Institutions

Treasurers and controllers often use several types of financial institutions depending on the nature of the transaction at hand. Most often, asking an institution to do something in which it isn't expert ends up costing you. Choose your bank and your bankers carefully. Rely on their advice only to the extent they've proven themselves. Don't hesitate to get a second opinion.

Remember, the federal government regulates the banking industry for good reason. Bank personnel receive no professional certification as do doctors, lawyers, and accountants. There's no continuing professional education requirement for bankers. Further, many of them sell their bank's services and look upon you and your company merely as consumers.

Commercial Banks

If you're looking for high-volume transactions and cash management expertise, go to a large commercial bank. Usually the major money-center banks offer every kind of banking service available. By money-center bank, most people mean those with national and international operations such as Citicorp, Wells Fargo, Continental Illinois, and Chase Manhattan.

The downside of using a major commercial bank is that smaller companies have less influence and get less attention.

Most large commercial banks have five divisions of service:

- Credit
- Operations
- Trust
- Investment
- Consulting

Some of the largest banks function as servicers for certain operations of smaller banks. For example, large banks provide trust services and escrow on behalf of other, smaller institutions.

The types of services offered specifically to controllers and treasurers by large commercial banks include:

- All types of loans
- Brokerage services
- Investment services
- Investment banking
- Safekeeping and other custodian services
- Transfer agent
- All types of cash management services

Regional Banks.   The regionals specialize in particular areas of the country. They're not as big as money-center banks. Their services aren't as extensive. Still, many of the regionals such as C&S Sovran, Crocker, First National of Maryland, and Wachovia are all fine regional banks. They have a large and diverse client base.

Depending on your requirements, a good regional bank can serve very well as your company's lead bank. Further, your company may get the kind of individualized attention at a regional that it wouldn't get at a money-center bank.

Local Banks.   Smaller businesses gravitate to local banks. These are commercial banks that specialize in particular market segments. Construction lending or professionals (doctors, lawyers) are two common areas to which the locals cater. They seldom offer corporate services such as electronic funds transfer and cash management.

Members of the Federal Reserve System.   All of the money-center and regional banks are members of the Federal Reserve system. Most local commercial banks are as well. State-chartered banks have the option of Fed membership.

Membership in the Fed guarantees regulatory oversight of the institution. Each member bank must meet strict capital requirements, operational practices, and lending specifications. Further, check clearing among member banks is much faster owing to the 12 regional Federal Reserve banks around the country.

Thrifts

Savings banks, savings and loan associations, and thrift and loan institutions all carry the classification of thrifts. Typically, thrifts lend out on the long end of the yield curve—15 to 30 years. Their loans are collateralized by hard assets expected to last for the life of the loan. Real estate lenders are typically thrift institutions.

Lending long on the yield curve means that a thrift's interest expense rises faster than the yield on its loan portfolio. The long-term loans don't roll off as fast as the short-term deposits they take in to fund the loans. That's why thrifts periodically suffer profit squeezes as interest rates spike up.

Thrifts have solved that problem to a great extent with the injection of variable-rate loans. Now as interest rates move, so too does the institution's interest income. The remaining issue seems to be the refix date of the loans. Thrifts cannot change them frequently enough to maintain their profit margins.

Thrifts don't usually offer much in the way of corporate banking services. However, they do offer long-term asset-based loans. That alone is often enough to justify corporations maintaining a relationship with their local thrift.

Mortgage Banks

Mortgage bankers often serve as the agent between the borrower and lender. For companies seeking to originate a large loan, mortgage bankers structure the deal and locate the lenders. They often form a syndicate of lenders for very large loans in order to spread the credit risk.

Mortgage bankers secure their deals with hard assets—usually real estate, but sometimes valuable and durable machinery and equipment. Their clients are commercial enterprises, insurance companies, thrifts, banks, and pension funds—anyone with large amounts of money willing to invest.

Insurance Companies

Insurance companies have become more sophisticated. Many have diversified into several types of investment categories. Corporate treasurers and controllers sometimes look to insurance companies for long-term funding of asset-based projects. These are typically beyond the ability of banks to fund. They don't have the size and they can't handle the duration of the loan needed.

Pension Funds

Three public pension funds—the California Public Employees Retirement System, California State Teacher's Retirement System, and New York State Teacher's

Retirement System—are among the largest financial institutions in the world. Each has assets well over $30 billion.

As far as corporate treasurers and controllers are concerned, insurance companies and pension funds offer nothing in the way of corporate services. Like insurance companies, pension funds assist companies by providing investment capital. Still, even the pension funds are growing more sophisticated. Many of them have a percentage of their investment portfolio set aside for worthy companies in which they're willing to take a venture stake.

Pension funds are major investors in stocks and bonds. Indeed, many large pension funds have such significant holdings in public corporations that their stock-voting powers swing election of their companies' boards of directors.

Investment Banks

These are the deal makers. Companies seeking to float a public securities offering hire investment bankers to make the deal happen. Investment bankers bridge the gap between the public and the offering company. Their job is to facilitate the deal, arrange for the financing, execute all the public regulatory compliance and filing requirements, and put together the investment syndicate.

Securities Brokers

Companies use securities broker/dealers to execute their investments. Treasurers call on brokers to initiate all types of purchases and sales of corporate securities. Further, brokers float certain types of financing for corporate treasuries such as repurchase agreements and commercial paper. They assist in the buyback of publicly owned stock into the company's treasury.

Maintaining Banking Relationships

Modern bankers do much more for their business clients than simply float loans. They provide cash management expertise, safekeeping, trust, collection of foreign payments, and escrow services, to name just a few. Treasurers of larger companies usually manage the overall banking relationship. Absent a treasurer, the controller takes over the function.

Management of banking relationships includes a variety of things:

- Borrowing
- Compensating balance maintenance
- Payment for banking services
- Deposit availability schedules
- Investment

- Funds transfers
- Collection of incoming electronic transfers
- Cash concentration

Communicating with Lenders

Companies with borrowed funds keep their lenders well informed. This is an important part of the banking relationship. The treasurer and CFO usually meet with the bankers regularly to review the firm's financial performance. If there's a problem adhering to the terms and conditions of a lending covenant, it's the treasurer's responsibility to inform the bank officer. Usually it's best to warn them well in advance of a possible breach.

Bring them into the decision-making process. They just may be able to help. Make sure they understand the nature of the problem. Perhaps it's just a financial ratio the firm failed to meet. Show them how the firm intends to remedy the situation. Well-informed bankers are far more likely to grant a *written* waiver of default. Make sure that waiver is in writing. Without it, the company risks calling the loan despite any verbal promises to the contrary.

Additionally, it's always a nice gesture to inform your bankers of the firm's upcoming business plan. Often, clearly defined goals and objectives accompanied by a concrete plan of attack add a level of comfort to lending decisions. Further, it's that much more credible if you can back up your current business plan with a solid track record of hitting past targets.

Last, the board of directors should meet with the firm's bankers at least once a year. Companies often invite the senior bank officers to a portion of a board meeting. There, they discuss the firm's financial results and future plans. They answer any questions from the bankers. Then the bankers leave.

The objective is to preserve an amicable relationship with your bankers. Report bad news just as readily as you do good news. If there's a problem, offer the company's solution at the same time. You want the banker to trust you. They can't unless they're confident of the communications link.

Negotiating Price

Bank services aren't cheap. Further, many company treasurers and controllers have little idea exactly how much they pay for bank services. That's because it is common banking practice to pay for services using a fee credit arrangement from collected balances or from compensating balances. Such fees not paid in hard dollars allow very little control for the company.

However, there's a way to identify the amount paid if you're on a fee credit arrangement. Insist on a monthly statement itemizing the service costs and compensation paid to the bank. Often corporate treasurers and controllers find they've been overcompensating banks.

If that's the case, then arrange an orderly scheduled withdrawal of compensating balances. This gets back some of the overpayments while preserving your banking relationship and more closely adhering to the original intent of the services agreement.

Payment Options

Many companies negotiate payment for their banking services in hard currency. The bank renders an invoice just like a regular vendor. The controller reviews it for accuracy and enters it into the accounts payable system. This method forces the firm to track bank costs and question charges appearing out of line.

Direct Debit.   Many banks offer to automatically debit their customers' checking accounts for the amount they think they've earned. This takes away some of the control that payment in hard currency offers. However, if your company allows this practice, make sure the bank submits a monthly statement itemizing the bank charges and services rendered. Additionally, even though the treasurer or controller doesn't actually write out a check in payment, make sure the statement gets properly reviewed.

Banking Services

Banks offer a diversified array of services for their corporate customers. The major money-center banks frequently have separate divisions specializing in the particular needs of business customers. Here are the types of services most useful to companies:

Electronic Funds Transfer (EFT)

EFT provides a convenient way to send and receive payments without writing a check. It reduces the guesswork associated with bank float. Many money-center banks offer EFT services. Some even provide EFT consulting for their cash management customers. The three most common EFT services include:

- Wire transfer of funds
- Corporate trade payments
- Preauthorized debits

Wire Transfers.   This is the least sophisticated form of electronic funds transfer. It merely consists of one bank wiring over the *FEDWIRE* or *BANKWIRE* system an amount of funds into another bank. No information regarding the nature of the payment such as invoice numbers and items purchased transfers with the payment.

A bank wire is an expensive and laborious way to make a vendor payment. Except in unusual cases, don't use a wire transfer to pay your bills.

Corporate Trade Payments

In contrast to wire transfers, corporate trade payment (CTP) is the most sophisticated form of electronic funds transfer. It uses a commercial data translation facility—often the bank itself—to enter payment information from the payer. The payer electronically tells the payee what the invoice the payment is for, how much, and any other information that would go with a normal payment by check.

They do this by entering the payment information through a data translation facility. The information then electronically transfers to an automated clearinghouse (ACH). This is the link between the buyer's and seller's banks. The ACH sends the appropriate debits and credits to the customer's and vendor's accounts through the banking system. Banks record the entries the same day. Figure 16-1 shows how the system works.

However, the real benefit to using corporate trade payments is that vendors receive *information* regarding the payment electronically. This allows them to record the payment on their accounts receivable system electronically. The process is faster and less expensive for both parties. The most common uses for corporate trade payments include:

- Payroll
- Employee expense reimbursements
- Dividend payments to shareholders
- Interest payments to bondholders

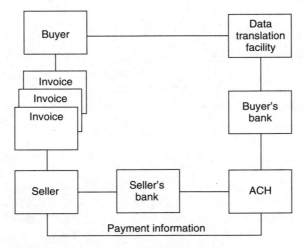

Figure 16-1. Corporate trade payments.

- Vendor payments
- State and federal tax payments
- Electronic payment using point-of-sale debit cards

Preauthorized Debits.   Chapter 12, "Accounts Payable," described how preauthorized debits (PADs) work. Briefly, the buyer allows the seller to pay itself by drawing funds from the buyer's bank account. Like the corporate trade payment system above, this system can use the electronic funds transfer facilities of the automated clearinghouse.

Alternatively, some companies simply give the vendors checks from a special checking account and allow them to write their own payment checks. The two restrictions are:

1. The vendor writes a check or electronically debits the account for only a limited amount.
2. A monthly statement goes to the customer from the vendor itemizing each transaction.

Of course, the customer reconciles the checking account each month. However, in certain instances where customers make a large number of small purchases every month, preauthorized debits save money for both parties. The most commonly used preauthorized debits include:

- Loan payments
- Sending cash from operating divisions to the corporate cash concentration account
- Membership dues
- Rent and lease payments
- Insurance premiums
- Utility payments
- Recurring monthly fees

Direct Debit

Some companies may want the advantages of a direct preauthorized debit arrangement but don't want to accept the risk of possible abuse by their customers. In these cases some sophisticated banks offering cash management services provide direct debits.

Under this arrangement the *bank*, not the vendor, debits the customer's account for routine or recurring payments. To accomplish this the vendor submits a list of direct debit items to the bank. The bank then initiates an electronic fund transfer through the automated clearinghouse to debit the customer's account and credit the vendor's.

There's another method to accomplish the same thing. It uses preauthorized drafts rather than the more sophisticated EFT. Banks without the necessary electronic equipment employ such drafts on behalf of their customers. Though the drafts are subject to the clearing bank's funds availability schedule, it's still better than waiting for your customer to receive your invoice, process it, wait a while, cut a check, mail the check, and then go through your own bank's check deposit and collection process.

Direct Deposit

We see this service most often in companies' payroll systems, payments for annuities, royalties, dividends, and pensions. It works almost the reverse of the direct debit above. Instead of having a vendor submit a payment list to the bank, you (the payer) authorize your bank to debit your account and credit the account of your payees. This system works most effectively when the following are true:

- Invoices aren't involved.
- Payments are regular.
- Payments are the same amount each time.

Advantages of Operating "Checkless" Payment Systems

All of the EFT, direct debit, and direct deposit mechanisms have one thing in common—they don't require use of a check. Further, the corporate trade payments system doesn't even use a paper invoice. Instead, the system records transactions at both ends using electronic entries to the company's payables and receivables systems.

The efficiencies resulting from elimination of all those checks floating around for just the payroll system include the following:

- No provision is required for lost or stolen checks.
- No special treatment is necessary for sick or vacationing employees.
- Costs of operating the check disbursements system are eliminated.
- Employees don't leave work on payday to do their banking.

Lockboxes

Many companies employ one or an entire system of strategically located lockboxes. Their purpose is to receive customer payments. Most lockbox systems place the box in close proximity to the customers. Doing this reduces mail float. The lockbox receives the payments. It then processes, deposits, and often electronically transfers them to the company's cash concentration bank account in the headquarters city.

Most banks offer basic lockboxes. The most common services include:

- Receiving checks
- Processing checks received
- Depositing checks
- Payment reporting
- Returning payment information for credit to the receivables system
- Transferring funds to the concentration account

Some of the more sophisticated banks capture payment remittance information for their corporate customers. They enter this onto electronic media that goes directly into the company's receivable system.

Using lockboxes in this manner reduces the float involved in payment processing. Further, it eliminates the manual entry often done at the company to record customer payment receipts. Additionally, the most sophisticated lockboxes use the automated clearinghouse to transfer the daily receipts directly to the bank account of their corporate customer.

Some take this one step further by using the *electronic data interchange* feature of the automated clearinghouse to upload the customer payment information directly into the company's computer system.

Returned Item Lockboxes.   Some companies use lockboxes for a special application—receipt of dishonored payment checks. Often a collection agency operates this special lockbox. This reduces the time between rejection of a check and the beginning of collection procedures.

Remittance Intercept Lockboxes.   This is a hybrid of a bank-operated lockbox. This method doesn't have the bank process the payment as with a regular lockbox. Instead, a post office box used as a collection point receives payments. The checks are then couriered to the corporate office. Some companies having sophisticated payment-processing equipment receive the payments directly. Others send it directly to their banks for processing.

Of course, we lose transit time between the intercept box and processing point. However, large companies (or courier services specializing in this) receiving millions in payments each day often employ a combination of jet aircraft and helicopters to execute these critical payment transfers.

Controlled Disbursement

Banks are experts at helping their customers control funds flowing from their accounts. This benefits both the customer and the banks since the funds stay put longer. Most controlled disbursement services really combine several reporting techniques. These include:

- Check presentment
- Special zero-balance disbursement accounts
- Investment accounts

Chapter 12 identified the features of check presentment reporting. Essentially, this service simply reports to the controller each morning the amount of checks scheduled for clearing against the account that day. Knowing this information allows the controller to move money around and perhaps invest excess funds overnight.

Clearing Subsidiary's Checks.   A more sophisticated spin-off of the controlled disbursement bundle of services assists companies with more than one operating division. For these firms, the treasurer's objective is to minimize excess funds in the division's operating accounts. Here's one way to employ your bank's disbursement control services to accomplish that goal:

1. Each morning the bank polls company divisions' checking accounts for the amount of checks to be presented that day.
2. The bank transfers funds from the corporate cash concentration account into each division's checking account. The amount is exactly that required to fund all checks clearing that day.
3. At the end of the day, each division's account has a zero balance.
4. The corporate cash concentration account is automatically swept clear of excess funds (net of presentment for *that* account).
5. Invest excess funds either in an overnight repurchase agreement or in the company's interest-bearing money-market fund.

Maintaining Compensating Balances.   Funds kept on balance in non-interest-bearing accounts compensate the bank for their services. However, this opposes the purpose of controlled disbursement account services. The solution is not to take the account balance down to zero. If the disbursement account pays for bank services using deposit credit, then instruct the bank to take the balance down just to the agreed compensating balance.

Balance Reporting

Most banks offering corporate services provide account balance information via computer terminal. From their offices, corporate customers quickly obtain the following information for each account:

- Lockbox deposits
- Automated clearinghouse debits and credits
- Availability schedule for deposited funds
- Opening and closing balances
- Checks clearing that day
- Line of credit available

The most sophisticated banks provide this information not only for accounts at their own institution, but for accounts at other banks their clients deal with as well.

Consulting Services

The money-center banks offer a variety of consulting services to their corporate clients. Most likely you can find the services you need at the corporate divisions of:

- Citicorp
- Continental
- First Chicago
- Mellon
- BankAmerica
- Wachovia

Further, many of the smaller regionals offer specific banking services often tailored to their customers.

Figure 16-2 shows a list of typical bank consulting services.

- Assessment of country risk for international companies
- Foreign exchange exposure and risk management
- Interest rate risk management
- Trade credit policies and procedures
- Analysis of cash inflow system
- Analysis of controlled disbursement program
- Analysis of cash concentration system
- Installation of electronic funds transfer system
- Installation of electronic data interface system
- Collections of international accounts receivable
- Clearing foreign checks
- Business planning
- Cash flow planning
- Float studies
- Lockbox studies
- Payment processing studies
- Analysis of vendor credit terms
- Assessment of compliance with discounts taken policy
- Training

Figure 16-2. Bank consulting services.

Fees.   Many banks run their consulting divisions as profit centers. Their fee structures are competitive with those of other top consultants in the banking field. Fees depend on the nature of the engagement. Lockbox location studies and implementation of lockbox systems, for example, often quote their fee from a schedule. The number of locations analyzed drives the service cost.

Other types of bank consulting such as acceleration of cash inflow using bar-scanning payment-processing equipment quote fees as a custom engagement. Chances are the bank quotes the job on an hourly basis extended by the number of hours worked by the consultants involved plus out-of-pocket expenses.

When you engage a bank consultant—or any other consultant, for that matter—be sure to get an engagement letter. It should contain the consultant's:

- Understanding of the task
- Scope of the work
- Approach to the problem
- Expected work product
- Estimated fees
- Estimated completion date

Make sure your agreement informs you of any changes to material aspects of the engagement (such as fees) *before* they occur.

Determine the bank consultant's mission for the bank. Some banks don't run their consulting divisions as profit centers. Often their purpose is to drum up business for other divisions. Others are out to demonstrate their abilities to prospective customers. Still others are really selling their bank's services.

Matching Your Need with the Capabilities of a Consultant

Clients like to think that no one knows a bank's capabilities like a banker. That's why they're so popular as consultants for banking-related matters. Nevertheless, financial consultants such as the international CPA firms argue that bank consultants aren't always independent of the conclusions they draw.

Identifying Need.   Many managers hesitate to engage a consultant. Some feel that it's an admission of inadequacy. Nothing could be further from the truth. The sophisticated banking operations of many companies—particularly those dealing in foreign countries—require specialists. The most successful consulting situations have these five ingredients:

Need for objectivity.   Sometimes there's disagreement among the company's managers on a particular course of action. An objective professional with the background and resources to evaluate the problem and recommend specific solutions can help make the decision.

Clear target.   Never hire a consultant without first knowing exactly what needs to be done. Sometimes the real problem isn't always clear. A good consultant's first task is to identify the problem and gain agreement that everyone understands the objective.

Cost.   The estimated cost of the consulting engagement must be a fraction of the expected contribution to overall profitability. Bank consultants often use a multiplier of around 4. That is, benefits must be at least four times the cost of the engagement.

Availability of information.   Consultants require specific information about the company's operations. Be sure that the information needed exists in a form and with sufficient accuracy to make the project worthwhile. Further, make certain you have figured obtaining the information into the overall cost of the project.

Durability of the decision.   Consultants solve specific problems and help make decisions. The solution must have the probability of lasting long enough for the company to obtain an adequate return on its investment. For example, don't engage a consultant for work on a problem with specifications that might change in a month or two.

Selecting a Bank

Treasurers and controllers place a premium on performance and price. Certain banks have reputations for expertise in particular areas. Often, within a region, some banks have a particular strength that their money-center competitors cannot match. There's a lot of competition out there for your company's banking business. Use the following criteria to identify the banks your company needs.

Identifying the Services
Your Firm Needs Most

Rank in order of importance the bank services your company requires from its bank. Are they cash-management-related? Perhaps you need funding. Your cash concentration system may need an injection of electronic funds transfer expertise.

Next determine if this is a one-time requirement or if it's ongoing. Needs that recur may necessitate a higher ranking than issues permanently solved by one week of a consultant's time.

Then identify those banks with a capability in those services that rank highest.

People Servicing Your Account

Definitely interview the team that the bank proposes for your account. Chances are they'll come from various areas of the institution if your requirements are diverse. The team should be under the overall supervision of one senior officer. You should have access to that person as well as every member of the banking team.

Pay particular attention to these people's backgrounds. Find out their credentials. Avoid insisting on credentials not needed on your account. However, if, for example, your needs focus on cash management, ask about professional designations and memberships such as:

- Certified Cash Manager
- NCCMA—membership in National Corporate Cash Manager's Association
- NACHA—membership in the National Automated Clearing House Association

Generally, people active in professional associations have the most up-to-date information and are serious about what they do. Find out if your bankers have worked before on the problems your company faces. How did they solve them? Would those same solutions work for you? Talk with *their* clients and find out how satisfied they are with the bank.

Technological Resources

Many treasurers require specific types of equipment from their banks. These may include high-speed optical scanners for payment processing or sophisticated computer interface software for converting payment records to a format acceptable to your receivables system.

It might require advanced telecommunications equipment for use in electronic funds transfer, electronic data interface, and automated clearinghouse operations. If your bank doesn't have this equipment and your company needs a bank with that capability, this isn't the bank for you.

Make sure the data downloaded from the bank's computers is compatible with your own computers. If not, and if conversion is difficult, then you'll miss the advantage of what you're paying the bank to provide.

Servicing Customers

Determine the bank's commitment to customer service. Find out how easily you can reach the person with the answer to your questions. Often banks have small pieces of information required to answer a question scattered around the institution. An example is reporting of incoming deposits. You want all incoming deposits reported on one page. However, banks not committed to servicing their corporate customers may have incoming deposits dispersed on separate reports from the:

- Automated clearinghouse
- Wire transfer desk
- Depository transfer check-clearing operation

Though a minor inconvenience, this may be just the beginning of larger problems.

Commitment to Your Particular Needs

Some banks offer services to treasurers as an accommodation while waiting to float them a loan. That's not what you want. A professional bank is proactive in getting, servicing, and retaining the business that's important to you. Without that commitment, the department that services you could be wiped out by one manager's decision.

You want your bank to earn a reasonable profit from your business. Without that profit incentive, the bank soon grows weary of supporting a loss leader just so it can originate some loans.

Banking Agreement Contract

Some banks negotiate multiyear contracts with their corporate customers. These often include specific caps on price increases. Certainly, your contract should include these things:

1. *Float computations.* The contract should describe how the bank computes float and how it figures into cost of services.

2. *Performance guarantees.* We want the bank to perform at a particular level. The best way to assure that is to explain what you want in the contract. An example would be the guaranteed funds availability schedule from daily deposits.

3. *Penalties.* Your bank's standard contract may charge you for specific violations of the banking agreement. Two of the most popular are minimum balances and number of transactions. If your bank does this, make sure the agreement specifies any penalties.

17
Capital Expenditures

Overview

Chapter 17 demonstrates the methods used by treasurers and controllers to evaluate major capital purchases. These decisions are usually so large both in terms of dollars and in what they do for the company that they require extensive analysis. The analytical methods demonstrated throughout this chapter deal not only with the mathematical examination but with the business evaluation of such expenditures, too.

We'll identify a structured method of proposing capital projects. Then we'll show how to choose among several seemingly competitive projects. After making the decision, we'll illustrate a monitoring program to ensure the project accomplishes its task.

Reasons for Capital Expenditures

Many companies develop a gap between the profit capabilities of their present assets and the benefits that newer, larger, or just *more* assets can provide. The capital investment decision is simple:

Does the cash inflow from the assets purchased exceed by a large enough profit margin the cash outflow of the expenditure?

If it does, then buy the assets. If not, then pass. All the analytical procedures and senior company executives involved make the decision complicated.

What do companies count as capital expenditures? A new production line qualifies. So do the machines that go on the line. Warehouses are capital expenditures. Often just expanding the existing storage facility requires treatment as a capital project.

Capital projects use the company's spending power to create a flow of future profits for a period of several years. Projects whose profit benefits span only one year are not capital projects. Instead, treasurers designate these as expense investments or simply operating expenses. Do not depreciate them since benefits inure for only the current accounting period.

Benefits from capital projects vary among companies. Some type of equipment, for example, reduces manufacturing costs. Modern computer-aided production machinery lowers labor and energy used for each item made. Acquiring another enterprise or just its production assets immediately increases production capacity. In this case it answers the sales staff that says, *we can sell every one of these things right off the warehouse floor.* Now they can—let's just hope at a profit.

New products often require capital programs for producing the item. Sometimes governmental agencies require pollution-control equipment to satisfy stricter laws. These produce no return on the investment. The company really has no choice in the capital expenditure decision. However, most firms still treat such expenditures as capital programs.

Normal Capital Expenditures

By far the most common capital expenditures are those classified as "normal." These are the routine replacement of durable goods required to maintain the company's present level of operations. They don't usually require huge outlays. Purchase of a new forklift to replace one that's worn out is a good example.

Often there's no financial analysis done to justify the expenditure. Approval comes from the executive whose department wants the expenditure. Reasons cited are often no more than *because we need it.*

Normal capital expenditures seldom receive extensive senior management review. The capital expenditure plan identifies each normal program, then subtotals all normal expenditures. Usually the approval process focuses on justifying the purchases. Once assured, discussion usually turns to the nonroutine expenditures that can really make some profit for the company.

Special Expenditures

These are the money-making projects that grab everyone's attention. Different companies treat nonroutine capital projects with varying degrees of formality. Generally, special capital projects involve:

- Large amounts of money
- Long-term commitment
- Replacement of entire categories of equipment
- Major reductions in cost

Often just the study of the project requires significant expenditure. For example, evaluation of an additional production facility may require outside engineering and construction professionals. The decision process leading up to approval of the capital expenditure at a company having a structured approval process might proceed like this:

1. Division production manager recognizes need for an additional facility. The manager guesses that the cost is approximately $5 million.

2. The division manager evaluates this seat-of-the-pants estimate and justification for the expenditure. Division manager appoints an evaluation group including people from engineering, marketing, finance, production, and operations. Division manager allocates a fixed budget for the initial evaluation. This covers any outside experts required.

3. The group generates a capital program proposal for $5.3 million. This goes up to the corporate director of capital expenditures for evaluation.

4. Depending on the level of authorization the board of directors gives senior executives, the board may vote on the proposal or simply leave it up to the company's management.

5. Construction begins. Reports progress periodically to the board. This review includes costs and returns on the investment. The board approves cost overruns as well.

Evaluating Risk

The risk related to capital projects involves three areas:

- Expected return
- Cost overruns
- Financing risk

Coping with Risk

Treasurers and controllers manage capital project risk from the initial evaluation through implementation and monitoring. One way to control risk is by making the project return its original investment within a short period. The higher the risk, the shorter the required time needed for repayment. This reduces some of the influences from longer-term market fluctuations.

Range of Error.   Astute treasurers and controllers analyze capital projects using three different sets of assumptions: best case, most likely case, and worst case. Some analysts get more sophisticated in their assessments. They attach a probability of each scenario occurring. From there, they arrive at the *expected value* of the project's return. Figure 17-1 shows one such computation. Ginger's expected return amounts to the weighted average return from each of three case scenarios. In this case, the expected value of the industrial oven project is $865,000. That's the number Ginger uses to compute how closely the project comes to covering cost of capital, profit, and risk.

Ginger Partners, Ltd. Capital Project Analysis—Industrial Oven Expected Value of Return			
	Return	Probability	Expected return
Best case	$1,000,000	35%	$350,000
Most likely case	850,000	50%	425,000
Worst case	600,000	15%	90,000
Total			$865,000

Figure 17-1. Computation of expected return.

Alternatively, some companies take a more gloomy view of all projects. They assume the return never rises above that projected in the *worst*-case scenario. If the project passes even under the worst assumptions, chances are the company's capital is safe. The firm views any results better than that as a windfall.

Assessing Risk of Particular Assumptions. Often projection of financial results for capital projects uses many assumptions—particularly if the project requires several years before earning back the initial investment. Analysts frequently take apart the assumptions, searching for those that *drive* the project's profitability.

Such driver assumptions control the outcome of the project more than other assumptions. A technique called *sensitivity analysis* reveals these superassumptions. It involves testing the outcome of the project under different ranges for each assumption. Some variables don't move profits much, regardless of where they fall on their range. Others cause huge swings if moved only slightly. These are the driver assumptions.

Using a computer model, it's easy to develop a quick sensitivity analysis for capital projects. Figure 17-2 shows a simple sensitivity matrix.

Ginger Partners, Ltd. Capital Project Analysis—Industrial Oven Net Income Sensitivity Analysis—Sales Volume versus Interest Rates			
	Sales volume		
Interest rates	100,000 units	150,000 units	200,000 units
12%	$75,000	$85,000	$100,000
11%	85,000	95,000	110,000
10%	95,000	105,000	120,000
9%	100,000	110,000	125,000

Figure 17-2. Sensitivity analysis.

Notice how Ginger's net income fluctuates depending on these two driver variables. Using the sensitivity table, we can quickly estimate projected net income over the likely ranges of our assumptions. The treasurer or controller can now assess risk using these specific driver assumptions over their three case scenarios. This technique zeros in on the risk associated with various assumptions the firm accepts with a capital project.

Risk-Reward Matrix.   Theoretically, we view the risk of capital projects as having a level of reward for every level of risk. The more risk, the more compensation we demand. Ideally, we want projects with low risk and high reward—the upper left quadrant of Figure 17-3. Unfortunately, many firms find themselves in the lower right quadrant—high risk, low reward.

Preparing Capital Expenditure Proposals

Each capital project stands on its own merits. Most treasurers and controllers insist that initial evaluations and ongoing monitoring of projects separate one program from another. For example, if we have five capital projects going in various areas of the company, we evaluate each independently. Chances are the same manager isn't responsible for all five. Without independent evaluations of each project, there's no accountability for performance among the five project managers. Further, independent monitoring allows us to make changes and corrections on one project without disturbing the expectations and performance of the others.

Proposal Contents

Capital project proposals have one purpose: *Clearly describe the project considering all the issues important to the decision makers.* We want to see the reasoning behind the recommendation. Readers must understand the assumptions used and their likelihood of fulfillment.

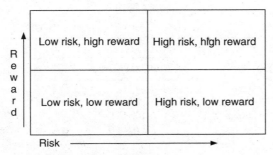

Figure 17-3. Risk-reward matrix.

Above all, we want *realistic* proposals. If a project is marginal, once reduced to the proposal format, we don't want window dressing and fluff to make it look better than it really is.

Highlight all the options available for the project. If there's an unknown or a soft number used in the assumptions, communicate that in the proposal. We don't want to mislead the reader. This damages the analyst's credibility for presentation of future projects. Here's a list of the sections usually helpful in presenting major capital project proposals:

- Executive summary and highlights
- Background of the project
- Statement of the need
- Analysis of alternatives
- Benefits of the project
- Economic justification
- Assumptions used
- Risk and opportunities
- Implementation plan
- Plan for periodic monitoring

Dos and Don'ts of Capital Project Proposals

Proposals are factual accounts, not embellished attempts designed to persuade the reader. The facts, numbers, and computations do the persuading. The text explains and amplifies on the numbers. It doesn't influence.

Preparing for the Audience. Every proposal talks to a specific audience. Determine the things your audience requires to make a decision on the project. Then deal with them point by point. Don't prepare analyses over the heads of your readers. Don't waste everybody's time with long explanations. Be brief.

Maintaining Objectivity. Keep the project in perspective. The proposal presents an objective description of all aspects of the project. Chances are the company won't go broke if it rejects the project. Avoid turning into an advocate of the project. Your readers can't make an unbiased evaluation with a proposal attempting to convince them of its validity.

Providing Comparisons. Often capital projects are new to the company. The decision makers lack a frame of reference for the project. Give them one. Compare the assessments and analyses with things familiar to the readers.

Keeping the Context.   Good proposals communicate the context in which their project works. Describe how it fits into the company's overall business plan. Tell the readers if it's an isolated investment made just once. Alternatively, perhaps it's just the first step in a series for one huge ambitious project. Given this context, readers want to know what happens to their investment if they get halfway through the project and decide to abort. How much does the firm lose? What happens to the equipment purchased so far?

Defending the Proposal.   Don't do it. Analysts who win the battle may end up ultimately losing the war. Often successfully defended proposals fail because the project was weak to begin with. The person who successfully defended suffers loss of credibility. Everyone looks at their next project proposal more carefully. It may be a good one, but those already burned hesitate before taking another chance.

Specify.   Avoid generalizations. Employ summary tables that describe the point quantitatively. Use graphs to visually demonstrate concepts. Explain how these items work if it's not obvious. Do not litter your text with adjectives. What may be *huge increases* to one person may not be to someone else. Instead, talk in terms of absolutes—an increase of $45,000, for example.

Computing Hurdle Rates

Not only must companies recoup their original investment, the expenditure has to compensate the company for the risk it's taking and several other things. Many firms call this the *hurdle rate.* If the cost of capital is, say, 10 percent, then the hurdle rate rises to some point above that. Many companies require that capital projects return 20 or 25 percent and more before they clear the hurdle rate and they approve the project. The difference between the cost of capital and the hurdle rate compensates the firm for its risk.

Building the Hurdle Rate

Some companies just arbitrarily establish a minimum rate of return for capital projects. This isn't very analytical and often quashes projects that could provide a good return for their low level of risk. Most companies, however, derive hurdle rates from a variety of input items. Building a hurdle rate usually considers the following factors:

- Cost of capital
- Profit margin
- Compensation for risk
- Compensation for management's time and effort

Cost of Capital.   Cost of capital isn't difficult to figure. Many companies use a *blended* or aggregate cost of capital that includes all the company's financing. They use this percentage in arriving at all types of capital projects regardless of financing method.

The blended cost technique also works for projects not requiring special financing, but drawing funds internally. In these cases it makes sense. Where did the money come from in the first place and what did it cost? There's no way to tell since all the funds aggregate into one pool. Therefore, use the aggregate cost of funds.

Other companies treat each project individually. They determine the financing method for a particular project. The cost of capital *using that financing method for that project* becomes the first component of the hurdle rate computation.

Profit Margin. At the very least, the minimum return for a capital project should make us back our normal profit margin after costs. Otherwise, let's just stick with our normal line of business rather than try anything new.

For companies with several divisions the profit margin component may be different for each entity. Some divisions receive a break on the minimum profit margin, making it easier to get capital project approval. Firms do this to channel money into strategically important areas of the company.

Compensating for Risk. Here's where the concept of hurdle rates gets fuzzy. There's a rate for every risk. Everyone has his or her own concept of risk and what it's worth to the firm. One way to gauge risk is by comparing it with other investments with a known return. Take a treasury bond for instance. It has a known return at any point in time. It also has a known risk—none. A T-bond, then, is at the bottom of the risk scale.

Second mortgages fall somewhere toward the top of most investors' risk scales. These too have a known return—considerably above that of T-bonds. Further, there's a ready market for both second mortgages and T-bonds. Fill in the risk scale with other types of investments having a known return and an active market to prove that return.

Liquidity should enter the equation somewhere. The less liquid an investment, the greater the risk factor. Choose comparison investments having a similar liquidity factor. This isn't always easy. For example, how liquid is a bottling plant production line? Not very. However, we did say that risk was the most fuzzy of the hurdle rate components.

Soon, the capital project under consideration falls between two investments having similar assessed risks. From this we gauge the return needed for the risks taken of the particular program we're looking at.

Management's Time. The company wants compensation for management's time and effort in overseeing the capital projects. This is similar to another overhead burden allocated to a division profit plan. Nevertheless, consider what else management could be doing to earn the company a profit if it didn't have to fiddle with the capital project under study.

Put in that context, there's an *opportunity cost* to involving management in any capital project. The firm wants compensation for that foregone opportunity.

Putting the Hurdle Rate Together.   Now that we have the four components of a hurdle rate, let's put it all together. Figure 17-4 shows how one company built its hurdle rate. Observe that the skip loader project must return at least 23.5 percent for its justification.

Problems with Hurdle Rates

Hurdle rates have several problems—even those carefully arrived at as in Figure 17-4. First, they make no allowance for cash flow. Investments that don't return anything until the last period are more risky than those that return money steadily. Yet an arbitrary hurdle rate doesn't consider periodic cash flows. The risk portion of the computation might give something to a project that throws off cash toward the repayment of its capital. However, such detail tends to be rare.

Second, many hurdle rates end appreciably above the going rate of return. Soon the cost of projects and the risk undertaken by the company rises. Without consciously doing so, the firm places itself at even greater risk by demanding higher and higher return on its capital projects. Remember—there's a rate for every risk.

Evaluating Return on Investment

This isn't a finance book. However, there are several financial analyses used to evaluate the return on capital projects. These are simple to compute. Nevertheless, don't use them as a substitute for common sense. Frequently, capital projects don't meet the hurdle rate of return. Yet, they have other merits that cause their justification. One such circumstance might be the project that puts the company into a new market—one strategically targeted for entry.

T-D-O Excavators, Inc. Capital Project Proposal—Skip-Loader Replacement Hurdle-Rate Computation	
Hurdle-rate variable	Rate
1. Cost of capital: skip loader is purchased using an installment loan from Citicorp	8.75%
2. Profit margin for Digging Division last year	7.75%
3. Risk: similar to that of a class A preferred stock	5.00%
4. Compensation for management efforts	2.00%
Computed hurdle rate	23.5%

Figure 17-4. Building a hurdle rate.

Discounted Cash Flow Rate of Return

Most capital projects have cash outflows and inflows. Since we're dealing with durable goods, these take place over a number of years. We must consider the time value of the money flowing in and out of the firm over the duration of the project. That's why we put the cash flows into terms of *present value*. The other discounting technique, called *internal rate of return*, identifies the rate that repays the project's initial investment out of discounted future cash flows.

Net Present Value.   Our objective using net present value (NPV) analysis is to convert the future value of the project's cash inflows into today's dollars. If we've two different projects to compare, the one with the greater NPV is the winner—in this particular measurement.

Assume we're deciding between two projects for T-D-O Excavators:

- A new skip loader
- Another conveyor system for removal of rocks from out back

T-D-O's cost of borrowing money is 12 percent. Let's assume the following about both projects:

- *Skip loader.*   Cost is $500,000 and cash inflow for the next 10 years is $75,000 per year.
- *Conveyor system.*   Cost is $400,000 with cash inflow of only $65,000, but for the next 15 years.

Use the NPV tables in any finance book or any good financial calculator (such as an HP-12C). The NPV of both projects is:

- Skip loader: $423,767
- Conveyor: $442,706

Therefore, from this standpoint, the conveyor appears to be a better investment. However, let's compute the return on investment for both projects:

$$ROI = (NPV / \text{initial cash outlay}) / \text{no. of years}$$

Skip loader: ($423,767 / $500,000) / 10 = 8%

Conveyor: ($442,706 / $400,000) / 15 = 7%

Therefore, the skip loader, even though it's more expensive, has a smaller NPV, and lasts only 10 years, has a better return on investment. Note also that these calculations consider the 12 percent cost of funds by discounting the future cash inflows back to present value.

Internal Rate of Return

The internal rate of return (IRR) differs from net present value computations in that it discounts the future cash inflows back to present value so that they exactly equal the initial cash outlay. We use two steps in computing IRR:

Step 1: Determine Annuity Factor of Future Cash Inflows.   Find the table factor for the present value of an ordinary annuity of $1. We'll use this in the annuity table for step 2. Compute the table factor using this formula:

Annuity table factor = net cash outlay / average annual net cash inflow

The factors used for T-D-O's two projects are:

Skip loader: $500,000 / $75,000 = 6.67
Conveyor: $400,000 / $65,000 = 6.15

Step 2: Use the Annuity Table for IRR.   Look up the two factors using the table for present value of an ordinary annuity of $1. Use the row corresponding to the correct number of years in the projects. Then look up the column to find the IRR that discounts us back to the initial cash outlay. Here are the results:

- Skip loader: For 10 years, the factor was 6.67. This gives an approximate IRR of 8 percent.
- Conveyor: For 15 years, the factor was 6.15. This provides an approximate IRR of 14 percent.

From an IRR perspective, the conveyor is a better project.

Accounting Rate of Return

Analysts use another method of evaluation called the *accounting rate of return*. It uses net cash inflow or net profits and the average investment to measure the project's productivity. Some analysts focus on net profit rather than cash flow. In these cases, we call the computation *return on net assets* (RONA). The equation for the accounting rate of return is:

Cash return = average annual net cash inflow / cash outflow

RONA = net income + after tax interest expense / total assets − current liabilities

For T-D-O's project compute the cash return as:

Skip loader: $75,000 / $500,000 = 15%
Conveyor: $65,000 / $400,000 = 16%

Payback Period

This is a very quick method used to gauge a project's *liquidity* rather than its actual return. Payback measures the number of years (or payment periods) it takes to return the initial investment. Compute payback as:

$$\text{Payback period} = \text{cash outlay} / \text{constant cash inflow}$$

The payback periods for T-D-O are:

Skip loader: $500,000 / $75,000 = 7 years
Conveyor: $400,000 / $65,000 = 6 years

This method ignores the time value of money. For example, say one project has a constant cash inflow over five years and another pays the same amount for just two years, then stops. Both projects have the same initial costs. The payback periods for both may be identical. However, the one with a continuing cash inflow is certainly better.

General Rules

There are three rules analysts go by when working with discounted cash flow, IRR, NPV, and the accounting rate of return:

1. If NPV (in dollars) equals cash outlay (also in dollars), the project is at a breakeven and shouldn't be done without special circumstances. The same holds true when IRR (in percentage) equals cost of capital (also in percentage).

2. If NPV is negative, don't do the project. If IRR is less than the cost of capital, don't do the project.

3. If NPV is positive and IRR exceeds the cost of capital, the project bears further investigation.

Ranking Projects

The most difficult thing when ranking different capital projects in order of priority is converting each to a common denominator. We *must* compare apples to apples.

Usually, two projects have different cash flows and their initial payments are different as well. Most likely, the financing requirements aren't similar either.

Use the criteria in Figure 17-5 to compare two different projects.

Monitoring Project Performance

Capital projects are too expensive and their benefits too important to allow differences between expectations and actual performance. Astute treasurers and controllers monitor the performance of their capital projects. The company's attitude toward such programs should focus on accountability of the people who proposed a project in the first place.

Too often companies make a proposal unjustifiably attractive just to get it pushed through. They worry about how they're going to hit those targets later. Controllers prevent that with postcompletion audits of each project. Benefits of such reviews after completion of a project include:

1. Identification and reporting differences between projections in the proposal (on which authorization to proceed was based) and actuals.

2. Provides a basis to make corrections to the program if necessary.

3. Creates a forum in which to hold project management responsible for the accuracy of their proposal estimates. This serves as a deterrent against excessively ambitious proposals.

4. Involves senior management in the investment process.

Description of the project
Is this a new project, a replacement, or a repair?
Benefits: Increase in output, decrease in production costs, quality enhancement?
  What does the project do for us?
Cost of project
Schedule of cash outflows (if more than one)
Schedule of cash inflows and all assumptions used to arrive at the schedule
NPV
IRR
Payback
Hurdle rate required
Estimated useful life
Residual value
Risks
Opportunities

Figure 17-5. Comparison of capital projects.

Who Does the Audit?

Capital projects are complicated. Frequently everyone is on unfamiliar ground. The audit team shouldn't try to reinvent the wheel. Avoid that by including on the team those most familiar with the project. Additionally, include at least one person who wrote the original project proposal. However, make sure that one member of the team is completely independent (and objective) of the project. Finally, the audit team reports to an executive independent of the project.

What to Audit?

Certainly audit the most important and expensive projects of the company. From there, if your firm has many smaller projects, select particular projects to audit. It might be a good idea to select one project from each person who submits proposals. That way, if there's a consistent flaw with the performance estimates, we can find it and fix it. Figure 17-6 illustrates the sample outline of a capital project audit.

Preparing a Capital Projects Plan

Capital expenditure plans usually integrate with the company's business plans. They serve to bridge gaps in the company's capacity to achieve some part of the

1. Name of project and designation
2. Names of those who proposed the project
3. Names of the audit team
4. Description of the project as submitted in the proposal
5. Assessment of the completed project compared with the proposed description
6. Total actual costs compared to proposed costs
7. Actual elapsed time to complete compared to that proposed
8. Actual cash inflow compared to that proposed
9. Comparison of actual financial indicators compared to that proposed, including NPV, IRR, payback
10. Explanation of all material variances
11. Lessons learned from the project; analysis of changes required by the proposal and decision-making process

Figure 17-6. Capital project audit.

plan. Since capital projects span a number of years, many companies include their plan as a section of the overall business plan.

Once the capital projects plan is in place, other parts of the company become involved. The finance group must determine how best to pay for the project. The division conducting the project identifies the impacts to its own business plan the project has now and in the future.

Components of the Capital Projects Plan

We've proposed and approved all capital projects by the time we've reached the planning stage. All that remains is integrating each into the company's business plan. Parts of the capital projects plan most interesting to business plan participants include:

- Identification of all projects
- Financial schedules associated with the capital plan
- Demonstration of how each project integrates into the company
- Assessment of the impacts on the company each project makes

Identifying Projects.   Include in this section of the business plan a brief description of each capital project. Outline all major projects having a material effect on the company, its costs, and revenues individually.

Describe why the company accepted each project. Don't shortcut this part of the plan. Part of the monthly assessment that tracks planned results against actuals includes the capital projects plan. We want enough detail to assess progress each month. We also want to know immediately if the programs deviate from their planned course.

Scheduling the Projects.   The financial schedules associated with each project interest the treasurer and controller. List all capital projects on a monthly schedule that spans the time covered by the overall business plan itself. Include on this schedule:

- Projected cash inflows, revenues, and any other income item listed individually by project
- Projected cash outflows, costs, and expenses listed individually by project

Additionally, include milestones scheduled for completion at particular points in time. For example, if the firm builds a new warehouse, show on the schedules when the foundation was *actually* poured compared to its target pouring date.

Integrating the Capital Plan with the Business Plan.   Many departments must plan for the impact of capital projects. This part of the capital plan identifies likely changes for each department as a result of each capital program. For example, if the company builds a new production line, either current production stops during construction or the old line moves elsewhere. The business plan must communicate these impacts to all affected departments.

Assessing Impacts on the Company.   Capital projects affect the company as a whole. Otherwise, we wouldn't spend all that money doing them. This section of the capital plan describes the impacts on various parts of the company for each project. It's not the economic justification—the plan described that earlier. However, we do want to discuss how each project assists in moving the company that much closer to the overall targets described in the firm's business plan.

Detailing Each Program.   The last part of the capital projects section provides the detail for each program. Most companies just include the forms they submitted to the capital projects review committee. These provide a detailed reference base for each project right in that section of the business plan.

18
Financing and Borrowing

Overview

Financing ongoing operations and borrowing funds for expansion are among the most important jobs of treasurers and controllers. Chapter 18 describes some of the many financing vehicles available to companies of all sizes. Astute financial managers often find the most readily available money sources right there in their own companies. Chapter 18 points them out and shows how to tap into them.

Sometimes the company's business plan requires capital assets too expensive for outright purchase. When this happens, questions of financing or leasing quickly arise. Chapter 18 demonstrates computations designed to determine the best decision.

Long-term funding arises from a variety of sources. We'll discuss the strategies involved in private and public placement of equity and debt securities. Treasurers and controllers do not limit their funding sources to just this country. Often international sources provide less expensive and less restrictive money. Finally, high-risk, high-reward companies can tap venture capital funds when more conservative sources turn a deaf ear.

Recognizing Internal Sources

Most treasurers and controllers count sources either within the firm itself or those with whom it has a strong relationship—such as its bank—as internal sources. This is usually the first source of funding companies look to before going to outside investors. These internal facilities provide money faster and less expensively than any other source. Further, the terms of repayment are the most flexible since the company exerts more control.

However, most internal funding sources provide only short-term money. The firm cannot rely on them to provide the core financing around which it builds a capital structure. Long-term funding comes from owners' and partners' contributed capital, stock, long-term loans, and debt securities issued by the firm.

The most commonly used short-term sources of funding include:

- Working capital
- Trade credit
- Bank lines of credit
- Installment loans

Liberating Working Capital

The quickest way to free cash held within the company is to reduce working capital requirements. Once liberated, the company transfers this money where it's needed most. Tap sources of additional funds from any of the working capital components. Here's how we compute working capital:

Cash

plus accounts receivable

plus inventory

less accounts payable

less accrued liabilities

equals working capital

Decreasing either component of the asset side—receivables or inventory—frees cash invested in working capital required to run the firm. For example, if the collections department figures out a way to permanently reduce the average collection time from 35 days to 25 days, that's a source of internally generated funds. The working capital no longer absorbed by receivables moves back into the firm.

Likewise, increasing working capital components on the liability side—accounts payable and accrued liabilities—provide an interest-free loan to the company. For example, say that the purchasing department successfully negotiates a change in its purchase contracts that results in extending payment terms from an average of 30 days to 45 days. This reduces working capital invested in the firm's ongoing operations.

Clever treasurers and controllers establish programs that routinely search for ways to liberate cash from working capital. Every time they free this valuable asset, they put it to work elsewhere within the company.

Figure 18-1 illustrates how to compute the value of purchase terms and payment dates.

Factoring Accounts Receivable

Factoring refers to sale of accounts receivable to a factoring company. This takes place at a discount to compensate the factor for risk and allow a profit. For the discount paid, the company receives its money faster than if it waited for the receivable to age through its normal collection cycle.

Assume three vendors offer the following terms.

- Vendor 1: Payment is due in 30 days or else, no discount, and vendor offers a $10,000 credit limit.
- Vendor 2: Payment is due in 45 days, no discount, and vendor offers a $20,000 credit limit.
- Vendor 3: Payment terms are 2 percent discount if paid in 10 days, otherwise full payment in 30 days or else, and vendor offers a $10,000 credit line.

Assume monthly purchases are $10,000. Determine profit contribution of each vendor's terms.

- Vendor 1: All this vendor provides is a $10,000 interest-free loan for one year. If cost of funds is 10 percent, this is a contribution to the firm's profit of $1000.
- Vendor 2: Terms of purchase *doubled* the credit facility *and* extended the payment terms. This vendor provides a $15,000 interest-free loan for one year and contributes $1500 toward profitability.
- Vendor 3: The 2 percent discount separates this vendor from vendor 1. However, this alone provides a $2400 increase in profitability ($120,000 in annual purchases × 2% = $2400). The $667 cost of funds incurred by paying 20 days "early" to get this discount is computed as:

$$\frac{[(\$10,000 \times 10\%) \times 20 \text{ days per month}] \times 12 \text{ months}}{360} = \$667$$

However, vendor 2 allowed 45 days to pay. The extra costs by taking the discount compared to a 45-day payment term were $778, computed as follows:

$$\frac{[(\$10,000 \times 10\%) \times 35 \text{ days per month}] \times 8 \text{ payments}}{360} = \$778$$

Therefore, the net contribution by choosing vendor 3 is $1622 ($2400 − 778 = $1622). Vendor 3 still offers the best deal.

Figure 18-1. Determining value of purchase terms.

Factors purchase receivables with recourse and without recourse. With recourse means that the seller retains liability for uncollectible debts. The discount isn't as steep for recourse purchases. Without recourse requires the factor to bear the risk of bad debt. Factors include this risk in their discount percentage.

Cautions When Using a Factor. Some sales of accounts receivable allow the customer to know of the transaction; others do not. Consider how notice of such a sale could affect your customer relationship. For example, few prestigious law firms would allow their clients to know about any factoring of their receivables.

Second, factoring is one of the most expensive sources of cash. Use factoring as a last resort. Finally, before selling your receivables, be sure to check the loan covenants and restrictions. Some banks secure their loans with assets of the company—often using accounts receivable. Under such circumstances, factoring receivables could cause a condition of default.

Unsecured Credit Lines

Treasurers often call these *revolvers*. They amount to unsecured lines of credit that have a definite repayment date. The bank makes the funds available on demand. Treasurers and controllers use revolving lines for short-term cash deficits. Companies with seasonal business draw the LOC down during the slack time and repay it when the business cycle cranks up again.

Pricing Credit Lines.   LOCs are more expensive than regular loans. The interest rate is usually a multiple based on the prime lending rate. Additionally, since the borrower has the right to draw funds on demand (with just a phone call or fax), the bank charges a commitment fee. After all, the bank must keep enough cash available to fund the entire commitment at all times. Commitment fees usually range from ⅛ to ½ a point of the available balance.

Cleanup Provisions.   Most credit lines require the borrower to repay the entire balance for one month out of every twelve-month period. This ensures that the borrower isn't misusing the LOC for its permanent financing requirements. Additionally, LOCs usually run for only 12 months. At the end the bank has the option of renewing the line or calling for repayment and canceling the agreement.

Single-Payment Loans

These are the traditional working capital loans. Companies use them for the same purpose as a line of credit—to fund temporary working capital shortfalls caused by fluctuations in the business cycle. However, companies must repay single-payment loans on the day specified in the loan agreement. Some lenders fund the loan on an *as needed* basis, as with a credit line.

Single-payment loans usually have a predetermined and certain source of repayment. An example of the proper use of a single-payment loan is a special deal offered a company on its raw materials. Normally the firm doesn't buy such a large quantity, but the deal is too good to pass up. The company draws a loan with the intent of repayment at the end of the sales and collection cycle.

Installment Loans

Companies often finance their capital equipment using installment loans. The idea is that the equipment will throw off cash sufficient to repay the principal and interest owed each month on the installment note.

Installment loan terms run between one and five years. Longer terms usually require the lender to have a mortgage interest in the asset.

Computing Annual Percentage Rates—Add-on Interest.   The actual interest rate paid by borrowers on their installment loans is tricky. Banks employ two payment methods for installment loans: add-on interest and declining balance.

Avoid contracts calling for add-on interest. They give the bank a higher interest rate than specified in the loan contract. They compute interest over the entire loan life. Then they add it to the loan balance as if it were principal. Monthly payments are figured on the total balance (principal and interest yet owed). The borrower pays monthly interest *on the interest it will eventually owe.*

Here's the equation to compute the *annual percentage rate* of an add-on installment loan:

$$APR = 12(95N + 9)I/12N(N + I)(4P = I)$$

where N = the number of loan payments made during the life of the loan
    I = the total interest charges
    P = the principal amount of the loan

Assume a borrower has an add-on installment loan of $10,000 ($P$ in the equation). The term of the loan is 24 months (N) and the interest rate is 9 percent. First compute I in the equation. Total interest charges are $1800 ([$10,000 × 9%] × 2 = $1800). Now, insert this and the other variables into the equation:

$$APR = \frac{(12(95 \times 24) + 9) \times \$1800}{(12 \times 24) \times (24 + 1) \times ((4 \times \$10,000) + \$1800)}$$

$$APR = 16.43\%$$

Notice how the computed annual percentage rate after the interest add-on is significantly higher than the contractual interest rate of 9 percent. That's why smart treasurers always compute the real interest rate of such contracts before committing their companies.

Computing Annual Percentage Rates—Declining Balance.   This is the more popular method of computing monthly installment payments. It bases the interest charge on the principal balance yet outstanding. This works in a manner similar to a normal home mortgage. The interest rate stated on the loan contract is much closer to the actual annual percentage rate.

Figure 18-2 shows a loan amortization for a two-year declining balance installment loan.

Lending Criteria Used by Banks

Banks look carefully at their corporate borrowers. Generally, the more seasoned lending officers deal with loans made to companies. Banks base their lending decisions on just three things:

Payment no.	Payment	Principal	Interest	Ending balance
1	$456.85	$381.85	$75.00	$9,618.15
2	456.85	384.71	72.14	9,233.44
3	456.85	387.60	69.25	8,845.84
4	456.85	390.50	66.34	8,455.34
5	456.85	393.43	63.42	8,061.91
6	456.85	396.38	60.46	7,665.53
7	456.85	399.36	57.49	7,266.17
8	456.85	402.35	54.50	6,863.82
9	456.85	405.37	51.48	6,458.45
10	456.85	408.41	48.44	6,050.04
11	456.85	411.47	45.38	5,638.57
12	456.85	414.56	42.29	5,224.01
13	456.85	417.67	39.18	4,806.34
14	456.85	420.80	36.05	4,385.54
15	456.85	423.96	32.89	3,961.59
16	456.85	427.14	29.71	3,534.45
17	456.85	430.34	26.51	3,104.11
18	456.85	433.57	23.28	2,670.55
19	456.85	436.82	20.03	2,233.73
20	456.85	440.09	16.75	1,793.63
21	456.85	443.40	13.45	1,350.24
22	456.85	446.72	10.13	903.52
23	456.85	450.07	6.78	453.45
24	456.85	453.45	3.40	0

Figure 18-2. Installment loan amortization schedule.

- Repayment capacity of the borrower
- Cash flow from operations
- Collateral

If your company meets the banks' standards in these three areas it will get the loan; if not, it won't.

Financial Statements. Historical financial statements provide all the information bankers need to evaluate earnings capacity and cash flow. They're looking for a demonstrated repayment history of prior loans. If your business plan produces prospective financial statements, the bankers may want to see these as well. However, prospective financials carry much less weight than a track record based on independently audited statements going back several years.

Evaluation of earning capacity reduces to just one number—times interest earned (net earnings/interest expense). Bankers want assurance that the company has a good margin of error in their operations and can still meet its payment obligations.

Times interest earned is usually a multiple—the bigger, the better. If earnings cover interest by just a factor of 1, the company barely meets its obligations. That won't fly. Indeed, the lending covenant may specify a minimum interest coverage ratio.

Cash Flow from Operations.   Banks look most carefully at cash flow. They want assurance that the company can meet all of its trade obligations *and* the terms of the loan under consideration. Further, trade payables aren't usually the only liabilities companies have. Chances are they have other debts such as financing leases, term loans, credit lines, and bond interest payments, to name just a few. Cash flow from operations must support these as well.

Finally, the bank wants a margin of error from cash flow. Cash must exceed all current obligations by a sufficient margin to absorb unforeseen problems and delays of cash inflow.

Collateral.   Hard-asset lenders demand collateral. They want assets (such as accounts receivable) sufficient to allow them a fast sell-off at distressed prices in the event of default. However, there's a problem with overcollateralizing a loan with strategic assets of the company, such as production machinery.

If the firm has a problem, the bank forecloses on the collateral. Unfortunately, the company needs these assets to continue in operation. Now the company faces closing down and the bank has an asset it knows nothing of how to employ, short of dumping it at a fraction of its value. Everyone loses.

Along with collateral, most banks require a minimum level of the owner's stake in the company. They measure this using the debt-to-equity ratio. If equity falls below the minimum 2:1, questions arise as to who really owns the company—the bank or the owners. The greater their stake in the firm, the less likely owners are to walk away if the going gets tough. Further, with their own money on the line, owners take fewer unnecessary risks.

Figure 18-3 shows some of the hot buttons bankers use to help make lending decisions. Companies' negotiating strength increases as more of these buttons are pressed.

Floating Commercial Paper

Commercial paper is an unsecured promissory note of a short-term maturity. Companies often use it as an alternative to short-term bank loans.

The commercial paper market continues to grow. In its infancy, only blue-chip companies floated commercial paper (or CP, as it's often called). Only the full faith and creditworthiness of the issuer backs CP.

Today, however, many types of firms issue CP. They often provide a guaranteed stream of payments—such as from accounts receivable—that *securitizes* the commercial paper. Using this technique, companies without the gilt-edged status of a blue-chip company can successfully issue CP.

Using Commercial Paper as a Funding Source

CP is by definition a short-term financing vehicle. It sells either at a discount to its face or with interest payable at the end of the term. Both of these customs allow CP

Financial stability. Lenders base the stability of borrowers on these financial indicators:

- Current ratio should be at least 2:1
- Quick ratio should be at least 1:1
- Times interest earned standard is about 2:1, but this varies among lenders and within industries
- Debt-to-equity standard is about 2:1. However, hard-asset lenders able to perfect a security interest in a readily marketable asset may go higher.

Subordination of loan. This identifies where the lender stands in the line of succession of creditors in the event of default. Naturally, lenders who stand first in line have less at risk. Along with position of the loan, lenders want sufficient collateral easily salable at a value even after the distress sale discount equivalent to the loan amount.

Management. Lenders want comfort in management's talent, experience, record of success, depth, and second-tier support staff.

Industry. Bankers lend into industries on the upswing. They want a demonstrated market demand for their borrowers' products. Ideally they want to see entry barriers that limit new competition. Further, lenders who demonstrate a long history of relationships with a diverse group of clients provide better stability and assurance of repayment.

Infrastructure. Bankers want the assurance that the borrower company has the physical assets in place to execute its repayment plan. Such assets include property, plant, equipment, systems for accounting, inventory control, and management information. They want to see a demonstrated control over the sales force and distribution channels.

Figure 18-3. Loan decision hot buttons.

to avoid SEC registration requirements *and* original-issue discount rules regarding recognition of imputed interest expense for the issuer and income for the buyer.

To meet both of these requirements CP maturities never exceed 270 days. The proceeds go to fund current operations.

Rolling CP Issues

Many companies depend on the funds from their CP issues. Indeed, some sell new issues of commercial paper in order to liquidate a previous issue that's maturing. Using this technique, they roll over CP issues continuously. This relieves them from the requirement of dipping into working capital to liquidate a maturing issue.

Companies that roll their CP issues often have a standby line of credit ready to meet any shortfall of the new issue if it fails to sell. Using a backup LOC, they sell whatever part of the new issue they can, then use the proceeds and the LOC to liquidate the prior issue.

Reducing Buyer's Risk

Smaller companies involved in the CP market need to make their issue more attractive to buyers. They can enhance the perceived strength of their balance sheet by obtaining a letter of credit from a top bank equivalent in value to the CP issue. A third party—such as a bank—holds the letter of credit for benefit of the CP buyers. The LOC pays off in the event the company defaults and cannot liquidate its issue on maturity.

Electronic Book Entry

The CP market has entered the electronic age. Much of the commercial paper now issued uses the electronic book entry system run by the Depository Trust Company under the supervision of the Federal Reserve. Electronic debits and credits to the buyers' and sellers' accounts replace actual paper notes. This system makes payment processing for CP buyers and sellers much faster.

Rating Commercial Paper

Independent agencies rate most commercial paper issues. The rating an issue receives determines both the interest rate the company must pay and how well it sells. Six companies rate commercial paper. These are:

- Standard & Poor's
- Moody's Investor Services
- Crisanti & Maffei
- Fitch Investor's Services
- McCarthy
- Duff & Phelps

Using Company Assets as Collateral

The size of asset-based loans falls somewhere between what's available from unsecured instruments and from long-term, fully collateralized mortgage loans.

The assets of the company used as collateral often change during the term of the loan. Accounts receivable and inventory are two. By using assets whose value changes, the amount of funding available also changes. For example, a company may draw an asset-based loan against its accounts receivable. As the firm collects its receivables, it repays the loan. However, it uses the loan proceeds to fund production that makes more product that, when sold, creates even more receivables. This way the loan balance never actually gets repaid. Bankers call this an *evergreen* or *revolving loan.*

When to Use Asset-based Loans

Most companies use asset-based loans when they require more funds than they can borrow on an unsecured basis. The need for these funds isn't long-term. Such companies are often:

- High growth
- Involved in seasonal businesses
- Seeking funds for an acquisition or major purchase
- Entangled in a turnaround situation

Companies seeking to grow rapidly often cannot turn their assets into cash quickly enough to support other growing parts of the firm. Alternatively, companies with a seasonal business require funding to carry them through the slow period. The loan repays during the peak season.

Companies seeking funds for an acquisition use the cash flow generated by the acquired company to repay the loan.

Often asset-based lenders provide the funds necessary for a turnaround. If the collateral is in place and the company's recovery plan is realistic, this type of loan often makes sense.

Qualifying Assets

Asset-based lenders use all kinds of collateral to make the deal work. Commercial asset-based loans typically advance funds against such collateral as:

- Accounts receivable
- Inventory
- Work in process
- Royalties
- Franchise rights

Some asset-based lenders view the last two—royalties and franchise rights—as nontraditional collateral. However, they both have the one characteristic that turns on lenders: cash flow. Take, for example, the royalty stream from a producing oil well. Independent professionals quantify the reserves. If the well is producing, there's no speculation as in exploratory wells. The market for oil is proven and liquid. This royalty-producing asset guarantees the cash flow. From a lender's perspective, there is no better collateral.

Valuing Assets.   Lenders look for tangible value in their asset-based collateral. They must quantify that value to determine the amount they can reasonably advance against it. For accounts receivable, they evaluate the quality of the receivable portfolio. They check on the creditworthiness of the customers. Composition of the portfolio (in terms of aging and the velocity accounts) rolls from one aging bucket to the next (please see Chapter 11, "Accounts Receivable"), providing additional information on the portfolio's value.

Inventory used as a base for asset loans raises questions of liquidity. After all, if borrowers default, lenders may end up owning the inventory. Since they aren't in the business of using it, they must find buyers. They base their lending on:

- Discount required to move the inventory
- Speed the inventory is sold
- Liquidity of the market—number of buyers
- Potential obsolescence—prevalent in computer equipment and electronic components

Few asset-based lenders advance funds over 50 percent of the estimated market value of inventory. Often they engage independent appraisers to determine value. These professionals value the inventory using a forced sale or liquidation basis. The appraisals often require specific technical expertise. Real estate used for collateral is one such asset. People make careers out of appraising real estate.

Ongoing Monitoring.   Just because an asset or a company qualifies for an asset-based loan today, doesn't guarantee that status for the duration of the loan. That's why banks usually require periodic evaluation and inspection of assets used as collateral. They want to protect their interests. At the very least, expect the lender to demand periodic financial statements.

Cost of Asset-based Loans

Interest rates vary depending on the lender's perceived risk. If the underlying assets have a ready market, maintain their value, and are liquid, the rates are better than for assets that don't contain these qualities. Usually the interest rates vary based on an index rate. These are usually the prime rate at a designated bank (usually the lending bank) or LIBOR (London Interbank Offered Rate).

From the index rate, the lender attaches a spread. The spread provides compensation for risk, fees associated with the transaction, and profit.

Additional Fees.   Most asset-based loans incur some fees. These vary depending on the type of asset monitored for sufficiency. An audit or appraisal fee often enters into the annual maintenance cost of the loan—paid for by the borrower, of course. The bank also charges back its borrowers for wire transfer fees every time it makes another advance.

Many banks include something called *float days*. This is a specified number of days allowed the bank after receiving payment to credit the borrower's account. If a lender is inefficient at crediting its loan payments, this amounts to the borrower paying for that inefficiency.

Financing Using ESOP

Employee Stock Ownership Plans (ESOPs) provide a significant tax break for closely held companies. Using an ESOP as a financing vehicle, a company can deduct not only the interest on its financing, but the principal as well. Within IRS Code 404, restrictions limit the amount of deduction to 25 percent of the annual compensation of the plan participants. However, for companies with large participating payrolls, this is a material consideration.

Figure 18-4 summarizes the tax advantages of an ESOP.

Mechanics of a Leveraged ESOP

Three parties participate in the funds flow associated with an ESOP:

- The company
- The ESOP itself
- The lender

The purpose of the plan is to allow the ESOP to purchase company stock using borrowed funds. The company then uses the proceeds from the stock sale for operations and general corporate needs. The company also funds the ESOP each year

---

1. Employer contributions are tax deductible to 25 percent of participant's annual compensation.
2. Lenders to ESOPs receive 50 percent of the interest income tax-free. Lenders that are *Regulated Investment Companies* also qualify for this exemption with the benefits flowing through to their shareholders.
3. ESOP dividends paid to participants are tax-deductible.

Figure 18-4. ESOP tax advantages.

in the amount needed to service the loan required for stock purchase. Figure 18-5 shows how this works.

Using this method, the ESOP pays the debt service using funds provided by the company. The company gets to deduct *all* of its annual contribution up to 25 percent of the plan participant's compensation. Naturally, as the corporate tax rate rises, the advantages of such employee stock ownership schemes increase.

There's another advantage. In the event of a hostile takeover, the ESOP owns the stock. Since the company directs the ESOP, it won't tender its shares to the unwanted suitor.

Acquiring Companies Using a Leveraged ESOP

ESOPs often acquire the stock of other companies on behalf of the benefactor company. The same tax advantages inure to this type of transaction. Here's how it works:

1. The ESOP borrows funds to purchase the stock of the target company.
2. The employer company guarantees the ESOP loan and contributes cash sufficient each year to pay the debt service.
3. The ESOP purchases the target company's stock directly, then exchanges it with the employer company for its own stock. Alternatively, the ESOP uses the loan proceeds to buy stock in the employer company that then uses the proceeds to

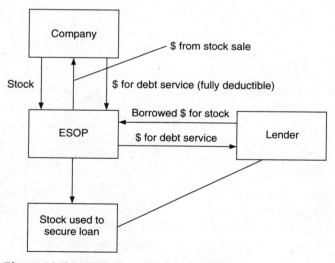

Figure 18-5. Mechanics of an ESOP.

buy the target company's stock. Either way it works out the same—the ESOP owns the employer company stock and the employer company owns the target company stock.

Conditions of ESOPs

If you're thinking of using an ESOP to enhance the tax advantages of financing your company, the IRS has certain specific requirements. The purpose is to prevent abuse of the tax advantages to financing through the ESOP. The key requirements include:

1. *Restrictive use.* Loan proceeds must acquire stock in the employer company. ESOPs cannot purchase and hold any other assets.
2. *Nonrecourse loan.* ESOPs cannot encumber any assets other than those purchased with the loan proceeds.
3. *Main beneficiaries.* The loan undertaken by any ESOP must primarily benefit the employees.
4. *Cannot reduce worth.* The interest rate and value of the securities acquired using the loan proceeds cannot reduce the worth of the company or the plan.
5. *Arm's-length transaction.* Both the interest rate on borrowing and the value of securities acquired must bear prevailing market rates and value.
6. *Related-party transactions.* ESOP transactions cannot be between related parties.
7. *Stock distribution.* Participants in an ESOP must receive stock distribution upon employment termination.
8. *Stock voting rights.* ESOP participants may vote their employer stock shares consistent with the way shares held by any other shareholder may vote. If the employer company's shares are not registration-class securities, ESOP participants may vote on corporate matters decided by a majority of the common shares voted.

Leasing Assets

Companies lease major assets for a variety of good reasons. Some companies cannot afford purchase of the capital assets needed to run their businesses. Others find that financing these assets cuts too deeply into their profit margins. Still other companies choose not to disburse the cash required for a purchase, even though they could.

Most often, leasing is more expensive than actually purchasing. Many treasurers and controllers suffer over the decision to lease or buy. This decision becomes even more difficult when the leasing rate looks more attractive than the cost of capital to buy.

Types of Leases

The first step in deciding to lease or buy requires determination of the type of lease under consideration. The two most common leases are capital leases (also called *financing leases*) and operating leases.

Operating Leases.   Ownership of the assets in operating leases remains with the lessor. The lessee is like a tenant paying rent. The contract never contemplates the lessee owning the asset. The complete lease payment is an ordinary and necessary business expense and, therefore, completely tax-deductible.

Capital Leases.   Capital leases provide for the lessee to eventually own the asset at the end of the lease. The lessor actually provides a vehicle for the lessee to purchase the asset. Of course, included in the terms of the lease are interest payments. Four tests distinguish a capital lease from an operating lease. Presence of any *one* of these qualifies the lease as a capital lease:

1. The term of the lease equals at least 75 percent of the total estimated economic life of the leased asset.
2. The lease contract transfers ownership to the lessee at the end.
3. The present value of the minimum lease payments is at least 90 percent of the fair market value of the leased asset.
4. The lease contains a bargain purchase option (defined as a below-market price).

Leases not meeting any of these four tests are operating leases.

Deciding to Lease or Buy

Taxes play an important role in this decision. Be aware of these two tax effects:

1. For capital leases, deduct the annual depreciation as an ordinary and necessary business expense. This is because the lessee is (or will be) the owner. Lessees of operating leases cannot take depreciation since they don't (and never will) own the asset.
2. Operating leases treat the entire lease payment as an ordinary and necessary business expense—completely tax-deductible. Capital leases treat only the interest portion as a deductible expense. Consider the rest of the monthly lease payment principal toward purchase.

Lease/buy analysis computes the present value of the *after-tax costs* of the lease. It compares these with after-tax costs of a leveraged purchase. Be sure to include these two items in your analysis:

1. *For leases.*   Depreciation, interest, and maintenance do not apply for operating leases. However, a portion may apply for capital or financing leases.

2. *For purchases.* Depreciation, principal paydown, interest, and maintenance costs are relevant.

Model Lease versus Buy Analysis

Here's a sample lease/buy analysis to illustrate the principles described above. Assume that MTH Industries is looking at a new industrial welding system for its San Diego pipe-fitting operation. The facts include:

- Cost of the welding system: $100,000
- Economic life: 5 years
- Residual value: none
- Interest rate if borrowed funds are used: 14%
- Annual maintenance expense on the welding system: $5000
- MTH's marginal tax rate: 30 percent
- Annual payment required to purchase: $29,128
- Depreciation method: MACRS
- *Operating* lease payments: $29,000 annually

This is a triple-net lease. Therefore, MTH pays for all maintenance. Since the $5000 annual maintenance fee exists whether MTH buys or leases, it is an irrelevant cost. Omit it from the analysis. The lease offered MTH is an operating lease. This allows full deduction of the entire lease payment as an expense. However, do not deduct depreciation from operating leases. Figures 18-6 through 18-9 show MTH's computations.

From Figures 18-8 and 18-9 it appears that the leasing alternative *is* indeed slightly more expensive. However, when two alternatives are this close, consider the cash tied up in a down payment. Many companies would rather have the money even if the lease option is a little more expensive.

Sale/Leaseback

Many treasurers and controllers find their companies hold substantially appreciated assets. They use these assets in daily business operations, so they can't sell

Payment no.	Payment	Principal	Interest	Loan balance
1	$29,128	$29,128	$ 0	$70,872
2	29,128	19,206	9,922	51,655
3	29,128	21,895	7,233	29,770
4	29,128	24,961	4,168	4,810
5	5,483	4,810	673	0

Figure 18-6. Purchase option: interest expense computation.

Year	Book value	Rate	Depreciation	Accumulated depreciation
1	$100,000	20%	$10,000	$ 10,000*
2	90,000	40%	36,000	46,000
3	54,000	40%	21,600	67,600
4	32,400	S/L	16,200	83,800
5	16,200	S/L	16,200	100,000

* MACRS requires acquisition year ½ the annual rate.

Figure 18-7. Purchase option: depreciation.

Pymt. no. (1)	Payment (2)	Interest (3)	Depreciation (4)	Taxable shelter (¾=5)	After-tax cash flow [2−(5×30%)=6]	Present value of costs (7)
1	$29,128	$ 0	$10,000	$10,000	$26,128	$26,128
2	29,128	9,922	36,000	45,922	15,352	12,085
3	29,128	7,233	21,600	28,883	20,478	13,822
4	29,128	4,168	16,200	20,368	23,018	13,628
5	29,128	673	16,200	16,873	24,066	12,499
						$78,162

Figure 18-8. Purchase option: computation of present value.

Payment no.	Payment	After-tax cost	PV of costs
1	$29,000	$20,300	$20,300
2	29,000	20,300	17,807
3	29,000	20,300	15,620
4	29,000	20,300	13,702
5	29,000	20,300	12,019
			$79,448

Figure 18-9. Lease option: computation of present value.

them. The question is how to extract the cash in these assets and employ it more profitably without losing use of the asset.

The answer is often a sale/leaseback. This works on such corporate assets as the headquarters office building or warehouses. The company may sell these appreciated assets to an investor and immediately lease them back. The company gets the profit from the sale (less capital gains tax) and retains use of the property through the lease. Now the firm is free to plow the funds back into the business to get a higher rate of return than it would by allowing the cash to sit buried in the slowly appreciating asset.

Placing Securities Privately

Private placement of securities involves a different set of rules and marketing strategies than the larger public offerings. Companies offer the placement of debt or equity securities to only a small number of private investors. The firm targets its effort to selected purchasers.

Under Regulation D of the SEC code companies may privately issue securities meeting specific criteria. This allows companies to avoid SEC registration normally required in public offerings. Regulation D placements require that investors meet at least one of these criteria:

- *Related party.* The investor is associated with the issuer in a capacity such as an officer, director, or partner.

- *Net worth.* Investors must have a minimum net worth of $1 million.

- *Percentage of net worth.* Investment of $150,000 paid over five years cannot exceed 20 percent of the investor's net worth.

- *Income level.* Annual income for each of the past three years must be at least $200,000.

Investors meeting any of these requirements are accredited, sophisticated, and knowledgeable about what they're doing. The SEC believes them able to make an informed investment decision without all the disclosure normally present in a public securities offering.

Filing with the SEC

Even private placements must file with the SEC. If the offer exceeds $500,000 the company must file a *private placement memorandum* with the SEC and provide it to the offerees. This document discloses all the material aspects of the offering necessary to make an informed investment decision.

Rule 505 of Regulation D governs limited offerings up to $5 million. It requires specific disclosures if any securities sell to *nonaccredited* investors. Further, it provides for an unlimited number of accredited investors who may purchase the securities. However, no more than 35 *nonaccredited* investors may purchase the securities.

Role of the Investment Banker

Investment bankers actually place the securities to private investors—often individuals or other companies. However, before that happens they design the entire structure of the deal.

Investment bankers manage the process of the offering. They assist in gathering the legal, accounting, and consulting talent necessary to prepare the private placement memo. Part of this includes the firm's business plan and financial forecasts compiled by an independent CPA firm.

If you engage an investment banking firm to work on your private placement, be sure to negotiate a *kill fee* from the start. This limits the costs in the event that the firm decides to rescind the offer prior to placement.

Going Public

The popularity of public equity and debt offerings fluctuates with the securities markets. During good times, when the stock market rises, investors take more risk. Frequently there's a surge of new stock offerings. When investors turn more conservative, the pendulum swings toward debt offerings such as bonds and some of their derivatives.

Either way, public securities offerings provide the funds necessary to launch companies on the next phase of their evolution. However, organizing and actually bringing such an offering to the public market is a monumental undertaking. It involves rigorous disclosure and filing requirements with the SEC.

Most firms doing a public offering form a team dedicated to the project. The team includes both inside and outside professionals experienced in the operation. Usually these people form the core of the offering team:

- Executives of the company, including its CFO and treasurer
- Internal legal counsel
- Outside specialist legal counsel
- Independent auditors
- Underwriters of the securities issue
- Bank note company
- Financial printer
- Transfer agent
- Registrar

With all these high-priced people involved, such an undertaking is expensive. However, the rewards are equally large. Few companies enter into public offerings without the intent of raising money at least into the seven- and eight-figure ranges.

Scheduling Activities

The process of bringing a securities offering to the public market takes time. Most firms allow anywhere from 6 to 12 months. To help coordinate all the tasks required, most projects schedule them on a calendar with due dates and people responsible identified. Figure 18-10 shows the tasks involved and those who usually do them. This was reprinted with permission of the publisher, Prentice-Hall, a division of Simon & Schuster, Englewood Cliffs, New Jersey, from *The Cash Management Handbook*, by Christopher R. Malburg, 1992.

Activity	Responsibility
Preparation of due diligence documents.	Offering company
Draft due diligence text.	Offering company, underwriter, legal counsel
Proof and accept due diligence printed copy.	Offering company, underwriter, legal counsel, auditors, financial printer
Audit of financial statements, compilation of any financial forecasts, and review of any financial presentations contained in offering prospectus and filings; preparation of auditor's opinion on fairness of presentation of financials and expanded notes to the financial statements; preparation of management letter.	Auditors, offering company financial executives
Draft, approve, and print SEC filing.	Legal counsel, financial printer
File registration with SEC.	Offering company and legal counsel
File press releases and compliance with blue-sky laws in the various states offering the securities.	Legal counsel and underwriters
Print prospectuses, filing packages, and offering documents.	Financial printer
Form underwriting group; establish share allocation and retention by underwriter group.	Underwriters
Negotiate price and terms with underwriting group members.	Offering company and underwriters
File with SEC and receive determination that the offering is "effective."	Legal counsel
Release offering announcement to the press; place tombstone ad.	Underwriters
Sell the offering.	Underwriters
Close the offering.	Offering company, underwriters, legal counsel, transfer agent

Figure 18-10. Schedule of tasks for a public offering.

Offering Requirements

Companies issuing public securities must comply with certain other internal and external requirements. These include:

- Specific records and accounting methods
- Board authorization
- Amendment of certificate of incorporation
- Compliance with NASD requirements
- Compliance with selling rights of existing shareholders
- Compliance with blue-sky laws in different states

Records and Accounting Methods.   Companies issuing securities to the public must have three years of *independently audited* financial statements. Additionally, their accounting methods must comply with the generally accepted accounting principals of their industry. An example is the software development companies springing up all over. Accounting rules for this industry require companies to capitalize some types of expenditures and expense others according to the standards in their industry. When they purchase software, they amortize the costs over a period not exceeding five years. Those companies going public must ensure their financial statements comply with these rules.

SEC enforces strict disclosure requirements regarding self-dealing and related-party transactions. Usually these require lengthy explanation. Therefore, companies planning a public securities sale begin the process at least three years in advance. They stop buying goods and services from the firm's principal owners. They don't make loans to officers and employees either.

Board Authorization.   The company's board of directors must resolve to issue securities whether it's a public or private placement. If the public already holds the company's stock, then the board resolution must specifically address an increase in issued and outstanding shares. The company's secretary records all such board resolutions in the minutes of the meeting.

Amending the Certificate of Incorporation.   If the company has already issued all authorized shares, then the board must resolve to increase the number of shares authorized. Further, existing shareholders must vote to increase the number of authorized shares. If the measure passes, then the company must amend its *certificate of incorporation* to increase the authorized shares.

NASD Requirements.   The National Association of Securities Dealers involves itself in all public securities issues. Prior to actually selling the new securities the company must attend to the little details that make an offering work.

The first such detail is providing the NASD with the registration documents. Usually the underwriters include the NASD on their list of agencies and individuals who need to see the registration and filing documents. The next item is a formal request by the company that the NASD list the stock (if it's an initial public offering) on whatever exchange the company has targeted.

Additionally, the company must choose a ticker symbol for its stock. The company or its legal counsel communicates this to the NASD via letter. Last, the final public issue documents from the company's legal counsel go to the NASD for permanent recording of the issue.

Selling Rights.   Existing shareholders have the right to sell a pro rata portion of their shares in the public offering. Usually the company assists in this. Shareholders wishing to sell appoint an attorney-in-fact to oversee their sale of stock. This attorney appoints a transfer agent (often the same one used by the company) to act as custodian of the stock sold by existing shareholders. After the stock sells, the attorney sends the proceeds to the shareholders.

Compliance with Blue-Sky Laws.   Each state has different laws regarding sale of securities to the public. The company must comply with *each* state's laws in which it offers the securities. The underwriters usually take care of this for the company. They conduct a survey of the blue-sky laws in each state the offering hits. The company makes any changes in the offering needed to comply with each state's requirements. Sometimes, certain state's laws don't fit the offering's requirements. The company may choose to omit them from the offering rather than make the changes necessary for compliance.

The company maintains careful records of the research and changes made to the offering to ensure compliance with state blue-sky laws.

Public Reporting Requirements

The SEC hits companies issuing securities for the first time with a raft of reporting and disclosure requirements. This throws open the privacy of once-confidential corporate affairs to public scrutiny. Figure 18-11 shows a list of the public reporting and disclosure requirements.

Funding from International Sources

The world's financial centers grow more active every year. Today, publicly traded markets exist in:

- New York
- London
- Paris
- Frankfurt
- Hong Kong
- Saudi Arabia
- Singapore

1. *Insider trading.* Specific restrictions govern insiders' trading of the company's securities. These restrictions include when insiders can sell, how much they can sell, and disclosure of the transaction.

2. *Changes in the company.* The SEC requires publicly held companies to disclose publicly any material changes in the company.

3. *Audited financial statements.* All publicly traded companies must engage an independent CPA firm to conduct a *certified* audit on their financial statements. The company reports results of this audit to the public.

4. *Annual reports.* The company must provide an annual report to each shareholder.

5. *Form 10K.* The company must file Form 10K with the SEC. The format for this report closely follows that of the annual report.

6. *Form 10Q.* Each quarter the company must provide all shareholders with quarterly financial statements. It also files these with the SEC under Form 10Q. CPAs do not usually audit these quarterly statements. However, an independent CPA firm usually compiles them and issues a disclaimer opinion.

7. *Annual meeting.* Once each year the company must hold a shareholder meeting. Shareholders of common stock vote on directors to the board as well as any other issues stated in the company's bylaws that require shareholder vote.

Figure 18-11. Public reporting and disclosure requirements.

- Tokyo
- South Korea

This list isn't exhaustive. Nevertheless, companies doing business internationally often tap the huge funds on these exchanges when issuing equity securities.

For international debt, Eurobonds are a popular vehicle. Usually Eurobond investors reside in countries with different currency than the bond's denomination. The company issues its Eurobonds in bearer form and they are free of withholding taxes. Further, Eurobonds don't require the lengthy registration procedures of the SEC or any European regulatory body.

Tapping into Venture Capital

Many companies began with the injection of seed capital from a venture firm. This was probably a small amount of money just sufficient to prove an idea or concept and get the company off the ground. However, many treasurers and controllers omit venture firms for their second tier of financing.

The expansion phase of a company's growth cycle doesn't have quite so much risk as the start-up phase. Many companies tap their original venture capital sources for expansion capital. These people already have a relationship with management. If the company is successful so far, there's a favorable track record.

Qualities Venture Capital Looks For

Risk capital above all looks for a high reward potential in a short time. Getting risk capital is expensive—either in a high interest rate or in terms of diluting ownership of the company. Risk capital also wants to ensure that this profit potential remains for a period of time. Therefore, *barriers to entry* in the industry put the company in a more favorable light. This reduces competition from entering the market and unseating the firm from its position.

Proprietary technology vital to the enterprise speaks loudly to managers holding venture capital. Patents provide a legally protected insurance policy for the company's profitability. It gives the company a head start on the competition and makes it more difficult, time-consuming, and expensive for others to enter the industry.

Cash flow provides risk takers with comfort that their investment has some means of repayment. Further, it demonstrates that they aren't throwing their money into a bottomless pit that has no hope of ever sustaining itself.

Competent management provides risk capital investors with assurance they won't foolishly misuse the funds. Venturists look for these qualities in the management of their companies:

- Intelligence
- Judgment
- Aggressiveness
- Determination, courage, and refusal to accept defeat
- Experience in the industry
- Honesty and strength of character
- Charisma

The last attribute, charisma, identifies management as a group that can attract and retain the best talent possible.

Most venture capital firms want a team relationship with management. Many want direct involvement with the company's operations. Some even demand a seat on the board of directors.

Market is another concern of venture capitalists. They look for markets just beginning to break into the stratosphere. Microcomputers were just such a market when Apple Computer Corporation began. This company had all the above ingredients for a successful venture relationship.

The last thing risk capital managers look for is an exit. They want a way to take their profits and move on to the next project. Often this means taking the company public and selling their shares. Without a method of reaping rewards, it's difficult to attract venture capital.

19

Investments

Overview

Chapter 19 identifies the issues associated with running a treasury investment operation. It shows how to establish performance goals and use the different investment vehicles to meet those goals.

Treasurers successful in freeing working capital often find themselves temporarily with excess cash. Some wealthy companies find this condition more the rule than the exception. Treasurers unsure of their cash forecasts don't want to pay these excess funds out to shareholders as dividends for fear of some unforeseen future need.

Regardless of where the funds come from or how long the treasurer has them, they must work for the company like any other asset. Think of the investment department more as a cost control center rather than a profit center. After all, if the treasurer could make more than the company by investing rather than from operations, then the company is in the wrong business.

Cash is an expensive commodity to hold. Treasurers measure its cost in terms of the company's cost of capital plus the forgone return on capital invested in the company. You can see why the income from investments merely offsets only some of these costs.

Establishing Goals

Carefully control the goals of the investment function. Short-term cash investments should undertake only the most conservative positions. Remember, the purpose is *cost reduction,* not profit. Let the sales force and operating divisions hit the home runs. The level of risk making that kind of return by investing is beyond the authorization of most treasurers. The three goals of the investment function—*in order of priority*—are:

- Safety
- Liquidity
- Yield

Safety

This is the most important corporate investment goal. It's difficult for the treasurer to accumulate excess cash not immediately required in the operation. Conservative investments should leave no doubt as to their complete redemption and liquidation of the position upon maturity. If the firm makes a competitive return on such investments, so much the better. However, above all else *we want the principal balance back on time.*

Linking Safety with Return.   There's a rate for every risk. Investments yielding above-market returns carry more risk. They have to—that's why the promoters must pay more to investors. The high return compensates for the added risk. If an investment sounds too good to be true, it is.

Crossing the Line Between Investing and Speculating.   Treasurers do not speculate with company's funds; they invest them. Often there's a fine line between the two. However, factors that control the safety and, therefore, the viability of an investment include:

- Term to maturity
- Track record of the security issuer
- Underlying collateral, if any
- Liquidity of the market for the security
- Risk

Use these indicators to define your firm's definition of investment versus speculation.

Liquidity

Even the most astute treasurer's cash forecasts suffer unexpected shortfalls. When that happens, the firm needs cash quickly. Investments with a future maturity may require immediate liquidation. Companies in securities without a ready market may suffer a loss of interest *and* principal if they need to get out quickly.

Trading Liquidity for Yield.   Due to the danger of unforeseen cash requirements, investments without an active secondary market pay greater yields. They have to in order to entice the buyers to undertake liquidity risk. Fixed-rate securities, such as bonds or bond funds, provide a case in point. Bonds not actively traded suffer declines in value if interest rates rise.

Yield

Rates offered by different securities vary depending on a variety of factors. Safety and liquidity are two. Additionally, there's supply and demand. Securities that everyone wants often trade at a premium above their face value.

Risk.   Risk and *perceived* risk are two factors that drive yield. Issuers with lower ratings (AA rather than AAA as published by Moody's Investor's Services, for example) must pay a higher rate because of the additional risk.

Maturity.   The maturity of a security is also a factor. When the yield curve slopes upward (positive) it means that investors expect rates to climb in the future. Therefore, longer-term maturities must pay a higher yield than their short-term counterparts to stay competitive.

Trading Between Safety, Liquidity, and Yield

Treasurers who establish investment goals do so by trading between safety, liquidity, and yield. They create balance among risks in the firm's investment portfolio by considering both safety and liquidity.

Usually the company includes its requirements in the investment policy manual. The board of directors approves these requirements in the authorization it grants the company's chief investment officer. This person is responsible for executing the investment function according to company policy.

Using these guidelines of safety and liquidity, the board identifies a range of targeted returns.

Identifying Safety.   How do most treasurers identify the safety required of their investments? It depends on the security. For bonds and other fixed-income instruments, independent investment rating services provide a measure of relative risk. The investment policy guidelines may specify a minimum rating below which the firm cannot invest.

Companies often purchase instruments that use underlying collateral (such as repurchase agreements). In these cases the investment decision turns on the safety of the *collateral*. Again, the investment policy may use rating services and a minimum level of collateral such as 105 percent or more.

Further, the policy may include instructions on safekeeping of the collateral. Many firms require an independent third party take physical possession of their collateral. Others feel better if *they* take physical possession themselves.

Liquidity.   Liquid investments are usually safer. Liquidity deals with two factors:

- Size of the secondary market
- Maturity

Corporate investment policy may dictate the maximum maturity for its short-term investments. The policy states these in terms of overnight, one day, one month, etc. Further, some companies identify maximum percentages of their investment portfolio invested in different maturities.

Safety also relies on the ability to quickly liquidate an investment position prior to maturity without suffering a loss. The size of the secondary market determines the ease of early liquidation. Naturally, publicly traded stocks and bonds maintain active markets. Commercial paper does as well.

Directing Investments

Prudent management provides definite direction for their company's investments. No matter how much they may trust the investment officers, they don't send them off without guidance and simply hope for the best. Further, they don't give one person absolute discretion over the entire investment function. Most companies seek the wisdom of more than one person when it comes to oversight of their short-term investments.

Investment policies established by the board provide formal written guidance. Periodically, someone independent of the investment function audits the actual execution of trades compared with management's written guidelines. The two should match. If they don't, there's a problem.

The strict guidelines established by management protect the investment officer as well. Investment strategies result from the judgment of more than just one individual. Additionally, the checks and balances maintained by the system of internal accounting controls reduces risk of fraud by creating a deterrent. It also identifies problems at the earliest stages. The most important of these controls include:

- Qualified personnel
- Use of qualified and reputable brokerage firms
- Dual control of investment assets
- Independent confirmation of transactions
- Periodic and independent investment account reconciliation
- Periodic independent audit of the entire investment function

Establishing the Investment Department

The decision to formalize a company's approach to investing excess short-term cash comes from the highest authority in the company. Usually this is the board of directors. The board creates the position of investment officer. It directs the staff to formulate the company's investment guidelines. The board then ratifies and accepts these guidelines and incorporates them into the investment department's charter.

Part of the process of creating a company's approach to investment management includes establishment of:

- Board of directors investment committee
- Standards for brokerage firms

- Trading authorization limits
- Standards for safety and liquidity
- Performance benchmark yields
- Requirements for investment personnel
- Standards for reporting

Establishing the Investment Committee.   The board of directors names an investment committee to oversee the firm's investment activity. Individuals knowledgeable in the investment markets and who are *independent* of the actual execution comprise the investment committee. Most companies require that a majority of the investment committee include outside directors. This committee oversees the entire investment function. It reports to the board as a whole. It recommends all investment policies and procedures to the board.

Standards for Brokerage Firms.   Prudent investors don't deal with just any brokerage firm that comes along. Most companies establish specific guidelines for the qualifications of their brokers. They want a brokerage firm with:

- Experience in securities relevant to the company
- Sufficient size to command accurate trading execution
- Financial stability
- A reputation as an upstanding, ethical company

Companies with large investment portfolios often employ several brokerage firms. They apply their written criteria to each brokerage firm used.

Trading Authorization Limits.   The investment committee establishes trading authorization limits in these categories:

- Amount at the discretion of individual investment officers
- Amount invested at particular brokerage firms
- Concentration of the portfolio in specific securities

Most companies stratify the authorization limits of their investment officers. Investments beyond a particular amount require approval by someone with higher authority. Beyond a higher amount, the investment committee votes on the positions. If the investment department wants a still larger position, approval must come from the complete board.

Few prudent investors load their portfolio with too much of a given security. The investment committee establishes guidelines and monitors the portfolio composition to ensure there's no *undue concentration* of investments in a particular security.

Standards for Safety and Liquidity.   When determining concentration of the portfolio in specific securities, the company weighs yield against risk. Most investment committees specify limitations on quality (such as no more than 10 percent of the portfolio in AA-rated or less-commercial paper). By doing so, it establishes the blended yield of the portfolio. The committee uses that as a benchmark to judge investment performance.

Another limit is the maturity of the portfolio. Again, most companies establish a percentage for the various levels of maturities the company may undertake. The amount of the investment portfolio maturing at any time ensures the liquidity of the company's excess cash.

Targeted Returns.   Policies regarding safety, maturity, and concentration help determine the return on invested funds. However, the firm needs to identify the return that these policies dictate, then use it as a target. It's one thing to set policies that establish the return. However, it's unacceptable to miss that target by not hitting the yields available. Targets help everyone reach the desired goal.

Requirements for Investment Personnel.   Most companies name at least two investment officers so that they can cover for each other if one is unavailable. The investment committee makes sure these officers meet specific minimum standards. They carefully check backgrounds and references. Those on the investment committee knowledgeable in the subject conduct the interviews and recommend hiring or firing the investment officers.

Some of the requirements for an investment officer may include:

- Minimum educational requirements such as a bachelor's degree or (less frequently) an MBA
- Five years' or more experience in an investment capacity
- NASD series 7 license—required by some large companies
- Clean credit history
- No criminal record
- No disciplinary actions by the regulatory bodies
- Clean NASD arbitration history (if applicable)

Standards for Reporting.   The investment department's responsibility includes performance reporting to the investment committee. Monthly performance reports provided by the investment committee generally include:

- List of all securities held at month end
- Schedule of investment maturities
- Aggregate yield
- Aggregate risk factor such as AAA, BB, etc.

- Comparison of risk and yield with investment guidelines
- List showing each transaction executed during the month

Additionally, each month someone independent of the investment function reconciles the brokerage statements against the investment accounts in the general ledger. Further, the confirmations of trades and the brokerage account statements go *unopened* directly to someone independent of the investment function. This person verifies compliance with company investment guidelines.

The reconciliation process brings discrepancies to the attention of the investment committee immediately.

Identifying Problems

The treasury department requires specific technical expertise to execute most of its responsibilities. This is especially true of the investment function. Unless you know what you're looking for, it's easy to overlook problems buried among all the technical jargon and paper that flies around an active investment trading operation.

By its nature, investment of excess cash is an opportunistic enterprise. Traders make decisions involving big dollars in a matter of seconds. Often the buy/sell agreements consist of a verbal understanding over the phone—repurchase agreements usually work like this. The paperwork doesn't catch up with the transaction for a few days. By then, chances are the investment has already matured and the cash moved somewhere else.

It takes an expert to dive into a trading operation to determine that it's running in accordance with management policy. However, the good news is that reckless trading operations usually generate other symptoms easily identified by lay people.

Evaluating Investment Personnel

Most investment problems start and end with people. Determine that all investment personnel have the appropriate qualifications. See if their backgrounds and education match those specified by the investment committee in the investment policy manual. If they don't, there's already a problem.

Uncomplementary Duties

Too many investment duties done by one person, without offsetting control procedures, open the door for problems. Look for jobs performed by the same person or two related people that compromise internal controls. For example, sometimes reconciliation of complicated investment transactions (such as hedges and swaps) with the investment account in the general ledger requires an investment expert. Some companies just have the investment officer reconcile the accounts.

This verifies that the transaction was done as the investment officer intended. *However,* it negates the internal control provided by the reconciliation process. If the investment officer was hiding losing transactions or executing trades outside company policy guidelines, no one would ever know.

Another control frequently bypassed is the confirmation process. Some companies allow both the investment confirms and the brokerage statements to go directly to the investment officer for verification. This places the investment officer in the position of both executing the trade *and* receiving the only independent verification of what actually occurred. This paves the way for the erroneous entry of trades not conforming with company policy.

The rule to remember is: *never delegate execution and recording or verification functions to the same person.*

Internal Controls

The atmosphere of control, procedures, and adherence to authority must exist in the investment operation. Further, it must exist in management's respect for the *system* of controls. Without a well-maintained control system, investment employees may or may not follow company policies.

Some companies get around restrictive trading policies and controls without ever actually breaking the rules. The person with the authority to circumvent a control simply authorizes overstepping a policy or procedure. What was at first an exception soon becomes the rule. The authorization process for circumventing the rules turns into the rule itself.

Such an atmosphere of management disregard for internal control procedures breeds sloppiness in the trading function. It gets even worse if the investment committee provides rubber-stamp approval of all the breaches in internal control. This happens easily as managers explain lapses in control with the opportunity they had. Frequently, time is the excuse for not following the internal control and authorization procedures. *The market won't wait* is a common explanation.

Sometimes the transaction that caused the breach of internal control to begin with works out as planned. The company makes a higher rate of return on a security that exceeds its risk-taking guidelines. Such success makes the next decision to invest outside company policy easier. The problem comes when the trades crater. The board discovers investment risk way out of the range authorized and they never knew it was happening. Adherence to internal controls prevents this from happening.

Written Investment Policies

Problems most often occur in investment departments without written policies and procedures. These should specify exactly what the investment committee and the board of directors expect in terms of:

- Performance
- Risk
- Reporting
- Authorized transactions
- Dual control of assets
- Internal accounting control
- Personnel qualifications
- Policies related to fidelity bonding

Deviation from these policies requires a *prior* board resolution. Deviation without a prior board resolution is cause for termination. Companies not following these guidelines send the wrong signal to their investment officers.

Performance Standards

Everyone needs some goals to shoot for. Investment professionals are no exception. In this business, however, we measure performance in terms of portfolio yield. The board determines yield targets when it establishes guidelines relating to risk and maturity.

If the investment department stays within these guidelines, it hits established performance standards. Problems occur when the board fails to set performance (yield) standards. Suddenly the investment department must guess how much return is enough. Most traders err on the high side. This often requires them to take more risk than the board contemplated.

Another problem occurs when the board fails to match established performance standards with the risk and maturity guidelines already in place. If the board holds the investment department to a standard average yield above what risk it allows the treasurer to take, there's a problem. Either the treasurer must disregard risk standards and meet the yield targets, or average yield comes in below the targeted minimum yield. Either way, the treasurer fails.

Treasurers seeing this dysfunction between yield targets and risk policies must bring it to the investment committee's attention for correction.

Monthly Reporting

A sure sign that a problem in the investment department currently exists, or will shortly, is lack of regular monthly reporting. Without accurate monthly reports, the company merely trusts that traders comply with company policies. Monthly reports prove that investments follow company policies. Further, they establish a deterrent against noncompliance. After all, few people disregard rules if they know they'll be caught.

Collateral

Lack of adequate policies and procedures regarding investment collateral is another sign of impending problems in the trading department. A firm can do 1000 trades using collateral. Let's say that the first 999 are fine. However, if the last one goes sour and the company loses its principal, it wipes out all the income from the previous 999 trades.

Make sure the board establishes guidelines for collateralized investments such as repurchase agreements. These guidelines should address:

- Quality
- Term
- Amount
- Possession
- Procedures for transfer of ownership

Using Investment Vehicles

Corporate treasurers have a myriad of investment vehicles to choose from. Each offers its own unique combination of yield, maturity, risk, and liquidity. Most investment departments balance their portfolios in terms of different securities. They stagger the maturities to comply with company policies of liquidity. They mix the levels of risk to maximize yield while remaining in compliance with risk guidelines. The most common investment vehicles used include:

- Mutual funds
- Money-market instruments
- Stocks
- Bonds

Mutual Funds

Treasurers new to the investment field often use mutual funds. This relieves them of having to pull their own investment trigger. It's done for them by the fund managers. Further, this spreads the risk among a variety of securities meeting the fund's requirements.

Mutual funds exist for every combination of maturity, safety, and liquidity. Here are the types of mutual funds most companies use:

Load Funds.   The *load* is a fee the fund charges its investors for investing their money. Funds charge loads either on the front end or the back end. Funds that charge a front load deduct this fee from the cash invested. So if a firm puts

$100,000 into an 8.5 percent front-loaded fund, it actually only gets a yield on $91,500. The fund takes the other $8500 as its fee.

Back-end loads allow investors a yield on their entire principal amount. The fund extracts its fee when the investor redeems the shares. If the fund performs, its fee goes proportionately higher. Additionally, many back-loaded funds offer a declining scale for their loads over time.

No-load Funds. Many mutual funds don't impose a load fee on their investors. Instead, they extract their fees from the yield. Additionally, some add entry and exit fees. Further, some no-load funds extract an assessment fee. This allocates each investor a proportionate percentage of the fund's operating expenses.

Beware of assessment fees based on expense ratios. These work in conjunction with the load to determine total compensation to the fund. For example, take a no-load fund with a 2 percent expense ratio. The cost to the investor is 2 percent of total assets under management. Over 10 years, that's 20 percent. Contrast this with a 7 percent front-loaded fund with only a 0.75 percent expense ratio. Over the same 10 years the cost of this fund is only 14.5 percent even though it's front-loaded.

Closed-end Funds. The value of each share of a closed-end fund varies with the value of its securities portfolio as well as the *market's perception* of its future value. Bylaws of closed-end funds limit the number of shares it can issue. Often they're publicly traded just like stock in a company.

Open-end Funds. These funds issue shares constantly. They make a market in their own shares and redeem them on demand.

Types of Mutual Funds

Mutual funds market themselves based on the objectives and securities the fund buys. Most large mutual fund companies like Vanguard and T. Rowe Price offer many different types of funds based on specific strategies, yield, and maturity requirements. Here are some of them:

Money-Market Funds. Begin with the safest type of mutual fund. Safest, because they are the most liquid and generally invested strictly in U.S. government securities and high-grade commercial paper. Most treasurers use money-market funds as a parking place for their temporary excess cash. Commercial banks catering to corporate customers often combine their cash management sweep account services with a money-market fund. This makes it easy for the bank to invest daily excess funds for the treasurer.

Growth and Income Funds. These mutual funds invest in stocks that receive dividend income. Usually banks, public utilities, and insurance companies form the core of their investment portfolio. However, most treasurers don't use growth and income funds unless they have a longer-term excess cash position. That way they take advantage of the appreciation of the growth and income fund.

Growth Funds. These funds concentrate on securities with long-term growth potential. They don't pay regular dividends. Companies involved in research and development projects prove attractive holdings for growth funds.

Commodity Funds. Commodities are a specialized field. Few corporate treasurers have the expertise or the time to manage a commodities portfolio. Buying into a commodity fund allows them to participate in the market with the help of seasoned professionals at the helm.

Bond Funds. Two categories exist for bond funds: taxable and nontaxable. The taxables invest in the bonds of blue-chip corporations, U.S. Treasury and agency funds, U.S. mortgage funds, and on down to junk bonds.

The nontaxables include more than 400 funds with assets exceeding $1 billion. These invest in municipal bonds.

Capital Gain Funds. This is the volatile, risky side of mutual funds. When the stock market soars, so do the capital gain funds. When it tanks, they quickly follow. Those funds purchasing stocks on margin further enhance the risk. Margin has a multiplier effect on both gains and losses. Few treasurers place a significant percentage of their excess investable money in capital gain funds.

Index Funds. Index funds follow the performance of the stock market. Fund managers buy the Dow industrials and other performance indices. This assures treasurers that the Dow never outperforms them. The majority of index purchasers time their entries and exits into the funds to take advantage of over- and under-valued situations in the stock market.

Money-Market Instruments

The money market is a catchall term for short-term, very liquid securities. Maturities range anywhere from overnight in the case of repurchase agreements to a year for U.S. Treasury bills. Here are some of the most commonly used money-market securities:

Repurchase Agreements (Repo or RP). These represent a safe parking place for temporary excess cash. They're easy to buy and even easier to liquidate. Once the company establishes a repo account with a bank or brokerage firm, all it takes is a phone call. Repos or RPs really amount to a short-term loan made *to* a bank or a securities brokerage firm by the investor. The loan is collateralized by U.S. government securities equal to about 105 percent of the loan.

In the event the loan fails to repay on maturity, the lender/investor simply liquidates the underlying collateral. It's liquid and there's a ready market for it. The problem comes if the investor failed to insist on actual transfer of title and delivery of the collateral to a third-party depository. Some repo purchases go one step further—they insist on physical delivery of the collateral to their company and they hold it themselves.

Commercial Paper.   These are more risky than repos since they carry no underlying collateral. The full faith and creditworthiness of the issuer back them. However, there's a ready market for most blue-chip company's commercial paper. Banks generally can accommodate whatever maturity term in commercial paper a client wants. Due to the added risk, interest rates for CP are higher than for repos.

Banker's Acceptances.   Banks issue banker's acceptances to finance foreign trade and the storage of goods. They amount to the bank's guarantee (acceptance) that they'll pay the face amount on maturity. BAs sell at a discount to their face rather than pay interest. Because they always mature in less than 270 days, they don't require tax treatment as original-discount securities. Few BA issues have defaulted owing to the superior credit rating of the issuing banks and the underlying collateral that supports them—usually the goods being transferred or shipped.

Certificates of Deposit.   Certificates of deposit (CDs) are not usually sufficient in size for most corporate cash positions. FDIC insurance limits the amount of funds in one institution to $100,000. Further, the yields are often low. Finally, the maturities aren't nearly as flexible as with other investment vehicles such as commercial paper or repurchase agreements.

A secondary market exists for top-rated CDs that allows them to compete with T-bills and commercial paper. Depending on your appetite for risk, choose from three types of CDs:

1. *Eurodollar CDs.*   Off-shore branches of United States, Canadian, Japanese, and European banks issue Eurodollar CDs. They represent U.S.-dollar-denominated certificates actually issued by the foreign institution. Eurodollar CDs pay a higher interest rate than their domestic counterparts due to the added risk of exchange controls and trade sanctions involved with dealing off-shore.

2. *Yankee CDs.*   These represent CDs payable in U.S. dollars but issued by *foreign bank branches located in the United States.* Yankee CDs are the reverse of Eurodollar CDs.

3. *Domestic CDs.*   U.S. banks and thrifts issue domestic CDs. Buy issues only from the top-rated institutions. Many investors use the Moody's or Standard & Poor's rating of the issuing institution as an indicator of a CD's relative safety.

Treasury Bills.   The Treasury issues T-bills every Monday for maturities of 91 and 182 days. Once a month the Treasury issues bills having a 52-week maturity. Because of these short durations they aren't subject to original-issue discount rules. Rather than pay interest, the Treasury issues T-bills at a discount to their face. T-bills come out in $10,000 denominations with increments of $5000.

Agency Discount Notes.   As their name implies, these securities come out at a discount rather than pay interest. Agencies of the federal government such as the Federal National Mortgage Association (FNMA) issue discount notes to finance their short-term cash requirements. Maturities don't exceed 270 days, so they don't require original-issue discount treatment. Agency discount notes carry a high-quality rating, though not so high as securities *actually* issued by the U.S. Treasury.

Quasi-Money-Market Instruments

Quasi-money-market instruments commonly come in three categories:

- Floating-rate instruments
- Packaged securities
- Options on U.S. government securities

The risk here is slightly higher than in conventional money-market instruments. However, the liquidity is still there and the yield is often as high as 500 to 800 basis points greater than in the securities of the U.S. government.

Floating-Rate Instruments.   The industry calls them *floaters* because the securities carry an adjustable rate tied to the T-bill rate or LIBOR (London Interbank Offered Rate). They have a definite maturity date as well as periodic *refix* dates (when the interest rate adjusts). These range from weekly to annually and everywhere in between.

Interest rate risk comes if a treasurer has locked in a floater and rates go up. The investor must wait until the next refix date before taking advantage of the higher rates. Sometimes this can be as long as one year.

Unwinding this unhappy event requires purchase of a swap contract. This instrument is a contractual obligation between two *counterparties* to swap fixed-income cash flow for adjustable-rate cash flow. This is how many financial institutions fine-tune their interest rate risk.

Packaged Securities.   FNMA packages their mortgage obligations for sale to institutional investors. During periods of declining interest rates the Fed's cost of funds usually lags that of the spot markets. When rates rise again, astute treasurers usually switch out of the adjustable-rate mortgages and into floaters.

Options.   These aren't options on stocks. Aggressive treasurers with authorization to take more risk often enhance their portfolio yields by purchasing options on Treasury bond futures. This strategy is not for amateurs. There's a lot of money on the line. It takes a savvy, experienced professional to correctly time T-bond put-and-call transactions. However, with the right support from the board and a disciplined investment strategy, options on T-bond futures provides a method to enhance portfolio yields.

Long-Term Investments

Many companies have enough excess cash that they invest in long-term *core* positions. These often include stocks and bonds specifically targeted to give a long-term yield above the money-market rate. Further, many of the positions are in securities of companies with a strategic advantage to the firm. For example, a company that's dependent on the price of a particular commodity such as gold may invest in the stock of gold mining companies. This helps hedge the upward price pressure.

Stock Index Futures.   If a company loads its investment portfolio heavily with corporate stocks, they often hedge the risk using stock index futures. Stock futures trade on the Chicago Mercantile Exchange—usually in the form of the S&P 500. Using this security, treasurers bet that the entire S&P 500 moves in a particular direction.

The S&P 500 is quoted at 500 times the price. For example, shorting one S&P future contract at 500 places at risk $250,000 (500 × 500 = $250,000). Such a position would insulate a long-stock portfolio of at least that value. Four things drive the value of stock index futures:

- Interest rates
- Dividends paid by the underlying stocks
- Movement of the stocks in the index
- Expiration date of the futures contract

Box Spreads.   This is a sophisticated stock-hedging technique not advised for amateurs. Its intent is to lock in return while reducing market risk—nice ideas if they work. Under a professional's guidance, they do. Here's how a box spread operates:

1. The investor buys and writes S&P 500 index calls and puts. Each has the same strike price and expiration date. These positions exactly offset one another.
2. If the index rises, the position profits from the long calls. Loss from the short puts prior to closing them out partially offsets the profit. The opposite works in the event the index drops. Theoretically, the profits are greater than the losses.

Money-Market Preferred Stock.   This stock carries a floating-rate dividend periodically reset during an auction. The dividends compete against the money market for investors' attention. The tax advantage to this type of stock is the dividend exclusion.

Adjustable-Rate Preferred (ARP).   This stock carries a dividend rate based on the average yields of 10- to 30-year Treasury bonds. Their price is based on a discount (for top-rated issuers) or a premium on the T-bond index. ARP stock fluctuates with market supply and demand. Companies averse to market risk should steer clear of ARP stock.

Bonds

Bonds provide more security than stocks in the sense that they carry a definite return. Failure to pay timely interest results in default and throws the issuer into bankruptcy. However, bond prices fluctuate with the market's expectations of interest rates, the issuer's stability, and future prospects.

Volume on the bond market is larger than all of the stock traded on the NYSE, the ASE, and the OTC markets. Computations associated with bond transactions really aren't that complicated. Here are the five most basic concepts treasurers need to understand about bonds:

Current Yield. The prevailing market price affects a bond's return. Use this equation to compute current yield:

$$\text{Current yield} = \text{coupon income}/\text{market price}$$

For example, say a company owns an International Harvester bond of 8.875 percent due 6-15-99 that currently trades for 97.559 (that's $975.59 per bond). The current yield is 9.11 percent ($88.875/$975.59 = 9.11%). Notice how the market discount drives the current yield higher. If the bond had sold for a premium, the current yield would be *less than* the coupon rate.

Coupon Rate. This is simply the annual interest rate stated on the face of the bond. The example of the International Harvester bond above has a coupon rate of 8.875 percent. Only when the bond sells at par ($1000) does the coupon rate equal the current yield.

Computing Accrued Interest. Accrued interest is the interest income or expense (depending on whether you're a buyer or seller) when trading a bond *between* interest payment dates. Most bond transactions on the secondary market involve the computation of accrued interest since they pay interest twice yearly. The chances of actually trading a bond on the date of payment are slim.

Remember these three rules regarding accrued interest:

1. The *seller* of a bond receives accrued interest (income) through the sale date from the buyer.

2. The *buyer* pays the seller the bond purchase price *plus* accrued interest (expense) through the sale date.

3. The total amount paid (purchase price *plus* accrued interest) is the buyer's basis in the bond.

Here's how to compute accrued interest:

1. *Determine the interest per day.*   Use this equation:

$$\text{Interest per day} = (\text{face amount} \times \text{interest rate})/360 \text{ days}$$

Say a company sells on July 15 a bond with a standard $1000 face value, yielding 10 percent payable on December 1 and June 1. Interest per day is $.278 ([$1000 × 10%]/360 = $.278).

2. *Determine the number of days involved.* This includes the number of days since the last payment *plus* the day before settlement date. In the above example, count the number of days between June 2 and July 19—assume settlement date of July 15 *plus* the day before a standard 5-day settlement period. The number of days is 47. Many financial calculators (such as the HP-12C) can computer the number of days for you. Alternatively, you can get counting calendars that provide the numbers of days.

3. *Compute accrued interest.* Multiply the daily interest (item 1) by the number of days (item 2). In our example, accrued interest is $13.07 per bond ($.278 × 47 = $13.07). The buyer pays the seller the accrued interest. However, the buyer receives the next entire interest payment from the bond issuer when it comes due (on December 1). This makes the buyer whole, though it takes the time from purchase date to the next interest payment date.

Yield to Maturity (YTM). Yield to maturity (YTM) includes the time yet running on a bond. The complexity of manually computing YTM is beyond the scope of this book. However, many financial calculators (including the HP-12C and the Monroe Bond Calculator) have a preprogrammed YTM facility. Additionally, bond-yield tables in some books provide this same information.

Converting Municipal Bond Taxable Equivalent Yields. Many treasurers invest their core positions in nontaxable municipal bonds (*munis*). However, these bonds compete against taxable bonds issued by corporations. Investors need a quick method of converting the yields for taxable and nontaxable securities. That way they compare apples to apples.

Here's the equation to convert yield from a tax-exempt bond to one that's fully taxable:

Taxable equivalent = tax-exempt yield / 1 – combined federal and state tax rate

To demonstrate how this works, assume you see a tax-exempt bond (issued in your firm's domicile state) with a yield of 6.255 percent. Your firm's federal income tax rate is 34 percent and its state rate is 11 percent. The *taxable* equivalent yield to you for this bond is 11.37 percent (.06255/(1 – [.34 + .11]) = .1137). This means that taxable bonds must yield at least 11.37 percent to compete with this tax-exempt bond on an after-tax basis.

Tax-Advantaged Investments

Many treasurers mix taxable with nontaxable securities in their investment portfolios. Governmental entities issue nontaxables. These include:

- Municipal bonds
- Tax-exempt paper and notes

- T-bonds and notes
- Money-market munis

Municipal Bonds. State and local governments issue munis. The interest income is free of federal *and* state taxes to residents of the state of issue. Investors buying munis from states other than their resident states must pay state tax on the interest income. Capital gains (if any) resulting from their sale, however, are always taxable.

Be especially cautious when purchasing bonds issued by cities. Many carry ratings as junk bonds. The risk of default for some municipalities is just as high as for many corporations.

Tax-Exempt Paper. Municipalities often issue commercial paper just as do many corporations. However, the commercial paper issued by municipalities is *tax-exempt* just like their bonds. Their maturities are usually between 30 and 270 days (thereby avoiding original-issue discount treatment). Municipalities issue tax-exempt paper in anticipation of the receipt of specific revenues. Typically these issues comprise:

- BANs: bond anticipation notes
- TANs: tax anticipation notes
- GANs: grant anticipation notes

The problem, however, comes when the issuing municipality's creditworthiness diminishes to the point where these municipalities cannot sell such anticipatory issues any longer.

T-bonds and Notes.   Many treasurers confuse the maturities of treasuries. Here they are:

- T-bills: less than one year
- T-notes: issued for between 1 and 10 years
- T-bonds: issued for between 7 and 30 years

T-bills sell at a discount. T-notes pay interest only once a year. T-bonds pay interest semiannually, just like a corporate bond. All are taxable only at the *federal* level. They are exempt from state tax.

Money-Market Municipals.   These combine the best characteristics of mandatory tender bonds with commercial paper—and they're tax-exempt. Municipalities issue these bonds for any time period between 1 and 365 days. At expiration, the buyer tenders the bond and receives back the money plus accrued interest.

Alternatively, the buyer may establish a new tender date and interest rate—similar to rolling over commercial paper. Some issues allow for mandatory conversion to a fixed rate at a time specified in the bond indenture.

Using Futures to Control Investment Risk

Savvy treasurers and their investment committees effectively use futures to reduce the risk inherent in their portfolios. This allows them to obtain higher yields while remaining within their prescribed risk threshold. However, futures trading often carries a bad image. That's because too many people confuse its proper use for hedging with raw speculation.

When used properly, T-bill futures provide an insurance policy against three things:

- Changes in interest rates that cause price changes
- Loss of liquidity
- Risk of default

Like any insurance policy, we hope the futures positions expire worthless. That means the main positions did what we wanted and we didn't need the insurance. However, if the market goes against us, the insurance helps offset the loss.

Taxation Issues

Treasurers and investment officers must understand the tax implications of their portfolio. Bring your firm's tax professionals into the investment policy-setting sessions. The most common taxation issues associated with corporate investments include:

- Capital gains
- Dividends-received deductions

Capital Gains

Buying and selling investment securities triggers capital gains and losses. Net capital gains and losses offset one another, short-term with short-term and long-term with long-term. Use five steps to compute net capital gains or losses:

1. Separate short-term from long-term capital gains or losses.
2. Net like-term gains and losses against one another.

Ownership percentage	Percent of dividend deductible
Less than 20%	70%
From 20% to 80%	80%
More than 80%	100%
For companies designated as *small business investment companies*	100%

Figure 19-1. Dividends-received deduction percentages.

3. Add the net of long-term results with short-term results.

4. If a gain results, include it with the firm's other income.

5. If a net capital loss results, it is subject to capital loss limitations.

Corporations use capital losses only to offset capital gains—not ordinary income. However, companies may carry the losses back for three years and forward for five years.

Dividends-Received Deduction

This tax rule reduces the amount of double taxation on corporate earnings. Within specific guidelines a corporation may exclude certain dividends from stock of other companies it holds. The amount of the exclusion depends on the ownership percentage held in the company's stock. Figure 19-1 shows these percentages and the dividend deductible.

IRS Code Section 246(b) provides another limitation on the *amount* of the dividend allowable. It focuses on the amount of the dividend recipient's taxable income. The amount of the dividend deduction cannot be greater than the dividend recipient's taxable income multiplied by the dividend deduction shown in Figure 19-1.

For example, say company A owned 25 percent of the stock of company B. Company A received an $80,000 dividend and it had taxable income before dividends of $65,000. Compute company A's dividend exclusion as follows:

- The exclusion *potentially* deductible is $64,000 ($80,000 × 80% = $64,000).

- The amount of the *actual* exclusion is just $52,000 ($65,000 × 80% = $52,000).

20
Corporate Communications

Overview

Chapter 20 identifies the investment community to whom the treasurer communicates the company's:

- Press releases
- Financial results
- News

Corporate communications involves more than presenting just a polished image for public relations purposes. Handling of investors, partners, shareholders, and lenders directly affects a company's ability to raise capital. It also influences the firm's stock price.

Chapter 20 identifies the company's responsibilities in the area of corporate communications. It shows how to prepare a press release and where to send it. Additionally, this chapter identifies the legal requirements for issuing news that the public needs to know in order to make prudent investment decisions.

Very large firms usually have separate investor relations and corporate communications departments. This task usually falls to the treasury department of small- to medium-sized companies. Regardless of where in the company it's done, servicing shareholders is an expensive task. The good news is that proven techniques exist to control those costs. Finally, Chapter 20 demonstrates the steps necessary to form a crisis management team and to plan for specific contingencies that could affect the company.

Good corporate communications can enhance an already solid balance sheet. It promotes the company's strengths and admits its weaknesses.

Composition of the Investment Community

The United States has more than 5000 corporations competing for investors' attention. The New York Stock Exchange lists over 1600 of these. Close to 900 companies trade on the American Stock Exchange. The NASDAQ over-the-counter market lists about 3000. With all of these companies to choose from, the top 25 brokerage firms monitor less than 500 companies. Further, analysts from several different firms often watch the same company. This further diminishes exposure of the aggregate total.

The investor-relations department must compete for the attention of a segmented investment community that includes:

- Individual investors
- Brokerage firms
- Pension and retirement funds
- Analysts
- Newsletter writers
- Insurance companies
- Mutual funds
- Foreign investors
- Banks and other lenders

Each is important to the company. Further, your company competes against other companies for investors' attention. You may consider membership in the National Investor Relations Institute (2000 L Street NW, Suite 701, Washington, DC 20036, 202-826-0630). This organization can tell you about your competition as well as provide a wealth of information regarding the practice of investor relations.

Individual Investors

This often represents the largest group of investors, but they usually hold the least amount of company stock compared to other segments of the investment community. Certain communications from a company often target individual investors. The annual meeting is a good example.

Few firms release information relevant to professional investors and securities analysts at annual meetings. Consequently, attendance is largely from individual investors. The format of the meeting follows legal requirements and provides general information of specific interest to individual investors. Management seldom dives into the technical aspects of company operations as it does with professional securities analysts.

Brokerage Firms

The nation's largest brokerage firms can swing public sentiment about a company just by their recommendations to clients. Investor relations treat large brokerage firms very carefully. They provide informal meetings with analysts from these firms. This provides the analyst an opportunity to ask specific questions relevant to his or her particular investors and investment strategies.

Often regional and national brokerage firms broadcast these conferences to their outlying offices. However, management must take care to avoid disclosure of information not available to the general investment public. This is illegal and places both those who give this information and those who act on it in jeopardy. Instead, companies release sensitive information to all parts of the investment community at the same time in the form of a press release.

Pension and Retirement Funds

Such institutional investors are among the largest in the world. For example, in California the State Teachers Retirement System and the Public Employees Retirement System together manage over $80 billion. If they were banks, they would be among the largest in the world. As investors, they are big hitters.

Companies pay close attention to how much of their stock such pension and retirement funds hold. Acquisition or sale of the size these organizations deal in definitely affects the market price.

Further, many of these investors now demand a voice in the management of the company. Some want special communication with company executives. Others demand a seat on the board. They frequently have the stock-voting muscle to make these happen.

Analysts

Respected securities analysts often form public opinion on specific companies. The recommendation of a handful of top analysts can send a stock price soaring or into the tank. Some are independent and write their own newsletters. Others work for large brokerage firms.

Buy-Side Analysts.   These are analysts employed by institutions, portfolio managers, and large individual investors. They provide information on securities of interest to their employer/investors. They constantly comb the financial community for new, undiscovered investment opportunities. Many specialize in undervalued securities. Others focus on specific industries.

Buy-side analysts take a longer-term view of the market. The broad economic future of the company interests them.

Sell-Side Analysts.   These specialists generally work for large brokerage firms. They track particular issues and industries. Sell-side analysts provide the precise timing required for their employer's clients to leg in or out of their securities positions. Because of that interest, sell-side analysts usually want hard data—numbers. Their orientation is short-term performance.

A formal report recommending the stock issued by a sell-side analyst indicates a clear following of the company. The fact that an analyst is in the process of preparing a report on a company is inside information. The company may not disclose its knowledge of this fact.

Independent Analysts.   The investment community includes a variety of independent investment analysts who write their own newsletters and often have their own television shows. They help shape the investment strategies of thousands of individual investors. When combined, the independent analysts influence a segment of the investment population not easily ignored by investor relations departments.

Institutional Investors

These are the mutual funds, insurance companies, and pension and retirement funds. These institutions account for more than 70 percent of NYSE trading volume. This segment of the investment community receives plenty of attention from the corporate communications departments of most publicly held companies.

Foreign Investors

Trading publicly held stocks is a worldwide proposition today. Many companies court the analysts who shape opinions and strategies of foreign investors. Of course, investor relations departments bend over backward to determine the kind of information about their company that interests this group. Much of it involves the company's international relationships. Failure to pay attention to foreign investors leaves untapped a viable and growing segment of the worldwide financial community.

This is even more true as American companies successfully float debt and equity offerings on exchanges in London, Paris, Frankfurt, Stockholm, Brussels, Tokyo, and Hong Kong.

Professional Fund Managers

This institutional group takes huge positions in stocks of publicly held companies. The way investor relations and corporate communications handles them determines in part how they invest their fund's money. A small but growing number of fund managers make all investment decisions from computer models. These are the so-called programmed traders. Investor relations managers don't waste their time contacting these fund managers.

Investment Advisers

These people provide recommendations regarding investment of their clients' money. Certainly those with substantial clients have the ability to influence a company's stock ownership. Many investor relations professionals include investment advisers on their list of people receiving the company's information.

Banks and Other Lenders

Lenders consider themselves investors of sorts. After all, they've given their money to a company and hope to make a return on it. Isn't this the definition of investment?

Therefore, companies who value their access to the debt market make sure they treat these lenders with all the care of any other large and valued investor. This means the corporate communications department sends them all the investor information about the company they desire. Some firms even include major lenders on the invitation list of financial analysts for whom they host conferences.

Beyond Regular Investors and Pundits

Though not really investors or people who form the public's financial and investment opinions, there's another group that consumes material distributed by the corporate communications department. This group includes:

- Employees and prospective employees
- Customers
- Suppliers
- The community at large
- Industry trade associations
- Regulatory agencies

Generally, this group finds its most valuable information in the company's annual report. They want to know about the longer-term prospects of the company. Also of interest to them is the firm's history so they can draw their own conclusions regarding its future.

Responsibilities

Corporate communications and shareholder relations have two responsibilities to the company:

- Facilitate capital formation.
- Determine that the company's stock price matches realistic performance expectations.

Companies accomplish this by providing the information investors require to formulate an opinion about the company's stock price. When this occurs, investors drive the stock's market price so that it is always fully and fairly valued. Three things that affect stock price include investors' attitudes toward:

- Investing in stocks in general
- Your particular industry
- Your particular company

True investor-relations professionals also have a responsibility to their profession: provide complete, timely, and truthful disclosure of events materially affecting the company.

Legal Responsibilities

Two legal responsibilities exist for corporate communications:

- No misleading information is disseminated.
- Material information is made equally available to all investors at the same time.

The objective of SEC laws regarding insider trading focuses on existence of an unfair advantage by providing corporate information not generally available to the public. In certain cases the Justice Department has asserted that people outside the company receiving such *material nonpublic information* were *temporary insiders.* Justice prosecuted these people under the insider trading laws as well as certain of the RICO statutes.

Rules of Disclosure

Follow the disclosure rules of the exchanges trading your firm's stock. If you don't know them, then call the exchange and request a copy—do it now; we'll wait. Generally the order of disclosure for material inside information goes like this:

1. *Contact the listing exchanges.* They probably want the nature of the news, method of release to the public, and timing of release.
2. *Issue a press release.* This goes to the wire services and other news media.
3. *Contact institutional investors.* It makes sense to give special consideration— *after fulfilling all public disclosure requirements*—to those holding major blocks of your stock.

Eliminating Insider Information. Generally, material corporate information changes its status from *inside* information to *publicly available* information when the company issues press releases or equivalent public statements containing the information.

Timing is critical. For example, the CFO may wish to present the company's earnings forecast to a meeting of securities analysts. However, *before* doing so the firm must issue a press release stating the earnings forecast. It doesn't matter if the news media ignore the press release. At least the company attempted to notify the public. After the forecast is public knowledge, the CFO is free to discuss it with analysts.

Once a forecast is made public, the company must disclose any anticipated material deviations. Furthermore, the company is obligated to continue disclosing its forecasts from that time forward—not a good position when earnings fall.

Trading Patterns.   The securities markets are very efficient. The public quickly sees changes in trading patterns. So does the sponsoring exchange and the SEC. They may call the firm to find out the reason for a departure from normal trading patterns. Possibly they'll recommend the company issue a press release. They also have the power to stop trading pending an announcement.

Rumors and Leaks.   This is a delicate topic. If rumors cause a change to stock trading patterns, the company needs to find out their origin. If the source of true rumors comes from within the firm itself, then many attorneys advise issuing a press release. This discloses the inside information to the public. It also stops further damage to the investment community.

If the rumors are still true but sources outside the company leaked them, management has a choice. Legally, the firm is not obligated to issue a release. However, many companies do. This prevents the impression the firm is stonewalling the press.

When volunteering information to the public under such circumstances, make sure of the following:

- It is accurate.
- It is complete.
- It is not misleading.
- It corrects or updates prior statements.

Figure 20-1 provides a guide for deciding when to disclose material information.

Commenting on Analysts' Reports.   Stay away from analysts' reports. Most investor relations professionals refuse to read, edit, correct, approve, or comment on analysts' reports. However, sometimes an analyst's report is so far off the mark that it could damage the public.

When that occurs, management may discuss methods the analyst used to arrive at the wrong conclusions. Without disclosing material nonpublic information, the analyst is shown the error. However, the company leaves any corrections up to the analyst.

Respecting the Silence Period.   During the registration period of a new securities issue the company cannot tout itself. The investment banker usually provides guidance on communication procedures and content. Take care to ensure the

1. *Rumors and leaks.* Depends on source and materiality. If the leak is true, material, and from *within* the company, then issue a release. If not, then it's probably not required.

2. *Updating prior statements.* Business is dynamic. Often things change that affect the accuracy or completeness of prior public statements. When that occurs, issue a release.

3. *Company stock transactions.* This is considered a material event in the company and requires public disclosure.

4. *Exchange requirements.* Most exchanges have disclosure requirements. Study them. Follow them.

5. *Stock trading patterns.* A marked change in stock trading probably requires disclosure of the reasons. If management doesn't know the reasons, then it should so state.

Figure 20-1. Disclosure guidelines.

company doesn't break regular communication patterns. Maintain things such as normal advertising, brochures, press releases on regular business matters, routine financial results, shareholder reports, and previously scheduled meetings.

Avoid clearly optimistic communications that could jack up the price of a pending securities issue. Examples include:

- Bullish earnings projections
- Predictions on the future success of new products
- Sales forecasts
- Favorable opinions on the company's valuation

Presenting Fairly

The company's responsibilities include fairly stating the company's financial position. The firm's communications department must have a reputation of honesty. They earn that reputation by presenting bad news as well as good news. Credibility of investor relations requires candid discussion of the company's weaknesses as well as its strengths.

Indeed, often the firm's current problems provide less interest to investors. Here's why. The securities markets are very efficient. More often than not, the stock market has already discounted the bad news and reflected it in the current market price even before it's formally released to the public. At that point investors want to know *what management is doing about it.* If investors believe management and their solution, the stock price rebounds. If not, it continues to slide.

Elements of a Fair Presentation.   Corporate information fairly presented carries five attributes:

- Discusses issues honestly
- Does not minimize problems or overstate successes
- Discusses the options available
- Discloses management's strategy
- Describes expected results

Analysts can see through management's attempts to soft-peddle corporate problems and failures. When it finds out, the investment public reams management. This loss of credibility often finds its way to the firm's stock price.

Avoiding Uncertainty

The stock market reacts negatively to uncertainty. Therefore, the investor relations and communications department must always present the impression that management:

- Anticipated the issue or event
- Has a plan of action
- Knows exactly what it's doing

Indeed, this should be the case anyway. Companies who don't disclose bad news soon develop a reputation among investors for hitting the market with:

- Negative surprises
- Unforeseen liabilities
- Unexpected competitive actions
- Adverse product developments

All these things create uncertainty regarding management's ability to maintain present earnings levels. Predictions of improved conditions and earnings fall on deaf ears. Indeed, such news may actually move the stock price down as management loses more credibility.

The message investors send to those who run their companies is clear:

The fewer surprises of any kind, the better the chances for long-term stock appreciation

Maintaining Consistency

Consistency of information disclosed to the public is equally as important as its credibility. Investors quickly drop interest in a stock they believe moves based on information known only to a few. Therefore, make sure all corporate communications treat every segment of the investing public fairly and equally. That's the law anyway.

Never make information selectively available only to some analysts. This is sometimes difficult when addressing the research department of a *particular* brokerage firm. Nevertheless, most analysts respect managers who decline to disclose certain material information for fear it is not generally available to the investment public. Further, they understand and accept that they really don't want inside information they can't legally use.

Indeed, even if disclosing such information to a select group, they still wonder, *what else has this person told to others and not to me?* Ultimately, such inconsistency breeds loss of faith. Further, it can get all parties into trouble.

Stonewalling

This is a term that grew out of the Nixon White House. When dealing with the investment public, it has to do with rumors and questions regarding answers potentially damaging to the company. Rather than answer such questions honestly, the firm's spokesperson comes back with *no comment* or *just trust us.*

Such answers only serve to fuel the fires of speculation. A better tact is to discuss such potentially negative issues openly. If they involve information material to the company's future performance, then issue a release *before* commenting. Actions other than these impugn credibility as well as generate a deserved reputation for inconsistency of information.

If you really can't discuss the answer to a question, rather than the standard *no comment*, try using *I can't help you with your story right now.* It isn't stonewalling. Indeed, it isn't a formal refusal to comment. You're acknowledging the reporter's right to do the job while saying that you also have a job to do. Most people respect that.

Fulfilling Information Requirements

Different segments of the investment community have special information requirements. Professional securities analysts, for example, require detailed information on such things as order volume, production backlog, and capital investments, to name a few. Bombarding individual investors with such data, however, would likely waste everyone's time.

Analysts want sufficient information to formulate their own opinions on the company's profit potential. Individual investors, on the other hand, often want the opinion of others they view as having more knowledge or insight. They want support for these experts' opinions in a form understandable to someone who doesn't make a living as a financial analyst.

Technical Analysts

This is a term for stock followers who base their opinions on a stock's history of performance. The firm of William O'Neil & Company in Los Angeles is one of the foremost technical analytical firms. Companies' investor relations departments often supply some graphics on stock price history to such analysts. However, that's not the type of information they present best.

Fundamental Analysts

These analysts believe that a stock moves based on certain performance aspects of the company. For example, a fundamentalist would look for development of a new product to drive the stock price up. These analysts consume the most often published information from the corporate communications departments.

Publications and Publicity

Corporate communications departments publish lots of material on their companies. The larger the firm, typically the more paper their communications people put out.

Annual Reports.   By law every publicly held company must publish an annual report. It doesn't have to be the fancy publications produced by the *Fortune* 100. SEC Form 10-K supplies the format of information for corporate annual reports. Each firm must file a Form 10-K with the SEC each year. Many investor-relations departments keep quantities of these for distribution to investors and analysts who ask for them.

Quarterly Reports.   The SEC also requires quarterly reporting of every publicly held corporation. These mostly consist of unaudited financial statements and management discussion. Each company must file its quarterly reports with the SEC using Form 10-Q.

The quarterly report provides a formal opportunity to communicate with shareholders, analysts, and the investment community. It clarifies issues that cannot wait for publication of the annual report.

Corporate Data Book.   Professional securities analysts use this more than individual investors. These provide in-depth information regarding:

- The company
- Markets
- Products
- Management
- Financial structure

- Schedules of debt and their maturities
- Capital expenditures
- Research and development programs
- Depreciation schedules
- Analysis of each operating unit
- Competitors
- Facilities

Data books generally get mailed to analysts and brokerage firms automatically. Institutional investors may receive them as well. Naturally, like all corporate communications, the firm makes it available to anyone who asks. Still, its target audience is the analysts and money managers who need such detailed information.

Newsletters.   Some investor-relations departments publish newsletters for their companies and send them to large institutional investors as well as analysts. When done quarterly, these provide a forum in which to update investors on issues such as:

- Progress toward forecast performance
- Market conditions
- Maintenance of price and cost levels
- Technological advances
- Impacts from economic changes

Press Releases.   Throughout this chapter we've discussed the use of press releases as the preferred method of disseminating information to the public without favoring one segment over another. Later in this section we'll show the parts of effective press releases and where to file them.

For now, however, be aware that corporate communications specialists must have the resources to generate clear, accurate, and timely press releases. Further, they need a quick way to deliver them. The fax machine has greatly assisted in sending press releases.

Accessing Senior Executives.   Controlling access to the company's senior executives often falls to the people of investor relations and corporate communications.

The purpose of this control is to grant fair access by analysts and groups needing to hear from the firm's senior executives. Each individual speaking to the public must understand the Justice Department's definition of material and inside information. Steer clear of topics qualifying as insider information. Don't be afraid to explain why you cannot answer specific questions.

Alternatively, many firms present their senior executives to analysts' groups for the purpose of announcing material inside information. *However, they issue a press release before the conference to eliminate the insider qualification.*

The groups most often extending invitations to senior executives include:

- Securities analysts societies
- Industry trade groups
- Broker groups

Some companies invite small groups of analysts to their headquarters to talk informally with senior executives. Often the firm makes a transcript of the session and provides it to whomever wants it.

Many firms with their stock traded on worldwide exchanges send senior executives on tour to the foreign financial centers. Often companies in these countries assist in organizing the presentations. These usually include:

- Local brokerage firms
- Investor relations consultants
- Investment bankers

Of course, foreign analysts who follow the firm's stock should receive all of the company's mailings. Additionally, foreign analysts often emphasize the importance of direct communication with the chief executives of the company. They like to see the decision makers.

Establishing Effective Investor Relations

The investor relations staff is the primary point of contact between the company and the investment community. The key to establishing effective investor relations is to make sure the staff has sufficient information and authority to answer questions posed by the investment public.

If the financial press sees the investor relations staff as just a barrier to company executives, they bypass it. They soon initiate direct contact with executives not authorized to speak on behalf of the company. This makes communication difficult on all sides.

Creating the Staff

The objective of investor relations is to create a staff that is a valuable and effective resource for company information. Further, those authorized to speak on behalf of the firm carry senior management's trust and have current, accurate information they can discuss.

Professional analysts don't tolerate mere puppets authorized only to mouth communiqués prescribed by manipulative executives. They always seem to find the real truth, then blast the company for attempting to hide it. Once that happens, it's difficult to regain the public forum (or trust) to refute the charges.

Positioning Investor Relations.   The senior investor-relations executive must have a sufficiently high position in the company to enjoy the trust and respect not only of management but of the financial press. This pays for itself in the person's ability to speak for the company rather than taking valuable time away from the CEO and CFO.

Further, the more highly placed are investor-relations executives, the more of the company they understand. They must have the background to discuss issues such as:

- Marketing strategy
- Pricing
- Backorders
- Production costs
- Financial matters
- Technology

Without the necessary background or access to information, the investor-relations staff is useless to the investment community. Worse, it gives the impression the firm has something to hide—not only from the financial public, but even from its own employees.

Establishing Policies

Financial analysts as well as business reporters want information instantly. The markets won't wait while a lowly corporate communications clerk seeks authorization to answer a simple question. This creates uncertainty. Sometimes, rather than wait for the answer, analysts take the risk out of a decision for their followers by simply recommending they dump the stock.

Therefore, the investor-relations department has two primary policies. It must be:

- Accessible to anyone requiring company information
- Responsive and accurate

Designing the Chain of Command.   Inevitably the investor-relations staff receive questions whose answers *might* fit the definition of inside information. After all, every analyst and investor is seeking a leg up on the competition for their constituents. Handling such detailed questions goes with the territory.

However, there's a way to minimize the risk of talking about matters that could hurt the investment public because its announcement fell short of prescribed SEC guidelines. Figure 20-2 shows the policy regarding chain of command. Such policies ensure the information provided by the firm is:

- Timely
- Consistent with previous releases
- Accurate
- Legal according to guidelines established for disclosure of inside information

The most likely inquiries received by the investor-relations department revolve around requests for the company's standard publications such as annual and quarterly reports along with Forms 10-K and 10-Q. Additionally, analysts call wanting clarification on press releases and the effect of current events on the company. Often they ask for interviews with particular executives.

The chain of command should fulfill these routine requests quickly and efficiently.

Public Reporting Requirements

Most public reporting requirements focus on the controller's and treasurer's responsibilities. These include the annual and quarterly report. Additionally, financial accounting and reporting standards require specific disclosure of things such as:

- Inflation
- Changing prices
- Foreign currency translation
- Unfunded liabilities
- Contingent liabilities
- Related-party transactions

Where the company's financial statements disclose such issues, be sure to inform the investor-relations department.

---

1. All inquiries are referred to the investor-relations specialist.
2. Analysts gain access to company executives through the investor-relations department.
3. Investor-relations experts attend executive interviews with analysts.
4. Refer questions to the company's legal counsel involving disclosure of material inside information not available to the general public.

Figure 20-2. Investor-relations chain of command.

Assign a single individual as the contact point on specific issues most likely pursued by analysts. Provide him or her with accurate answers to the most likely questions. Identify the company's policy regarding the issue. Determine its effect on key company performance indicators such as profitability and earnings per share. Provide him or her with management's plan of action and the expected effects when successful.

The best time to prepare for questions from the investment community is *before* release of the financial statements.

Filing Press Releases

Publicly held companies issue press releases for two reasons:

- To announce news about the company
- To stop uncertainty associated with news that could affect the company

Well-timed press releases bracket bad news to reduce its damage to the company's stock price. It does this by removing the uncertainty about events. Often the actual impact of bad news isn't nearly so serious as the speculation that goes on before management comes clean with the investment public.

When to Issue Press Releases

When is the proper time to release news? *As soon as the information is certain and complete.* Not a minute before and not after. The most common reason for issuing a press release is when there's news of a material nature that could affect investor decisions regarding the company. By law the company must make such news available to the general public before discussing it with individuals. Press releases fulfill legal requirements. Indeed, that's how the government's own Department of Commerce announces its periodic economic statistics.

Additionally, some companies forecast their earnings for the public. As a matter of routine they issue a press release stating their forecast.

Preparing a Press Release

The media receive hundreds of press releases. They don't have time to read long epistles. Convey what you want quickly, precisely, and end it. Here are some guidelines to follow:

Length.   Keep your press release as short as possible. One page is preferable, two is the maximum. Make them easy to read by double spacing the text. *Never* use a tiny font to squeeze more space out of a page or two. It takes more time to write something concisely. However, your chances of it actually getting published increase.

Style. The most effective press releases use a brief style. They convey facts and figures. If the readers want more information they can always call the company's office of corporate communications. Don't forget, the purpose is to communicate an event, not necessarily write the article.

We want our press release to communicate four things:

- Who sent it (use the company's letterhead)
- Who to contact for further information
- What's up
- What it means to the company

Figure 20-3 shows the accepted press release format.

Recipients. Where do you send the press release once it's completed? We want it disseminated as widely as possible. There should be no question that the company made every attempt to inform the *entire* investment public equally. Therefore, all press releases go out at the same time to all recipients. Most firms fax their press releases.

Sandwiching Information. Never sandwich bad information between two items of good news in a press release. The technique is transparent to even the most naive reporter. Instead, make each release stand on its own. If possible, many companies issue the bad news first. They allow the public to digest it, then issue the good news.

Broadcast Media. Radio and television provide an excellent source of coverage for fast-breaking corporate news. There's so much happening in the world of busi-

---

Press Release

<u>For immediate release</u>
Contact: Chris Malburg, Senior VP, Corporate Communications
    (234) 456-7890
                              Headline Title or Subject

Lead paragraph. State the news item.

Second paragraph. Cite the impact to the company. Give facts and figures. Provide graphics if necessary. Quote company executives.

Third paragraph. Identify management's options. State the solution(s) management intends to pursue. Identify the likely results of management's action.

####

Figure 20-3. Press release format.

ness that most of the broadcast media are happy to receive press releases. Include these sources on your press release list:

- ABC TV
- NBC TV
- CNBC (cable)
- CBS TV
- CBS radio news
- CNN
- Business Radio Network (in Colorado Springs, Colorado)

Another list sometimes forgotten in the rush to release news includes:

- Key shareholders by individual name
- Board members
- All senior executives of the company
- Division executives separated from corporate headquarters

Wire Services.   Most radio, television, and print news media subscribe to the wire services. Therefore, issue your press release to:

- Associated Press
- United Press International
- Reuters
- Dow-Jones Capital Markets
- Quick Nikkei News
- Market News Service
- Knight-Ridder Financial News
- Bloomberg Business News
- Business Wire
- PR Newswire

Newspapers.   Public companies often send releases of an event that could have a material impact on a company to the following newspapers:

- *Wall Street Journal*
- *Barron's*
- *Investor's Business Daily*
- *Financial Times of London*

- *The New York Times*
- *Los Angeles Times*
- Local newspapers

Magazines.   Many corporate communications executives ignore magazines because they're too slow. However, some of the business magazines have deadlines tight enough to allow for news within a week of their deadline. Further, a press release may prompt sufficient interest for an in-depth story that the wires and newspapers would miss. Therefore, send your press releases to:

- *Forbes*
- *Fortune*
- *Businessweek*
- *Inc.*
- *Financial World*

Using Photos

Inclusion of photos does not increase the likelihood of seeing your news item in print. The quality of a photograph coming over the fax is not sufficient for most media to use. However, inclusion of the phrase, *photographs available on request*, within the press release often gets results.

Using Video News Releases (VNRs)

The media use short videos for everything. Why not use them for press releases as well? Often companies hire professional public relations firms and advertising agencies to produce their VNRs.

The lead time required for such production precludes the use of VNRs for communicating news that affects a company's stock price. However, VNRs often provide a vehicle for companies to present their story to analysts and institutional investors using a state-of-the-art method.

Wariness of News Organizations.   The news organizations are careful to avoid accusations of reporting bias. Therefore, most are skeptical of professionally edited VNRs coming from publicly traded companies. If they're going to use visual media from a company, they much prefer *unedited B-roll film footage*.

If you submit videotapes to news organizations for use in their broadcasts, follow these three tips:

1. Minimize visual and verbal mention of the company. The intent is to provide a source of news to the media, not free advertising for the company.

2. Use third-party spokespersons with a perspective different from that of the company. It can still be favorable to the firm—just different from that of its executives.

3. End with a summary of tips or information useful to the targeted viewing audience.

Using Press Conferences

Press conferences work to a company's advantage only if produced by people familiar with the forum. They cannot appear too contrived. You must allow the media to ask questions and get sufficient information to write a story. Absent these ingredients, reporters feel they've wasted their time and the company attempted to manipulate them. Both of these attitudes may appear in black and white.

Scheduling the Event.   Few things companies have to tell the news media can compete with most real news stories. Therefore, schedule the event on a slow news day. The first objective is to provide as little competition as possible to *attending* the firm's press conference. The second objective is to limit the number of stories likely to compete with the news *obtained from* your press conference.

Planning for Equipment.   Reporters and photographers have lots of equipment. They have sound and light requirements as well. Make it as convenient as possible for them to set up and take down their equipment. While they are with you, make sure that your environment is one where all their equipment works its best. For example, don't schedule a press conference next door to a building being torn down.

Many firms use special rooms for press conferences. These have sufficient electrical outlets. The lighting is designed for videotape equipment. Air-conditioning is sufficient to counter the heat thrown off by the added lighting.

Be sure to schedule sufficient time *before* the event to allow for setup and testing of the equipment. Additionally, allow the news team sufficient time to take down their equipment afterwards. Some veteran press conference organizers even carry a few spare parts, extension cords, and cables for the news crews.

Additionally, make sure you know everything relevant about the facility. Include such information as the locations of:

- Restrooms
- Loading docks
- Personnel to assist in loading
- Freight elevators
- Secretarial services
- Telephones

- Setup areas for broadcast trucks
- Entrances for odd-sized vehicles

Brief Speakers on Broadcast Procedures. Once the lights are on and the cameras are rolling, you are on your own. Everything you say can and will be used against you. Make sure everyone appearing before the media understands their subject. Never allow them to think they can be anything less than completely honest.

Often microphones at the podium cannot pick up questions from the press. Determine this before the press conference begins. If that's the case, then make sure the speaker repeats the question before attempting to answer it.

The best way to conduct an orderly press conference is to control the format. Begin with an introduction as to the reason for calling the press conference. Next, the firm's experts elaborate on the news items. Make sure they speak in plain English, not in engineering or financial jargon. Be sure to pass out a prepared text describing the news.

The next phase is the toughest—questions from the press. Questioners allowed simply to shout their questions with the loudest prevailing turns the press conference into a free-for-all. A more organized way is for a company spokesperson (not the person answering) to call on questioners who have raised their hands. The White House conducts its press conferences this way. Make sure the person calling on the reporters does not show any favoritism. The proctor must allow both friendly and hostile questions.

Organizing Annual Meetings

The law requires that publicly held companies conduct annual meetings. This is the one public forum that allows individual investors a voice before senior management. Organize the annual meeting to provide a chance for individual investors to identify their concerns. Additionally, be sure to allow management a forum to:

- State company policies
- Make known its intent and plans for the company
- Explain recent developments
- Identify their effects on the company
- Fulfill legal and procedural meeting requirements

Answering Shareholder Questions

Questions from combative shareholders give senior management fits—especially when the press anticipates such questions and chooses to cover the annual meeting. The best way to deal with this is to do the following:

- Anticipate these questions and have facts to support your answers.
- Answer honestly.
- Never try sidestepping the issue.

Shareholder questions fall into six general categories:

- Company performance
- Management
- Social responsibilities
- Mergers and acquisitions
- Control issues
- Financial issues

Company Performance. Any time the economy swings (and when is it ever static?), shareholders question the firm's performance. They're afraid the firm's performance was below what an economic downturn should have caused. Otherwise, they're concerned that the company didn't rise to the level that an economic uptrend should have caused.

Here are some questions often heard from shareholders regarding company performance:

1. How does current performance track with management's plan?
2. Has the company experienced difficulty in obtaining additional financing? Has it successfully rolled over existing financing?
3. What exactly has the company done to slash costs? To improve operating margins?
4. Since interest rates have fallen (or risen), why has interest expense still gone up (or grown at a disproportionate rate)?
5. What is management doing to stop the company from losing even more market share?
6. Why does the company's stock price continue to slide even when the market goes up?
7. What is the company doing to improve its bond rating?
8. Why are current inventory levels so high (or low—they're never just right, are they)? How will it affect operating performance?

Management. Executive compensation is always a lively topic of conversation at annual meetings—even more so when the company's earnings and stock price are down. Here are some of the questions you should prepare for:

1. Describe how the firm's executive incentive plan enhances shareholder value.

2. How many outside directors sit on the board's compensation committee?

3. What was the average increase in total compensation for senior executives including stock options exercised and exercisable along with other noncash compensation? How does that compare with the year's increase (or decrease) in stock value?

4. What perks does the firm provide for its executives and their families? What is the dollar value? What dollar amount *is not* tax deductible by the company?

5. What percentage of outstanding stock do senior executives own?

Social Responsibilities.   Many stockholders use the annual meeting as a forum to vent concerns of special interest to them. The most likely questions touch on topics such as:

- Environment
- Sexual harassment
- Elderly
- Health care
- Racial policies
- Inner-city crisis

Prepare for questions like these:

1. How does the firm's manufacturing facility protect the environment?

2. Does the company's insurance policy cover liability for environmental damage?

3. Have any of the company's products been investigated or targeted by the Consumer Products Safety Commission?

4. How much did the firm contribute to political candidates and PACs? Which ones were they?

5. What precautions does the firm take on humane treatment for its test animals?

Financial Issues.   Shareholders are increasingly knowledgeable about their company's finances. Prepare for questions regarding changes in accounting policies and contingent liabilities. Here are a few:

1. What new accounting policies were adopted during the year? Why?

2. Has the firm adopted new accounting standards for postretirement benefits and income taxes?

3. What accruals for bad debt, contingent liabilities, and asset write-offs occurred during the year? What was their impact per share?

4. Why aren't the company's pension plans fully funded?

5. Why are the company's pension plans overfunded? What steps is the firm taking to recover the overfunded amount?

6. Why isn't the 10-K distributed with the annual report? What information does the 10-K contain that the annual report does not?

Voting Proxies

This is the most serious part of the annual meeting. Each share of common stock receives one vote. Most shareholders cast their votes using proxies. That way they can vote without actually being present. The company's secretary is responsible for counting the votes and proxies. Often the company's independent CPA firm is engaged to conduct and certify the count.

Shareholder Voting

Different companies have various provisions in their bylaws allowing common stock shareholders to vote on various issues concerning the company. Keep in mind, shareholders don't run the company; management does. As a result, shareholders don't vote on management issues. They entrust such issues to the directors for whom they vote.

The other most common voting issues shareholders vote for as specified in most company's bylaws include:

1. *Appointment of the firm's independent auditors.*   This is important to shareholders since the auditors provide their opinion on the fairness of presentation of the financial statements. It is these statements that provide the basis for investors' decisions.

2. *Executive compensation.*   Shareholders increasingly demand a vote on how they pay the management of their company. This extends only to the very senior management of the firm—the CEO, CFO, and directors, for example.

3. *Stock options issued to employees and directors.*   Along with executive compensation goes the performance incentives provided to senior management. Most commonly these are in the form of stock options.

4. *Mergers and buyouts.*   Shareholders often have the right to vote if their company is the target of a corporate merger or buyout. However, they generally don't vote if management elects to acquire another firm.

5. *Changes in stock.*   Issues such as stock splits and an increase in the amount of stock authorized and issued requires shareholder approval. This is logical since it affects the holdings of individual shareholders and could dilute their investment position.

6. *Proposed amendments.*   By law the company cannot omit from shareholder voting proposed amendments by the shareholders themselves. Additionally, the

corporate secretary must provide information on just how a shareholder gets a measure on the ballot.

Controlling Shareholder Servicing Costs

It's expensive to service shareholders. The company must send out all their publications to them. It also solicits proxies and distributes dividends. Shareholders of 100 shares or more don't present a problem. However, those holding less than 100 shares—the so-called odd-lotters—quickly drive up shareholder servicing costs.

It costs the company just as much to service the odd-lotters as it does shareholders with larger holdings. This catches treasurers in a dilemma. On one hand, it's good for the company to have a widely diverse shareholder base. This makes it more difficult to mount a takeover attempt. Further, the loss of faith from one shareholder segment (such as pension funds) won't affect the stock price to such a great extent. On the negative side, odd-lotters are expensive to service.

This group may include former employees to whom the company gave a few shares of stock. Others received some shares as a gift or from an inheritance. Many odd-lotters have such minor holdings they've lost interest in the company. Some don't even know they own the stock. Others have lost their stock certificates. Many would like to sell their few shares, but the brokerage commissions make it prohibitive.

Further, most odd-lotters simply discard the materials so faithfully sent them by the company. The solution is to conduct an odd-lot buyback.

Buying Back Odd-Lot Stock

About one-quarter of publicly held companies engage in formal odd-lot buyback programs. Cost control is the primary reason. Treasurers surveyed during the second quarter of 1993 indicated that it costs slightly less than $20 a year to service odd-lot shareholders.

If a treasurer can reduce the number of odd-lot shareholders by just 5000, this saves $100,000 in the corporate communications budget for the year. Given such potential savings, an odd-lot buyback program might provide a net saving.

Keeping It Simple. Too many treasurers allow the company's attorneys to make the odd-lot buyback offer too complicated. By the time the poor shareholders read through the pages and pages of legalese, they're so confused they can't make a decision.

Instead, keep the offer simple. Tell the shareholders only what they need to know to make their decision. You don't need all the additional material that goes into public offerings made to knowledgeable shareholders.

Figure 20-4 shows a list of the items most odd-lotters need to know when making their decision to sell back their few shares of stock.

> The company wants to buy your stock.
>
> Sale of your stock under the terms of this offer is *commission-free*.
>
> The purchase price per share in the offer is: $_____.
>
> The offer expires on: _____.
>
> Mark the enclosed form in the box saying *yes* (you will sell) or *no* (you won't sell).
>
> Use the enclosed self-addressed stamped envelope to return the form.
>
> For questions, call _____ at _____.

Figure 20-4. Information contained on an odd-lot offering form.

It's that easy. For shareholders who don't respond, many companies follow up with another letter or a phone call.

Managing Crises

Crisis. The nature of the word has a negative connotation. Uncertainty of what the crisis situations bring creates fear of the unknown. Recall earlier we established that investors perceive uncertainty—any uncertainty—as bad news. From an investor-relations standpoint, the worst part about a crisis is uncertainty.

Crisis points are really situations that have reached a critical phase. They require decisions by senior management. Professionals offer speedy resolutions to crises. Their companies must eliminate the uncertainty surrounding a crisis by answering these questions:

- What's the problem?
- What's the impact to the company?
- What are the alternatives?
- What does management propose?
- What is the likely outcome?

Once management answers these questions to investor's satisfaction, the crisis is manageable.

Creating a Crisis Management Team

Since crises don't happen with any regularity and since you never know what area of the firm they'll involve, how do you select a crisis management team? The answer is to plan for the worst. Assign the best people in the company specific responsibilities during the crisis. Delegate a single person authorized to communicate with the public. Make these assignments before the crisis occurs.

Many companies organize their crisis management teams as shown in Figure 20-5. This line of authority ensures the firm's announcements to the public all come from one source, the VP of corporate communications. The CEO and the board have ultimate authority; however, rarely should they speak on behalf of the firm during a crisis.

Planning for Contingencies

Many well-managed companies plan for the eventuality of a crisis. Public disaster agencies such as cities, police, fire, and the Red Cross plan for crises. Most have specific plans for such disasters—like earthquakes, civil unrest, airplane crashes, and major fires—already in place before they're needed. Airlines have specific crisis intervention teams in the event one of their planes crash. So does the FAA and most of the airplane manufacturers. They staff these teams with professionals and maintain them on alert around the clock—just in case.

Such extreme measures usually aren't necessary for companies not in high-risk businesses. However, use these questions to determine the most likely area from which a crisis in your company may come:

1. Identify the public's greatest exposure to damage from your company. It may be from toxic emissions, explosion, computer failure, or faulty products, to name a few.

2. Of the areas identified as having the greatest risk, which will escalate in intensity? How intense will it get? How quickly will it reach a critical mass?

3. Who escalates the crisis? Is it a governmental regulatory agency such as the EPA? Is it the SEC? Do the national and local newspapers scrutinize your industry and your company?

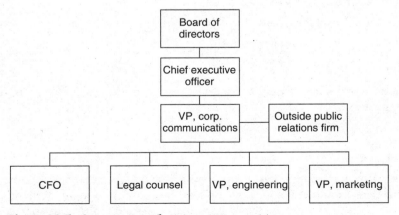

Figure 20-5. Organization of crisis management team.

4. How much will the crisis interfere with normal operations? For drug companies and meat packers, a contamination crisis brings sales to a stop. Indeed, the companies desperately seek to *remove* their products from store shelves.

5. Is your company the victim or the culprit? Sometimes a company is both. This happens in cases where an incompetent subcontractor makes a mistake on a part that later causes injury to the public. The company *was negligent for using that subcontractor.* Determination of victim or culprit helps form a strategy to deal with the crisis.

6. To what extent does the crisis damage the firm's profit? Measure this not just in terms of hard dollar costs. Identify such intangibles as employee morale, hiring, productivity, stress, workers' compensation claims, and erosion of community support.

Designating the Head of Crisis Communications

When a crisis hits, everyone—the media, the regulatory agencies, the public, *and* the firm's executives—wants to hear what happened from someone who really knows. Management should never send a lowly, inexperienced, and ill-informed sacrificial lamb before the press.

Select a true professional in the field of corporate communications and investor relations as your spokesperson. This individual must be a senior officer of the company. He or she should enjoy the full faith and trust of top management. There should be nothing that goes on in the company that's too confidential for this person to see.

The person should have this type of background and personality:

1. Professional training in an area of importance to the company. If your firm is a bank, for example, then the head of corporate communications should be an experienced banker.

2. Understanding of the SEC's insider trading and information disclosure rules.

3. Experience in public relations. This includes relationships and contacts with all parts of the media worldwide.

4. Excellent communications skills. This is the first person shareholders use to judge the security of their investment in your company. The person must be an excellent writer. He or she must be an outstanding and credible speaker.

5. The individual must exude an aura of honesty and believability. When he or she says something, it must not only *be* the truth, but *sound* like it as well.

6. The ability to acquire cooperation from all areas of the firm.

7. Flexibility to adjust priorities as events dictate.

8. Knack of communicating corporate strategy coming from multiple sources within the company.

9. Respect of the media.

10. The skill to operate within a budget.

11. Open-mindedness.

Dealing with a Hostile Press

Every morning as the sun peaks over the African veldt an antelope awakens. It knows it must run faster than the fastest lion or be eaten. At the same time, a tiger opens its eyes. It knows it must outrun the slowest antelope or it will starve. It matters not whether you're an antelope or a tiger: when the sun comes up, you'd better be running. . . .

The same goes for confronting a hostile press during times of crisis. The best way to deal with hostility is to face it and let them know three things:

- What happened
- What the impact is
- What management is doing about it

After reporters settle that, they begin their investigation. They want to tell the public why the crisis happened in the first place. The primary questions are:

- Could this have been avoided?
- Who is responsible?

Getting Your Facts Straight.   Nothing produces hostility in the press faster than information purported as fact, only to have it "corrected" later. Management loses credibility. It makes the reporter look bad as well. Often the media reports "corrected" news with a far different slant than the original version.

Before stating anything to the press during a crisis, make sure it's correct. Further, make sure the company's spokesperson knows more about what happened than the press.

A good example of how *not* to present the facts came with the radioactive release from the Three Mile Island nuclear power station. The press already suspected the company of withholding information. They were in no mood to hear anything short of the complete truth from some company underling. Nevertheless, when company spokesman John Herbein arrived at the press pool's room everyone knew the release was already measured at 1200 millirems per hour. Everyone, that is, except Herbein. He opened his remarks by stating that aircraft flying over Three Mile Island had just measured the release at just 300 millirems per hour.

The press conference deteriorated from there. All because Herbein's company placed him in an impossible position by failing to furnish him with the latest facts. Second, Herbein exacerbated the problem himself by becoming hostile with the press.

Taking Control of the Message. Astute companies learn a valuable lesson from politicians: seize control of your message. That means that the company proactively solicits invitations to present their case to the public. Instead of fearing the press, they grant one-on-one interviews. They go on the national talk shows. They provide press releases and articles to the print media. Always the message contains three characteristics:

- It is the truth.
- Management knows how to fix the problem.
- The damage is quantified and controlled.

Turning Questions Your Way. People answering questions can easily turn them to their own advantage. Here are three pat phrases every experienced communicator can use:

1. Usually when someone asks a question like that, people really want to know . . .
2. That's an interesting question. Before answering, I believe people should know . . .
3. Yes. That's certainly one way to look at it. However, let's first examine the situation this way . . .

These allow the answerer time to think as well as gain control over the session.

Identifying Red-Flag Questions. Be careful of the way a hostile interviewer phrases questions. Many people in the press would rather spout their own opinions than report yours. Beware of these openings:

- Isn't it true that . . .
- Aren't you really saying . . .
- _____ reported you said . . .
- How do you respond to allegations that . . .
- Are you aware . . .

Obviously you can't ignore such questions. However, before answering, turn such a negatively worded question into one more positively worded. Be sure to bring out the good things your company has done before this crisis. Above all:

- Be honest.
- Take your time and think about your answers.
- When you do answer, speak as the authority you are.

21
Risk Management

Overview

Chapter 21 describes the best methods to manage risk. The objective is to protect profits and financial stability. In this section we'll cover risk assessment and management techniques.

Elements of Uncertainty

Every financial executive deals with uncertainty. Uncertainty creates risk and vice versa. It also creates opportunities. Most treasurers and controllers isolate uncertainty and quantify the risk associated with it. Using this information they make an informed judgment on the wisdom of taking the risk. Often they discover ways to reduce the risk, while leaving the opportunity substantially in place.

Sources of Risk

Risk and uncertainty come from such areas as:

- Possibility of casualty loss
- Interest rates
- Financing sources
- Economic environment
- Product demand
- Legislative and regulatory actions affecting profitability
- Demand for product
- Technological breakthroughs affecting sales

Decision-making Process

Dealing with uncertainty and the associated risk requires clear thinking. It also lends itself to analytical techniques. Deal with risk using these steps:

- Identify options available.
- Project possible events occurring from each option.
- Determine likelihood of these events occurring.
- Identify results.
- Forecast results on impact to profitability.

Identifying Options.   Each decision usually has several options. Some require different levels of risk. Others have various risk–reward ratios. The first step is to determine the different ways to approach a decision to get the desired results.

Projecting Events Occurring from Each Option.   Each option carries with it a set of possible events that can occur as a result. The risk assessment process identifies the likely outcomes of each option. Often careful analysis reveals results you may not have anticipated after just an overview.

Assessing Probabilities of Events.   The probability of specific events occurring affects the risk of each option. Assess the probabilities of events resulting from different options using three gradients:

- Highly probable
- Possible
- Unlikely

Alternatively, assign each outcome a probability percentage of actually occurring. Use this probability to compute the expected value of an outcome. Here's how: Multiply the estimated probability of an event occurring by the profit that results from it. The product is the expected value of profit from the outcome. For example, say we estimate the probability of selling 1000 units of a product at 33 percent. If we accomplish that, the profit is $100,000. The expected profit value of the outcome is $33,000 ($100,000 × 33% = $33,000).

Identifying Results.   Most people forced into making decisions that involve uncertainty want to know the worst that could happen. Few managers would risk an outcome that puts the company out of business, regardless of its probability. That's how insurance companies make their living. They sell coverage for events having a hugely negative outcome, but a very low probability of it actually happening. The expected value of the insurance company's risk is less than the premiums they charge plus their investment income.

Predicting the Impact on Profit.   Every risk decision has at its core reward for taking the risk. If the reward isn't adequate for the risk, the decision should be negative. Therefore, we need to determine the profit resulting from the outcome of each option under consideration.

Margin of Error

Every company's tolerance for risk is different. It hinges on the reward for taking the risk and the probability of success. Additionally, the margin of error a company tolerates has to do with its management. Some people are naturally conservative. For these individuals, reward must outweigh the risk by a greater margin than the risk takers accept. Figure 21-1 shows the relationship between reward and tolerance for risk.

The concave shape of the curve identifies tolerance for risk at various reward levels. As the reward rises, so does the tolerance for risk. However, at level 3 the curve begins to flatten. That's the point of diminishing return. The company is willing to take on less risk for the same reward. Eventually, no amount of reward entices the firm to incur more risk. At this point, management is *risk-averse.*

Adjusting the Margin for Error

Risk management decisions undertaken by financial executives often deal with adjusting the company's risk tolerance. For example, borrowing often entails guessing where interest rates are going. Treasurers who believe interest rates are rising may borrow at a fixed rate. Others who see rates possibly falling go for adjustable financing. Some fine-tune their rate strategies by selecting the index that serves as a base for their financing rate.

However, most company controllers and treasurers don't see themselves as interest rate experts. They don't want such decisions to affect profitability. Their risk management strategy maintains the possible impacts to profit within the company's margin for error. Using methods such as hedges and other financial instruments, they control interest rate risk. If the strategy is effective, rates can go anywhere within a prescribed range and the firm's decision to undertake the financing alternative would still be the same.

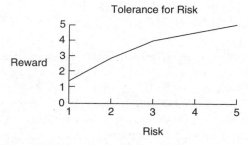

Figure 21-1. Risk-tolerance curve.

That's how professionals control risk—they utilize methods that keep the outcome within a range that's acceptable to the company.

Types of Risk

Most treasurers and controllers deal with two types of risk for their companies:

- Interest rate risk
- Risk of loss or damage

The theory of assessing the risk and possible outcomes is the same for both. Additionally, each employs commonly used tools for controlling the risk associated with various decisions. Once you understand how to identify risk, quantify its effects, and properly use the tools to control it, risk management isn't difficult.

Interest Rate Risk

Companies incur interest rate risk as the following change with fluctuating interest rates:

- Market value
- Earning power
- Value and cost of assets
- Amount of liabilities

Learning that they have a certain amount of control over the impact of changes in interest rates on their companies surprises some treasurers and controllers.

Management of interest rate risk unquestionably concerns financial institutions. They balance the interest income of their assets (loans) against the interest expense of their liabilities (deposits). Typically, commercial banks borrow funds long and lend them short. Therefore, their interest-earning assets gain value when rates move up. This increases their profit spread. The cost of the liabilities rise as well; however, it lags that of the assets. The reverse works when rates fall.

However, companies other than banks have entered the field of interest rate risk management. Insurance companies typically invest in rate-sensitive assets. Businesses requiring borrowed funds for operations often incur rate-sensitive liabilities. Certainly, real estate companies with mortgages on their properties incur interest rate risk.

The Concept of Rate Risk Insurance

The purpose of interest rate risk control is to ensure a tolerable profit within the range we expect interest rates to move. Some argue that the techniques used to manage interest rate risk are expensive if rates move in your favor. They cut off part of the upside potential. These people are gamblers. Few companies pay their financial executives to gamble with company funds.

Rate risk control measures *do* cost money—just like any other insurance policy. Further, we hope that we never need the insurance because rates move in our favor. However, if rates move against us, the insurance instruments at least partially offset the losses we incur. This preserves our profit projections.

There are four steps to managing interest rate risk:

- Determine the likely *range* of interest rate change.
- Determine risk without management help—the so-called *embedded risk.*
- Simulate the effects of these changes.
- Formulate and implement risk-reduction strategies.

Identify the Range of Rates.   Few treasurers and controllers are also experts at forecasting interest rates. For that matter, few economists are either. Surveys indicate they're wrong more than 80 percent of the time. However, the same surveys reveal when economists project a *range* of rates over a period of time they're right 80 percent of the time. Therefore, we go with their strength. Base interest rate risk strategy on a *range* of likely interest rates.

Large companies with much to lose if interest rates go against them often purchase professionally prepared interest rate forecasts. Chase Econometrics is one such forecasting firm. Data Resources, Inc., is another.

Look for three different interest rate scenarios: rising, falling, and most likely. Use these to create a range of rates for risk-reduction strategies.

Simulate Rate Movements.   Most companies serious about controlling interest rate risk use automated techniques to forecast results of changes. The more sophisticated companies simulate the change caused by movements in interest rates in their balance sheets, income statements, and cash flows.

Simulation is not as complicated as some think. For many companies, the spreadsheet model used to forecast financial statements for planning purposes is sufficient. For financial institutions, canned rate risk simulation software is available. Regardless of how it's done, make sure your simulation technique does these things:

- Forecasts earnings under different assumptions
- Allows for easy entry of multiple interest rate scenarios
- Provides for easy entry of different risk-reduction strategies

Identify the Embedded Risk.   Embedded risk results from the three rate scenarios run *without* any risk-reduction strategy. This yields the interest rate risk currently *embedded* in the company. Use this as a starting point. The problem won't get any worse than this. From here use the simulation model to design risk-

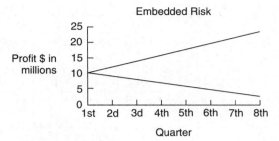

Figure 21-2. Embedded interest rate risk.

reduction strategies that insulate against the embedded risk. Figure 21-2 shows what embedded interest rate risk looks like.

The space between the lines defines embedded risk. The graph shows a total embedded interest rate risk of almost $25 million over the entire two-year period. The rising line assumes a *falling* interest rate scenario. This is typical of a company with adjustable-rate financing. As rates fall, interest expense falls and profit rises. The falling line represents profits resulting from a rising interest rate scenario.

Formulating Risk-Reduction Strategies.   Different companies use a variety of interest rate risk-reduction strategies. The objective is to bring interest rate risk into the company's *range of tolerable risk.* If this is a large company, perhaps a $25 million risk over two years isn't out of the question. For smaller companies, even a $5 million risk is often too much.

Formulate risk-reduction strategies to limit downside risk. As much as possible they should also preserve the upside potential for favorable movements in interest rates. Let's say a company has adjustable financing and the treasurer worries about a rise in interest rates. One risk-reduction strategy is to create a maximum ceiling over which the interest rate on the borrowed funds won't rise. This reduces downside risk. It also limits to some extent the upside potential if rates move in the company's favor. The amount of the reduction in upside potential is the cost of implementing the risk-reduction strategy—the cost of insurance, in other words. Figure 21-3 shows the result of this strategy. The two horizontal lines show the

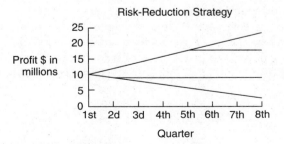

Figure 21-3. Risk-reduction strategy.

amount of interest rate risk reduction. In this case, the strategy removed about $15 million in risk.

Here are the four most often used interest rate risk-reduction instruments. There are others, but begin with these:

1. *Interest rate swaps.*   These are off-balance-sheet contracts that "swap" fixed-rate cash flows for variable rates and vice versa. Since these are actually contracts between two parties, they swap only the cash flow, not the actual asset or liability. However, auditors may view such contracts as contingent liabilities. If they're material to the firm's financial position, they may require footnote disclosure. Swaps don't usually require a cash outlay. However, if rates go against you, they may end up costing more than either a floor or ceiling position. That's because the contract locks you into paying a higher rate for the duration of the agreement's term.

2. *Floors.*   A floor is the sale of a put option purchased on an interest rate index such as LIBOR (London Interbank Offered Rate). It guarantees a minimum interest rate. If rates fall below the floor, the owner receives the difference between the floor rate and the actual rate. Use floors to reduce the risk of interest-rate-sensitive assets.

3. *Ceilings.*   Ceilings are the reverse of floors. Calls purchased on an interest rate index protect against rising rates on adjustable-rate financing. Both floors and ceilings require a capital outlay to put into place. After all, they are put and call options. The company's risk is limited to the cost of the position.

4. *Collars.*   Enter a floor and ceiling simultaneously and you have a collar. Unlike floors and ceilings done separately, collars usually have little if any cost—the revenue from the floor put option about equals the cost of the ceiling call option.

Risk of Loss or Damage

Many companies charge the treasurer or controller with purchasing insurance for the company. Some call it *risk management*. Insurance is a complicated subject. Millions of dollars are often at stake—both for premiums and the assets insured. If you aren't an expert in insurance, seek the help of a qualified professional. The best are those who don't sell insurance, but provide their expertise on a consulting basis. That way they are independent of the decision.

As with interest rate risk management, we don't insure the company for every possible loss in order to reduce risk to zero. Such an objective is far too expensive. The rule many treasurers follow is to insure against catastrophic losses that could cause material damage to the financial stability of the company. A loss that halts operations certainly qualifies.

Analyzing Insurance

Insurance professionals recommend annual review of insurance coverage. Things change. The firm's business expands or contracts. It purchases assets that require insurance. During the annual review the treasurer analyzes claims made by and against the company. The objective is to reduce risk of loss or damage to the range of tolerable risk. Further insurance beyond that point is unnecessary.

The results of insurance analysis sometimes reveal the company is overinsured. By raising deductibles, the firm enjoys substantial savings on premiums while maintaining risk at a tolerable level. When conducting an insurance review, note these items:

- Level of risk for the company's business(es)
- Number of employees
- Inventory—value and type
- Value of assets covered by policies
- Actions against the company for insurable liabilities

Administering the Details

Insurance administration is detail-oriented. It involves deadlines, expiration dates, premium payment dates, and specification of assets or events insured. Here are four administrative tips to use in the insurance function:

Listing Policies. Large companies have many insurance policies. Maintain a list of all policies. Include on the list for each policy:

- Name of carrier
- Policy number
- Asset or event covered
- Amount of coverage
- Premium
- Deductible

Constantly check for redundant policies. It's surprising how many companies over the years purchase insurance whose benefits overlap assets or events. Sometimes the cumulative total of these policies results in a condition of overinsurance.

Safekeeping of Policies. Just like any other valuable corporate document, maintain all insurance policies in a safe place. Some companies use a fireproof vault on the premises. Others rent a safe-deposit box at a bank.

Periodically compare the actual policies with those on the list. They should match exactly. If they don't, obtain another copy from the carrier—if it is still in force.

Determining Adequacy of Coverage. Risk managers often ask the question, *What would happen if . . . ?* The "if" is usually a damaging event. Then they determine how much of the loss their present insurance policies cover. If the amount of loss borne by the company falls into the area of unacceptable risk, then expand the coverage. Sometimes this amounts to no more than lowering the deductible. Other times the firm should restructure its insurance coverage.

Coinsurance.   Insurance companies created coinsurance clauses to transfer some of the liability for loss to the policyholder. This helps reduce the premiums and makes insurance more affordable. The coinsurance clause usually limits coverage to a specified percentage of the asset replacement value. Policies with 80 percent coinsurance clauses are common. Use this equation to compute the amount of claim collectible from an insurance policy containing a coinsurance clause:

$$\text{Allowable claim} = \frac{\text{face amount of policy}}{\text{coinsurance } \% \times \text{asset value}} \times \text{loss}$$

Types of Insurance

Businesses purchase every type of insurance product ever invented. Indeed, they buy some policies custom-designed for their unique needs. Here are some of the most common policies:

Umbrella Policies.   This type of policy insures against risk not covered by any other policy owned by the company. Insurance professionals use umbrella policies for coverage of catastrophic events. Umbrellas pay when the liability of an event exceeds the coverage provided by the specific policy. For example, say a company incurs a $1.5 million liability that requires its errors and omissions policy to pay up to its $1 million limit. The umbrella covers the additional $500,000 in liability that exceeds the E&O policy limit.

Fidelity Bonds.   These are specific bonds normally used to cover the actions of employees. Some companies cover only certain employees with jobs in high-risk areas. The treasurer's office is one such area of the firm. There, employees have access to liquid assets. Other firms purchase a comprehensive fidelity bond that covers *all* employees. This eliminates generating virtually the same paperwork for each employee.

Workers' Compensation.   Workers' compensation laws vary from state to state. Check the laws pertaining to the specific states in which your company has employees. Some states require that employers carry workers' compensation coverage with the state itself. Others don't recognize so-called blanket policies the firm purchases for all employees in all states. Errors in workers' compensation policies are expensive not only in terms of premiums but from the exposure to employees and their attorneys.

Business Interruption Insurance.   Companies that depend on the cash flow generated from ongoing operations with little margin for error need such insurance. It covers loss of profits from such catastrophes as:

- Flood
- Storm
- Computer failure
- Loss of computer data
- Leakage (especially important for computer installations)
- Civil commotion
- Explosion
- Supply of goods from specific critical vendors

Shipping Insurance.   If your company purchases critical and expensive goods FOB shipping point, it bears the risk of loss while in transit to the company. Shipping insurance is common sense. Additionally, expensive shipments transferred over water require special marine cargo policies.

Commercial Property Insurance.   Most companies own or lease commercial properties from where they conduct their business. They usually cover such facilities as:

- Warehouses
- Manufacturing facilities
- Equipment within facilities
- Offices

The comprehensive coverage for these facilities usually includes such things as fire, theft, and personal injury.

22
Managing Bankruptcy

Overview

Chapter 22 identifies the various sections of the bankruptcy code and illustrates their uses. From that point, we detail the rules associated with transfer of property owned by bankrupt companies. Failure to follow these rules may place both the transferor and receiver in jeopardy.

Chapter 22 also illustrates the steps taken during the bankruptcy process. It's complicated and takes time. However, when financial executives know what to expect, they can greatly reduce the cost to creditors. Along with the actual bankruptcy process, we'll explore:

- Managing creditor relations
- Alternatives to filing bankruptcy
- Tax implications of bankruptcy proceedings and forgiveness of debt
- Emerging from bankruptcy protection

Sections of the Bankruptcy Code

Bankruptcy. The very term conjures up images of mismanaged enterprises leaving faithful employees waiting for paychecks that never come. Indeed, the term originated from the medieval practice of smashing workbenches and outdoor stalls of merchants who failed to pay their bills. *Banca rupta* literally means "broken bench."

Today, however, bankruptcy laws protect both the debtors and creditors of businesses whose fortunes have taken a turn for the worse. Skillful uses of the bankruptcy laws provide time for a troubled company to get back on its feet. Emerging from bankruptcy protection with sufficient capital to operate the company often results in repayment of a greater portion of the firm's debts. Sometimes creditors receive all moneys owed them.

United States bankruptcy laws focus on specific chapters within the U.S. Bankruptcy Code. Each chapter provides for certain remedies to protect debtors and creditors. The most common bankruptcy code chapters used for businesses include:

- Chapter 7: Liquidation
- Chapter 11: Reorganization

Depending on the company's situation and the assets involved, filing under one chapter of the Code serves everyone's purposes better than another. Both chapters will be discussed.

Chapter 7

For the debtor company, this is the worst-case scenario. Chapter 7 bankruptcy closes down the firm. It no longer has the ability to operate and earn its way out of financial calamity. Chapter 7 has one intention: to satisfy as many creditors as possible. It requires the debtor to forfeit all nonexempt assets. In exchange for this forfeiture, the bankruptcy court releases the debtor from all liabilities associated with the business.

Most of the public auction of assets formerly belonging to a bankrupt company results from Chapter 7 liquidation. However, this step occurs in the middle of things. Prior to actual sale of nonexempt assets, the company takes two steps:

- Filing a petition for bankruptcy protection
- Marshaling assets

Filing

The debtor files a petition for protection under Chapter 7 of the bankruptcy code. This makes the filing a voluntary action. However, under certain circumstances, creditors may file against a debtor. Such an *involuntary* bankruptcy must meet these requirements:

1. The filing must include at least three creditors if there are more than twelve creditors total.
2. The debtor must owe at least $5000 in aggregate unsecured claims.
3. Creditors must show the debtor isn't paying debts owed.

After filing an involuntary petition, there exists a gap period. During this time the debtor is free to run the business. The bankruptcy court oversees material transactions if fear exists that the debtor may fail to preserve assets. The process of filing stops all attempts by creditors to collect debts and enforce debt obligations.

Marshaling Assets

Once filing is complete, the court appoints a trustee. The trustee's job is as follows:

- Locate the debtor's assets.
- Value the assets.
- Determine any avoidable conveyance or transfer of assets.

In this case, *avoidable* means that the bankrupt's estate has the legal right to void the asset transfer. This places more assets in the pot used to repay creditors.

When marshaling a debtor's assets, the trustee looks for these types of assets:

- Real and personal property
- Equitable and legal interests
- Causes of action against another party
- Intangible property
- Assets owned by the debtor but in the possession of a third party

Trustees also marshal assets that the petitioner acquires or is entitled to within 180 days after filing. Such assets include:

- Insurance proceeds
- Earnings from the company
- Rents
- Settlement of law suits
- Assets received from conversion of the estate's property

Liquidating Assets

This is the part of Chapter 7 bankruptcy proceedings most familiar to people. Except for those assets subject to a lien, the trustee sells all the assets included in the bankrupt's estate. There are specific rules of procedure contained in the bankruptcy code that govern how the trustee liquidates estate assets.

Once the liquidation has occurred, the court directs the trustee to file an accounting of all funds received. From these funds, the trustee distributes the estate to the creditors.

Distributing Proceeds

Chapter 7 of the bankruptcy code provides for a specific order of priority when distributing the estate. Figure 22-1 shows the order of priority for distribution of liquidation proceeds.

1. Priority claims—see below for order of priority
2. Unsecured, timely filed claims
3. Unsecured but claims were filed tardy
4. Secured and unsecured claims for:
   - Fines
   - Penalties
   - Forfeitures
   - Punitive damages
5. Interest from the date of the petition on debts owed
6. Amounts owed debtors

Figure 22-1. Priority for distribution of liquidation proceeds.

Priority Claims. Priority claims rank the merits of specific types of obligations owed by the bankrupt company. Since they are the first liabilities paid after liquidation, the order of priorities is meaningful to creditors. Here is a list of the order of priority claims and what they mean:

Priority 1. Administrative expenses and fees required to run the bankrupt's estate. These include fees paid to the trustee, lawyers, and accountants. Additionally, it includes the costs incurred to protect and preserve the estate's assets.

Priority 2. Creditors involuntarily extending unsecured credit after the filing of an involuntary petition but before appointment of a trustee and an order for relief is entered.

Priority 3. Persons to whom the bankrupt firm owes wages, salaries, and commissions. These can exist up to 90 days *prior* to the date of petition or the date the company ceases doing business, whichever is earlier. However, the code limits each such unsecured third-priority creditor to a maximum of $2000. Such wage claims include income earned but withheld along with Social Security taxes, vacation pay, sick time pay, and severance pay.

Priority 4. This makes good the payments a bankrupt company should have paid into benefit plans for the services employees rendered. The time limit is up to six months prior to filing the bankruptcy petition or the date of ceasing business. Like priority 3, there's a limitation of $2000 per employee *less the amount already paid in wages.*

Priority 5. Those who produce grain and store it with a grain storage facility that goes bankrupt reside in this priority. Likewise, included in priority 5 are fishers with claims against bankrupt fish storage or processing facilities. However, the code limits this to the same $2000 per individual.

Priority 6. This slot provides protection to consumers who gave the bankrupt company deposits on yet undelivered goods. However, the maximum is $900 per individual.

Priority 7. Taxing authorities enjoy the seventh priority. This includes most types of taxes such as income, property, employment, social security, all excise taxes as well as customs duties.

Discharging Debts

After liquidation and distribution of the estate, the court discharges the bankrupt's debts. Legally, under Chapter 7, corporations and partnerships don't receive a written discharge. Instead, the entity is liquidated, then dissolved. The effect is the same as a discharge of debt.

Discharging debts acts as an injunction that prevents further creditor actions against the bankrupt company. However, even the bankruptcy code does not discharge some debts. These include:

- Debts arising from embezzlement while the debtor acted as a fiduciary
- Fraudulently incurred debts
- Debts resulting from a prior bankruptcy or where the debtor was denied discharge
- Taxes and customs duties
- Governmental fines and penalties
- Debts resulting from willful or malicious injury

Chapter 11

This is one step removed from the finality of Chapter 7. The bankruptcy code provides for reorganization of an insolvent company under Chapter 11. This frequently makes sense to creditors since a company that continues operations has a better chance of repaying its debts than if it were simply liquidated. There are many success stories of companies seeking the protection of Chapter 11. This provides time to reorganize the company's financial structure—perhaps to secure additional capital. Through the reorganization comes a repayment plan acceptable to the firm's creditors.

As the company operates under its reorganization plan, it generates the cash needed to repay its obligations. If successful, the company emerges from Chapter 11 protection, probably much smaller, but stronger as well. Most Chapter 11 bankruptcies involve five steps:

- Filing
- Operations

- Formulation of the reorganization plan
- Creditor acceptance of the plan
- Confirmation of the plan and its acceptance by the court

Filing

Debtors file most Chapter 11 petitions. However, creditors may also file, creating an involuntary bankruptcy. In that case, the debtor must answer the petition. The court then conducts a hearing. Usually there's a time lapse between filing and the hearing date. Bankruptcy experts call this the *involuntary gap period*. The requirements for filing an involuntary petition for Chapter 11 are the same as those for Chapter 7.

Once the debtor files a petition the court automatically issues a stay from all creditor efforts to collect debts against the petitioner.

Operating the Company

The common term used in Chapter 11 bankruptcy when the company continues to operate under court protection from collection efforts is *debtor in possession*—DIP for short.

The debtor in possession runs the business as if it were the trustee. It has all the rights, duties, powers, and obligations of a trustee appointed by the court. However, the DIP isn't compensated. Additionally, the DIP cannot investigate its own acts for fraud, gross mismanagement, and financial affairs. Further, all DIP agreements require periodic reports to the court on the business, its financial affairs, and property.

Powers the DIP exercises include:

- Operate, use, sell, and lease property.
- Obtain unsecured credit on behalf of the company.
- Incur obligations.
- Exercise a trustee's power to avoid prior conversion of assets.
- Recover preference and other property transfers.
- Power to object to creditor claims.

A frequent requirement contained in DIP agreements is the reduction of executive salaries. It doesn't make sense to further enrich someone who caused such problems at the expense of good-faith creditors.

Appointing a Trustee. Sometimes the courts must overturn a DIP agreement due to fraud, incompetence, or plain mismanagement. Often the court appoints an examiner as an interim step prior to appointing a trustee. The examiner looks at the DIP's actions and informs the court of transactions contrary to the best interests of the creditors or security holders. If necessary, then the court appoints a trustee.

Formulating a Reorganization Plan

The *reorg plan* demonstrates to the court and creditors how the company intends to repay its debts and conduct the business of the company. Often such plans contain strategies on selling specific assets or even entire divisions of the firm in order to generate cash. They justify the expenditure of funds to remain competitive in the marketplace.

Most reorg plans contain extensive financial analyses that project the balance sheet at specific points in time. They also concentrate on cash flow. That's usually the area of deepest concern to creditors. They want to know how the company intends to repay them and when they can expect the cash.

Items Required in the Reorg Plan.   The court allows the DIP great latitude in formulating a reorg plan. However, the bankruptcy code does require certain things as a framework:

1. Specify the classes of claims and interests.
2. Identify those assets not impaired by the reorganization plan.
3. For impaired assets, specify their treatment.
4. Demonstrate methods to avoid discrimination between treatment of claims and interests within the same class.
5. Demonstrate how the DIP intends to implement the plan.
6. Amend the corporate charter where necessary.

Opposing the Plan.   The bankruptcy code provides the debtor every opportunity to file a reorg plan. During the first three months after filing the Chapter 11 petition, the debtor has the exclusive right to file a reorg plan. If that time limit is met, then the court grants an additional three months for creditors to study, amend, and accept the plan.

If the debtor fails to file a plan within three months or if the creditors refuse to accept the plan within six months after filing the petition, then any party may file an opposing plan. Creditors' ability to file a competing plan gives them a voice to use against debtors. Suddenly, the debtor faces accepting a lopsided plan created by the opposition because it didn't submit a fair plan the first time around.

Accepting the Reorganization Plan

The code emphasizes full disclosure of the plan by the debtor. To accomplish that the DIP must furnish creditors not only the reorg plan but also a written disclosure statement already reviewed and approved by the court as adequate for the purposes.

Accepting by Unimpaired Classes of Creditors.   Unimpaired claims get 100 percent of what is owed them. The fact that the debtor is bankrupt did not hinder payment in full. The law views claims not impaired by the reorg plan as automatically approving it. Therefore, the code does not require the DIP to obtain acceptance of the reorg plan by the unimpaired creditors.

Accepting by Impaired Classes of Creditors.   These are the creditors to whom the reorg plan pays less than what the company owes. Each class of creditor gets to vote on acceptance of the reorg plan. The plan is accepted if a majority of the impaired class *and* two-thirds of the money represented in the class accepts it.

Confirming Acceptance by the Court

The final step in the Chapter 11 process is confirmation of the reorg plan by the court. To accomplish this the court conducts a formal hearing. Any party may object to confirmation during the hearing. The SEC also has the right to object for publicly traded companies under their jurisdiction.

The court uses several guidelines to determine its confirmation. These include:

- Feasibility of the plan
- Satisfaction of the best interests of the creditors
- Fairness of the plan to all classes of creditors
- Acceptance by the impaired classes of creditors
- Adequate provisions for priority claims and administrative expenses
- Adequate disclosure of directors, officers, and trustee
- Proposal of the plan made in good faith
- Compliance of the plan with the bankruptcy code

Confirming a Cramdown.   Sometimes all classes of creditors can't agree on a reorg plan. However, the court believes that the plan is *good enough*. In this case, the court confirms the reorg plan without the consent of one or more classes of creditors. It essentially forces the dissenting creditor classes to accept the plan. We call this a *cramdown*.

Cramdown confirmations must meet two different tests:

1. *Best-interest test.*   Under the proposed reorg plan, each creditor receives at least the amount it would have received in a Chapter 7 liquidation.

2. *Absolute-priority test.*   Those classes subordinate in priority to the dissenting class(es) cannot receive any payment under the proposed reorg plan until the dissenters receive full payment.

Once the court confirms the reorganization plan it discharges all debts incurred prior to filing the petition except those retained in the plan and sometimes in the confirmation order.

Transferring Property

The bankruptcy code treats the term *transfer* broadly. Within the context of moving around assets and interests in the bankrupt company's estate, it can mean:

- Giving security interest
- Attaching a lien
- Bank deposits
- Entry of judgment
- Sale of property
- Gift of property
- Payment of money or property to satisfy creditors

Property transfers have two sides: the trustee and the creditors. The court stands in the middle acting as referee. The trustee wants to void certain transfers the company executed before or after the petition filing date. This puts more assets in the estate for use in satisfying creditors. Naturally, those paid by *potentially avoidable transfers* want them to stand. Otherwise, they would have to return the money.

The governing date regarding transfers is the date the company or creditors filed the petition for Chapter 11 protection. This is the effective date the company entered bankruptcy.

Prepetition Transfers

The bankruptcy code provides five types of avoidable transfers:

- Preferences
- Fraudulent conveyance
- Secret transfers
- Transfers avoidable under state laws
- Statutory liens

Preferences. It's dangerous for a creditor to deal with companies teetering on the brink of bankruptcy. The code generally allows for the voiding of transfers made that give a *preference* to creditors either within 90 days of filing the petition or when the debtor is in fact insolvent. The trustee may void the transfer and demand repayment to the estate. This particularly holds true if the preferential transfer gives the creditor a greater payment than it would get in a Chapter 7 liquidation.

The trustee must prove that a preferential transfer took place. Most are indisputable. However, identifying the time a company became insolvent is tricky. From there the trustee can attempt to void transfers taking place 90 days prior. However, a debtor's insolvency creates a rebuttable presumption under the law. The transferee then has the burden of rebutting the date of insolvency.

Note that it doesn't matter if the payment was for an ordinary debt current in its payment schedule or overdue. Indeed, a regular payment on an installment loan could be an avoidable preference item if the payee received more than it would have under a Chapter 7 liquidation.

Within the code section dealing with preferences, seven exceptions exist. These give the trustee power to avoid transfers. Here they are:

1. *Payments made within 45 days and incurred in the ordinary course of business.* An example is something like a telephone bill.

2. *Consumer goods.* The company has the right to purchase and pay for consumer goods with a value less than $620 and not have the transfer payment voided.

3. *Statutory liens.*

4. *Contemporaneous exchanges.* These are the simultaneous exchanges of goods or services for payment. A transaction that contains a span of time between transfer of goods or services and payment or transfer of a security interest as collateral voids a contemporaneous exchange. This makes the payment avoidable by the trustee.

5. *Inventory and receivables.* Vendors who sell the bankrupt company inventory and continue their security interest until paid are unavoidable by the trustee. However, that changes if the payment improves the creditor's position to the detriment of other unsecured creditors. Again, the key date is 90 days prior to filing the petition.

6. *Purchase money security interests.* The seller has responsibility for perfecting these. If that occurs, then the payment is not avoidable by the trustee.

7. *Newly extended unsecured credit.* Companies often purchase items on a revolving credit basis. Say the *prepetition* bankrupt company buys goods continuously from a company, then pays down the account and receives additional credit. The vendor's payment is unavoidable by the trustee only to the extent of the amount paid by the company. For example, say the beginning accounts payable balance is $10,000 and the company pays $4000. Any additional credit granted by the vendor is protected only to the amount of the payment, $4000 in this case.

Fraudulent Conveyance

A trustee may void fraudulent transfers made by a company within a year of petitioning. These three general categories define fraudulent transfer in the code:

- Transfers intended to hinder, delay, or defraud creditors
- Transfers made to a general partner when the firm is already insolvent
- Transfers exceeding the amount reasonably owed the creditor

The last category is often abused. For this, the code includes these additional caveats:

- Transfers made while the debtor was insolvent
- Transfers made that *caused* the debtor's insolvency
- Transfers that left the debtor with too little operating capital
- Debts incurred that the debtor knew it could not repay

Each instance provides a cause for the trustee to avoid the transfer and place the funds back in the estate.

Secret Transfers

Most often such transfers of property are not recorded. Debtors in danger of going under sometimes transfer property out of the firm in order to preserve it for later access. Often such premeditation falls under the fraud statutes.

At issue is the recording of the transferee's security interest. Timing of the recording is critical. Transfers recorded within the 90-day period preceding filing of the bankruptcy petition are avoidable by the trustee. Additionally, secret transfers for fraudulent purposes can occur *prior to one year* before the filing and still be voided. Companies in dire straights may transfer assets but wait to record the transfer until just a year before the filing. In these cases, the date of recording acts as the actual date of transfer. The transfer is avoidable.

Transfers Avoidable Under State Laws

Many state laws grant trustees the right to void unfiled, imperfectly filed, or incomplete transfers of interest. Further, the trustee acts on behalf of the estate as a bona fide real estate buyer. Therefore, the trustee may void unrecorded or unperfected transfers of real property.

Statutory Liens

Statutory liens result from actions of law. Often the act of filing a bankruptcy petition triggers an automatic lien on the petitioner's property. The trustee may void certain of these liens. Liens arising from nonpayment of rent or from property seized due to nonpayment of rent are two instances where statutory liens are avoidable.

Transfers After Filing

Assets transferred to the bankrupt company *after* filing the petition belong to the debtor, not the estate. While the debtor is in possession of the estate's assets, the law protects the transferees. Usually the court must approve such transfers anyway. This provision allows the company to transact its business and grants automatic relief to those vendors helping the firm deal with its problems.

Managing Creditor Relations

Creditors' committees are powerful in cases of bankruptcy. However, they are governed by the bankruptcy code. Further, the court has the ability to cram down a reorganization plan even though not all classes of creditors accept it.

The first step in joining the creditors' group is to file a claim. The code gives creditors of companies under Chapter 7 only 90 days to file a claim after the first date set for the creditors' meeting. The court itself sets the filing time limit for creditors of companies protected under Chapter 11.

Most courts require a creditor's claim filed on an approved form complete with documentation proving the claim. The claim may also include interest and service charges. The trustee receives all claims and has the right to object. The court conducts hearings on claims to which the trustee objects.

Disallowing Claims

The bankruptcy code generally disallows creditors' claims in the following categories:

- Evidence of prior agreement that the claim is unenforceable
- Interest not yet due
- Payment for services that exceed their value
- Damage from termination of a lease
- Credit for employment tax

Superpriorities

Sometimes the court grants creditors a *superpriority*. Often this happens when a trustee deliberately acts to diminish a secured creditor's interest. This can result from a trustee:

- Making cash payments to a creditor that diminishes the amount of collateral allowed
- Giving a creditor an additional lien that reduces the amount of collateral allowed
- Granting some other sort of relief that diminishes the value of the creditor's claim

In these cases, the court grants the affected creditor an administrative expense claim that is superior to all other claims in that creditor class. It also may review the trustee's qualifications.

Another more desirable superpriority is the debts incurred by the trustee. A trustee's job is difficult. It usually requires specialists and professionals to assist in the often monumental workload. No such professionals would work for a bankrupt company unless the court granted them superpriority to pay for their services.

Finding Alternatives

Bankruptcy is the last resort for troubled businesses. Depending on the case and the assets left to the business, other alternatives may provide a better result to creditors. The most common alternatives include:

- Appointing a receiver
- Agreement of composition and extension
- Voluntary liquidation
- Transfer of assets
- Mediation between debtor and creditors
- Maneuvers of assets and liabilities

Appointing a Receiver

Designating a receiver stops short of actually filing for protection under the bankruptcy codes. Debtors not eligible for bankruptcy protection for whatever reason may request that the court appoint a receiver. The receiver conducts an orderly liquidation of the firm's assets.

Agreement of Composition and Extension

This requires communication between debtor and creditors. If attorneys with their clients' best interests at heart are involved, they can often hammer out such agreements at little cost.

Composition.   This term simply means the creditor agrees to take an amount less than what was originally owed. Both parties agree that the partial payment satisfies the debt in full.

Extension.   This is exactly what the term means. The creditor agrees to extend the term of payment for the debt. Often, troubled companies seek to combine both composition and extension agreements for their major creditors.

Those creditors not in accord with the agreement always have the option of filing a petition for involuntary bankruptcy. However, the court often dismisses such petitions if the proposed combination and extension agreement better serves creditors and debtor alike.

Voluntary Liquidation

Many different liquidation plans exist. Creative debtors and creditors usually can come up with a plan that makes sense to everyone involved. Three of the most common methods include:

- Assignment of assets
- Assignment governed by statute
- Assignment under common law

Assignment of Assets.   Usually this plan requires a trustee or receiver of the debtor's assets. The trustee receives all the debtor's property in assignment for the benefit of the creditors. Most states require that a majority of the creditors agree to the terms and conditions of the assignment. As usual, those creditors who disagree with the assignment plan can always file an involuntary petition for bankruptcy.

Assignment Governed by Statute.   Many states have statutes that address assignment cases. Some offer more comprehensive guidelines than others. The New York State statutes governing assignment read almost like the bankruptcy code itself. They contain provisions for avoidance of transfers, preferences, court supervision, and documentation requirements. If assignment is an issue with your case, be sure to consult your state's unique treatment of the requirements.

Assignment Under Common Law.   Some states have no statutes governing assignment. In these cases, look to the common law. Debtors have the inherent common-law right to make an assignment of assets.

Transfer of Assets

This plan refers to the bulk sale of the debtor's assets and property. The proceeds can go to a third-party trustee who distributes it to the creditors. Alternatively, it can go directly to the creditors themselves. Bulk sales are most effective with debtors having a large number of unsecured creditors.

Bulk transfer requirements are simple: creditors must receive at least 10 days prior notice of the sale. The debtor/seller must provide the buyer with a list of the creditors.

The risk to a buyer involved in a bulk transfer is the possible existence of *unlisted creditors*. These parties may claim a distribution from the buyer or, if the amount remaining is unacceptable, file an involuntary bankruptcy petition.

Mediation Between Debtor and Creditors

This method of resolving disputes is gaining popularity. Many states have laws governing formal statutory and binding arbitration and mediation. The agreements hammered out usually meet the requirements of both the debtor and creditors. Mediation is a fast and less expensive alternative to costly bankruptcy proceedings that usually take years to resolve.

Maneuvering Assets, Liabilities, and the Company Structure

Companies in financial trouble often attempt a restructuring on their own. Sometimes these measures work. Their success requires a competent management acting in good faith along with trusting and reasonable creditors.

Maneuvering Assets. Insolvent companies are not without valuable assets. Management can use these assets as collateral for additional loans. It can sell some or all of these assets to satisfy debts. Often announcement of the sale of entire divisions or product lines signals the beginning of financial problems for companies.

Maneuvering Liabilities. Many of the liability maneuvers were discussed above. These include composition and extension agreements. Some troubled companies actually issue debt securities to raise needed capital. Another alternative is to sell stock in the firm to its creditors. Often these agreements allow the creditors a seat on the board as well.

Structuring the Company. Changes in the company's structure address specific problems. Often they involve changes in management as well as the product lines and markets the company serves.

Tax Implications

Bankruptcy and the less drastic alternatives discussed in this chapter carry income tax implications. The most evident one is the inclusion of debt discharge and cancellation in taxable gross income. Compute the amount of debt cancellation included in taxable income as the difference between the debt reduction and the amount paid to obtain the reduction.

For partnerships filing for protection under Chapters 7 and 11 the petition creates a new taxable entity. Corporations that file for bankruptcy, however, do not create a new entity. Here are some of the tax implications associated with bankruptcy proceedings:

1. *Reporting regular income.* Corporations that receive income from ongoing operations, gains and losses from transfer of assets, and discharge of debt must recognize the income as it would under more normal circumstances.

2. *Taxable transactions of the estate.* Property that reverts to the bankrupt company's estate can incur tax consequences as it is operated and disposed of. The tax liability belongs to the *estate* and is included on bankrupt entity's fiduciary income tax return. It is not an obligation of the debtor.

3. *Unpaid tax obligations.* After the bankrupt's estate is disposed of, any remaining tax obligations unpayable from remaining assets are discharged. *They do not revert back to the debtor.*

4. *Closing the tax year.* The tax code allows individuals to close their tax year with the filing of a bankruptcy petition. This allows them to use some of the tax provisions in the short year. These may include net operating loss carryovers that would otherwise flow straight through to the fiduciary tax return of the estate. Such benefits are useful to offset the debtor's taxable income during the year of bankruptcy filing.

Tax Effects of Insolvency

The IRS doesn't treat gain or loss on property transferred by an insolvent company any differently for tax purposes than if the firm were solvent. However, it makes a difference whether the company qualifies for treatment as insolvent when computing the tax effects of a debt discharge.

Companies meeting IRS qualifications for treatment as insolvent may avoid tax liabilities for discharge of debt. Generally, the qualification for insolvency revolves around the firm having an excess of liabilities over the fair market value of its assets. The company must meet insolvency criteria *both before and after the debt discharge.* If the discharge of debt suddenly makes the company solvent, then treat the discharge as taxable income.

Cancellation of debt from income tax liabilities proportionately reduces the tax benefits of these items:

- Carryover of net operating losses
- Capital loss carryovers
- Carryover of credits

Additionally, the basis of the firm's remaining assets is reduced. However, the basis reduction is limited to the aggregate amount of undischarged liabilities.

23
Personnel Management

Overview

Chapter 23, "Personnel Management," may seem unusual in a book for treasurers and controllers. However, mastering the technical part of your financial responsibilities isn't enough. Modern treasurers and controllers are senior executives in every sense of the word. They deal with more than just computer systems and the flow of money.

Today, employees and the way companies treat them represent a significant portion of every executive's responsibilities. The law requires minimum standards and levels of behavior accorded to personnel by their employers. Often the law orders standards that aren't always in the company's best interests. Indeed, some managers see certain rules as illogical and contrary to the way they have always done business.

Nevertheless, proper, *legal* treatment of employees not only makes the workplace more productive, it reduces the risk of a lawsuit by agitated employees.

Interview Techniques

Financial executives conduct many different types of interviews. The job interview is only the most obvious. Included among the more common interviews are:

- Performance appraisal
- Grievance
- Counseling

Your legal counsel will tell you that anything you say during these interviews can and will be used against you. Keep extraneous topics out of the conversation. Stick to the point of the interview. Many people write down their agendas to keep them on track. Document the conversation. After the interview, draft a memo to the file indicating:

- Date and time
- Participants

- Subjects discussed
- Resolutions
- Deadlines for improvement, change, or projects

Some companies ask the participants to ratify the written record of the conversation by signing it. This is a formal procedure, usually only employed if an executive expects the interview to result in legal issues or proceedings.

Preparing for an Interview

The amount of preparation required for an interview depends on the objectives. If there's little possible chance of legal action resulting from the interview, then a written agenda is unnecessary. However, even seemingly innocent conversations with employees have a habit of being twisted around by plaintiff attorneys. The best rule is, *when in doubt, document.*

Privacy.   Select a meeting place that is private. People do not always respond as honestly if they don't know who can hear their conversation. Additionally, choose a neutral place if the interview warrants it. For some interviews, such as performance counseling, managers need a two-way conversation. The boss's office isn't always the most conducive place for freedom of speech.

Timing the Interview.   Allow enough time for a full discussion. The financial department of most companies is a busy place. Deadlines are common. Identify the amount of time the conversation should take and make sure both parties' schedules can accommodate it.

Homework Prior to the Interview.   If you're talking with a job applicant, be sure you've already read the résumé. Perhaps the applicant has already had other interviews in the company. Find out the results and impressions the person has made so far. Read the job description for the position so you can judge the technical qualifications you're looking for. List the information and questions you want answered that haven't been discussed in prior interviews.

Asking Questions.   One objective of an interview is to establish a dialog with the person. You can start the ball rolling by asking open-ended questions. These are questions that don't allow a simple *yes* or *no* answer. For example, *What aspects of your present position do you like best? Why?* The answer from this question reveals a lot more than simply asking, *Do you like your present job?*

Avoid leading questions—those signaling a particular response. You want to know what the person thinks—not what he or she thinks you want to hear. Additionally, don't react negatively to the responses. There's time to evaluate the candidate after accumulating all the information. Shocked or negative responses only stifle honest answers.

Try not to take notes during the questioning session. People are uncomfortable not knowing what part of their responses you're writing down. Instead, wait until the interview is over, then record your impressions.

How to Legally Hire and Fire

This is the most sensitive area of labor practice. Companies cannot discriminate in *any* way regarding hiring and firing practices. Insensitive managers can expose their companies to huge liabilities by not following the rules. This is especially true of large firms with deep pockets. When in doubt regarding *any* issue concerning hiring and firing an employee, check with your firm's personnel specialist or legal counsel.

Hiring People

The job interview has three goals:

- To qualify the candidate
- To provide the candidate information about the job and company
- To generate goodwill about the company

The first step—even before interviewing candidates—is to establish a *job profile*. Put it in writing. This identifies the specific qualifications required to do the job. It also helps in the screening process.

After completing the job profile, use that information to create a sketch of the candidate most likely to successfully fulfill the job requirements. Be specific. Note background items such as:

- Education
- Employment history
- Related experience
- Temperament
- Technical qualifications
- Leadership skills and experience

Job profiles also help in making hiring decisions based on factors unrelated to the job's requirements. This is often a cause for discrimination suits. Further, it helps in seeking similar information from competing candidates. This makes the hiring process more uniform. It allows you to compare people with similar qualifications for a job that requires those exact qualifications.

Legal Aspects of Job Interviews.   Discrimination suits require the plaintiff to establish only *preliminary* proof of their accusation. After that, the burden of rebuttal falls on the defendant company. The employer must establish some legitimate business reason for its actions. Once the employer presents its case, the plaintiff has a chance to prove *the real* reason for the discrimination—evidence of the employer notwithstanding.

Proof of a preliminary discrimination accusation requires only three things:

1. Plaintiff belongs to a protected class. The law bases class on:
   - Race
   - Sex
   - Religion
   - National origin
   - Handicap
   - Age
   - Anything else claimed by the plaintiff

2. The plaintiff is connected with the company in some employment context.

3. The company damaged the plaintiff within the context of the employment relationship. This extends to hiring, firing, raises, promotions, and disciplinary action.

Questions to Avoid.   Do not ask potentially discriminating questions of job candidates. Avoid questions whose answers could categorize an applicant in a *protected class*. Even if it is not your intention to discriminate, an imaginative plaintiff lawyer will ask *why you wanted that kind of information in the first place if for no other reason than discrimination*. Figure 23-1 shows eight questions and categories of conversation to avoid when interviewing job candidates.

Conducting Employment Searches.   Employers have the legal obligation of conducting a full and fair employment search. This means that the pool from which it draws job applicants is not unfairly or discriminatingly limited. When advertising for jobs, place the ad in generally circulated media available to *all* potential job candidates. Stay away from those periodicals that cater to a particular class or group.

Checking References.   Check references of *each* candidate in which you have a serious interest. Many employers wonder what's the use. Few companies provide any real information on former employees for fear of being sued. However, you never know what the person on the other end of the line will reveal.

Many savvy recruiters listen carefully to what *isn't* said when checking references. For example, say that an employee sued her former employer for wrongful termination. The case settled out of court. Part of the settlement agreement included a gag order on the company when prospective employers checked the plaintiff's references. All the company needs to tell an employer checking references is, *Our legal counsel recommends we don't discuss the case of Ms. _____ with anyone*. This sends a message loud and clear that something out of the ordinary occurred in the relationship.

On the other hand, be very careful of what you say when employers call *you* requesting information on former employees. Here's what you can safely provide

---

Avoid These Job Interview Questions and Topics

1. *Age and date of birth.*   There can be no possible relation to age and a candidate's qualification for the job.

2. *Arrests.*   Unless an arrest led to a conviction it has no relation to the candidate's qualifications. Additionally, some states disallow inquiries regarding criminal convictions unless it has direct relevance to a candidate's job responsibilities.

3. *Weekend work.*   This has to do with religious discrimination. Employers must reasonably accommodate employees' work hours around their religious requirements.

4. *Citizen of which country.*   The answer could lead to a suit based on discrimination of national origin. Further, the answer probably makes no difference except to the CIA, NSA, FBI, or defense contractors.

5. *Handicaps or physical impairment.*   Employers cannot discriminate based on handicaps. They must make an effort to accommodate handicapped employees. Instead, it's OK to ask: *Do you have any physical limitation that will keep you from performing the work as described?*

6. *Physical stature.*   Don't ask for physical statistics such as height and weight unless you can prove their relation to job performance. Further, they could be protected under the handicapped rules.

7. *Marital status.*   This has nothing to do with job performance. However, a plaintiff lawyer could argue that the client wasn't hired because of the employer's moral concern about a particular marital status.

8. *Pregnant or planning on children.*   Since employers cannot refuse to hire a woman who is pregnant or wants children, why even ask the question? It only opens the door for a discrimination suit.

Figure 23-1. Questions to avoid.

without a *signed release* from the former employee allowing you to disclose specific information:

- Dates of employment
- Job title
- Confirm or deny salary levels stated by the inquirer. *Do not volunteer salary information.*

Sexual Harassment

This is a serious matter. Almost 50 percent of the financial work force is female. Further, statistics indicate that women bring 90 percent of all sexual harassment claims against men. That makes sexual harassment—regardless of who initiates it—a potentially huge exposure. Executives have the responsibility to create a work environment that is not conducive to an atmosphere that allows sexual harassment.

Types of Sexual Harassment

Two categories of sexual harassment exist in the workplace:

- Quid pro quo (something for something)
- Hostile environment

Neither is acceptable in a modern work situation.

Quid pro Quo.   This is the standard trade-off. A supervisor may tell a subordinate that he or she will get a raise if that employee goes along with the supervisor's suggestion. Alternatively, an office manager may threaten to block a subordinate's promotion unless the subordinate submits to an affair (regardless of the gender of either).

Hostile Environment.   The law defines a hostile environment as *regular and repeated actions or things displayed that unreasonably interfere with job performance.* A hostile environment creates an intimidating or offensive workplace. Ingredients of a hostile environment may include:

- Sexual pictures
- Calendars
- Objects
- Graffiti
- Offensive language
- Jokes
- Gestures
- Comments

Hostile environments come in many varieties. For example, a female truck driver is subjected to sexual remarks every time she pulls into the garage; a male office worker is embarrassed by the beefcake photos his female coworkers post around the office.

Federal Law

Federal law uses the following guideline to determine if an employee has acted in a sexually harassing manner:

. . . if an employee's behavior toward another employee has the purpose or effect of unreasonable interference with the individual's work performance or creates an intimidating, hostile, or offensive working environment.

Not only do plaintiffs name the company in resulting sexual harassment suits, but they also name the coworker responsible. Courts have required coworkers perpetrating the harassment to pay all or a portion of damages awarded.

Intent versus Impact

Unwelcome attention, advances, touching, or even looking constitutes sexual harassment regardless of intent. The plaintiff is the one who determines what is *unwelcome.* If the impact of such attention causes interference with the individual's work performance or creates an intimidating, hostile, or offensive working environment—and they can prove it in court—then sexual harassment occurred. The company will pay dearly.

Creating Company Policy

Draft a company policy regarding sexual harassment. Define sexual harassment using examples. State that the company has zero tolerance for behavior considered sexually harassing. Many firms present this policy at employee assemblies. They often include them in the employee manual.

If your company has no policy regarding sexual harassment, Figure 23-2 provides a guideline.

Enforcing Company Policy

It's not enough to pay lip service to preventing sexual harassment. The company must actively *and consistently* enforce its policies. It cannot discriminate in disciplining employees who choose to remain in the dark ages.

Company Policy Regarding Sexual Harassment

1. The Company will not tolerate any behavior that qualifies as sexual harassment.

2. Employees should notify their supervisor immediately if they feel they are sexually harassed.

3. The Company will investigate the complaint promptly. If it finds a case of sexual harassment the Company will take corrective action immediately.

4. The Company will notify both parties of the results of its investigation.

5. Employees have a right to present their claim to the Equal Employment Opportunity Commission (EEOC) or the state's department of employment.

Figure 23-2. Sexual harassment guidelines.

Enforcement of the company's policies extends not only to employees. The firm has an obligation to provide an environment free of sexual harassment. For example, say the company's biggest client likes to come over to the office and make suggestive remarks to workers. That's sexual harassment. The company has an obligation to its employees to tell anyone—even its largest client—not to harass its personnel.

Acting on Policy

Chances are most employees don't know how to respond to an incidence of harassment. Figure 23-3 shows the steps your firm can recommend to assist.

If you are the supervisor dealing with a harassed employee, remember:

- Respect your employee's rights and dignity.
- Don't jump to conclusions.
- Act in the company's and employee's best interests.
- Never forget that *No means No.*

Internal Control Issues

The financial departments in companies control liquid assets and record their transactions. Most well-run firms have specific systems of internal control to prevent theft and conversion of company assets. A cornerstone of most internal control systems is the checks and balances afforded by dual control.

However, what happens when the two people designated to provide each other's checks and balances become too close? Suddenly a potential control problem exists. How does this happen? Office romance is one way. In a California bank the branch manager and chief teller fell in love. Together they embezzled well into the six figures before being caught. In court the teller claimed her lover/manager had complete control over her willpower.

Respond to Sexual Harassment

1. *Respond immediately.* Make your feelings crystal clear immediately after receiving unwanted sexual attention from anyone in the workplace. You have the right to say no and make it stick.

2. *Record the incident.* Write down the date, time, place, those involved, witnesses, and the particulars for each incident.

3. *Involve your supervisor.* Report harassment to your supervisor. If the harassor is your supervisor, go to the person responsible for your supervisor's actions.

Figure 23-3. Steps to respond to sexual harassment.

Another problem is the change in two people's relationships. Say the accounting clerk responsible for reconciling the checking account and the supervisor responsible for review of the reconciliations suddenly become in-laws. It happens. Maybe they hate each other and will always hate each other. But maybe they don't. Now, by virtue of their family relationship, they have compromised control over the checking account.

Problem situations don't even have to result from legal relationships. Two people who suddenly decide to live together present similar risks. The point is, we want our internal control systems operated by people *independent* of one another. An astute manager pays close attention to the relationships between people who provide key internal controls. The manager knows how these people feel about one another. The manager observes behavior that might indicate a less-than-independent relationship. As soon as this happens, the manager takes steps to reinforce the control now compromised.

Bonding

Most financial departments purchase fidelity bonds at least for those employees with access to liquid assets. This allows the company to share some risk of loss from employee actions with an insurance carrier.

Additionally, information provided by employees necessary for approval by the bonding company is useful from a personnel viewpoint. For example, the bonding application can ask questions that an interviewer cannot legitimately ask. This provides yet another level of information about the employees hired.

If the bonding company refuses to issue a bond on a particular employee, it raises an immediate red flag.

Safety

Some controllers and treasurers scoff at the issue of safety. *What's the worst that can happen,* they ask, *a hell of a paper cut?* Wrong. One petrochemical company, for example, had vertical file cabinets whose drawers failed to close automatically. An employee working on a bottom file drawer rose, unaware of the still-open drawer above him. The sharp metal corner of the drawer smashed through his skull and into his brain, permanently disabling him. The settlement was in the millions.

Financial personnel often work late and on weekends. It is the manager's responsibility to make sure the workplace is safe for these employees. Often the solution merely requires additional lights installed in the parking lot. Some companies provide a security guard who escorts employees from the building to their cars.

Make security and office safety an issue in the financial department. Many companies include in their employee manuals statements, policies, and procedures regarding safety. Astute managers conduct safety meetings with their staff. They want to know if there's a potential problem before it turns into a lawsuit.

Working Conditions

Every company has different attitudes toward the conditions they provide workers. This extends from the physical environment to stress and respect given to employees.

Physical Environment

Few financial operations require interior design and decoration by the world's top professionals. Indeed, they usually emphasize function and efficiency. After all, few customers or clients ever see the treasury or accounting departments.

However, the workplace must be appropriate for the company and its employees. It should provide sufficient space for workers to perform their jobs. If treasury personnel are negotiating terms of the company's bank line, all parties are probably more comfortable in a private office or conference room.

Computer workstations should provide *ergonomic* sensitivity to:

- Blue-spectrum rays from computer screens
- UV rays from fluorescent lights overhead
- Chairs with arms to prevent carpal tunnel syndrome

Some companies hire ergonomic consultants to evaluate their work environment. This not only prevents lawsuits from disgruntled employees looking for an excuse to nail the company but it provides tangible evidence of good faith and an interest in employee well-being.

Emotional Environment

Be sensitive to people's feelings. Admittedly, the office is no place for anarchy. However, be aware of what employees want and need to do their jobs. Honor reasonable requests. Don't forget, you all want the same results.

This extends to what people wish to be called. That's right. Consider how a female worker feels after going through a messy divorce. She may want her maiden name back. Make sure you honor that simple request. *Ask her what she prefers.* Print her new business cards. Instruct the telephone operator to answer with her new name. Do this without the employee having to ask.

Financial departments get tense around month-end and year-end closings. Manage the deadlines to reduce that stress as much as possible. Anticipate the need for overtime and don't keep it a secret. People appreciate some control over their work environment. They respect managers who respect their employees' personal time requirements. Unannounced overtime and continual emergency weekend sessions undermine a manager's grasp of his or her job.

Employee Privacy

This is a growing concern for employee activist groups such as Nine to Five. It's also turning into a lucrative practice area for plaintiff attorneys. Issues of employee privacy include:

- Work environment—the employee's desk or office
- Background investigation during hiring
- Polygraph testing
- AIDS testing
- Narcotics testing
- Inspection of purses and briefcases
- Monitoring telephone calls
- Audio/video monitoring of job performance

Work-space Privacy

Employers cannot rifle through an employee's personal work space unless there's a legitimate business reason to do so. For example, if you suspect an employee is storing computer disks containing proprietary information in his or her desk, can you search the desk? Probably not. However, if the employee normally keeps something routinely needed during the course of business (such as the check-signing-machine signature plate), you *can* search the desk for it. If you come upon something else the employee is not authorized to possess, then that's a legitimate search. Be sure to have a witness present when searching an employee's private work space.

Preemployment Investigation

The rule is that employers must limit their investigation of employees to information required to determine their qualifications for the job. Few jobs require the company to hire a private investigator to tail a prospective employee.

Some companies have strict policies against drug abuse. They state in their employment application the company policy of screening all employees for drugs. Knowing this going in, a prospective employee is free to make the decision to pursue employment.

The law frowns on AIDS testing, or even asking if the prospective employee has AIDS. Unless there's something specific to the job that requires a worker to be free of the AIDS virus, it's irrelevant to the hiring decision. You may find yourself in a discrimination suit if you make an issue of AIDS in prospective employees.

Inspection of Personal Baggage

Many companies require inspection of all employees' purses and briefcases upon exit of the building. This helps prevent theft. Some companies include personal computers in this inspection policy.

If such inspection procedures are a policy of your company, be sure to apply it to *all* employees. You cannot discriminate in any way—including baggage inspection.

Monitoring Employees' Work

Companies employ all sorts of methods to monitor employee performance. These include telephone monitoring and video cameras in areas containing liquid assets. Some firms even employ surveillance techniques in their computer areas—such as the wire transfer room.

To avoid employee complaints about surveillance, follow these rules:

- Inform the employees of the surveillance.
- Do not single out employees for surveillance.
- Identify the specific business reason for the surveillance.
- Provide employees access to surveillance results.

Counseling

Financial managers aren't known for their human resources skills. They deal in facts and figures. Answers are either right or wrong. There's always the press of time and deadlines. However, by necessity, our society requires even financial managers to exercise at least minimal level of employee-relations skills.

The most effective skill in managing employees is the ability to constructively counsel behavior. When done well, this helps both the company and the employee. It also provides a written record of the firm's good faith attempt to communicate and correct employee behavior in the event of a subsequent wrongful termination suit.

Counseling Unacceptable Behavior

Regardless of the behavior or offense, there is a right way and a wrong way to counsel employees. Design a policy that gives employees a chance to correct behavior and supports the company's right to determine job procedures. Here is a list of the phases a company might go through when counseling a problem employee:

First Discovery.   When first noticing a problem, talk with the employee in private. Explain company policy and how the employee broke that policy. Describe the correct procedure. Keep the conversation constructive. This is the time to give an employee the benefit of the doubt.

To let them know how seriously the firm takes a breach of its policy, document the conversation, give a copy to the employee, and put a copy in their personnel file. Finally, explain the firm's next step if a repeat of the offense occurs.

Second Offense.   This is more serious. A pattern of behavior is developing along with a disregard for company policy. Conduct a more formal counseling session. Follow these steps:

1. Notify the person that this is the second offense.
2. Summarize what was said before.
3. Repeat instructions on the proper procedure.
4. Establish deadlines for change.
5. Explain the reasons for this policy.
6. Issue a written reprimand.
7. Explain the consequences if the infraction occurs a third time.
8. Document the session. Give the employee a copy and put a copy in their personnel file.

Third Offense.   If the same problem occurs a third time some companies suspend the employee without pay. Others initiate immediate termination proceedings. Regardless, make sure the company applies its policy consistently to all employees.

Keep in mind that the company's actions may come under scrutiny by a professional arbiter or by a judge and jury. Seek legal counsel if necessary. Additionally, be sure to document the third counseling session in the employee's personnel file.

Rules for Counseling

Supervisors have their own individual styles when counseling employees. For most, this is an uncomfortable task. However, when done properly it helps both parties. Indeed, frequently supervisors find that a shortcut instituted by a well-meaning employee actually *increases* work flow without diminishing internal controls. Without the counseling session, this might not have been discovered. Figure 23-4 provides some rules for use in counseling.

Mentor Programs

All of us learn from those senior to our position. If we're lucky the most qualified teacher becomes our mentor. Some companies go so far as to establish mentor programs that match senior people with those more junior. Mentors guide their protégés through the assimilation process of their new jobs. Many companies report lower turnover and better-qualified employees as the result of their mentor programs.

Formalizing Backup and Cross-training

Some mentor programs result in a generalized knowledge of the company. Lucky employees enter a program of formalized backup and cross-training designed to teach them, at the same time allowing them to contribute their special talents. As employees grow, they often enter a planned line of succession. The designated backup person works toward the time when a superior rotates out of the job and needs a qualified replacement. The mentor often assists in designing the track that allows the protégé to progress. This not only includes progress in the firm and cross-training, but extends to outside classes as well. These specific courses prepare a person for the possibility of entering the backup function.

Rules for Employee Counseling

1. Document company policy and communicate it to employees.
2. Determine a clear statute of limitations for use between offenses. Incorporate it into the employee manual.
3. Be certain of the facts before counseling an employee.
4. Be consistent with counseling.
5. Listen to the employee. Make the counseling session a two-way conversation.
6. After the session, treat the employee just like any other employee.
7. Never try to trap employees breaking the rules.

Figure 23-4. Rules for counseling.

Figure 23-5 shows the qualities to look for when selecting participants for a mentor program.

Professional Presentations

If enough people require a specific skill, it often makes sense to plan for in-house instruction by professionals. Even small companies find this more cost-effective than sending people to individual seminars.

Skills Inventory

An inventory of people's special skills comes in handy for larger companies and those that employ a number of people in different locations. Often the company needs a particular skill and doesn't know that they have it within their own ranks. Need for fluency in foreign languages is a frequent occurrence. Special knowledge of generally accepted accounting principals, procedures, and rules often comes in handy.

Continuing Professional Education (CPE)

Many companies include CPE as part of their skills-enhancement programs. Often the courses offered provide specific knowledge required to fulfill goals established in the business plan.

Mentor Qualifications

1. A superior performer
2. Sets an outstanding example
3. Supportive and helpful to subordinates
4. Not didactic and closed-minded
5. Understands how to delegate responsibility and authority
6. Establishes two-way communication
7. Good teacher
8. Patient
9. Has a genuine interest in the company and the protégé

Figure 23-5. Qualities of a good mentor.

Reasons for Turnover

Companies turn over their employees. That's a fact of life. However, excessive turnover robs the firm of training it has provided departing employees. It often seems that just when employees reach their peak performance levels, they leave the firm. The reasons vary. However, it's important to understand why.

Conduct exit interviews with employees who leave. Find out their reasons. Track the answers. Even if done informally, finding out exactly why someone left the firm contributes to controlling costly employee turnover. Perhaps too many people leave because of low wages. Maybe the firm loses valuable professionals due to limited advancement opportunities. Particular supervisors may have a disproportionate turnover rate due to their management style. Whatever the reasons, the company needs to know them. Hard numbers are the best way to identify problem trends.

Job Descriptions

Written job descriptions assist in:

- Establishing ranges for pay rates
- Defining qualifications for prospective employees
- Evaluating employee performance

It may seem a waste of time at first. However, what better way to communicate to an employee the company's performance expectations?

If you're creating job descriptions for the first time, include these items:

- Duties
- Supervision
- Authority
- Special skills, knowledge, or qualifications required by the job

Duties

List the tasks of the job. Describe the level of complexity, difficulty, frequency of each task, and the importance to the firm. For example, the tasks associated with an accounting clerk might include:

- Total daily cash receipts.
- Post cash receipts in accounts receivable subledger.
- Transfer receivables subledger entry to general ledger.
- Account for $1 million of monthly income.

Supervision

Describe the supervision required of the job and that given others by the job. This brackets the relative level of authority and responsibility. Be sure to identify the other job titles related to supervision given and received. Also, include the number of people supervised under this job description.

Authority Levels

Describe the level of authority the job has. For example, an assistant treasurer may have authority to invest up to $100,000 of excess cash in specific securities. Investments beyond that level require review and approval from a higher authority. Authority levels also identify where the job description fits in the company's hierarchy of responsibility.

Special Requirements

Include all special skills, knowledge, and extraordinary demands of the job. Perhaps the job requires knowledge of foreign currency hedging. Maybe the person must speak a foreign language when dealing with the firm's foreign subsidiaries. Some jobs in the treasury and accounting areas require odd hours or long hours during peak seasons. Be sure to include these as well.

Once drafted, be sure to keep the job descriptions current. Changes *will* occur. Some firms include discussion of employees' job descriptions in their annual performance review.

Index

About the Author

Christopher R. Malburg, CPA, MBA in finance, has more than 15 years of experience working for the Fluer Corporation and Citicorp as well as consulting in planning and control for Ernst & Young and Spicer & Oppenheim, two of the world's largest public accounting firms. In his practice as a management consultant based in Palos Verdes, Calif., his clients include banks, securities brokerage firms, and service companies. Author of *The Professional Investor's Tax Guide, The Cash Management Handbook,* and *Business Plans to Manage Day-to-Day Operations,* Malburg is also executive editor for AICPA's "Guide to Good Practice Series."